*The American
Immigration Collection*

Immigration:
Cultural Conflicts
and
Social Adjustments

LAWRENCE GUY BROWN

Arno Press *and The New York Times*

NEW YORK 1969

IMMIGRATION

CULTURAL CONFLICTS AND SOCIAL ADJUSTMENTS

IMMIGRATION

CULTURAL CONFLICTS AND SOCIAL ADJUSTMENTS

BY

LAWRENCE GUY BROWN

ASSOCIATE PROFESSOR OF SOCIOLOGY
OHIO WESLEYAN UNIVERSITY

LONGMANS, GREEN AND CO.

NEW YORK · LONDON · TORONTO

1933

LONGMANS, GREEN AND CO.
55 FIFTH AVENUE, NEW YORK
221 EAST 20TH STREET, CHICAGO
88 TREMONT STREET, BOSTON
128 UNIVERSITY AVENUE, TORONTO

LONGMANS, GREEN AND CO. Ltd.
39 PATERNOSTER ROW, LONDON, E C 4
6 OLD COURT HOUSE STREET, CALCUTTA
53 NICOL ROAD, BOMBAY
36A MOUNT ROAD, MADRAS

BROWN

IMMIGRATION

To My Wife
VIVIAN ROWSE BROWN

PREFACE

THE UNITED STATES has been one of the greatest immigrant-receiving countries of the world, with a consequence that it always has had a problem of immigration which began even before the thirteen colonies on the Atlantic seaboard became an independent nation. There has been an almost uninterrupted stream of immigrants whose life adjustments have been in terms of a culture that is very different from that in the United States. Not only has there been a conflict of cultures but adjustments in America have become increasingly difficult with the transition from a simple rural environment to a complex industrial society.

At first the problem tended to center around undesirable immigrants — social variants who were socially and economically maladjusted in their native habitats and thus reached America poorly equipped to make a satisfactory accommodation to a strange cultural milieu. The problem has grown more involved as the social organization in America has become more intricate and the contrast greater between the culture of the immigrant and the culture in the United States.

The purpose of this book is to analyze the problem of immigration with special reference to the nature of human nature. Because of the character of human nature and its inextricable relationship to the culture in which it developed, there would be a problem of assimilation no matter what the invading nationality might be. Americans of the same economic, social, and educational level would experience similar difficulties in a European or Asiatic environment. So the discussion revolves around what takes place because of the nature of human nature when a people of a strange culture invades the social heritage of another group.

It is not the aim of this study to evaluate the present system of regulation or to show just what the effects of immigration have been. We are too near the movement to know what the ultimate outcome is to be. We do know that it is changing the character of the United States as a nation; whether for better or for worse we cannot say and shall never be able to say, since a United States without immigration is not a reality as a means of comparison.

This text is not designed to show that immigration should be checked, but will deal with the immigrants already in the United States who at present number nearly fifteen millions. They have come entirely ignorant of and unhabituated to our customs, our cultural organization, and our laws. We are interested in the process of adjustment; that is, we are concerned with the manner in which the cultural heritage of the immigrants helps or hinders their adjustments in the American social order.

Volumes have been written to show that the recent immigrant is inferior and an undesirable acquisition. Dr. E. D. Reuter has refuted this stand in his scientific study, *The American Race Problem*. On page 95 he has said: " For approximately two decades there has been virtual agreement among scholars; all accept as a provisional but fairly well-founded working hypothesis the position that the various races and peoples of the world are essentially equal in mental ability and capacity for civilization." Consequently this book does not concern itself with the mental capacity of the immigrants.

Scientific investigations have revealed that there is not a pure race in existence. Racial mixture, therefore, has produced the present population of the world, but has left enough diversity in different regions to develop a racial ethnocentrism and arouse fear regarding racial mixtures. Not only is there not a pure race, but there is not a pure culture. Progress, or at least change from a simple to a complex social order, has taken place through cultural diffusions.

Our attention in this text, then, will be centered on the cultural conflicts that have resulted from a continual stream of aliens into the United States. The ramifications of the immigration problem will be viewed from the standpoint of the character of human nature and the social process by which it develops, along with the fact of industrialization and urbanization in the United States.

This book is based on the fact that there are two phases to the problem of immigration: the social nature that the immigrant brings with him and the social situation in which he makes his adjustments. The first aspect is discussed in Chapter I, *Immigration and Human Nature.* The second aspect is considered in Chapter XVIII, *The Problem of Immigration.*

The discussion of human nature is placed in the first chapter for orientation purposes. It will give the student a knowledge of human nature which will serve as a necessary mental content for a scientific consideration of the problem of immigration. The mental organization resulting from this information should take the place of the lay mind that ordinarily defines the question of immigration. Furthermore, this chapter on the character of human nature serves as a frame of reference for keeping the discussion of immigration in the field of sociology.

It will not be possible to acknowledge my debt to all those who have contributed to the development of the ideas in this text. I have been greatly stimulated by the following teachers in the field of Sociology: Drs. E. W. Burgess, Ellsworth Faris, J. E. Hagerty, F. E. Lumley, C. C. North, and R. E. Park. Other men in Sociology who have helped in various ways are Dr. E. T. Krueger, Dr. E. C. Hughes, Professor H. W. Zorbaugh, Mr. Clifford R. Shaw, Mr. Henry McKay, and Professor Fred Zorbaugh.

I wish to thank especially Professor Ernest R. Groves, editor of the series in which this text appears, for his critical reading and editing of the manuscript.

LAWRENCE GUY BROWN

CONTENTS

IMMIGRATION
Cultural Conflicts and Social Adjustments

Part I. Introduction

CHAPTER I
IMMIGRATION AND HUMAN NATURE

THE PROBLEM of immigration in the United States is rooted in the character of human nature and its relation to the cultural complex in which it is produced. As we shall see later, the nature of human nature and the process by which it develops place the problem of immigration definitely in the field of sociology. Like most other social questions immigration has its economic, political, biological, and historical aspects; but the problem of cultural conflicts and adjustments so characteristic of immigration falls in the field of sociology.

Human nature is everywhere the same, and everywhere it is different. Call this a paradox, if you will. Everywhere we find identical units of behavior regarded as essentially human — religions, manners, language, morals, etc. — hence human nature is everywhere the same so far as the number of units is concerned. However, since these units of behavior tend to vary in content in various situations because they have developed in different cultural complexes, human nature differs everywhere.

The similarity of human nature everywhere (that is, the same units) is the social phenomenon which makes possible social intercourse, social adjustments, diffusion of cultures, and therefore, immigration. Only from this similarity in the number of units does accommodation or assimilation become possible at all. On the other hand, the different content of these units of human behavior makes the adjustment processes of accommodation and assimilation difficult. Widely varying languages, different customs, and traditions, dissimilar habits and manners, all tend to operate against a ready social adjustment.

The character of human nature makes it possible to portray immigrant cultural backgrounds in general without a specific discussion of each group, despite the fact that each nationality has developed in a different social situation. This is practicable, since the units in human nature which make for adjustments or maladjustments of the immigrant in the American cultural complex are the same units in general for the Poles, the Germans, the Bulgarians, the Greeks, or any other group.

In any immigrant group the individuals have built up habit systems and attitudes which make for a complete adjustment in the cultural complex in which these factors developed, but make for disorganization in any other social situation. Therefore habits and attitudes are such, in so far as adjustments are concerned, no matter what the nationality may be.

These habits and attitudes do not have the same content with each group, but they all differ from the same attributes of human nature in American society. The language of the Germans is not the same as the language of the Turks; the food habit systems of the English are not the same as the food habit systems of the Poles; the religious customs of the Italians are not the same as the religious customs of the Russians; yet they all function alike to prevent a ready adjustment in American society and, therefore, can be discussed in a general manner.

There are at least six ways in which human nature is everywhere the same and everywhere different. In the discussion of these similarities and differences the best method of understanding immigrant cultural backgrounds will be found. Furthermore, there will be demonstrated the reason for such a tremendous problem of adjustment for the immigrant when he reaches the United States. (1) Human nature is everywhere the same so far as the number of units is concerned, because human groups universally have similar needs and similar life problems to meet. The contents of the units are different because the situations in which these problems are solved are not the same. (2) Each individual of any nationality or race starts life without a trace of culture but has the capacity and potentialities to acquire any culture and any life organization. This versatility disappears, however, once the individual has acquired culture and human nature. (3) While culture and human nature are acquired by identically the same social processes everywhere, the result is never the same. (4) A life organization of habits, attitudes, and interests is contingent upon the cultural complex in which it develops and fails to function effectively in other social situations. (5) Ethnocentrism (that is, emotional attitudes concerning the value of one's own culture and habits) results from the social process in which human nature and culture are acquired and makes the appreciation of any other culture almost impossible. (6) Human nature, once it has developed, resists change.

These six statements concerning human nature seem so important in understanding the adjustment problem of immigration that a detailed discussion of each point follows. This analysis will serve as an explanatory frame of reference for many of the intricacies of the immigration question.

(1) *Human nature is everywhere the same so far as the number of units is concerned, because human groups universally have similar life problems to meet.* Scientific study has given man a monogenetic origin which was followed by a long period of dispersion in which racial differentiation took place as each group made the physical adaptations postulated by a particular situation. It is of little interest to us here how divergent types were produced, but it was probably through biological mutations and inbreeding in isolation.

Divergent characteristics through racial differentiation have more to do with cranial and other anatomical measurements, skin pigmentation, hair color, etc., than with organic needs and the capacity to acquire a particular culture, which is our chief interest in a sociological discussion of immigration. Whatever may have been the biological process in producing divergent types, it has developed in every group a commensurate capacity for acquiring any culture, and has given each group the same organic needs. Consequently, assimilation into any culture is not checked by the biological process, as many authors would have us believe, but by the social process in which the undefined impulses in the organism have become habits of activity.[1] As we shall see later, the resulting attitudes and habits developed through the social process in one cultural situation make assimilation in any other cultural complex very difficult, in fact, make complete assimilation impossible.

While biological adaptations were being made, cultural accommodations were also taking place and have continued as a form of social adjustment down to the present time. Despite the fact that the process of diffusion has been very important in cultural manifestations, there have been enough isolation and segregation and variations in environmental situations to result in dissimilar contents for each unit of human behavior in different localities.

As has been said, the individuals of any group have similar needs and similar situations to meet. There is a universal need for food and drink for the satisfaction of the hunger and thirst impulses. Everywhere there is a sex impulse to be gratified and a need for relaxation in sleep. In every cultural group, situations have been met by some form of government; a political, economic, and religious system; a moral code; and some form of communication. With the same needs to satisfy and similar situations to meet, there have developed the same units of human nature and the same units of culture. But since the methods for working out a way to meet these needs have varied with the environmental conditions, human nature and culture differ, so far as the content of these units is concerned. This means that the traditions, customs, beliefs, ideals, standards, and ideas, as well as the personal life organizations, will vary with every group, since experiences are never the same.

Consequently, America's immigrant population, no matter what its source may have been, has reached the ports of the United States with a background of the same number of cultural units as the native Americans have. These units

[1] For a discussion of this social process, see L. Guy Brown, *Character Education*, published by the Children's Village School of Printing, Dobbs Ferry, N.Y. 1929.

include habits, attitudes, customs, and traditions, which were developed without direct contact with or any reference to the social situation in the United States. The arrival of each group has meant a conflict of cultures, followed by a process of disorganization for the invading group because these units of human nature and culture have a different content. It is this problem of adjustment, involving the social processes of migrations — isolation, segregation, competition, conflict, accommodation, and assimilation — that interests the sociologist.

(2) *Human nature is similar everywhere and yet different, not only because there are similar problems to meet, but because each individual, no matter what his racial or nationalistic affiliations may be, starts life without a trace of culture or social nature. He has, however, the capacity to acquire any culture and any social nature peculiar to any culture. But once he acquires a culture, this versatility is lost and he is held by his particular cultural complex.* Each individual starts life without the attributes we regard as essentially human: language, religion, code of morals, sense of beauty, political beliefs, prejudices; that is, the units of culture that one finds everywhere with different contents.

What the infant of any nationality does have at the outset is a random behavior capital out of which it is possible to build an almost unlimited number of habits. He has undefined activity in his organism which at birth is not directed toward any particular adjustment end but which can be molded by social training into behavior patterns for every field of activity.

It is the social heritage into which an individual is born which makes his hereditary movements and capacity significant at all, and these hereditary movements could have developed in any cultural setting. Culturally speaking, the Italian is not an Italian because he belongs biologically to the Mediterranean branch of the Caucasian group, but because he was born into the Italian cultural complex. Culturally, the Italian infant might become a German, a Frenchman, a Spaniard, or a member of any other group. But once he is an Italian, culturally speaking he will never be a Ger-

man, Frenchman, Englishman, or an American.   He may
be an Italian-German or an Italian-American, but he will
never get completely away from his cultural experiences as
an Italian.   This description would hold true for an individual of any racial or nationalistic group in the world.

Plasticity in development exists at birth, as has been indicated already, but once a culture has been acquired as a
world in which to live and attitudes and behavior patterns
have been formed in relation to this culture, the behavior
mechanisms in the organism of the individual are never
again the same.   The attitudes and modes of behavior tend
to resist change and often lead to demoralization in a new
social milieu.   This all becomes important in immigration
as the migrants attempt to accommodate themselves to a new
cultural complex.

Adjustments in the United States must always be in terms
of the background of experience of the immigrant and they
can never be so complete as with an American-born person
who has not had experiences in any other social situation.
Although an infant starts life without culture and a social
nature and could acquire any culture and any social nature
at the outset, that is not true of the adult immigrant who
has already built up a world in which to live as well as a life
organization of habits, interests, desires, and attitudes.

(3) *Human nature is similar everywhere not only because each individual starts life without a culture or a social
nature, but because both are acquired by identically the same
process whether the individual be Negroid, Mongoloid, or
Caucasian.*   Since the social process is the same, the difference in the human nature and culture acquired depends on
the experiences a person will have in a particular location.
The social process is a matter of defining objects through
experience and developing attitudes concerning these objects.   The attitudes created in respect to an object become
the basis of the behavior patterns that an individual will
have in relation to that object.

Let us see how the social process operates everywhere to
produce human nature and to give a person a cultural
habitat.   The individual comes in contact with an object

through random, often emotional behavior. This social experience leads to some definition of the object, thus creating an attitude which is the foundation of his life organization. While objects are acquired by the same social process in Europe as in America, they will without exception have a different meaning.

So the immigrants, like native Americans, have had social experiences in which objects have taken on meaning and become social values; experiences in which attitudes have been developed and behavior patterns formed. The definition of objects, the social values acquired, the attitudes developed, and the habit systems built up, are all contingent on the encounters the immigrant has in a cultural complex. In all cases these objects have a different significance from the one they would have had if the immigrant had been born in America. These early formalizations are the important ones because they establish the life tendency of the individual and are very difficult to change.

In the social process where the immigrant acquires objects to make up the world in which he lives, he acquires his parents who have a different philosophy of life from American parents; he acquires his sisters and brothers, other relatives, playmates, and teachers — all of whom have habits and ideas unlike those found in America. All of them have developed in a world similar to the one he is constructing and their human natures determine in no small way his behavior patterns. In the process of acquiring these personal objects in his world there is nothing more important than the attitudes of these individuals since the child either comes in conflict with their attitudes or accepts them for his own. With the peasant child in his native habitat there is little conflict with the attitudes and social values of others for he is not associated with people who are following any other cultural pattern. Consequently the immigrant has come to America without having realized that objects could have a different meaning from the one his experiences have created.

In addition to these personal objects he must experience and acquire impersonal objects; ritual, religion, home, school, law, church, manners, morals, ceremonies, etiquette are some of these. His experience in the acquiring of these social values is greatly enhanced by the ready-made, traditional definitions in society. Objects have come to him already defined in terms of the social heritage in some European or Asiatic situation.

This matter of developing human nature, behavior patterns, and acquiring a cultural habitat, all goes on in the social process at the same time. When an attitude has been developed, it means that some object has been defined or redefined and the behavior pattern of the individual has been molded so that the person acts toward this object in accordance with his attitude and his definition of the situation. In every case the experience with an object might have been different with the development of other attitudes and another pattern of behavior. Any person, no matter what his social universe may be, could have built up a quite different world in which to live, since there is nothing specific in the organism of an individual that decides how objects are to be defined. But once definitions have been made and habits built up in relation to these objects, a sudden change to an environment with other meanings demands a re-orientation in behavior patterns; in the new situation old habits fail to function, and the result is social disorganization and often personal demoralization. This is the experience of an immigrant when he comes to the United States.

Had any immigrant of any nationality been born in a situation of American customs, he would not have developed the traits he brought with him to the United States, since there is no such thing as the inheritance of social traits, beliefs, or attitudes. The immigrant comes with a personal organization pattern that is an adjustment to life, and is, therefore, difficult to change — but no more difficult to change than an American behavior pattern.

The acquisition of a world in which to live and the development of human nature always involve the utilization of organic impulses or undefined activity that exist in the individual at birth. We may take language as an example of how all people of any nationality develop through the same social process, and how this development fails to function in a strange society but is the outstanding form of adjustment in the cultural complex of the native habitat. At the outset the new-born of all nationalities start life with only random vocalizations which become an articulate language in the social process. While the random vocalizations are defined as only one language, say the Greek, we know that they could have been eventuated as either the Chinese, the German, the French, the Japanese, in fact any language spoken anywhere. But once the Greek had been learned through the definition of random vocalizations, the emergence of any other language was partially blocked. The Greek language used sounds necessary for that language and neglected some sounds needed for other languages. Years have been spent in building up this language through a slow unconscious process until it is a habit system which can be used without effort, while any other language must be learned with difficulty through a conscious process.

In the same manner the other undefined impulses become habit systems through socialization. The vague hunger impulse will be defined as a food habit system corresponding to the dietary interests of the nationality in which the immigrant is born. But this hunger impulse could have been satisfied by the food habit system of any other nationality. The important thing for immigration is the fact that a food habit system has been developed, which tends to exclude all others and makes adjustment in a new cultural complex very difficult.

One might run through the whole gamut of human habit systems since the great majority of immigrants have arrived as adults with complete, well established behavior patterns in every phase of life. There are habit systems in religion, in dress, in relationships between the sexes, involving both courtship and marital status. There are economic, political, occupational, and social habit systems — all well formed and operable in a European or Asiatic cultural complex. These behavior patterns and many more have a genuine functional value in the native habitat of the immigrant but are sure to be at variance with the similar modes of activity in another social order.

The accumulation of social experiences of a group dating back many centuries is represented by these behavior patterns. Experiences in this cultural complex have led to the building up of many sentiments around all existing behavior patterns. For this reason the control over the individual is practically complete, especially with the peasant who makes up the greatest part of our immigrant population. The peasant's life is quite largely a matter of routine activities in primary groups — the family and the community.

So the process of acquiring a personal life organization and social milieu goes on uninterrupted, and the immigrant's life patterns are well established before he leaves his native land. Even when the immigrant comes as a mere child, positive behavior trends have already developed. Since one's thinking can function only in terms of his experience, the immigrant naturally has a different type of mental life. His conception of home, marriage, chivalry, law, and of God and religion will naturally be different from that found in America, even though he has developed in the very same social process.

(4) *Human nature is everywhere the same because the life organization of the individual is contingent upon the culture in which it has developed.* While the life organization fits this cultural situation perfectly, the attitudes, habits, and sentiments built up here will not be of the same service in a strange situation where there are different social values, different definitions of objects, and different attitudes.

In order to see the close relationship between the life organization of habits and attitudes of an individual and the social milieu in which he lives, one has to realize that one's culture really becomes a part of him through mental imagery. The personality of the individual is the subjective aspect of his culture so the individual and his culture are inseparable. It is the subjective aspect of the culture that is most important since it is possible in this way for one's culture to go with him and condition his behavior even when he may move away from the physical or objective phase of his social organization.

So when the immigrant comes to the United States his

life organization is a subjective aspect of the physical culture that he left in his native habitat and is not directly related to the American social order. Consequently he is not adjusted in America. The greater the number of artifacts, modes of living, and traditional elements that he can bring with him, the better he will accommodate himself in his new environment. His church, his coffee-house, his fraternal organization, all facilitate a ready adjustment. If he could not live with his countrymen in an environmental replica of his own customs, habits, and traditions, he would be without a world in which to live and the result would be social upheaval and personal demoralization. What actually happens is that the immigrant, culturally speaking, does not live in America. If he did, he would find himself much disorganized, since his life personality, the subjective aspect of his world, would not find its complement in the United States.

From the standpoint of adjustment, it is fortunate that the immigrant can come with a part of the objective aspect as well as the subjective aspect of his culture, as he cannot, even if he wish, slough off his past mental organization. It is his very soul, his personality — it is his mental organization that gives him human nature at all. With the physical aspects of his culture present, he makes a better adjustment than he could if he were thrown entirely into the American cultural complex.

As a new-born, the immigrant, like any other individual, did not have any culture or characteristics of human nature and could have acquired the subjective and objective aspects of any culture. But as an adult, the immigrant finds it impossible to get away entirely from the subjective aspect of the culture of his original experience and is fortunate when he can acquire by degrees a new cultural world where his new mental content can actually correspond to some extent with the objective aspects of the social order in the United States.

Soon enough, even in immigrant colonies, the European peasant finds his well established mental life at variance with his new environment. The religious mental content of the peasant which was related to arcadian life does not find an objective complement in the slums of an industrial city, which are quite void of all the aspects of nature.   In his native habitat the Polish peasant, for instance, had a religious life which is an essential part of the immediate physical world in which he lived.   " Here every man in his practical life is continually in touch with the religious reality, is supported and surrounded by it, is an integrate part of the religious world." [2]   One can readily see how the religious mental content of the Polish peasant would be a hindrance to his adjustment in an American industrial city.   So it is with every phase of the subjective aspect of his native culture; it is at variance with the social order and ideas in the United States.

Through segregation the immigrant makes a desultory adjustment, an accommodation with those from his native village.   Then, if denationalization and renationalization are allowed to be a process, he gradually accommodates himself to a mixture of American culture and the culture he brought with him.   Thus his mental content, the subjective aspect of his culture, is modified and he is no longer a German or an Italian or a Pole; neither is he an American.   He is a German-American or an Italian-American or a Polish-American.   The character of human nature makes it impossible for him to be anything else.   Those interested in Americanization need not expect any more.   Human nature that has developed for several decades in the life of an individual can never be left behind.   Human nature at any point in the life of a person is always a combination of experiences from the past and from the present situation.   Consequently a complete change can never be the experience of an immigrant of the first generation.   It can come only with the second, third, or fourth generation.   An American of the same cultural, economic, and educational level could never become a German, an Italian, or a Pole.   He could never be more than an American-German or an American-Italian or an American-Pole.

[2] Reprinted from *The Polish Peasant in Europe and America*, by William I. Thomas and Florian Znaniecki (1918), by permission of and special arrangement with Alfred A. Knopf, Inc., authorized publishers. I, 232.

The thing to remember is that no matter what the racial affiliation of the individual, his personality, that is his life organization, will fit the cultural situation into which he is born, and the world he builds up will be coextensive with the same cultural situation. Furthermore, this fact makes the immigrant a cultural problem once he is outside the world he acquired, since his life organization will not fit another cultural complex. If a Bulgarian baby were taken at birth by an American family and reared in the cultural complex of the United States, its behavior patterns and attitudes would be American and the world it acquired in which to live would be American; it would experience a problem of disorganization and reorganization if it were later transferred to the cultural situation of Bulgaria. This close relationship between the life organization of an immigrant and his cultural complex is a cogent factor in the maladjustment found among immigrants. This would be true of any nationality.

Many cases on record show that racial affiliation does not determine the human nature of the cultural pattern of the individual. Cases given here are those of Orientals so that there will be a racial heritage very different from the one that is connected with the American cultural complex.

A Japanese infant, left an orphan in Oakland in 1896, was reared in an American orphanage. While her biological heritage, accordingly, was entirely Japanese, her social heritage was entirely American. On going to school she proved to be a bright student and surpassed her American schoolmates. But she developed an abnormal dislike, even hatred, of Japanese. Although her body and face were Japanese, her spirit and mind were markedly American and there was constant war in her soul. . . Her biological heredity is pure Japanese, but this has not given her a single Japanese idea or word or a particle of Japanese patriotism.[3]

Another illustration has been related by Dr. Robert E. Park from his experiences in the racial survey made on the Pacific Coast:

I recently had the curious experience of talking with a young Japanese woman who was not only born in the United States,

[3] Sidney L. Gulick, *The American Japanese Problem* (New York: Charles Scribner's Sons 1914), pp. 126–127.

but who was brought up in an American family, in an American college town, where she had almost no association with members of her own race. I found myself watching her expectantly for some slight accent, some gesture or intonation that would betray her racial origin. When I was not able, by the slightest expression, to detect the oriental mentality behind the oriental mask, I was still not able to escape the impression that I was listening to an American woman in a Japanese disguise.

A few months later I met this same young woman after she had returned from her first, and perhaps her last, visit to Japan. She was unusually reticent about her experiences, but explained that it was impossible for her to remain longer in Japan, although she had had every intention of doing so. She had found herself at a peculiar disadvantage there, because, though she looked like a Japanese, she was unable to speak the language; and besides, her dress, her language, everything about her, in fact, betrayed her American origin. The anomaly struck the Japanese public as something scandalous, almost uncanny. When she appeared on the streets, crowds followed her. They resented, perhaps even more at the time because of the recent passage of the Alien Land law, the appearance of a Japanese woman in the masquerade of an American lady.[4]

(5) *Human nature is everywhere the same because the process by which human nature and culture are acquired results in the individual developing the idea that his culture, that is, his ways of behaving are natural ways, and that all others are unnatural and inferior.* Thus a person of any nationality, whether he be of the most retarded or the most advanced cultural group, whether he be Negroid, Mongoloid, or Caucasian, feels that his way of doing things is the best way.

This fact is responsible for the ethnocentrism, the racial or nationalistic egotism, that one finds everywhere. According to Dr. Sumner:

Ethnocentrism is the technical name for this view of things in which one's own group is the center of everything, and all others are scaled and rated with reference to it. . . Each group nourishes its own pride and vanity, boasts itself superior, exalts its own divinities, and looks with contempt on outsiders. Each group thinks its own folkways the only right ones, and if it observes that other groups have other folkways, these excite its scorn.[5]

[4] Robert E. Park, "Behind Our Masks," *Survey Graphic*, 56 : 136. (May 1926)
[5] William Graham Sumner, *Folkways* (Boston: Ginn & Co. 1906), p. 13.

This attitude of ethnocentrism is so significant that it cannot be stressed too much; it is most important in adjustments to be made by immigrants in both their native habitat and their new environment. Dr. Faris describes it in the following manner:

Ethnocentrism, as ordinarily used, is the emotional attitude which places high value on one's own customs and traditions and belittles all others, putting as least valuable those that differ most. The universality of ethnocentrism is evidenced from the discovery that all preliterate peoples who have considered the question have worked out the answer in the same terms. It is obvious to a Nordic that the African and Mongol are inferior to himself, and hardly less obvious that the Mediterranean is intermediate between his own highness and the low-browed tribes of the tropic forests. But for more than a generation it has been familiar to specialists that Eskimos, Zulus, and Pueblos have exactly the same feeling towards us. The customs with which we are familiar are best. Mores which differ most widely arise from the social life of an inferior people. We are supremely human; they are only partially so.[6]

Ethnocentrism, then, is essentially narrowness. It is enthusiasm for our own due to ignorance of others. It is an appreciation of what we have and a depreciation of what differs. It is essentially a lacking of sympathetic dramatization of the point of view of another.[7]

Any immigrant group coming to the United States brings with it a background of ethnocentrism. The individuals of any nationality may think of the United States as a place to better their economic, political, social, or religious status, but they never think of the United States as having a culture superior to their own. Little does an immigrant group realize how great is the ethnocentrism which it will have to face, an attitude which by the definition of native Americans makes the culture of the immigrant inferior to that of the United States. One who realizes this situation expects Americanization to be a process long and difficult.

Every social trait has been strengthened by ethnocentrism.

[6] Ellsworth Faris, "The Nature of Human Nature." *The Urban Community*, edited by Ernest W. Burgess (Chicago: The University of Chicago Press 1926), p. 28.
[7] *Ibid.*, p. 30.

Language is not only a means of communication but in many cases a "symbol of freedom and self-respect," as with the Czechs. In many instances there is a complex of sentiments built up around a language so that when a group hangs tenaciously to its own language, there is more involved than merely difficulty in learning English. It is more convenient, and sentiments have made it the best language on earth, just as the social process has given us English, in our opinion the best language spoken anywhere. In a lesser degree, this is true of all immigrant groups.

With the immigrant, this ethnocentrism has a chance to function in the United States, since there is segregation and cultural isolation, except in a few situations, and there the immigrant sees American culture at its worst. It is no wonder that the immigrant with his ethnocentrism clings to his own culture when he compares it with American culture of the slums of our great cities where he is forced to live. This ethnocentrism is evidenced by the fact that many immigrants expect to return to their native land when they are financially able to do so, and are therefore not vitally interested in Americanization. While ethnocentrism works against assimilation, it does have an important function. We must not lose sight of the fact that ethnocentrism has its cultural value. It is a cogent rationalization of one's own culture and is an invaluable means of social control, resulting in a high degree of stability. Without it, the immigrant would probably experience immediate disorganization in American society, as is the case with those of the second generation when they tend to depreciate the culture of their parents.

The development of ethnocentrism seems to be a necessary by-product of the process of socialization. There must be economy of time in this social process. One could not learn to do things as they are done everywhere throughout the world. Consequently the educational system of the home, the neighborhood, and the school presents to the individual the "right" way of doing a thing — there is no choice. To the individual, it comes to be the natural way and any group that does it differently is doing it the unnatural way or certainly by an inferior method. One learns that his language is the natural language and all others are babble. The Arabians, for example, regard their language as the language of the angels. One's food habit systems, modes of dress, etiquette, courtship and marital relationships, in fact all one's modes of behavior are conceived by the individual as the very best way — in fact, the only intelligent way of doing things.

The following well demonstrates how the socializing process operates through formal education to produce ethnocentric attitudes:

I remember, in the house of my parents we used sometimes to have Slovak servants. We were very democratic and treated them almost as our equals — as servants. But, of course, being a Slovak, that was different. Being a Slovak, that was a sort of a practical joke. A gentleman would never have thought of being born a Slovak. Slovaks were so ridiculously meek and docile, and they spoke Magyar with a perfectly funny accent.

I entered the gymnasium with the notion that a gentleman might be a Magyar, a German, or even a Jew; but a Slovak? The idea!

We were taught that Slavs were hardly human. Some of them, like Russian generals and pan-Slavist agitators (whatever they were), were devils incarnate. The rest, the bulk of the Russian people, Czechs, Slovaks, Slovenes, Serbs, were simply an inferior and uncivilized race and worse. The Poles were the exception that confirmed the rule. They were a chivalrous and unfortunate nation, lovers of music, wine, and fighting, like the Magyars. But even they displayed Slavonic characteristics in being unable to organize a strong state, and it was quite natural that they should have fallen the prey of such a genius as Frederick of Prussia.

I remember with what resentment our class first learned the fact . . . that when the Magyars invaded the Hungarian plain from the north, the Moravian Slavs had the damned impudence to be already there! Our sense of the fitness of things was greatly relieved when we were told that their army was beaten to shreds.

Our teacher in history — by the way, an Armenian from Transylvania — always emphasized the fact that one of the best stunts ever perpetrated by the Magyar nation was the historic stroke of driving a wedge into the body of Slavdom that in the ninth century was stretching from the Baltic to the Ægean, thereby separating North and South Slavs forever. This was not only fine sport, but admirable statesmanship as well. Among those most immediately benefited by the event were the Slovaks, who thus got a chance to live under Magyar rule and enjoy the blessings of Magyar civilization, and whom we Magyars intended, in the long run, to elevate to our own level by Magyarizing them altogether.

Magyar civilization, we were told, was the heir and outpost of Rome on the eastern frontier of Europe. Latin culture was our precious heritage to defend against German violence, Slav barbarism, and Mahometan conquest. Had Latin not been the official language of the country until 1825, and one of the strongest bulwarks against the Germanizing tendencies of the Hapsburgs?

The Rumanians of Transylvania, who claimed that they were the direct descendants of the Roman legions, were, of course, a lot of preposterous liars. Imagine the Wallach yokels speaking of Roman culture! Why, our teachers would tell us, they lived like swine in their huts on the Transylvanian hills, were poor, dirty, and illiterate, and rightly, too, because they were born stupid and lazy.

We were told that Slovaks, Rumanians, Serbs, and Croats were enjoying perfect liberty and equality, and ought to be enthusiastic for Magyar rule. We were also told that to Magyarize them was to promote their own interest, because by becoming Magyars they would enjoy privileges from which, as Slovaks or Rumanians, they were naturally barred. Not one in ten of us began even faintly to suspect that the two statements implied a contradiction.[8]

Ethnocentrism must not be thought of as attitudes that are peculiar to the relationships between races and nationalities. Everywhere one turns he discovers sectionalism. In the United States we have the ethnocentrism of the Northerner, of the Southerner, of the New Englander, and of the Westerner. With the immigrant this sectionalism seems even more pronounced. The Italians furnish an excellent example of sectional ethnocentrism. In discussing the background of the Italians, Mr. Roselli says:

. . . the Italians living in Italy and those of America . . . are still subject to deep lines of regional cleavage, especially between the Northern and the Southern group. Their divergence is so great — divergence not only of speech, but of viewpoint, of training, and in short of everything pertaining to mores.[9]

    [8] Eugene S. Bagger, "A Rotten Education," *The Public*, August 3, 1918.
    [9] Bruno Roselli, "The Italians," reprinted by permission from *Immigrant Backgrounds*, edited by Henry Pratt Fairchild. (Published by John Wiley & Sons, Inc. 1927), pp. 100–101.

The Italians are used here as an example, but they are not the only immigrants who exhibit this pronounced trait of sectionalism, ethnocentrism. It is found throughout the world, and is very significant in our immigration problem. The same situation exists with the Jews. The Spanish Jews, some of the first to reach the United States, evidenced this attitude concerning those from Germany, and the German Jews reacted in the same way to those from Russia.

There was a time when a Spanish Jew or Jewess who married a German or Russian co-religionist would be promptly disowned; the hostility to such alliances was much stronger than it has ever been between Protestant and Catholic. The Sephardim have always had their own graveyards in which German and Russian Jews have not found rest.[10]

The early arrivals of any nationality have displayed ethnocentric attitudes concerning later arrivals from their own native country. They have called them " green-horns " and often refused to associate with them because their human nature was still so entirely foreign and because they were totally unfamiliar with even ordinary American ways. Even though the early migrants have not been assimilated and are antagonistic to many customs in the United States, still they have changed sufficiently to have attitudes of ethnocentrism concerning those who are still entirely alien in their habits and manners.

The attitude of ethnocentrism is vitiated by the fact that people tend to condemn others for being as they are. Sinclair Lewis not only described the individuals of Main Street but he censured them for being " Main-Streeters " when they could not be anything else. We blame Jews for being Jews and criticize Italians for having Italian manners. They could not be other than they are — yet we show our reprehension.

(6) *Human nature is everywhere the same because it resists change.* This fact in itself makes the assimilation of the adult immigrant impossible. Habits and attitudes once developed, rationalized, and strengthened by ethnocentrism,

---

[10] Burton J. Hendrick, "Jews in America," *World's Work*, 45 (1923), p. 152. Reprinted by special permission of *World's Work*.

tend to persist. So the student of human behavior sees at once that there will be a great social problem of adjustment connected with immigration. Having some understanding concerning the character of human nature and the social process by which it develops, he will know that the adjustment made by the adult immigrant of the first generation will not be assimilation but accommodation in terms of his native culture and the social situation in the United States. The student of human behavior keeps the problem in better perspective than the common observer and does not think of the immigrant as unique or inferior, since he is aware that if Americans of the same social, economic, and educational status were transferred to a European or Asiatic culture, the problem of adjustment would be just as great.

The immigrant comes to the United States with his life direction already established through experiences in the cultural complex of his native habitat and, psychologically speaking, his nationalistic character will always be partly European or Asiatic. It is difficult for an immigrant to become an American because one's reactions depend on the totality of his experiences, and the American cultural pattern does not contain the experiences that the immigrant has had in his native land. It is an insuperable task to attempt complete denationalization and renationalization of an immigrant, which is what is involved in Americanization. The immigrant has already spent his formative years and his human nature has developed with a certain life direction of attitudes, habits, and manners that cannot be forgotten.

Professor Fairchild has said:

This cultural accumulation becomes profoundly infused with sentiments of loyalty, devotion, patriotism, justice, truth, and rightness. To depart from any of its canons involves not only the pain of the unfamiliar, but also the guilty sense of treachery. The fact that an exceptionally emancipated or sophisticated individual may criticize certain features of his own group culture on rational grounds does not destroy the hold that it has upon him in general.[11]

[11] Henry Pratt Fairchild, "What Is an Immigrant Background?" Reprinted by permission from *Immigrant Backgrounds*, p. 11.

For the immigrant peasant in his native habitat there is little if any departure from the prescribed method of behavior. It is in the United States or some other strange social situation where there is a conflict of cultures that there is a break with customary behavior. The Jewish apostate and *allrightnicht* are notable examples.

One could take an immigrant at birth from any national group and let him develop in the American cultural complex and he would be an American, speaking the English language; he would have our food habit systems, our sex and family life, as well as all the other habit systems peculiar to our culture. But once the immigrant has gone through the socializing process and has developed human characteristics in a different social situation, the problem is quite different. Try as he will, he can never get entirely away from his background.

The immigrant is forced to act, if he acts at all, in terms of the cultural situation that he left in Europe or Asia. If he comes alone his reactions are to his native cultural situation as it exists in his mental imagery. If his friends come and they are able to bring artifacts, customs, ritual, traditions, etc., and settle together, then he makes a fairly normal adjustment, hindered only by the elements of American culture that he cannot avoid. If this cannot happen, his social nature, the subjective aspect of his culture, becomes a handicap because American culture is not a true objective complement of his personality.

While the immutability of human nature and the accompanying attitude of ethnocentrism apparently make immigration a great problem from the standpoint of adjustment, the problem would be much greater if there were no stability to human nature once it had developed. Immediate disorganization and demoralization are prevented if the process of Americanization is not hurried by people who do not understand human nature. No matter what may be our wishes and no matter what may be the desires of the immigrant, if he has developed the life organization of the Italians, or the social nature demanded by the customs of Poland, or human nature as the subjective aspect of the German culture, he will always remain in part, at least, an Italian, or a Pole, or a German. An immigrant who has lived for some time in America, and who has altered somewhat his national character, always finds himself maladjusted if he returns to the country of his birth.

We have considered in general the facts concerning human nature which give the United States its problem of immigration. The immigrant reaches America with a cultural complex involving his own language, religion, habits, manners, and customs. He has his own ideas concerning law, God, the state, chivalry, marriage, and the home. He has his own traditional superstitions, his idea of leisure time, and his own philosophy of life. Consequently he has a different type of mental organization and different standards of human values. One can think only in terms of his own experience and that is what the immigrant does.

Those who condemn the immigrant because he does not become entirely assimilated into the American cultural complex admit that they do not understand human nature and its inexorable relationship to the social heritage in which it develops. Those who criticize the adult immigrant for not becoming Americanized are indirectly rebelling against the fact that human nature is what it is. So the question of immigration is based not only on the character of human nature but on the fact that the average person does not understand it. If human nature were such that it could be sloughed off with ease, there would be little stability in society. Human nature is produced in terms of loyalties and prejudices, everywhere. Activities in life are conditioned by human nature as it has developed, or by the mental organization of each person, and every new accomplishment is based directly on past experience; thus the life organization of an individual takes a particular trend in the social situations in which he lives.

These facts become more intelligible and less disconcerting when we realize that the social nature of an immigrant is not any harder to change than the mental organization of the physician, lawyer, minister, or the human nature of the criminal or any other social variant. Human nature as it develops in any individuals or the members of any group tends to complete its existence in a particular direction once it is well established.

READINGS

Bogardus, E. S., *Immigration and Race Attitudes.* 1928
Fairchild, Henry P., *Immigrant Backgrounds.* 1927
Faris, Ellsworth, " The Nature of Human Nature," *Proceedings of the American Sociological Society.* 1926. Pp. 15–29
Groves, Ernest R., " Socializing Human Nature," *The Child, the Clinic and the Court.* 1925. Pp. 189–203
Lasker, Bruno, *Race Attitudes in Children.* 1929
Park, Robert E. and Miller, Herbert A., *Old World Traits Transplanted.* 1921
Thomas, W. I. and Znaniecki, Florian, *The Polish Peasant in Europe and America.* 1920. Vols. I, II. Shows the cultural background and human nature that an immigrant group brings to America.

IMMIGRANT AUTOBIOGRAPHIES

Antin, Mary, *The Promised Land.* 1912
Cahan, Abraham, *The Rise of David Levinsky.* 1912
Cohen, Rose, *Out of the Shadows.* 1918
Hasanovitz, E., *One of Them.* 1918
Lewisohn, Ludwig, *Up Stream.* 1922
Morgenthau, Henry, *All in a Life-time.* 1923
Panunzio, C. M., *The Soul of an Immigrant.* 1921
Patri, Angelo, *A Schoolmaster in the Great City.* 1917
Pupin, Michael, *From Immigrant to Inventor.* 1923
Ravage, M. E., *An American in the Making.* 1917
Riis, Jacob A., *Making of an American.* 1901
Steiner, E. A., *From Alien to Citizen.* 1904
—— *Against the Current.* 1910
Stern, E. G., *My Mother and I.* 1917
Thomas, W. I. and Znaniecki, Florian, *The Polish Peasant in Europe and America.* 1920. Vol. III
Tobenkin, Elias, *Witte Arrives.* 1916

CHAPTER II

INTRODUCTION TO PERIODS OF IMMIGRATION

T HE DIVISION of immigration into *old* and *new* is not being made because the process of adjustment, as a process, has been any different at any time. The same units of culture have been important in making accommodations with both the old and the new immigrants. The most outstanding reason for considering immigration in two divisions is the rapid change in the cultural organization in the United States where the immigrants have to make their adjustments. Of almost equal importance is the change in the composition of immigration. The new immigrant developed his human nature in a cultural organization unlike that of the old immigrant in many ways. The content of each unit of culture and human nature with the Slavic and the Mediterranean groups varies more from the same units in the United States than did the units with the northern and western Europeans. A third reason for a division of immigration into old and new is the change in the methods of control. The immigrants from northern and western Europe migrated in the greatest numbers when control was exercised by the various states; on the other hand, the immigrants from eastern and southern Europe have been supervised in their settlements in the United States by federal legislation.

The United States has changed from a country characterized by a simple rural environment to a complex industrial and urban society. This has taken place in a very short time, since the United States is not an old country — it has been an independent state for fewer than two hundred years. The change has been both cultural and economic. This has made the problem of adjustment much more difficult for those immigrants who arrived after the social order in the United States became more intricate and complex. Early, too, there was not a great population, but within the last century the population of the United States has increased to more than a hundred million, a fact which has greatly augmented the problem of immigration.

The cultural complex in America during the colonial period and a few subsequent decades, was based directly on the cultural organization of northwestern Europe. Consequently the immigrants coming during this early time did not find the necessary social adjustments so difficult. In many cases they moved beyond' established settlements and created their own social milieu. At that time they came largely from a life of agricultural pursuits and settled in the rural districts of America.

With the new immigrant the situation has been difficult from the outset. Industrialization, along with the fact that free land is no longer available, has sent the recent arrivals with a rural social heritage to great urban centers where the problem of adjustment has been increasingly arduous. With the recent arrivals settling in an urban center, there is a proximity with American culture that results in a conflict that could be avoided during the early years of immigration in rural America until an adequate adjustment had been made.

The old immigrant came in the greatest numbers when there was little formal control or state regulation. In fact the migrant from northwestern Europe reached American ports during several periods when there was an active interest in stimulating immigration, when there was a need for workers and settlers to help develop the United States as an independent nation. The new immigrant in his movement to America has been supervised by federal control. Agitation for federal regulation came quite largely during the invasion of the old immigrant and as a result of the problems attending his journey, his invasion, and process of adjustment. So while the application of federal control has had to do with the adjustment of new immigrants, it was instituted as a result of problems attending old immigration.

It is evident that no situation in the past can be compared with recent developments; the contrast in every aspect is too great. Had the Slavic and the Mediterranean immigrants come to the United States when its environs were largely rural, their problem of adjustment would have been quite different. If the arrival of the old immigrants had been confined to the last forty years, the process of accommodation for them would have been very unlike the experiences they have had.

The adjustments of any group must be considered in terms of the social situation in which the accommodation is made. Problems attending adjustments in one social situation would not have been the same in another period. It would not be possible to compare the colonial American with native Americans of today, with the purpose of showing that one group was superior to the other. They have made adjustments to contrasting situations and are, therefore, very different. Old immigration cannot be compared with new immigration in its accomplishments in the process of Americanization. This is not possible since there has not been a single constant aspect, except the fact that human nature as it develops anywhere is contingent upon the cultural situation in which it developed. Authors who have compared the two groups have exercised very little scientific caution. A comparison cannot be made where most of the chief elements have changed at an unprecedented rate.

There has been social disintegration for the immigrant in the Americanization process partly because of the manner in which this process is directed. But this social disorganization is not peculiar to immigration; it takes place in any changing milieu; it is only a part of the great industrial growth and urbanization in the United States. Immigration has been a tremendous factor in this growth, but the disorganization with the immigrant has not been different, except in degree, from the demoralization with rural Americans who have suddenly entered industrial and urban life.

Rapid change produces disorganization, and since there have been rapid changes in the United States involving thousands of immigrants, naturally we have a problem of immigration as well as problems of poverty and vice — because we have experienced social transition. Perhaps this change could have taken place without immigration and perhaps it could not; no one knows. The fact is that it took place through the utilization of immigration so that the immigrants have become a problem through the change they helped to produce.

There has been a great deal of interest in immigration; legislative chambers, pulpits, public halls, and club-rooms have been places for vehement discussions of the effects and the solution of the problem. Often the reactions have been emotional rather than rational. In many cases these reactions have been to wishes or prejudices. Facts concerning human nature have usually been neglected. Immigration has permitted patriotic organizations to become self-conscious; it has enabled individuals to define themselves as important persons interested in the welfare of a great commonwealth, as they have proclaimed that the native stock, American institutions, and social standards were endangered. It has revealed more about the nature of human nature than it has about the problems of immigration. This interest in immigration has always involved the idea of Americanization, but there has not always been a realization that Americanization of the colonial period would not be Americanization at the present time; neither is Americanization the same for every region in the United States; an adjustment is always to a specific situation and there are great variations in the many localities.

Every phase of our social life has been touched by immigration. Since the immigrant has been in close proximity to many social problems he has often been defined as the cause of these problems. One aspect of careless thinking about human behavior is the practice of saying that one thing has caused the other when two things are found together in society. When we find European peasants and low wages together we assume that these immigrants are responsible for low wages. Actually low wages are caused as much by the attitudes of American employers and the organization of modern industry as they are caused by the presence of immigrants. Immigrants have been closely associated with crime, vice, and poverty, but so have any population groups who have lived in the same areas of urban life now occupied by the recent immigrant. Then, too, the pathological aspects of any problem always receive more attention than the normal aspects. This text is an effort to understand each group in terms of its cultural heritage and the social situation into which it comes. It will therefore be descriptive of immigration anywhere as far as social processes are concerned.

The problem of immigration has been complicated by the fact that the United States is a new country and has been constantly in the process of establishing itself. There have not been precedents in other countries as a guide for many of the experiences through which the United States has had to pass. The adjustment of the immigrant has been to a kaleidoscopic situation to which not even most Americans were adjusted.

Since the United States has been constantly in transition and since the composition of immigration has changed and has come under a new technique of control, European migrations will be considered as old and new immigration. For further convenience the scheme of division as used by Professor Fairchild [1] has been adopted in this textbook. He has aptly divided immigration into the following periods: (1) Colonial; (2) Unrestricted Immigration; (3) State Regulation; and (4) Federal Control. The colonial period extends to 1783 when the thirteen colonies became an independent state. During this early era the American colonies had very little control over immigration. After the Revolutionary War from 1783 to 1830 the United States had not worked out any means of control, so there was a period of unrestricted immigration. From 1830 to 1882 the question of immigration was under the supervision of the various

---

[1] See Henry Pratt Fairchild, *Immigration* (New York: The Macmillan Company 1925), Revised edition, pp. 31–32.

states. Finally, through the decisions of the Supreme Court, immigration was made a matter of federal control in 1882. Old immigration came quite largely during the first three periods and the early part of federal control. It has continued down to the present, but since 1896 it has been greatly eclipsed by new immigration.

In each period immigration will be considered under the following aspects of the movements from the native habitat through a period of adjustment: (1) Composition; (2) Causes; (3) Journey; (4) Distribution; and (5) Social interaction and adjustments.

READINGS

Barnes, H. E., *Living in the Twentieth Century.* 1928
Beard, Charles A. and Beard, Mary, *The Rise of American Civilization.* 1928
Chapin, F. Stuart, *Cultural Change.* 1928
Dixon, Roland B., *The Building of Cultures.* 1928
Fish, Carl, *The Rise of Common Man.* 1928
Ogburn, W. F., *Social Change.* 1923
Reuter, E. B., *Population Problems.* 1923
Sullivan, Mark, *Our Times: The United States, 1900–1925.* 1927

Part II. Old Immigration

CHAPTER III
THE COLONIAL PERIOD

INTRODUCTORY STATEMENT

SOME AUTHORITIES have considered the entire period prior to the Revolution as an era of colonization, but there was a gradual infiltration of immigrants very soon after settlements were established, if one thinks of population movements as does Professor Fairchild. He makes this distinction between colonization and immigration: ". . . colonization refers to movements of people from a central state to its dependencies, while immigration is a movement from the territory of one nation to that of another." [1] Many of those who arrived before the development of an independent nation were from countries other than England, the central state, so there was immigration.

Colonies in America were founded by the younger sons and others of the aristocracy, and members of the lower classes, as well as the Puritans and Separatists from the Church of England. These groups left England when there were social discriminations, religious dissension, political upheavals, and economic disturbances. The struggle between agrarianism and the new capitalistic order was a transitional period that produced many who were socially and economically inadequate, undesirable groups that migrated with the more ambitious of all classes to establish colonies in America.

These colonies reproduced, in so far as their strange and wild surroundings permitted, the towns, the estates, and the homes of Englishmen of that day. They were organized and governed by

---

[1] From H. P. Fairchild, *Immigration*, revised ed. p. 32. The Macmillan Company, publishers.

Englishmen under English customs and laws; and the English-man's constitutional liberties were their boast until the colonists wrote these rights and privileges into a constitution of their own.[2]

So the immigrants coming into these colonies on the Atlantic seaboard, in so far as they accommodated themselves to any culture, had to make their adjustment to an English social order as it had been modified by the many vicissitudes of experiences in America. The plan of social organization in the colonies represented the crystallization of the attitudes of the settlers as to what was the proper pattern of behavior for everyone. Their experiences in Europe made them self-conscious groups; they had left their native soil to protect certain social values. All of them had suffered during the voyage and on the frontier, that their ideals might be put into operation. Each experience of hardship increased the sentiments built up around their beliefs and it was not to be expected that any group that endangered their newly acquired, hard-earned privileges would be welcomed.

The immigrants of the colonial period had two adjustments to make. They had to accommodate themselves to an undeveloped physical environment and to the newly established colonial culture, the religious unit of which caused the most concern. Despite the fact that the early settlers had come for freedom, there was just as much intolerance, just as much ethnocentrism, with the possible exception of Pennsylvania, as one ever found in any location and during any period. Consequently the immigrants coming during the colonial days faced, in a very minor degree, all the social problems of adjustment of any era. Most of the objections, especially cultural objections, ever raised concerning immigration were discussed as important at this time.

To study the process of adjustment made by the immigrants during any period, one must know the composition of the stream of migrants as well as the cause for the movement from one cultural situation to another. These are equally important with the nature of the social order into which the immigrants came in determining the adjustment

[2] From "Our Foreigners," by S. P. Orth. Volume 35, *The Chronicles of America.* (Copyright, Yale University Press 1921), p. 6.

that would be made. Of equal significance are the experiences the migrants have after they leave their native habitat, during the journey, at the port of debarkation, and especially in the section of the country where they have to make the final adjustment.

COMPOSITION OF IMMIGRATION FOR THE COLONIAL PERIOD

THE TWO outstanding groups reaching the seaports of America during the colonial period were the Germans and the Scotch-Irish. True, the Scotch-Irish arrived from the British Empire, and, strictly speaking, were colonists since they came from a " central state to its dependencies," but they were not accepted as such by the colonists, neither were they treated as equals by the English in the United Kingdom. As far as the attitudes of the Americans were concerned, they were immigrants. In fact, nearly all late arrivals during the colonial period were given the status of aliens by those who were well established in the United States. However, the attitude toward those from England was one of tolerance when compared with the attitude concerning those from other regions. Even a slight variation between the contents of cultural units for this early period was defined as different by the reactions of the early settlers.

The Scotch-Irish had at one time resided in Scotland and had gone to Ireland when James the First was determined to make a Protestant country out of Catholic Ireland by sending settlers from Scotland and England. Although they had lived in both Scotland and Ireland they were not Scotch-Irish in the sense that the term indicates.

They are in fact the most composite of all the people of the British Isles, being a mixture of the primitive Scot and Pict, the primitive Briton and Irish, and a larger admixture of Norwegian, Dane, Saxon, and Angle.[3]

The Scotch-Irish constituted about one-sixth of the population in the colonies at the time of the Revolution, having sent a greater number of immigrants than any other nationality. In some cases a pastor and his entire congregation

---

[3] From H. P. Fairchild, *op. cit.*, p. 40.

came as a group, thus bringing with them a complete scheme of living which became valuable in the matter of adjustment.

The Germans came largely from the lower part of the Palatinate, an area on both sides of the Rhine extending from Cologne to Mannheim. The majority of them were persecuted Protestants, many of whom were helped by England in finding a home in America. Religiously, they were composed of a variety of sects but the greatest numbers were Lutherans. There were, however, Mennonites, Dunkers, and Moravians in the migration from Germany. By the end of the colonial period there were probably close to seventy-five thousand in the various regions, out of a colonial population of two and a half million.

While these two dominant groups furnished the main influx of immigration, there were at least a few from practically every country in Europe. Of the minority groups the French Huguenots were perhaps the most important, many coming to America through Holland and England. The Huguenots or French Protestants had at one time been a strong political party in France. Before the influx to the United States, many had gone to England and Prussia after the revocation of the Edict of Nantes and the persecutions that preceded this move. The Huguenots, like the Palatines, had come to America for religious freedom.

In a discussion of the composition of immigration during the colonial period, there is a certain class which should be considered here: the indentured servants and redemptioners. The indentured servants came under contract made in Europe to serve a definite number of years; they were quite largely from the British Isles. The redemptioners were in the main Germans who were sold by the ship captain at some American port. In each classification there were people who wished to reach America but were financially unable to do so without some kind of aid. Since labor is necessary for the development of a new country, settlers in the colonies were willing to pay the passage of individuals or purchase them from those who had been responsible for their transportation.

The demand for these workers came chiefly from Maryland, Virginia, and Pennsylvania. The indentured group included not only common laborers, but schoolmasters and people of every trade and occupation, as well as many social variants, paupers, and criminals. It is recorded that a Lutheran minister was held under indenture in York, Pennsylvania,[4] and doubtless there were other cases. Schoolmasters served one or several families and often a community. Until about the middle of the eighteenth century the greatest number of indentured servants had come from the British Isles, but from this time on many were secured from Germany. In some cases, even when they had passage money and enough to establish themselves in a small way, the Palatinates allowed themselves to be sold so that they might become familiar with the English language and the customs and habits in America, thus preparing themselves for a better adjustment. In some instances individuals living in the colonies were indentured for misdemeanors, or when they had accumulated debts they could not pay. In all cases whether from Europe or America, they were really chattels during their period of service.

The pauper and criminal classes among indentured Europeans were the only ones who excited any comments against the system of white servitude. Transportation became the means of handling criminal classes, especially in England. Political prisoners were sent first of all. "Two shiploads of political prisoners were sent to Maryland as late as 1717, and of these eighty were sold as servants."[5] But it was the convicts who were sent year after year until the time of the Revolution that caused the colonists so much concern.

A further classification of colonial settlers could be made under religions since there were many sects, especially in Pennsylvania where there was a freedom of worship not found elsewhere. Mittelberger wrote:

We find there Lutherans, Reformed, Catholics, Quakers, Mennonists or Anabaptists, Herrnhuters or Moravian Brethren, Pietists, Seventh Day Baptists, Dunkers, Presbyterians, Newborn,

[4] See Cheesman A. Herrick, *White Servitude in Pennsylvania* (Philadelphia: John Joseph McVey 1926), p. 272.
[5] *Ibid.*, p. 117.

Freemasons, Separatists, Freethinkers, Jews, Mohammedans, Pagans, Negroes and Indians.[6]

Despite the variations in religious beliefs, there was a certain homogeneity, since the movement had been from northern and western Europe. As Professor Commons has said: "It is the distinctive fact regarding colonial migration that it was Teutonic in blood and Protestant in religion."[7]

CAUSES OF IMMIGRATION DURING THE COLONIAL PERIOD

THE ADJUSTMENTS that the immigrants made during the colonial period or any other time have their explanation partly in terms of the causes back of their migrations. As we shall see later, out of these causes came the attitudes, social values, and philosophy of life which became so important in the accommodation made to the situation in the new country.

Despite the fact that the immigrant had developed a social nature in keeping with his cultural complex, frequently there were economic, political, social, or religious conditions that became reasons for leaving his native habitat. In a complex social organization such as one finds in Europe, with cultural and economic interaction between countries, there are often competing elements for the social, political, and religious units of any particular social heritage. This often results in a conflict of culture in certain units whereby many minority groups find themselves unadjusted.

While the immigrant may be well oriented so far as language, family life, and many other cultural patterns are concerned, frequently he is unadjusted in one of the aforementioned aspects. Even then he may have partially accommodated himself to these factors and be fairly well satisfied, until there has been enough propaganda from without to lead to a migration from the cultural complex in which he has developed human nature.

Though the immigrants of the colonial period rebelled

[6] Gottlieb Mittelberger's *Journey to Pennsylvania in the Year 1750 and Return to Germany in the Year 1754* (Philadelphia, John Joseph McVey 1898), p. 54. Translated by Carl T. Eben. Reprinted by permission of the publisher.
[7] From John R. Commons, *Races and Immigration in America* (New York, The Macmillan Company 1920), new ed. p. 27.

against certain elements in their own cultural complex, still they were largely controlled, so far as attitudes, habits, and life philosophy were concerned, by their own native social organization.   This lack of orientation in a few units of their native culture did not mean that they were anxious to conform to another social milieu.   It meant only that they were desirous of finding some place to which they could bring the elements of culture in which they were adjusted, and continue their use; a situation which would give them an opportunity to work out to their own satisfaction the units of culture, religion, etc., in which they were maladjusted in Europe.   This gives us in brief the general explanation of the causes of colonial emigration.

There must always be some disturbing factor in the native land of the immigrant before he will leave a social situation in which his habits and attitudes have developed.   So, in discussing the causes of emigration, one must always look for some maladjustment in the cultural life of the migrant. For the colonial period it will be necessary to discuss the Scotch-Irish from Ulster and the Germans from the Palatinate, since they furnished the bulk of immigration during this period; some of the variant classes from all countries sending emigrants will also be considered.

There was a combination of economic, political, and religious causes lying back of the departure of the Scotch-Irish for the American colonies.   They had become successful manufacturers and exporters of textiles when the English merchants were influential in securing legislation which forced the shipment of all woolen goods as well as the raw wool to England, thus eliminating any further competition with the Ulster markets.   This discrimination affected the linen trade as well and greatly handicapped all the industries of northern Ireland.   With the expiration of their hundred-year leases the Scotch-Irish lost much of their land in competitive bidding with the Irish, who, because of their lower standards of living, could afford to offer a higher rent.

The rights of the Scotch-Irish were further curbed when they were compelled to take the vows of the Church of England if they wished to hold office. Refusing to become apostates from the faith and principles of the Presbyterian Church for political advantages, they lost much of their power of self-government.

The Scotch-Irish faced a crisis situation which to them meant a struggle to maintain their national character if they were to remain in Ulster. It involved new religious and political behavior patterns, as well as economic retardation, and a change in their cultural complex against which they rebelled. Movement away from a situation on the part of a minority group is often the only solution, especially when the situation means a change in habits, attitudes, customs, and traditions around which there have developed many sentiments in the way of ethnocentrism. In conflict with the Irish, the religion of the Ulsterites had been identified with nationality, so migration was to be preferred to a possible change in life organization and a loss of national character. They met this economic, political, and religious crisis situation by coming to America.

The Palatines in the Rhine region of Germany faced a similar crisis situation which to them was primarily religious, but was closely tied up with political and economic conditions.

The rulers of the Palatinate, the Electors Palatine, swung back and forth between Lutheranism, Calvinism, and Roman Catholicism, and since each successive ruler wished his subjects to conform to his religious views, the miserable people suffered accordingly. Both of the two great wars between 1684 and 1713, the War of the Grand Alliance and the War of the Spanish Succession, had borne heavily on the Palatinate, which had long been the object of Louis XIV's most covetous desire. The second ruthless devastation which the country experienced during the latter of these wars reduced the people to the lowest pitch of misery and desperation. Meanwhile their ruler, John William, was trying to force the whole of the people back into Catholicism.[8]

This forced shifting from one religion to another kept the cultural situation in a constant flux. While the inhabitants outwardly were followers of one faith, they still

---

[8] From H. P. Fairchild, *Immigration*, p. 38. By permission of The Macmillan Company, publishers.

cherished the content of another. True, religion represented only one unit of their cultural complex, but it was a very important unit since it was kept constantly in the minds of the people by these repeated changes, and the fact that it was closely related to all other aspects of life. Those who have observed the social disorganization that comes to an immigrant group which voluntarily abandons its religion, especially when the religion is closely allied to all other phases of the social organization, will better appreciate the condition when force is used. With religion often go standards of conduct and an inability to take over the content along with the form of another religion. Against this predicament the Palatines were struggling.

Each religion, Lutheranism, Calvinism, and Roman Catholicism, postulated to a certain extent a different pattern of behavior, different attitudes, and a different philosophy of life. In the minds of the Palatines the change was a tremendous one. The transition from one to the other, then, was not a simple matter since it became an undesired, conscious process and involved a mutation in personality, or a secretive pattern of behavior, something that rarely takes place without disorganization. The life organization so essential to one religion would be *de trop* in another. While religions, no matter what their names may be, represent the same unit of culture, the content may be very different and the transition from one surrounded by sentiments of ethnocentrism to one thought inferior is likely to be a demoralizing step.

It was the fight against these disintegrating changes along with economic and political conditions that led the Germans to leave their native habitat even when an edict threatening death was adopted by the Elector Palatine. Immigration in the face of this ultimatum shows how powerful attitudes may become when the esteemed elements of a culture of a people are involved.

What has been said regarding the Germans and Scotch-Irish applies to the smaller groups coming at this time; they left their native land because adjustments could not be made to certain units of culture without compromising the general life organization of the group. Especially was this true of the French Huguenots.

The real causes of immigration, then, are those factors which lead to maladjustment in the native habitat of the immigrant. There are factors in the country which is to be the destination of the migrants, but they are not causes, as many authors have called them, but rather conditions which offer a solution for the predicament in which the potential immigrant finds himself. Letters from people in the United States, and propaganda by agents may stimulate immigration, but they cannot be regarded as causes. There must be some distress, some problem for which migration offers a solution, or these techniques to stimulate immigration would not be effective.

So advantages in the United States cannot be thought of as reasons back of migrations. They merely offered a solution for the crisis situation and a chance to carry out the life philosophy of the immigrant as well as an opportunity to get away from political oppression and economic distress. The factor existing as a solution in the United States was the frontier with free land where these Europeans could leave the uncongenial life at home and settle as a group, and work out, unmolested, their scheme of life organization.

The causes lying back of emigration during the colonial period were of a nature that indicated that the immigrants had come to America to stay, and would be more interested, therefore, in making a definite accommodation. They had run away from an undesirable religious, social, and political situation. A brief stay in America would only accentuate the traits that put them at variance with their European culture. To return and be adjusted in their native habitat, they would have to take over the religious, social, and political patterns, the refusal of which had led to their migration. So there would be little incentive to return even if they could afford to do so. This fact should be kept in mind when a comparison is made with recent immigrants who expect in many cases to return eventually to their native lands.

There should be some explanation here of the causes that led to white servitude in the colonies. There would have to be some cogent reasons for one to sell himself into temporary slavery, in a strange land. In most cases the only difference between the indentured servant and other immigrants, so far as causes are concerned, was one of degree. Most of them came because of their unfavorable adjustments in Europe, especially from the economic standpoint. Not only were many dissatisfied with their social and economic predicament in the land of their birth, but Europe was anxious to dispose of its poor and undesirables. So the system of indenturing people for a period of years was soon rationalized and the practice was regarded as mutually beneficial to the colonies and the immigrants. It was considered a legitimate means of poor relief.

Such were the reasons for the migration to America of those who were willing to come. There were those who were forced to come because they were criminals or paupers. " It is estimated that possibly as many as fifty thousand criminals were sent to America from the British Isles, from the year 1717 until the practice was ended by the War of Independence." [9] It must be kept in mind that by present standards of criminality many of these so-called criminals of the colonial period would be only minor offenders and not stigmatized as criminals. Larceny of a small sum was punishable by death. Religious and political differences were excuses for deportation. Besides the criminals, many, especially children, were kidnapped and transported into servitude. Individuals were taken by force or enticed on board ships sailing for America. The extent of this practice is shown by the use of the colonial newspapers in advertising for those who had been lost in this manner.

THE JOURNEY

THE JOURNEY of the immigrant is important since it is his first experience beyond the narrow cultural world in which he has lived and every experience must be thought of as significant. Furthermore, the enervating nature of the voyage in sailing vessels, under adverse conditions during the colonial period, determined in many cases the success of

[9] *Ibid.*, p. 51.

the immigrant in making adjustments. The colonists were aroused to concerted action if the migrants were in any way incapacitated so that they became a burden when they arrived. This situation led to most of the legislation that was passed during the colonial period.

Immigrants who were healthy and economically secure when they left the port of embarkation often reached America impoverished, diseased, or physically incapacitated. This is shown by a discussion of the experiences of some of the German migrants.

Persons who left their homes in the Palatinate were, at every state of their advance, fleeced by agents, customs, duties, and other exactions, so that, although many left home with what might be considered ample resources to pay for their passage to Pennsylvania, they found their means entirely exhausted before they embarked at Rotterdam. Those who left the Palatinate were compelled to pass a total of thirty-six customs in the several principalities and cities before they reached Rotterdam. At these customs there were delays, and consequent use of provisions, and expenditure of the means brought from home; it was often four, five, or six weeks before the emigrants reached Rotterdam. After their arrival, there were further delays, the ship sometimes not sailing for weeks, and many of the passengers left Holland in debt. The ship company often paid debts in Rotterdam, but charged the amount paid and an additional item for interest so that the emigrant got deeper into debt.[10]

Records show that some ships were on the high seas for nearly six months when provisions were carried for a much shorter period, resulting in physical and mental suffering. The following is a vivid description of the conditions on some of the ships as portrayed by colonial observers:

. . . during the voyage there is on board these ships terrible misery, stench, fumes, horror, vomiting, many kinds of sea-sickness, fever, dysentery, headache, heat, constipation, boils, scurvy, cancer, mouth-rot, and the like, all of which comes from old and sharply salted food and meat, also from very bad and foul water, so that many die miserably.

Add to this want of provisions, hunger, thirst, frost, heat, dampness, anxiety, want, afflictions and lamentations, together with other trouble, as *c.v.* the lice abound so frightfully, especially on sick people, that they can be scraped off the body. The misery

---

[10] Cheesman A. Herrick, *op. cit.*, pp. 183–184. Used by permission.

reaches the climax when a gale rages for 2 or 3 nights and days, so that everyone believes that the ship will go to the bottom with all human beings on board. In such a visitation the people cry and pray most piteously. . .

Among the healthy, impatience sometimes grows so great and cruel that one curses the other, or himself, and the day of his birth, and sometimes come near killing each other. Misery and malice join each other, so that they cheat and rob one another. One always reproaches the other with having persuaded him to undertake the journey. Frequently children cry out against their parents, husbands against their wives, and wives against their husbands, brothers and sisters, friends and acquaintances against each other. But most against the soul traffickers. . .

At length, when, after a long and tedious voyage, the ships come in sight of land, so that the promontories can be seen, which the people were so eager and anxious to see, all creep from below on deck to see the land from afar, and they weep for joy, and pray and sing, thanking and praising God. The sight of the land makes the people on board the ship, especially the sick and half dead, alive again, so that their hearts leap within them; they shout and rejoice, and are content to bear their misery in patience, in the hope that they may soon reach the land in safety.[11]

The arrival at the port did not always end this deplorable existence, since no one was allowed to leave the ship unless he could pay for his passage or show evidence that he could soon do so. Many had to remain on board until they had been purchased. Those who had suffered most from the ordeal of the voyage, who had become sick and enervated, were not desired as servants and often died before they had a chance to leave the ship.

It is not surprising that a great number should become dependents at once in the United States following the experience of the transatlantic voyage. Not only were they destitute but physically incapacitated and thus unable to make a normal economic adjustment. As the burden on the colonists increased, there came a demand for hospitals and provisions for caring for these disabled individuals. In a message to the Assembly in 1741, the Governor of Pennsylvania presented a request made by the Germans for an immigrant hospital to care for their countrymen who had become ill during the long voyage.

[11] Gottlieb Mittelberger, *op. cit.*, pp. 20–25. Used by permission.

After reaching the port the indentured servants had to remain on the ship until someone came to secure their services. Mittelberger wrote:

The sale of human beings in the market on board the ship is carried on thus: Every day Englishmen, Dutchmen, and High-German people come from the city of Philadelphia and other places, in part from a great distance, say 20, 30, or 40 hours away, and go on board the newly arrived ship that has brought and offers for sale passengers from Europe, and select among the healthy persons such as they deem suitable for their business, and bargain with them how long they will serve for their passage-money, which most of them are still in debt for. When they have come to an agreement, it happens that adult persons bind themselves in writing to serve 3, 4, 5, or 6 years for the amount due by them, according to their age and strength. But very young people, from 10 to 15 years, must serve till they are 21 years old.

Many parents must sell and trade away their children like so many head of cattle; for if their children take the debt upon themselves, the parents can leave the ship free and unrestrained; but as the parents often do not know where and to what people their children are going, it often happens that such parents and children, after leaving the ship, do not see each other again for many years, perhaps no more in all their lives.

When people arrive who cannot make themselves free, but have children under 5 years, the parents cannot free themselves by them; for such children must be given to somebody without compensation to be brought up, and they must serve for their bringing up till they are 21 years old. Children from 5 to 10 years, who pay half price for their passage, viz. 30 florins, must likewise serve for it till they are 21 years of age; they cannot, therefore, redeem their parents by taking the debt of the latter upon themselves. But children above 10 years can take part of their parents' debt upon themselves.

A woman must stand for her husband if he arrives sick, and in like manner a man for his sick wife, and take the debt upon herself or himself, and thus serve 5 to 6 years not alone for his or her own debt, but also for that of the sick husband or wife. But if both are sick, such persons are sent from the ship to the sick-house (hospital), but not until it appears probable that they will find no purchasers. As soon as they are well again they must serve for their passage, or pay if they have means.

It often happens that whole families, husband, wife, and children, are separated by being sold to different purchasers, especially when they have not paid any part of their passage money.

When a husband or wife has died at sea, when the ship has

made more than half of her trip, the survivor must pay or serve not only for himself or herself, but also for the deceased.

When both parents have died over half-way at sea, their children, especially when they are young and have nothing to pawn or to pay, must stand for their own and their parents' passage, and serve till they are 21 years old. When one has served his or her term, he or she is entitled to a new suit of clothes at parting; and if it has been so stipulated, a man gets in addition a horse, a woman, a cow.[12]

After debarkation there are adjustments to physical conditions to be considered, but perhaps the most important factor is the public opinion the immigrant has to face, that is the attitude of those already living in the United States. The definition given the immigrant is all-important for the matter of adjustment in his new social environment. " A very different attitude was manifested in the colonies toward persons who came from the home state than toward those from any other country. The former were generally welcomed; the latter were regarded with suspicion, if not actual hostility." [13]   This statement was made regarding the colonial situation, the period now under discussion.

" Many of the stock arguments against immigration on the grounds of pauperism, criminality, and inability for self-support developed during this period." [14]   The attitude of the colonists and early immigrants is best found in the colonial immigrant regulations. Each colony tended to meet its own problems with legislative measures which must be regarded as a crystallization of the attitude of the way the matter should be handled, as well as one of the indices of the extent of the problem, or the imagined extent.

DISTRIBUTION

DISTRIBUTION is very important since it partly determines the type of adjustment the immigrant has to make. What the immigrant brings with him as a life organization as a result of past experiences, and the situation into which he goes, are the two factors that will decide what his immediate accommodation is to be. During the colonial period and all

[12] *Ibid.*, pp. 26–28.   Used by permission.   [14] *Ibid.*, p. 45.
[13] From H. P. Fairchild, *op. cit.*, p. 33.

subsequent invasions, the majority of the immigrants came with a rural heritage. During the eighteenth century and most of the nineteenth century, they were able to settle in a rural situation in America, making adjustments less difficult than those experienced by recent immigrants who have had to go into an urban environment with a rural social heritage. So the immigrant of the colonial period did not find a very great contrast between the units of culture in the United States and those he brought with him, but the colonists were looking for religious differences, so there was usually a slight conflict of culture. Even as early as the colonial period the distribution of immigration was largely a matter of attitudes on the part of the colonists and the immigrants. Neither group wanted to give up its national character, so the immigrants often had to move beyond the original settlement.

Distribution can be discussed in terms of the two main streams of immigration, the Scotch-Irish and the Germans from the Palatinate. The Scotch-Irish became frontiersmen as they had been in Ulster, where they had developed productive farms from the marshlands and had built thriving textile towns.

At the time of their arrival (in America) the lands along the Atlantic coast were already well occupied. . . Thus, due to the religious exclusiveness of Massachusetts and the well-settled character of the country, as well as due to a more or less general feeling of hostility of the English colonists toward certain types of immigrants, they chose as their destination New Hampshire, Vermont, Western Massachusetts, and Maine, and, most of all, Pennsylvania, and the foothill regions of Virginia and the Carolinas. By nature typical pioneers, they pushed into Western Pennsylvania, Ohio, Kentucky, and Tennessee.[15]

While the Germans settled in New York and in the south, by far the greatest number found a new home in Pennsylvania, and became the " Pennsylvania Dutch." The tolerant attitude of William Penn had made this a desirable place to settle.

He was the first American to advertise his dominions widely throughout Europe, offering to sell one hundred acres of land at

[15] From Roy L. Garis, *Immigration Restriction*, (New York, 1927), pp. 6–7. By permission of The Macmillan Company, publishers.

two English pounds and a low rental. His advertisements combined humanity and business, for they called attention to popular government and business; equal rights to all regardless of race or religious belief; trial by jury; murder and treason the only capital crimes, and reformation, not retaliation, the object of punishment for other offenses.[16]

The Germans settled also in Maryland, Virginia, North and South Carolina, and there was a settlement in Maine.

Although the discussion centers around the Scotch-Irish and the Germans, they were by no means the only Europeans coming to the United States during the colonial period as immigrants. "It was said that every language of Europe could be found in Pennsylvania." [17] The French Huguenots settled in Massachusetts, Rhode Island, New York, and North and South Carolina.

SOCIAL INTERACTION AND ADJUSTMENTS

IT HAS already been said that the adjustment made by any immigrant group in America is contingent upon two factors. These are the situation into which the members of a group settle and the social organization and human nature that they bring with them. The social organization and the human nature possessed by the immigrants can be discussed in terms of four general experiences. (1) When the immigrants reach America they have already developed social natures and acquired cultural worlds in which to live that are different from those found in America. (2) They have had experiences that led to maladjustments in certain units of culture which became the causes for their migration. Out of these experiences came potent attitudes and a definite philosophy of life that placed the emphasis on certain social values which they feel must be guarded even in a new situation. (3) They have developed other important attitudes in becoming courageous enough to break with the cultural milieu in which their social natures have been formulated; the beginning of a struggle to realize their philosophy of life. (4) There has been the suffering of a long, perilous

---

[16] From John R. Commons, *op. cit.*, pp. 29–30. By permission of The Macmillan Company, publishers.
[17] From Roy L. Garis, *op. cit.*, p. 20.

journey to the United States involving the horrors described above which often left the immigrants physically incapacitated for the strenuous adjustments in a new land and made them undesirable citizens in the opinion of the colonists. These, in general, are the experiences that immigrants had had when they reached America during the colonial period. The situation into which the immigrant comes is the second factor that becomes significant for adjustments. There are two important aspects: the experiences at the port of debarkation and the place of final settlement. As we shall see later there was a great contrast in the situation in various colonies. In some the immigrants were wanted because of their labor power; in others they were merely tolerated; and in a few colonies they were not welcome at all. The situation at the port of debarkation was greatly complicated by the arrival of the sick and destitute as well as the redemptioners who often had to be sold. The experience of some of the Palatinates at the port is shown by the following statement: " To the shame of the New York colonists, it is recorded that they were welcomed with privation, distress, fraud, and cruel disappointment. They were cheated and oppressed by the heartless and rapacious settlers, to whom their helplessness made them easy victims." [18] It was the attitudes of the colonists that made adjustments difficult, a condition which often could be met most successfully by isolation and segregation, out beyond well established settlements.

Much has been said about assimilation during the colonial period and the years subsequent to the Revolutionary War. Most authors, in making a contrast between the old immigration and the new have assumed that Americanization took place because the colonists and the immigrants formed a rather homogeneous group, so far as European origins were concerned. This conclusion has been reached because the accounts of few cultural conflicts were recorded after the immigrant had passed the port of debarkation.

What actually took place was the movement of new groups out beyond the periphery of old settlements where they resumed their European mode of living, modifying it only as

[18] From H. P. Fairchild, *op. cit.*, p. 39.

they made adjustment to a physical environment. Instead of becoming assimilated, they helped produce diversification in America's social organization, which even today is not the same everywhere. The term "Americanization" does not have a definite connotation. To be assimilated in American culture never did and never will mean the production of a definite cultural pattern. If assimilation is Americanization in one region, then it is something else in another section. Even a native during the colonial days had adjustments to make in passing from one colony to another. Isolation and segregation of immigrants were just as much facts during the colonial period as they are at the present time. Due to the existence of a frontier and a lack of a modern means of communication and transportation, it was possible for a group to move a little beyond a settlement and establish a colony in which old world opinions, customs, and habits could operate unimpeded. Even settlements in close proximity did not have social intercourse. Contacts were largely economic and secondary. Some of the settlements established at that time still show traces of European culture even at this late date. In some cases, the arrivals year after year from Europe prevented assimilation. In many sections of Pennsylvania the Germans are still known as "Pennsylvania Dutch," and there are American-born Germans who cannot speak English. Americanization is not a matter of nationality or racial capacity. It is a matter of the social situation and the process of interaction that goes on.

Americanization is a process that can be experienced completely only by the person who is born into the cultural complex of which this process is a part. Assimilation in the American cultural complex can be experienced only partly by those who have first been Germanized or Anglicized. Isolation and segregation hinder assimilation. Complete interaction at once in a strange culture usually results in social disorganization and personal demoralization; gradual interaction utilizing past experiences and the present situation means accommodation and partial assimilation. Where the process is gradual and carefully directed so that it does not become a painfully conscious operation, the adjustment is in terms of the American culture and the social organization brought from Europe. Thus, in some cases, it has been possible to save the best of each culture as they came together. Out of isolation and segregation during the colonial days came a stability that was taken for assimilation. It was, however, an accommodation in which the immigrant caused very little trouble for American-born citizens and the early colonists.[19]

The adjustments made by the Scotch-Irish and the Germans would not have been the same had they remained on the Atlantic seaboard. In the New England colonies where immigrants were not welcomed, there would have been many cultural conflicts and much talk of a lack of assimilation, while on the frontier and in certain other colonies no one objected to the content of any cultural unit; consequently it has been assumed that assimilation took place. However, the social organization brought by the Scotch-Irish and the Germans became segments in the mosaic of cultural areas that formed the colonial social organization, no division of which was the same. Assimilation which actually took place was confined to certain cultural areas, since there was not a colonial culture in general. Where the Germans and English were in close proximity the culture was German-English and even today in many places it is German-American.

Concern was shown regarding the lack of assimilation on the part of the immigrants by such men as Benjamin Franklin, as evidenced by some of his letters when he said:

Few of their children in the country know English. They import many books from Germany; and of the six printing-houses in the province, two are entirely German, two half-German half-English, and but two entirely English. They have one German newspaper, and one half-German. Advertisements, intended to be general, are now printed in Dutch and English. The signs in our streets have inscriptions in both languages, and in some places only German. They begin of late to make all their bonds and other legal instruments in their own language which (though I think it ought not to be) are allowed good in our courts, where the German business so increases that there is continued need

[19] Accommodation is a process whereby the minority group takes over enough of the culture to avoid conflicts. Assimilation is taking over all the culture, language, habits, customs, and traditions.

of interpreters; and I suppose in a few years they will also be necessary in the Assembly, to tell one half of our legislators what the other half say.

In short, unless the stream of their importation could be turned from this to other colonies, as you very judiciously propose, they will soon so outnumber us that all the advantages we have will, in my opinion, be not able to preserve our language, and even our government will become precarious.[20]

The fact that in certain cases the Germans had not developed any sentiments concerning the colonial culture or any attitudes of ethnocentrism, which is one of the indices of assimilation, is proof that Americanization was not taking place in the first generation. In the conflict between the English and the French, the Germans in some sections wanted to be neutral. They gave out ". . . one amongst another, and even in print, that, if they were quiet, the French, should they take the country, would not molest them." [21] This does not mean, however, that the second or third generations in this group did not become assimilated. In most cases they did. But the immigrants of the first generation of any nationality, strictly speaking, never become Americanized.

The problem of adjustment during the colonial days was not so great from a social standpoint as it is today in a complex industrial organization. A rural and village population from Europe could settle in a country district or a small town and not have the great contrast of situations that the European peasant has today when he takes a rural heritage to an urban environment.

There are many respects in which the matter of adjustment was simple as compared with the situation after the free land was gone and the urban trend in America was under way. Competition, which is one of the processes so important today and which is primarily an economic outgrowth, was virtually non-existent before the period of the Revolution. There was a great deal of opposition to immigration, but never on the basis of economic competition.

[20] Extract from letter of Benjamin Franklin to Peter Collinson, May 1753, from *Complete Works of Benjamin Franklin*, compiled and edited by John Bigelow (New York: G. P. Putnam's Sons 1887–1888), II, 297–298.

[21] *Ibid.*, p. 298.

There was an abundance of free land and room for everyone.

Whether one views the colonial period from the standpoint of the colonists or of the immigrants, he is impressed by the fact that the religious interests were the important cultural element in the thirteen colonies. The religious designations are evidence of this fact — the Puritans, the Quakers, the French Huguenots, the German Mennonites, and the Scotch-Irish Presbyterians.

From the standpoint of religion, immigration brought together two very self-conscious groups: the colonists and the later migrants. Most of the conflicts of cultures were on this basis. Fears concerning immigrants were often worries about the security of the dominant religion of the colony, as might be expected since the early settlers and many immigrants had left Europe partly for religious reasons. Some one has aptly said that the seventeenth century found the old world and its peoples so heartily tired of each other, that a partial separation was inevitable. The conditions in Europe were such that many of its inhabitants were moved to abandon their country, their homes, and their friends.

It could not be expected that the religious ethnocentrism developed in that situation would be sloughed off by crossing the Atlantic Ocean; consequently the ethnocentrism of the colonial period was primarily religious and only secondarily nationalistic. Protestantism would be tolerated anywhere, but Catholicism was very dangerous in the thinking of the colonists, except during the early days in Maryland. The attitude on the part of England in helping continental Protestants reach America was doubtless a factor in this opinion. Religious intolerance and religious ethnocentrism were the spirit of the time, despite the fact that religious freedom was one of the attractive inducements held out by most colonies. Colonists were not ready to welcome those who did not cherish the same beliefs that had become sacred to them.

The matter of social interaction and adjustments was not the same in the New England, middle, or southern colonies. In the New England colonies ". . . it was their avowed policy

and studied effort to prevent any considerable influx of foreigners, differing from them in language and customs. . .
In various ways, therefore, they set up barriers which repelled many who might otherwise have settled among them; and thus, while to the south there was developing a cosmopolitan nation, the inhabitants of New England lived on practically untouched by the great ethnic current until the present century." [22] This is evidence that the immigrants found themselves in a conflict of cultures when they elected to remain near the port of debarkation. They could, however, move out on the frontier, a privilege that does not exist today for the immigrant in industrial America.

In Massachusetts there was political franchise only for members of the established church, and as early as May, 1637, it was necessary to have the consent of authorities to entertain a stranger, manifesting an ethnocentrism equal to anything that could be found anywhere in any period of history. "Whippings, imprisonment, banishment, and in a few instances capital punishment" [23] were used to keep out the Quakers except in Rhode Island. The opposition to French Catholics found expression in legislative measures in 1647 making it impossible for them to become citizens. This attitude of exclusion was directed also toward the landing of those who might become public charges.

Connecticut was equally strict; only Rhode Island in New England showed any great tolerance for people who differed religiously. The early settlers in this region had left England because they had been persecuted or threatened as members of the Puritan party. Religious persecution does not fit a people for religious tolerance. Rather it builds up a set of attitudes that are impervious to any other religious ideas. When one knows how habit systems and attitudes develop, he can readily see that the experiences of the Puritans in their native country would not lead to religious toleration even outside the situation in England.

The middle and southern colonies were established at a slightly later period when there was some evidence of re-

---

[22] Emberson Edward Proper, *Colonial Immigration Laws* (New York: published by the Columbia Studies in History, Economics, and Public Law,1900), p. 22.
[23] *Ibid.*, p. 25.

ligious toleration. Though there was some opposition, it did not exclude immigration entirely as was virtually the case in New England. In speaking of the middle colonies E. E. Proper said:

At the close of the colonial period this group possessed the most mixed population of any of the colonies. Besides Englishmen, there were representatives from almost every country in Europe: Scotch, Highlanders and Lowlanders, Scotch-Irish, French Huguenots, Germans from various parts of the Empire, Dutch, Swedes, Finns, and a few Jews. Quite naturally, amid such a variety of nationalities, there existed a diversity of religious persuasions which shows clearly the tolerant spirit that must have existed in those colonies.[24]

Perhaps the most inhospitable treatment in the middle colonies was accorded the Germans in New York who left for Pennsylvania or the southern colonies. Pennsylvania was founded primarily for persecuted Quakers and others of the Christian faith, so it was there that the greatest religious tolerance was to be found. The generous attitude of William Penn helped to make Pennsylvania a colony composed of a heterogeneous population. This led to an influx not only of peoples of many religions but also of persons not socially and economically adjusted in Europe: criminals and paupers. The coming of these social variants was responsible for the opposition to the free admission of aliens on a social basis; that is to the exclusion of criminals and to a method of control of those who were likely to become a burden to the colony. So legislative acts in Pennsylvania were for the control of social variants and it was this group which found adjustments difficult to make. An act had been passed by the English Parliament to transport felons into the colonies in 1717 and five years later Pennsylvania imposed a duty on persons "convicted of heinous crimes" and imported into Pennsylvania. This was followed by a more inclusive act in 1730.

Despite the liberal views of William Penn there was later some consternation concerning the arrival of Germans in such great numbers who did not speak English and who were

[24] *Ibid.*, p. 38.

not familiar with colonial laws. In 1729 the Colonial Assembly passed an act which placed a duty on all " foreigners and Irish servants." This came following a great influx from Germany and Ireland.

There is considerable evidence that accommodation rather than assimilation was the process during the colonial period.

The pamphlets of that period contain frequent allusions to this prodigious immigration, and many fears, not unfamiliar in our own time, were publicly expressed. One writer expressed anxiety lest they " would produce a German Colony there. . ." Another writer of the period complains that they settle in communities, and have schools taught, books printed, and even newspapers printed in their own language, thus constituting a foreign colony, and likely to continue so for many generations.[25]

The establishment of the southern colonies embodied two periods, so far as religious attitudes were concerned. During their inception there was an attitude of religious exclusiveness, but later there was a trend toward toleration.

History leads us to believe that Maryland was founded as a mecca for Roman Catholics. Soon, however, acts were passed which took away protection and limited the religious and political activities of this group. S, from the standpoint of adjustment, the problem involved the Catholics and the criminals. The legislation passed failed to check the latter but diverted the influx of Irish Catholics to other regions.

Virginia displayed an intolerance for Catholics from the outset through its Charter. There was also opposition to the immigration of Dissenters or Non-Conformists; all must be members of the Church of England. Bringing a Quaker into the colony involved much consternation and a fine of one hundred pounds for the one who was responsible for the arrival of an individual of this sect.

An Act of 1699 is indicative of the religious intolerance of the times. A tax of 20s. was imposed on every servant brought into the colony not born in England or Wales. The object as set forth in the title purported to be the raising of funds to build a

[25] *Ibid.*, pp. 51–52.

capitol, but one cannot avoid suspecting that there were other motives in the case, not the least of which was the restriction of Irish Catholic servants.

The final struggle for supremacy in America between the English and French had the same effect in Virginia as in the other colonies, an intensified dislike for Catholics, especially the Jesuits, so that additional safeguards were provided to prevent their coming into the Province. This feeling was so strong that a company of neutral French Catholics, who had been conveyed into the colony by the home authorities, were ordered to be removed and their transportation paid for out of the public purse. It was believed that their presence would greatly endanger the peace and safety of the colony.[26]

The intolerance that marked the colonial days of Virginia was not in evidence in Georgia and the Carolinas, so the Huguenots came in considerable numbers to the Carolinas.

In its outstanding pathological aspects, the system of indentured servitude probably involved the greatest number of problems of adjustment. Still, the practice was accepted and in many cases the indentured servant did not suffer a loss of status because of his position. Nor did it in many instances seem so hard since there were so few opportunities in Europe. The whole plan was regulated, supposedly, by legislative enactments. "Under these laws servants were imported, they were bought and sold, they were held in servitude, and finally they secured their freedom." [27]

There was sentiment against Negro slavery in some of the colonies and as free labor was not available, the use of indentured servants was soon rationalized. It provided an opportunity for many unfortunate practices from the standpoint of both the servant and the master. Perhaps the most tragic aspect was the breaking up of families. "Even if a whole family were indentured to one man at the outset, there was no assurance that he would not later sell the indentures so as to cause separation. In any event the indentures were usually for unequal terms, so that freedom came at different times. In 1785, a Philadelphia butcher secured indentures for a father and mother with their two children, the parents being bound for five years and the children for ten years and

[26] *Ibid.*, pp. 65–66. [27] Cheesman A. Herrick, *op. cit.*, p. 286.

ten months and fourteen years and eight months, respectively." [28]   In some cases families were never reunited. Finally there was legislation to prevent the separation of husband and wife unless they gave their consent.

Servants could be inherited if the original master died or they could be sold any time before the termination of the period of servitude.   In some cases servants were badly treated.   The owner had the right to punish his indenture. If a servant married without the consent of his master he could be held for an additional year.   If women servants bore children they could be retained two years.   Certain individuals in colonial society capitalized on the fact that servants could not marry and kept disorderly houses where servants could congregate.   " Wherever white servitude was tried, it resulted in unsatisfactory social and moral conditions." [29]

Servants were often unfairly treated and many of them ran away.   They could be brought back, however, and forced into additional servitude for their behavior unless it could be proved that the master had not been fair.   If runaway servants were incarcerated and not claimed they could be sold to defray jail expenditures.   In some instances masters encouraged running away by mistreatment near the end of the period of servitude so that they might be able to hold the servant for an additional year.   Working conditions were such that the immigrant was often broken in health when he was released, and thus was forced into pauperism. We must not forget that purchasers often got worthless individuals as well as those with pernicious dispositions, so masters frequently suffered in the deal.

While the system of indentured servitude permitted many evils, there were many who became desirable American citizens who could not have reached the colonies without having had their passages paid.   " Of settlers in the early period, those who took indentures often fared much better than did those who bought land at once.   The indentured servants were trained to industry, familiarized themselves with the ways of the country, and many of them became rich,

[28] *Ibid.*, p. 212.   [29] *Ibid.*, p. 274.

while some of those who came with money and purchased estates immediately were not able to adjust themselves to the new conditions and lost their means." [30] Some settlers brought servants with them, often their relatives or friends. Masters had to pay freedom dues either in money or material. In Pennsylvania a servant received fifty acres of land when he was released.

Thousands of redemptioners achieved success. If a servant were a deserving man he lost no caste by reason of his service. Many of those around him were working as hard as he was to repay their borrowed money, or to pay for lands or other valuables which they had purchased. The servant's situation was not different; he was only paying a debt which had voluntarily been incurred. [31]

If a study were made of native Americans, it would be found that many highly respected and successful individuals could trace their origin in the United States to indentured servants. In fact the adjustment made by individuals who were owned by others was in many cases as satisfactory as with any other group.

In most of the colonies the English were the founders, so the culture was English modified through experiences in America. There was a desire to have all conform to the units of culture as established by these early settlers, but it is a mistaken idea to believe that they did. Isolation and segregation prevented cultural conflicts and made it possible for each group to realize to a certain extent the establishment of the cultural units to which it was accustomed in Europe.

Although there was considerable opposition to immigration during the colonial period, those arriving at that time, whether immigrants or colonists, helped produce the social organization that is now regarded as native American. Records do not reveal individual adjustments, but we know that each group had a problem of adjustment to face and that the result, through many generations, has been the production of many desirable and many undesirable citizens. In some instances the habits and practices of some of the

[30] *Ibid.*, p. 269.
[31] *Ibid.*, p. 270.

colonial settlers are still a mixture of European and American modes of behavior, resembling closely patterns of behavior that were brought with them.

READINGS

GENERAL

Armstrong, Edward, *Correspondence between William Penn and James Logan and others.* 1870–1872
Fairchild, Henry Pratt, *Immigration.* 1926. Chapter II, pp. 30–56
Johnson, S. C., *A History of Emigration; From the United Kingdom to North America,* 1763–1912. 1913
Mittelberger, Gottlieb, *Journey to Pennsylvania in 1750 and Return to Germany in the Year 1754;* translated by Carl T. Eben. 1898

COMPOSITION

Baird, Charles W., *History of the Huguenot Immigration to America.* 1885
Bittinger, Lucy F., *The Germans in Colonial Times.* 1901. Chapters IV, IX–XI, XV, XVII, XX
Bolton, Charles Knowles, *Scotch Irish Pioneers in Ulster and America.* 1910
Chinard, Gilbert, *Les Refugiés Huguenots en Amérique.*
Cobb, S. H., *The Story of the Palatines.* 1897
Dexter, F. B., *Estimates of Population in American Colonies.* 1887
Diffenderfer, F. R., *German Immigration into Pennsylvania through the Port of Philadelphia, 1700–1775.* 1900
Faust, A. B., *The German Element in the United States.* 1909
Fontaine, Jacques, *Memoirs of a Huguenot Family.* 1872
Ford, Henry J., *The Scotch-Irish in America.* 1915
Geiser, K. F., *Redemptioners and Indentured Servants in the Colony and Commonwealth of Pennsylvania.* 1901
Green, S. S., *The Scotch-Irish in America*
Hanna, C. A., *The Scotch-Irish.* 1902. Vol. I, Chapters XII, XVIII
Herrick, C. A., *White Servitude in Pennsylvania.* 1926
Hirsch, A. H., *The Huguenots of Colonial South Carolina.* 1928
Jacobs, H. E., *German Immigration to America,* 1709–1740
Kuhns, O., *German and Swiss Settlements of Colonial Pennsylvania.* 1901
MacLean, J. P., *Settlements of Scotch Highlanders in America.* 1900
Shaw, James, *Scotch-Irish in History.* 1899

CAUSES

Abbott, Edith, *Historical Aspects of the Immigration Problem.* 1926. Pp. 11–22

Baird, Charles W., *History of the Huguenot Immigration to America.* 1885. Vol. I, Chapters IV, V; Vol. II, Chapters VI, VII, VIII

Bittinger, L. F., *The Germans in Colonial Times.* 1901. Chapters I, II

Faust, A. B., *The German Element in the United States.* 1909

Ford, Henry J., *The Scotch-Irish in America.* 1915. Chapter V

Hanna, C. A., *The Scotch-Irish.* 1902. Chapters XXXVII, XXXIX

JOURNEY

Abbott, Edith, *Immigration: Select Documents and Case Records.* 1924. Pp. 6–9

Baird, Charles W., *History of the Huguenot Immigration to America.* 1885. Vol. II, Chapters IX, X

Mittelberger, Gottlieb, *Journey to Pennsylvania in the Year 1750 and Return to Germany in the Year 1754;* translated by Carl T. Eben. 1898

DISTRIBUTION

Faust, A. B., *The German Element in the United States.* 1909. Chapters II, IV–X

Ford, Henry J., *The Scotch-Irish in America.* 1915. Chapters VI–IX, XIV.

SOCIAL INTERACTION

Abbott, Edith, *Historical Aspects of the Immigration Problem.* 1926. Pp. 210–212; 415–422; 542–556; 702–703

Baird, Charles W., *History of the Huguenot Immigration to America.* 1885. Chapters XI–XIV

Bittinger, L. F., *The Germans in Colonial Times.* 1901. Chapters XVI–XXIII

Faust, A. B., *The German Element in the United States.* 1909

Ford, Henry J., *The Scotch-Irish in America.* 1915. Chapters X–XIII; XV–XIX

Garis, Roy L., *Immigration Restriction.* 1927. Chapter I, pp. 1–21

Hanna, C. A., *The Scotch-Irish.* 1902. Vol. I, Chapters I–VII

Mittelberger, Gottlieb, *Journey to Pennsylvania in the Year 1750 and Return to Germany in the Year 1754;* translated by Carl T. Eben. 1898

Proper, E. E., *Colonial Immigration Laws.* 1900

CHAPTER IV
UNRESTRICTED IMMIGRATION
1783–1830

INTRODUCTION

WHEN THE thirteen colonies became a separate nation, the Americans were interested at once in becoming self-sufficient, and since the former colonies were no longer subservient to the mother country, the immigration situation became strictly a national problem so far as America was concerned. With the establishment of a separate power, colonization was at an end and those arriving at the ports of the United States were regarded as immigrants no matter from what country they had come. While many new social complications developed during this period because of immigration, there was a demand for laborers, a need that could be supplied only through European emigration. Although the attitude toward immigrants had not changed, as evidenced by the fears of the leading statesmen in their discussion of naturalization and other immigration problems, the coming of immigrants offered a solution to problems of more significance than immigration itself. If the new state on the Atlantic seaboard was to be able to take its place among the nations of the world, it had to develop, and the many projects that had their inception at this time symbolized the determined attitude of the period. The West was being opened, railroads were begun, manufacturing was growing, and the Erie Canal was nearing completion.

For these new projects men were needed who were not available in America despite the rapid increase in the native population.   The letters sent back to Europe from America often revealed the opportunities for those interested in emigration.   The need for men, however, was in the West rather than along the Atlantic seaboard.   Numerous letters of the time stressed the fact that employment could be found throughout the Union for industrious mechanics, shoemakers, tailors, etc., but always the advice was given that on arrival in America emigrants should leave at once for some small town or village.   Those remaining in the seaport towns invariably spent a considerable amount of their small savings without achieving any progress toward their ultimate goal.

The government virtually lost sight of any need for regulation in this great forward movement and this epoch from 1783 to 1830 became a period of free immigration.   This passive attitude of the government finds its explanation in the fact that few immigrants were arriving at a time when industrial projects demanded a great labor supply.   The struggle for independence on the part of the colonies had aroused, momentarily, a new patriotism in the United Kingdom, and people were ready to stay at home.   The Orders in Council, the War of 1812, and the Embargo Act, all operated to curb any great influx of Europeans.   Then, all new arrivals were classed as foreigners and treated as aliens by the native Americans and the earlier immigrants. Throughout the entire period of immigration to the United States no group has been more ready to give a discreditable social definition to the new arrivals than former immigrants of the same nationality.

The tariff measures for the protection of the newly-founded industries of America not only prevented the shipment of English goods accumulated during the struggle for independence, but led to the development of manufacturing in the United States.   As productivity increased, there was a great need for the European laborer, especially the skilled or semi-skilled individual.   Opportunities in America became the occasion for a new stream of immigration with an annual influx of ten thousand a year by 1825.

COMPOSITION

AGAIN we need to consider the composition of the immigration stream since the nationality and the number always have a direct bearing on the process of adjustment. The arrivals for the period of unrestricted immigration were of the northern European stock or old immigration. The Irish furnished the greatest number for a single group and became an important element in the development of canals and railroads, as most of them were laborers or small farmers rather than tradesmen; especially was this true of those coming from the south of Ireland. The volume of immigration was small, the exact number being only a conjecture, since there had been no official count until the passage of an act that made necessary a complete report of the number of passengers carried. This act was passed on March 2, 1819, and in the year ending September 30, 1820, the first official statistics of immigration were collected. In addition to the Irish, a great many were coming from England, Scotland, Germany, and Switzerland. To those already mentioned, Timothy Dwight in discussing the population of New York City in 1812 has added " Swedes, Danes, Italians, Portuguese, Spaniards, and West-Indians." [1]

Indentured servants and redemptioners continued to be a factor throughout the period of free immigration. There was a decline in their importation as soon as there were enough free laborers available, but many came from Ireland and Germany early in the nineteenth century. The indentured system was not legislated out of existence as was Negro slavery, but merely disappeared when a more satisfactory plan could be adopted. Neither did it disappear because there was any appreciable sentiment against it; it was discontinued simply because it was not a good economic plan.

Undesirables were arriving in numbers great enough to cause some concern. Many parishes sent paupers to the United States during the period of free immigration.

---

[1] Timothy Dwight, *Travels in New England and New York* (New Haven 1822), III, 60.

I was down in the London docks, and there were *twenty-six
paupers* going out in the ship Hudson, to New York, sent by
the parish of Eurbarst, near Battle, in Sussex, in carriers' wagons,
who paid their passage and gave them money to start with when
arrived in the U. States; and other parishes must do the same or
they will be eat up by them. Many parishes are in that state
that the land is worth nothing to the landlord, and I see no
remedy except sending the extra population somewhere.[2]

As we shall see under the discussion of the causes for this
period, most of the arrivals were the destitute from the
various countries mentioned. The majority of them were
industrious members of the middle class who had once enjoyed a much higher standard of living than they had at the
time of their migration and made a normal adjustment on
the frontier of what was then America. Not all of them were
ambitious, however; some had developed attitudes of pauperism and came because they had been sent by their parishes.
Many of them were hand-workers, victims of industrialization; especially was this true of the hand-loom weavers from
Scotland.

THE CAUSES OF EMIGRATION

As WAS stated in the previous chapter, the causes of emigration for any period will help determine the type of adjustment the migrants will make. The experiences that the immigrants have had in their native land will determine their
philosophy of life. In 1783, the opening of the period of free
immigration, there had been enough emigration from the
continent and the United Kingdom to have established migration as a traditional method of escape from the social, religious, political, and economic conditions in these countries.
  While the economic cause of emigration was the most
potent, there were still social, religious, and civic conditions
that made life a miserable existence for many Europeans.

Europe is not only overburdened with poor, but oppressed with
servitude; so that the poor are not only unable to subsist by their
labour, but lie under great restrictions with respect to civil and
religious liberty. They are even, in a great measure, deprived of

[2] Extract from *Niles' Weekly Register*, XXIV, 113–114.

the satisfaction of expressing their feelings, of making complaints, or applying for redress of their grievances.[3]

This traditional means of escape became more alluring as letters were written by immigrants and colonists in America and sent to friends in Europe.   These epistles of good news were passed from family to family pointing out a way to escape the life of destitution in Europe.   But cisatlantic correspondence must not be considered as a cause of emigration, rather it offered a solution for the situation in which the real causes were to be found.

However, these letters are a good index to the real reasons for migrations.   It may be assumed that since they were written to proffer a solution to conditions in the United Kingdom and on the continent, they would stress those things which were a source of annoyance.   In a letter written by Joseph Priestley to a friend in England from Northumberland, Pennsylvania, October 4, 1796, is this rather extravagant statement:

The advantages we enjoy in this country are indeed very great. Here we have no poor; we never see a beggar, nor is there a family in want.   We have no church establishment, and hardly any taxes.   This particular state pays all its officers from a treasure in the public funds.   There are very few crimes committed, and we travel without the least apprehension of danger.   The press is perfectly free, and I hope we shall always keep out of war.[4]

A letter from Morris Birkbeck of Illinois written January 7, 1818, shows how communications from the United States could easily encourage those of England in financial straits to emigrate in order to better their condition.

I *own* here a far better estate than I *rented* in England, and am already more attached to the *soil*.   Here, every citizen, whether by birthright or adoption, is part of the government, identified with it, not *virtually*, but in fact; and eligible to every office, with one exception, regarding the Presidency, for which a birthright is necessary.[5]

[3] Extract from Dr. Joseph Priestley (see Doc. 4, Section I), *The Case of Poor Emigrants Recommended, in a Discourse, Delivered at the University Hall in Philadelphia, Sunday, February 19, 1797* (Philadelphia 1797), p. 257.
[4] Extract from letter written by Joseph Priestley to a friend in England.   It was first published in a newspaper in Leeds, England, and was reprinted by William Cobbett.   (See *Porcupine's Works*, IX, 312–313.)
[5] Morris Birkbeck, *Letters from Illinois* (Philadelphia 1818), p. 28.

These letters found a ready response because of the economic conditions in England, Germany, Switzerland, Scotland, and Ireland, which were the real causes of emigration. In many of the parishes in England there was a greater number than could be employed in agricultural pursuits, the chief occupation of the district. In each case the poor rates became a great burden. In order to relieve the distressing situations the parishes elected to encourage emigration, with a result that many came to America in destitute circumstances, many ready to work and make adjustments, but some who were to become objects of charity.

Not only was there distress in the agricultural districts but the mining and manufacturing districts were also centers of unemployment.

Several hundred persons have recently been discharged from the iron works and mines, in the neighborhood of Wellington, Ketly, Coalpit, Bank, Ironbridge, &c. in consequence of the depressed state of trade. At Wellington, in particular, the distress of the lower order is very great. On Sunday sen'night the town was literally crowded with persons out of employ, many of whom in vain applied to the recruiting parties.[6]

The economic depression early in the nineteenth century forced many in Germany and Switzerland to adopt a standard of living much below that to which they had been accustomed. Their inability to buy tended to demoralize the industries, which resulted in unemployment for many of the lower classes. There was a feeling that Germany and Switzerland were overpopulated, a condition that could be relieved only by emigration.

In some of the cantons of Switzerland, it was reported that there was complete unemployment for a large part of the population, making it impossible for people to have even the bare necessities of life, resulting in the death of thousands from hunger and want of every kind. Consequently, many left for Russia and America. The situation was not entirely a matter of unemployment. Goods could not be sold after

---

[6] Extract from the *Dublin Evening Post*, June 8, 1816; reprinted in *Niles' Weekly Register*, X, 408 (August 17, 1816).

they had been produced, in either Germany, Switzerland, or adjacent countries.

In Scotland, especially with the weavers, there was need for some relief in the economic distress. Petitions from these weavers were presented in Parliament, showing the extreme distress of those who were unable to earn enough for the bare essentials of life. Some were unable to secure employment at all, and those who worked long hours each day earned only a few shillings a week. The sufferers were not paupers but worthy persons many of whom were hand-weavers who could not operate the new power looms. In their appeal they did not ask for charity but for an opportunity to emigrate so that they might remove their families from the evils that would accompany such conditions.

In Ireland there was an even more deplorable state of affairs as shown by a discussion of emigration in Ireland in 1824–1826.

The land proprietors have taken up an opinion latterly, that the cause of their distress is the overstocking the land with people; and as the leases fall in, they get rid of the surplus population by turning them out entirely from their lands. Those poor people, not getting employment, either erect temporary habitations like sheds on the highway, or they come into towns, and crowd themselves into small apartments; perhaps four or five families will live in a garret or small hovel, huddled together there, without clothes or bedding, or food, living upon the chance of employment in the town as labourers. . .

. . . they have not the means to emigrate, nor can they get land· or employment at home. A poor man thus dismissed, with his family, from his dwelling and land, with perhaps one or two cows, a few sheep or a horse; the whole of which may not, at existing prices, be worth five pounds, seeks, in the first instance, to procure a lot of land from some middleman, who has cleared the farm of the pauper tenants whom he had previously ruined, and who is induced to take him as tenant, because he possessed a cow, a horse, or some sheep; the rent is such as the middleman chooses to impose, the tenant being willing to promise anything rather than go into a town, where he knows he cannot find employment, and hoping to get subsistence for a year or two, on his new holding; but at the end of a year, all that he has is seized for his new master, and he is ultimately compelled to seek an asylum in some hovel or town, trusting for his support to the precarious chances of daily labour.[7]

So the need for laborers in America offered an ideal solution for the lamentable economic and social situation in Europe.

THE JOURNEY

COMING from a situation of privation and destitution, the emigrants were in an enervated condition when they started on a voyage that in most cases entailed many weeks of suffering on board sailing vessels poorly adapted to carrying a cargo of human beings, not only from the standpoint of inadequate space and accommodations, but from the standpoint of the quantity and quality of food and drink. In many cases emigrants arrived in a deplorable physical condition and with attitudes that resulted in an adjustment of pauperism or temporary dependency.

Many accounts of suffering on the slow transports during the early part of the nineteenth century have been recorded. One of these publications [8] contained a letter from J. J. Mayersohn in St. Gall to the royal Prussian consul in New York, Herr J. W. Schmidt.

Almost every week we read credible accounts of hundreds (Swiss and German) who through their inexperience have become the easy prey of deceitful enlisting officers and dishonest ship captains. Some languished in Holland. Many were destroyed on ship board through want and by infectious diseases. Others came back home in the most pitiable condition, and of those who lived to see the longed-for shores of America, the promised land of their anticipation, how many found there only new misery and greater loneliness.

It was customary for emigrants to make arrangements with the captain of a sailing vessel for certain supplies for the journey, but there was no way by which a compliance to arrangements could be forced once the ship was on its way.

[7] From the Testimony of the Reverend Michael Collins. Extracts from the evidence taken before committees on the state of Ireland, 1824 and 1825. Reprinted in Great Britain, *Report from the Select Committee of Emigration from the United Kingdom* 1826, Appendix II, 314–315.

[8] Zuverlässige Nachrichten über die Vorbedingungen unter welchen Auswanderungen nach den Vereinigten Staaten von Nord Amerika ohne Vermessenheit versucht werden dürfen.

On some occasions continental emigrants were left in England and other countries even though they had arranged for their passage to America.

It was possible for those responsible for the transportation of immigrants to practice many forms of fraud. Redemptioners were often hurried from the ship in America before their friends knew they had arrived and could have a chance to rescue them from long periods of servitude.

Indeed it might be shown that emigrants have been actually induced to proceed to parts distant from that of their destination, by one or two thousand miles, under a belief that they were in the most direct road to the places of their intended settlements; nor does the evil stop here, for the emigrant is exposed to extortion on every hand, in the shape of charges for making out entries, taking charge of luggage, passing his name at the custom-house, frequently under the statement that he is of a trade which, by the existing laws, disqualifies him from going abroad, and that the broker has to provide another person to pass the examination for him (a practice not of unfrequent occurrence, though requiring a false oath), and for which service, whether real or imaginary, a high compensation is required, and thus the emigrant in reality often pays more for his passage than he would, were he to make his arrangement with the merchant, independent of these men.[9]

So during this period, thousands landed at the ports of America, in both the United States and Canada, in such a condition that only poverty and illness could be the early adjustments. Many of the objections raised against immigration were based on the fact that immigrants, through no fault of their own, reached America in a deplorable condition.

DISTRIBUTION

THE ATTITUDE concerning the immigrant depended on the locality in which he settled in America. This fact is illustrated by the following communication sent by an immigrant to his relatives in England:

You will please to notice, that this letter has no reference to the Atlantic States, there, everything is quite reversed: people had

[9] Extract from "A Report of a Committee of the American Chamber of Commerce in Liverpool 1822," reprinted in Appendix to *Report from Select Committee of Emigration from the United Kingdom* (1826), p. 296.

better stay at home than go there. I have travelled two thousand miles into the interior of America, where every European must come to do himself good. The people here want me to take the Oath and become an American, but I will not, unless you will come, then I shall have no objection; the people here are very benevolent and obliging to Englishmen.[10]

Advice to immigrants during the period of free immigration always contained instructions to go West and to avoid the large cities of the East. In many cases this advice was accepted and Illinois, Ohio, Indiana, and states of the Middle West were settled. Germans were found in Pennsylvania, Ohio, Virginia, Maryland, New York, North and South Carolina, Tennessee, Kentucky, Indiana, Missouri, and Illinois. Reports on immigration show that there was a tendency on the part of the Irish to remain in cities where they could secure employment, as many of them were very poor and had little capital. This meant that the Irish would present the greatest problem of adjustments of all groups coming to America, since in the cities the immigrants have always resided in the disorganized areas where major social problems are found in their most flagrant form.

SOCIAL INTERACTION AND ADJUSTMENT

AMERICA had just emerged from the Revolutionary War as an independent state with a feeling that this new sovereign freedom must be guarded, especially from monarchically-minded Europeans. It was the conviction of a great many statesmen during the Revolution and following that period, that it was incumbent upon them to preserve the newly formed state. There is always a self-consciousness following any war, and with the added impetus of newly won freedom and the establishment of a new state, there was bound to be a protective attitude on the part of governmental officials. This attitude of fear concerning foreign interference in the political life of America was crystallized in the Alien Bill in 1798 which gave the President power to deport any aliens who might by their behavior seem dangerous to the country.

---

[10] J. Knight, *Important Extracts from Original and Recent Letters Written by Englishmen, in the United States of America, to Their Friends in England* (2d series, Manchester 1818), p. 23.

Much concern was shown about the matter of naturalization, which was looked upon as a means of control for those who had designs on the destruction of the American government.

The period of residence required for naturalization was set at two years by the act of 1790, but this was raised to five years in 1795. The war excitement which marked the closing years of the century led to the passage of an act in 1798 requiring a residence of fourteen years for naturalization. This was repealed after four years, and the provisions of the act of 1795 were again put in force. They have remained unchanged in their essentials ever since. In addition to the period of residence required, there was much discussion as to the charge to be made for naturalization. It was proposed by some to set this at $20, but this was regarded by others as too high, and the amount was fixed at $5.[11]

A feeling of opposition to immigration was not limited to statesmen. American ethnocentrism showed itself in the reactions of many other citizens. In most cases, the immigrant was made to feel that he was an undesirable alien, as distinguished from the native-born, which is evidence that there was, even at this early date when men were needed, some problem of adjustment. An immigrant from Great Britain revealed this fact in the following statement: "There is one very unpleasant circumstance which attends us Englishmen here, which is, that most of the natives entertain the idea, *we quit our country for crimes,* and dare not return. I assure you I have been taunted with this already several times." [12] The early problem attending the arrival of criminals and paupers offered an excellent rationalization for the native American for his attitude of ethnocentrism concerning all foreigners.

The experience of another immigrant led to the following statement:

Throughout the States, I have remarked that there is a strong line of distinction drawn between *citizens of native and of foreign birth;* and, in some cases, where the latter have professed prin-

[11] H. P. Fairchild, *Immigration,* Revised edition, pp. 61–62. By permission of The Macmillan Company, publishers.
[12] Extract from *Look before You Leap; or A Few Hints to Such Artizans, Mechanics, Labourers, Farmers, and Husbandmen, as Are Desirous of Emigration to America,* etc. (London 1796), p. 103.

ciples of republicanism in Europe (a sin which might, at least, one should suppose, be forgiven them *in the United States of America*), they are treated with scorn, as out-casts, who ought to have remained in their own country, and have submitted to whatever form of despotism it chose to exert over them.[13]

Another instance of the reaction of Americans to foreigners has been recorded thus:

The old American (or Yankee) looks with the most sovereign contempt upon the emigrant; he considers him a wretch, driven out of a wretched country, and seeking subsistence in his glorious land. His pride is swelled, and his scorn of the poor emigrant doubled, not merely by this consideration, but by the prevailing notion that but few come here who have not violated the laws of their native realm. If a word is said of one returning, " Oh (says the Yankee), he'll none return: the stolen horse will keep him here."

With their insatiate thirst of gain, and these contemptuous notions of emigrants, they seem to consider them fair objects of plunder; and are prepared, in every transaction, to profit by their ignorance of the value of their goods, the customs and laws of the country, and the character of the people. Whoever comes here, should come with his eyes and ears open, and with the confirmed notion, that he is going to deal with sharpers. If he is not careful in purchasing necessaries for his inland journey, he will pay ten-fold for them; and when he is there, without equal caution, he will be liable to purchase land of a squatter: that is, a man who has taken possession of it, cultivated it without any title, and is subject to be ejected every day by the legal owner.[14]

With this reception following the treatment accorded them on the journey, it was quite natural that the immigrant should be interested in the preservation of his own customs, habits, and traditions, as well as in a chance to settle in a colony somewhat isolated from American life.

Despite the definition given the immigrants by native Americans, during the period of free immigration adjustments were not so difficult to make when compared with the present situation in American cities. The immigrants came as a group, settled as a group in most cases, and carried on their European patterns of behavior, many in rural districts

[13] Henry Bradshaw Fearon, *Sketches of America* (London: Longman, Hurst, Rees, Orme, and Brown 1818), pp. 346–347.
[14] E. Howitt, *Selections from Letters Written during a Tour through the United States, in the Summer and Autumn of 1819* (Nottingham 1820), pp. 217–218.

where there could be very little conflict of cultures.   In fact adjustments were not so difficult as they had been in Europe.   What happened in most cases was not assimilation since assimilation involves a complete change.   With those of the first generation the cultural attitudes were modified but they were as much European as they were American.

While the immigrants arriving at this time were condemned for their European human nature, there was not a demand for cultural changes.   Isolated colonies were responsible for their own habits and customs.   Adjustments were physical, since there were roads to build and water courses to bridge.   Land had to be cleared before it could be tilled.   In the last part of the eighteenth century, Benjamin Rush wrote a description of German life in Pennsylvania.   At that time they still maintained their European customs and habits, spoke the German language and had their own churches and schools.   Separate colonies gave the adult German a chance to make economic and social adjustments without any very important changes in his cultural organization and social nature, which resulted in stability rather than disorganization.   The adjustment was that of accommodation and not assimilation.

The immigrants brought with them during the period of unrestricted immigration their own scheme of cultural life. Where it was possible to live in isolation, as it was in most cases, there was very little opportunity for assimilation, and therefore little chance for cultural conflicts and disorganization.   It is when there is disorganization and the immigrant becomes a problem that there is talk of his unassimilability. Since the records show little evidence of conflict with the immigrant from northwestern Europe during this early period, it is assumed by many that assimilation had taken place.   But this was not the case.   Each group with its own culture created a section of a mosaic of rural cultures to which later immigrants had to make adjustments.

While the immigrant of the first generation made an accommodation through isolation, there was a tendency on the part of the second generation as well as those of the first

generation who accumulated wealth, to break with their
European traditions and develop an American social nature.
Just as the Jews of today try to get out of the ghetto as soon
as they have acquired sufficient capital, so some immigrants
of this early period made an effort to lose their identity as
a certain nationality and be known merely as Americans.
This situation is shown by the writings of Dr. Ernst Brauns,
a German traveler.

With the beginning of the nineteenth century a spirit of innova-
tion, very dangerous to their well-being, suddenly began to take
possession of the once quiet and peaceful German communities in
North America.   Some Germans who had become rich thought
that they were superior to their less prosperous associates, and
their children began to be ashamed of the German language, and
to look upon it as the language of the common people.   They
demanded that in addition to German the English language
should be introduced into the German churches, although there
were already enough English churches everywhere.   It had
already been demonstrated by experience that the two languages
could not be united in one church, since in such cases German
gradually disappeared.   This desire for change therefore caused
a violent cleavage in numerous settlements which sometimes
resulted in a split into two parties — the German and the Angli-
cized-German.   The latter party was supported by the Irish and
the Anglo-American allies, and when this party dominated the
situation, the Germans were completely absorbed.[15]

So the conflict of cultures during this early period was
between immigrants of the same nationality, those who
wished to be American and those who wanted to remain
European in habits and traditions.

When the transition from one culture to another is under
way, there is likely to be a reaction which is really a nationalistic movement to revive the language as well as an interest
in the literature, customs, and traditions of the group.   When
a sufficiently large group of Germans became interested in
American culture during the early part of the nineteenth
century, the reaction set in.   This is concrete evidence that
assimilation had not taken place, nor was it likely to take
place if it could be prevented by those of the first gen-

[15] Translated from Dr. Ernst Brauns, *Praktische Belehrungen und Rathschläge für
Reisende und Auswanderer nach Amerika* (Braunschweig 1829), pp. 351–352.

eration and the more conservative of the second and third generations.

The reaction in Pennsylvania is summed up in the following paragraph:

Since that time (1813) there has been an earnest endeavor to revive the German schools that had been so nearly absorbed, and splendid progress has been made in this important field. To these appeals and to the numerous German immigrants in this state, numbering more than 50,000 souls between the years 1813 and 1829, we owe the fact that now so much interest in the German language has been awakened in Pennsylvania that when the last legislature met (1828), a request was introduced to have the German language declared an official language of the state with the same rights as English. In spite of the fact that the educated Anglo-Americans favored this legislative proposal, it failed at this time on account of the anglomania of those who were of German blood but who voted against it. But so great was the number of those who voted to have German installed as an official language that only one more vote was needed to pass this measure. However people in Pennsylvania cherish a hope that this proposal will be renewed in the next legislature and will be victorious.[16]

The Irish made a ready adjustment in cities so far as work was concerned; but they were still Irish in manners, attitudes, habits, customs, and traditions. Forming the new element for this period, they had not had time to change their life organizations. " The Scotch Colonists preserve, unaltered, the character, which they brought with them. They are industrious, frugal, orderly, patient of hardship, persevering, attached to government, reverential to religion, generally moral, and often pious." [17] They were Scotch-Americans in so far as any change had taken place. It is a mistaken idea to believe that the resulting cultural complex was the same where they settled as a group as it was in the German, English, or Irish colonies.

The adjustment of the Welsh was an accommodation rather than assimilation. In "An Open Letter from Welsh Immigrants in Pennsylvania, 1800 " we find evidence of this fact.

[16] *Ibid.*, p. 368.
[17] Timothy Dwight, *op. cit.*, p. 533.

Our end in establishing this settlement was for the general good of the *Welsh,* particularly that they may have the privilege of hearing the gospel in their own language. There are in *Cambria* preachers of different denominations, living together in peace and amity. We have three or four Welsh sermons every first day in the week, and there are English preachers in Beula.[18]

The group that found adjustments most difficult was the indentured class no matter what their nationality might be.

The substance of what I have been able to collect is, that the poor creatures who have been induced to *indent themselves* are in situations the most pitiable; they are treated by their *masters* in a similar manner *to the felons formerly transported from England to Virginia.* Instead of being put in possession of portions of land, and quickly discharging their engagements, they sink deeper into debt, and this by the means of being obliged to purchase on credit at the most extravagant charges from their masters the stores and necessaries of which they stand in need. Thus situated they are never free from the landholder who is an absolute tyrant, while his miserable *indented servants are likely to remain slaves forever.* Great numbers die from the change of climate, want of proper sustenance, and the very unusual and laborious employ to which they are rigorously subjected by their vigilant overseers.[19]

This was the situation in certain cases even though there had been much legislation for their protection. We must not lose sight of the fact that the abnormal aspects of any social situation always receive the most publicity. Many redemptioners and indentured servants could not be distinguished from others in their ultimate adjustments.

There were certain pathological adjustments such as poverty, pauperism, destitution, criminality, and insanity, that must not be overlooked as forms of accommodation. This can be illustrated from the writings of the early part of the nineteenth century. Regarding dependency we have many authentic statements such as the one below.

. . . many emigrants have suffered extremely during the voyage. They are landed in a sickly condition, or soon become sickly by the change of climate; so that for a long time they are unable to do anything at all, and they find expenses at inns and lodging houses much greater than they had any idea of; so that the little

[18] Extract from a letter printed in America in 1800; reprinted by William Cobbett in *Porcupine's Gazette (Porcupine's Works,* IX, 411).
[19] Extract from *Look before You Leap;* etc. (London 1796), p. 119.

money they might bring with them is soon expended, and they are left wholly destitute. In this case, if they meet with no relief from the charitable and well disposed, they must inevitably perish. Whereas, with a little assistance and encouragement, which is often of more real use than money, they may soon recover their health, strength, and spirits; and with proper advice with respect to the disposal of themselves, they may, in a short time, become useful citizens.[20]

A " Society for Assisting Emigrants " was located in Philadelphia. It gave information to immigrants and helped them to secure employment. In certain cases money was provided for immediate use and for the purchase of tools. Those who were sick were given medical care and later located where they could earn their own living. Because of the conditions of destitution in certain parts of Europe and the suffering during the voyage, people could not be expected to arrive with the goods, money, and physical strength necessary for a satisfactory adjustment.

They are frequently found destitute in our streets; they seek employment at our doors; they are found in our alms-house, and in our hospitals; they are found at the bar of our criminal tribunals, in our bridewell, our penitentiary, and our state prison. And we lament to say, that they are too often led by want, by vice, and by habit, to form a phalanx of plunder and depredation, rendering our city more liable to the increase of crimes, and our houses of correction more crowded with convicts and felons.[21]

In summary we can say that adjustments at the end of the period of unrestricted immigration in 1830 were in the form of accommodations. Isolated situations on the frontier did not demand any more. Immigrants were not Americanized and little disorganized because they did not come into contact with a strictly American milieu. In the cities where there were cultural conflicts the process of disintegration was well under way, which seems to be an essential step in the process of Americanization where a group is under the tremendous handicap of having to live in two cultures.

[20] Extract from Dr. Joseph Priestley, *The Case of Poor Emigrants Recommended, in a Discourse, Delivered at the University Hall in Philadelphia, Sunday, February 19, 1797* (Philadelphia 1797), pp. 19–20.
[21] Extract from the *Second Annual Report of the Managers of the Society for the Prevention of Pauperism in the City of New York, December 29, 1819, to Which Is Added an Appendix, on the Subject of Pauperism,* pp. 20–21.

Some were maladjusted because they arrived poorly equipped to make the transition from one culture to another and were not able to transport themselves beyond the well settled areas. By the end of this period a larger number were coming, which resulted in much legislation as the various states tried to cope with the growing intricacies of the movement of so many Europeans to America.

READINGS

GENERAL

Fairchild, Henry P., *Immigration.* 1926. Chapter III, pp. 57–67
Johnson, S. C., *A History of Emigration from the United Kingdom to North America, 1763–1912.* 1913

COMPOSITION

Cobb, S. H., *The Story of the Palatines.* 1897
Faust, A. B., *The German Element in the United States.* 1909
Ford, Henry J., *The Scotch-Irish in America.* 1915
Green, S. S., *The Scotch-Irish in America*
Hale, E. E., *Letters on Irish Immigration.* 1852
Haltigan, James, *The Irish in the American Revolution and Their Early Influence in the Colonies.* 1908
Hanna, C. A., *The Scotch-Irish.* 1902
Herrick, C. A., *White Servitude in Pennsylvania.* 1926
Jacobs, H. E., *German Immigration to America.* 1709–1740
McGee, Thomas D'Arcy, *The Irish Position in Britain and in the Republic of North America.* 1866
MacLean, J. P., *Settlements of Scotch Highlanders in America.* 1900
Maguire, J. F., *The Irish in America.* 1868
O'Brien, Michael J., *A Hidden Phase of American History, Ireland's Part in America's Struggle for Liberty.* 1919
O'Donovan, Jeremiah, *A Brief Account of the Author's Interview with his Countrymen, and of the Parts of the Emerald Isle, Whence They Emigrated*

CAUSES

Abbott, Edith, *Historical Aspects of the Immigration Problem.* 1926. Pp. 22–84

JOURNEY

Abbott, Edith, *Immigration: Select Documents and Case Records.* 1924. Pp. 9–20

DISTRIBUTION

Faust, A. B., *The German Element in the United States.*   1909
Ford, Henry J., *The Scotch-Irish in America.*   1915.
Maguire, J. F., *The Irish in America.*   1868

SOCIAL INTERACTION AND ADJUSTMENT

Abbott, Edith, *Historical Aspects of the Immigration Problem.*
   1926.   Pp. 212–250; 422–436; 556–566; 703–733
——, *Immigration: Select Documents and Case Records.*   1924.
   Pp. 102–110
Faust, A. B., *The German Element in the United States.*   1909
Haltigan, James, *The Irish in the American Revolution and
   Their Early Influence in the Colonies.*   1908
Hanna, Charles A., *The Scotch-Irish.*   1902
Maguire, J. F., *The Irish in America.*   1868

CHAPTER V
STATE REGULATION
1830–1860

INTRODUCTION

EARLY IN THE nineteenth century the economic situation in Europe had produced so many destitute individuals that only emigration seemed a mitigating solution, and was urged by many of the parishes throughout Europe. The propitious agricultural opportunities in this country, along with the rapidly-developing industries, offered some amelioration from the great suffering. Americans were not anxious to give up the chance of becoming independent farmers for work in industries — which created a demand for foreign laborers. The influx that started in 1825 with about ten thousand immigrants reached a total of 215,009 in 1854.

This great stream of immigration resulted in a perceptible increase in social problems of pauperism, criminality, insanity, etc., as the new arrivals tried to adjust themselves to the American situation, greatly handicapped at the outset by many years of destitution in their native clime and a journey of hardships across the Atlantic. Political upheavals in Europe which became a cause for migration focused the attention of statesmen on the danger of the political activities of a large foreign element. America had just become an independent nation with a spirit and attitude of republicanism that had been crystallized into certain important institutions that might easily be destroyed. The importance of any political danger was greatly over-emphasized since those coming were not the agents of any foreign government but people who were anxious to get away from undesirable conditions in Europe.

The problems of this period, both real and imaginary, caused a demand for regulation. The issue of state rights, of more importance at this time than the problem of immigration, had not been settled. Consequently restrictive legislation became a matter for each state rather than for federal control. So the period of state control began about 1830 and ended in 1882 after important decisions had been made by the Supreme Court showing that Congress could regulate the problems accompanying immigration better than the various states.

Since the era of state regulation covers more than fifty years in which many changes took place, it will be considered in two periods. Conditions were different, to a certain extent, after the Civil War with the passage of the Liberal Homestead Act of 1862 which resulted in the voluminous trek to middle and western states and territories. The first period will include the years from 1830 to 1860 and the second from 1860 to 1882, when the problem of immigration became a matter of federal control.

COMPOSITION

EMIGRATION was still from northwestern Europe: English, Irish, Scotch, Welsh, German, Dutch, and Scandinavians. The largest number came from Ireland and here we have a good example of the need for considering the composition, since the Irish furnished the greatest problem of adjustment. Their numbers, their destitute condition, the attitude concerning Roman Catholics, and the fact that they settled quite largely in cities offered a partial explanation, as we shall see later. The Irish were chiefly farmers, farm laborers, and servants, many of whom had been tenants ejected from the various estates in Ireland and were quite destitute when they left for America. The large immigration was now from the south of Ireland rather than from Ulster. Their experience with the English government had given them what Dr. H. A.

Miller [1] calls the " oppression psychosis," a further explanation of their inability to make ready adjustments in America.

The emigration from Germany during the first part of the nineteenth century was chiefly from the " Upper and Middle Rhine, the Grand Duchy of Baden, Würtenburg, the two Hesses, and Bavaria." There was a change during this period in the composition of those from Germany. Previously they had been largely agriculturists. With the political upheaval in Germany involving a struggle for liberty, emigration included a more intellectual class that came not because of poverty but because they were socially and politically maladjusted. They brought with them in many cases enough wealth to make an immediate economic accommodation in the United States.

NATIVITIES OF FOREIGN RESIDENTS [2]

Natives of	*Census of* 1860	*Census of* 1850	*Proportions in* 1860	*Proportions in* 1850
Ireland	1,611,304	961,719	38.94	43.51
Germany	1,301,136	573,225	31.45	25.94
England	432,692	278,675	10.44	12.61
British America	249,970	147,700	6.05	6.68
France..............	109,870	54,069	2.66	2.44
Scotland	108,518	70,550	2.63	3.19
Switzerland	53,327	13,358	1.29	0.60
Wales	45,763	29,868	1.11	1.34
Norway	43,995	12,678	1.07	0.57
China	35,565	785	0.86	0.03
Holland	28,281	9,848	0.68	0.45
Mexico	27,466	13,317	0.66	0.60
Sweden	18,625	3,559	0.45	0.16
Italy	10,518	3,645	0.26	0.17
Other Countries	60,145	37,870	1.45	1.71
Total foreign-born	4,137,175	2,210,866	100.00	100.00

While the composition of the foreign-born in the United States was largely English, Scotch-Irish, Irish, and German, there could be found many other nationalities as well. There were 4,137,175 natives of other countries in the United States

[1] See Herbert A. Miller, *Races, Nations and Classes* (Philadelphia: J. B. Lippincott Co. 1924), Chapter IV.

[2] Extract from *Population of the United States in 1860*; Compiled from the Original Returns of the Eighth Census under the Direction of the Secretary of the Interior, by Joseph G. Kennedy, Supt. of Census, Washington, D.C. 1864. pp. xxviii–xxxii.

in 1860, made up chiefly of those mentioned above, but there were representatives of almost every nation on earth. Although the table on page 81 does not include just those that came during the period of state regulation, it does show the nativities of the foreign residents at the end of the period in 1860, and reveals the background of cultures in which future immigrants must make their adjustments.

Europe was still anxious to get rid of the maladjusted members of society and America continued to be the destination of great numbers of these paupers, destitute individuals, and "criminals." Paupers were frequently assigned as seamen to evade the state laws and prisoners were in chains on board a ship within a day's journey of the port of debarkation.

An English emigrant who had become a naturalized citizen felt that a great injustice was being done the United States

. . . because anybody, or everybody, may come without let or hindrance. The rogues and vagabonds from London, Paris, Amsterdam, Vienna, Naples, Hamburg, Berlin, Rome, Genoa, Leghorn, Geneva, &c. may come and do come. The outpouring of alms and work houses, and prisons and penitentiaries, may come and do come. Monarchies, oligarchies, and aristocracies may and do reduce the millions of the people to poverty and beggary, and compel the most valueless to seek for a shelter and a home in the United States of America, and they do so. And what are the consequences? The consequences are that about 400,000 souls, from Europe, chiefly Germans, Irish, and Dutch are annually arriving in this country and making it their permanent abode. That a vast number of these emigrants come without money, occupation, friends, or business; many, very many, have not the means of buying land, getting to it, stocking it, and waiting for first crops, and many others would not settle upon land if they could. That, go where you will in the United States, you find nearly all the dens of iniquity, taverns, grog-shops, beer houses, gambling places, and houses of ill fame and worse deeds, are kept by foreigners. That, at the various ports, the alms-houses and hospitals are, in the main, occupied by foreigners; and that numerous objects of poverty and destitution are to be seen crawling along the streets in every direction. That not a few become criminals, filling our prisons and putting the country to great expense.[3]

[3] Extract from *Emigration, Emigrants, and Know-Nothings,* by a Foreigner (Philadelphia 1854), pp. 30–31.

This reads like a philippic from a spellbinder, but other documents of the time show that it is not too extravagant for certain conditions of the time. Immigration had now reached the place where cultures were in conflict in urban centers where there was a chance for a great variety of accommodations, many of a pathological nature.

When W. Steuart Trench assumed the responsibility of managing Lord Lansdowne's estates in Ireland after the famine, he gave the destitute tenants of these estates an opportunity for free transportation to America.

The mode adopted was as follows: Two hundred each week were selected of those apparently most suited for emigration. . . This plan succeeded admirably; and week after week, to the astonishment of the good people of Cork, and sometimes not a little to their dismay, a batch of two hundred paupers appeared on the quays of Cork, bound for the Far West. . .

. . . And thus, two hundred after two hundred, week after week, departed for Cork, until the poor-house was nearly emptied of paupers chargeable to the Lansdowne estate; and in little more than a year 3500 paupers had left Kenmare for America, all free emigrants, without any ejectments having been brought against them to enforce it, or the slightest pressure put upon them to go.[4]

It has already been pointed out that the pathological aspect of any situation always attracts more attention than any other aspect — and so it was with immigration of this period. The social variants, especially the paupers, were discussed more than those who came with goods, money, and aspiration for making a normal adjustment at once.

The consternation regarding immigration revealed by the press in various parts of Europe shows that in many cases a highly desirable class was leaving for America. It was said of the English emigrants: " Some of these people carry more than two thousand pounds each with them. Three millions of gold will, this very year, go from England to the United States, by the means of emigration." [5] In Ulster the *Newry Examiner* said: " The honest, the industrious, the inde-

---

[4] W. Steuart Trench, *Realities of Irish Life* (Boston: Roberts Brothers 1869), pp. 103–104.
[5] Extract from a letter written by William Cobbett to Sir Robert John Wilmot-Horton, *Niles' Weekly Register*, XXXVIII, 296.

pendent, are quitting us, and going to enrich another land and add strength to another state." Like reports are to be found in the papers of every country and in most of the communities in each country from which people were emigrating. So, while many paupers were being sent to the United States, there was also an industrious element of even greater numbers.

CAUSES

ECONOMIC, social, political, and religious conditions were the chief causes for the increased departures from Europe during the first part of the nineteenth century. The economic situation in Europe was still a disturbing element, and agents were not slow to take advantage of this fact and propagandized these areas of mendicity with literature concerning America. This method of stimulating emigration is shown by the following statement made in 1837:

And this deponent further says, that there were hand bills, placarded on every corner, tree and pump and public place in the city of Dublin, and for 40 or 50 miles in the surrounding country, stating, in substance, that the people were fools not to leave the country, where there was nothing but poverty staring them in the face. That laborers were so much wanted in America, that even women were employed to work at men's work — that work was plenty in America, and wages high, to wit, 9 or 10 shillings a day, British money, and his diet. And deponent further says that William Wiley of Dublin, the agent of Rawson and McMurray of New York, told this deponent that he, deponent could get ten pounds British money per month, and his diet as wages; that every one was on a perfect equality in America; that the common laboring man received high wages, and sat at the same table and eat with his master, and gave deponent such a glowing picture of the wealth of America, and that with ease, an independent fortune could be made; that he, (deponent) determined to relinquish his situation on the grand canal and bring his family to America, expecting, and so stated to his employer, that he might expect to see him return again in three years a rich man.[6]

American conditions as portrayed in this propaganda offered a way out of the European situation.

[6] Extract taken from *N. Y. Mercantile Advertiser* and reprinted in *Niles' Weekly Register*, LII, 409 (August 26, 1837).

This epoch of emigration was signalized by the Irish famine exodus of 1847; the "unemployment" situation in Scotland; the "privation of the working classes" in England and Wales; and the material discomforts of many in Germany, as well as the political upheaval. Many writers viewed the political situation in Germany as more important than the economic situation. Citizens of this country were pictured as desiring absolute political and religious freedom. Other writers were of the opinion that the economic conditions were of equal importance.

The economic situation in England and Wales can be seen by the poor-rate for the two countries in 1838, when 4,406,907 pounds were raised to care for the needy. Most of those helped were able-bodied poor, which fact demonstrates the actual unemployment situation. In the Highland districts of Scotland there was not profitable work for everyone, resulting in destitution and suffering. Regarding Ireland, a Parliamentary Commission reported that " it might be computed that about 2,385,000 persons, connected with the labouring population, are in distress for thirty weeks in the year, from the want of employment." [7]

The United States provided an outlet from undesirable economic and political conditions in Europe.

In the political and social organization of the United States, the two laws, of public lands and of naturalization, have a combined influence upon the whole matter of emigration. If the law of naturalization places the alien in a probationary situation for five years, the law of the federal domain gives to him without delay abundant resources for using this period of probation to create an independent position for himself. [8]

THE JOURNEY

THE JOURNEY for the immigrant began as soon as he left his home. For many the trip to the port of embarkation included many hardships.

" It is a lamentable sight," says a French writer, " when you are travelling in the spring or autumn on the Strasburg road, to see

[7] Extract from speech of William Smith O'Brien in *Hansard's Parliamentary Debates*, Vol. LIV, col. 837 (3d series 1840).

[8] Extract translated from A. van der Straten-Ponthoz, *Recherches sur la situation des émigrants aux États-Unis de l'Amérique du Nord* (Bruxelles 1846), p. 29.

the long files of carts that meet you every mile, carrying the whole property of the poor wretches, who are about to cross the Atlantic on the faith of a lying prospectus. There they go slowly along; their miserable tumbrils — drawn by such starved, drooping beasts, that your only wonder is, how they can possibly hope to reach Havre alive — piled with the scanty boxes containing their few effects, and on the top of all the women and children, the sick and bedridden, and all who are too exhausted with the journey to walk. One might take it for a convoy of wounded, the relics of a battle-field, but for the rows of little white heads peeping from beneath the ragged hood." These are the emigrants from Bavaria and the Upper Rhine, who have no seaport nearer than Havre.[9]

The hardships of the journey from the home of the emigrant to the port of embarkation were not greater than those at the port. The following is a discussion of conditions at Havre, France:

There is to be found continually a set of men, who have been forced to quit Germany, and with the purpose of going to America or who can say by what other chance have got to this place, where they now seek to keep up their life by making themselves busy with the emigrants. In all our travels in different countries, we have never met with more miserable men, a class more destitute of morality, than these land sharks, who lie in wait for those that thus come by thousands from Germany, thrust themselves upon them as countrymen and friends . . . detain their victims, plunder them, and abuse their inexperience in the most shameful way. . . The same dangers and temptations, however, repeat themselves to a great extent in the American sea-ports; and here also it is mainly again German idlers and drunkards, that suck out of the emigrant both his money and his morals, and turn his head especially by their godless talk before him of liberty and independence, deceiving him and filling him with the most false conceptions of the new land of promise, its customs and its rights. There is no doubt but that the subsequent course of life for very many emigrants has been determined in a great measure by the companions into whose hands they fell during the first three weeks of their life in the new world.[10]

Then came the hardships of the ocean voyage. The situation during the early part of the period of state regulation was little improved so far as the journey on shipboard was

[9] Extract from *Chamber's Edinburgh Journal* (new series), V, 388 (June 13, 1846).
[10] Extract from "The Immigration," by W. J. Mann, in *Mercersburg Review*, II (1850), p. 628.

concerned. All the deplorable conditions set forth in the last chapter still operated until there was a change in the actual shipping equipment in the way of steam transportation and a new type of steerage accommodation. The Irish fever-ships from 1840 to 1850 perhaps presented the most demoralizing conditions at this time.

The ships, of which such glowing accounts were read on Sunday by the Irish peasant, on the flaming placards posted near the chapel gate, were but too often old and unseaworthy, insufficient in accommodation, without the means of maintaining the most ordinary decency, with bad or scanty provisions, not having even an adequate supply of water for a long voyage; and to render matters worse, they, as a rule rather than as the exception, were shamefully underhanded. True, the provisions and the crew passed muster in Liverpool — for, twenty years since, and long after, it was from that port the greater number of the emigrants to America sailed; but there were tenders and lighters to follow the vessel out to sea; and over the sides of that vessel several of the mustered men would pass, and casks, and boxes, and sacks would be expeditiously hoisted, to the amazement of the simple people, who looked on at the strange, and to them unaccountable operation. And thus the great ship with its living freight would turn her prow towards the West, depending on her male passengers, as upon so many impressed seamen, to handle her ropes, or to work her pumps in case of accident, which was only too common under such circumstances. What with bad or scanty provisions, scarcity of water, severe hardship, and long confinement in a foul den, ship fever reaped a glorious harvest between decks.[11]

Reports at this time show many cases of demoralization resulting from the immorality on the ships.

At the port of debarkation, the third stage of the journey, there were often experienced hardships and deceptions that frequently led to the complete disorganization of the immigrant. History is replete with instances of the development of a parasitic class along with the shift of population groups. At this time a new class of grafters was produced — runners, agents, brokers, etc., who lived on the immigrants, finding the new arrivals gullible because of their inexperience in the American situation. The Board of Commissioners of

[11] John Francis Maguire, *The Irish in America* (London: Longmans, Green & Co. 1868), pp. 180–181.

Emigration of New York organized in 1847 was created to meet this situation and protect the immigrant as well as examine him.

As soon as a ship loaded with these emigrants reaches our shores, it is boarded by a class of men called runners, either in the employment of boarding house keepers or forwarding establishments, soliciting custom for their employers. In order the more successfully to enable the latter to gain the confidence of the emigrant, they usually employ those who can speak the same language as the emigrant. If they cannot succeed in any other way in getting possession and control over the object of their prey, they proceed to take charge of their luggage, and take it to some boarding house for safe-keeping, and generally under the assurance that they will charge nothing for carriage hire or storage. In this way, they are induced to go to some emigrant boarding house, of which there are a great many in the city, and then too often under a pretence that they will charge but a small sum for meals or board, the keepers of these houses induce these people to stay a few days, and when they come to leave usually charge them three or four times as much as they agreed or expected to pay, and exorbitant prices for storing their luggage, and in case of their inability to pay, their luggage is detained as security. . .

Amongst the numerous frauds practised by these runners and forwarding houses, there is perhaps none greater than that which exists in the sale of passage tickets.

The emigrant is shown a neatly printed ticket, with a picture of a steamboat, railroad cars, and canal packet with three horses attached to it, and is given to understand that such a ticket will take him to a given place beyond Albany in a specified manner, and for a price to be agreed upon, and after disposing of the ticket for an exorbitant price, the emigrant is furnished with a steamboat ticket to take him to Albany, where he is to present his passage ticket to some person or company upon which it is drawn, where it is often either protested, or objections taken to the mode of conveyance, and the passenger, instead of going upon the railroad or packet boat, as agreed upon, is thrust into the steerage or hold of a line boat.[12]

Societies for the protection of the immigrant were formed for the various nationalities. These agencies were supposed to check on every detail of the problems of debarkation and the preparation for the journey inland. In some cases these societies did an invaluable piece of work; in other incidents

[12] Extract from "Report of the Select Committee to Investigate Frauds upon Emigrant Passengers," *New York Assembly Doc. No. 46* (1848), pp. 5–6.

the personnel included the usual individuals interested in private gains. The legislative committee investigating the frauds at the port of debarkation found cases of irregularities.

Whilst your committee are compelled to acknowledge that they have been very much aided in their investigations by the kindness and courtesy extended to them by the officers of various emigrant societies, yet a sense of duty compels them to declare that in their judgment some of these societies do not afford that substantial aid to their brethren upon their arrival in a strange land, which they have reason to expect, and your committee fear that there may be cases where the officers or agents of some of these societies have a more tender regard for the money of the emigrant than for their safety and comfort, but they do not intend to give this remark a general application, for they believe that many of them have too much respect for the places they occupy, if not for their kindred, to abuse the high trust reposed in them.[13]

In an effort to control the arrival of undesirables, most of the states receiving immigrants passed a bonding law making the shipowners and passenger agents responsible for those who were destitute or sick for a period of several years, five years in New York and ten years in Massachusetts. New York required a bond of $300, and Massachusetts, $1000. In New York the responsibility was taken from the shipowners by brokers who provided hospitals and poor-houses for the defective classes, but the

. . . proprietors of these establishments were always interested in giving insufficient and indifferent food and accommodation. In all cases their profits were measured by this economy, and in some instances when they had made a bad speculation in relation to a ship's entire passengers, cruelty, evasion, and neglect were resorted to as the only means by which they could escape bankruptcy. Under this system, the emigrant was utterly without protection of the law, the hopeless victim of private rapacity. . .

When famine spread over Ireland, and provisions became high throughout Europe, the ship-fever manifested itself among the emigrants, and the utter inefficiency, cruelty, and even danger of the system became apparent. The provision made for the sick in these miscalled hospitals was wholly inadequate. The buildings employed were usually selected in the suburbs of the city, rather for economy than for adaptation, and almost necessarily

[13] *Ibid.*, pp. 7–8.

deficient in ventilation. In a two-story dwelling house at Bloomingdale, 46 by 40 feet, the proprietors admitted that 120 patients had been crowded, though several of the rooms were exclusively occupied by the officers and servants. The food, clothing and attendance, insufficient; the sick and convalescent, the old and young huddled together, and police arrangements, so essential in such establishments to maintain health and morals, utterly disregarded. So odious did these places become that hundreds of sick and destitute quitted them in terror and disgust, and attempted to obtain admittance in the alms house, or the hospital at Bellevue, frequently representing themselves as citizens, or pretending that they had been in the country for a period that rendered the municipal authorities responsible for their support. When bonded emigrants, ascertained to be such, were admitted into the institutions of the alms house department, the bondsmen were notified of the fact, and became liable for the expense, and almost invariably attempted by their emissaries to induce the parties to withdraw, and while chairman of the committee of that department I frequently had occasion to forbid their interference with the sick.[14]

So, during the early part of the period of state regulation, the journey from beginning to end included many crisis situations for the immigrant, all operating to unfit the migrant for a ready adjustment, socially and economically, once he was in America. These facts should be borne in mind when it comes to the discussion of the adjustment made by immigrants.

Even at this early date the Germans and Irish were condemned for being clannish and living in foreign colonies, but their experience *en route* had often been such that their attention was directed especially to the preservation of their own culture and associations with their own people rather than with Americans or Americanized Germans and Irish.

DISTRIBUTION

WHILE ethnic groups tended to segregate themselves in certain areas, there was nevertheless a rather wide distribution of all nationalities in America. Despite the many localities in which immigrants could be found in this period,

[14] Extract from testimony of Alderman George H. Purser, of New York City, before a state legislative committee appointed to investigate the work of the New York commissioners of emigration. *New York Assembly Doc. No. 34* (1852), pp. 170–172.

distribution became important in another respect.   There
was a great deal of poverty and unemployment because immigrants tended to congregate in cities near the ports of
debarkation.   So for the first time immigration became a
real problem through a lack of proper distribution.   This
situation was not necessary since farmers were calling for
help that could have been provided by the idle individuals
in large cities.

Some idea of the distribution of immigrants up to 1860
can be seen in the following statements: The English were
found in the greatest numbers in the states of New York,
Pennsylvania, Illinois, Ohio, Wisconsin, and Michigan, while
smaller numbers resided in Florida, Arkansas, Oregon, North
Carolina, South Carolina, and Mississippi.   The greatest
number of Irish had found homes in New York, Pennsylvania, Massachusetts, Illinois, Ohio, and New Jersey, while
smaller groups had gone to Florida, North Carolina, Oregon,
Arkansas, Texas, and Kansas.   The Germans were most
numerous in New York, Ohio, Pennsylvania, Illinois, Wisconsin, and Missouri, while fewer of this nationality resided
in Vermont, Maine, New Hampshire, Florida, North Carolina, and Rhode Island.[15]

The attitudes of foreigners in opposing the institution of
slavery, which became important in their adjustment, may
have an explanation in the fact that " 3,582,999 — that is,
86.60 per cent of the whole number of foreign-born — were
inhabitants of the *free States,* and 533,176, or only 13.40 per
cent, of the *slave-holding States.*" [16]

With the exception of the Irish, most of the immigrants
took advantage of the free lands in the West.   The Irish had
been agriculturists, but their unfortunate experiences and
the fact that they had little wealth led to the acceptance of
work with immediate returns, so they settled in the cities
and towns in the United States.   This is the real beginning
of the problem of immigration in connection with urbanization.   The Irish arrived in a destitute condition, in many

[15] See Edith Abbott, *Historical Aspects of the Immigration Problem* (Chicago: University of Chicago Press 1926), p. 330.
[16] Extract from *Population of the Unived States in 1860,* p. xxx.

cases, and took the first work offered them, which was usually
in the cities in connection with public works, canals, railroads, and other transient occupations.

Any immigrant who remained in the city had at first to
live in the worst sections, where he became identified with
the disorganization of those areas, with little chance to change
his social position.   Americans objected to the presence of
immigrants in large numbers.   In an effort to secure the
passage of the Homestead Bill, it was said: "You will rid
your cities, New York, Philadelphia, Baltimore, and all the
large cities of the Union, of their surplus population — a
population weighing like an incubus upon those cities." [17]

In the same debate it was said: "What is the objection
to an increase of our foreign population?   I have heard but
one that is worthy of consideration; and that is, that they
congregate about our towns, oftentimes become unruly, and
too frequently swell the calendars of crime." [18]   It was in the
cities that the Irish became a political problem and attracted
general attention.

SOCIAL INTERACTION AND ADJUSTMENT

THROUGH the discussion of the composition, causes, and the
trials of the journey, we have a partial description of the
experiences and life organization of the immigrants of this
period.   For the processes of interaction and adjustments
this is only part of the picture.   Equally important is the
social situation into which the immigrants bring their social
heritage of attitudes and habits.   The cultural milieu into
which the immigrant migrates can best be studied through
the attitudes of fear, censure, and approbation of the native
Americans.   The attitudes of fear had come to include almost every aspect of life concerning the foreigner who was
reaching America with strange customs and habits.

For the first time since the inception of immigration into
the United States, cultural adjustments became just as portentous as the accommodation to the physical environs.

[17] Extract from debate on the Homestead Bill in the House of Representatives,
April 1852, *Congressional Globe*, Thirty-second Congress, first session, Appendix,
p. 520.
[18] *Ibid.*, p. 511.

This is shown by the discussion of the experiences of the Germans at this time:

The German in America is a complete stranger. Everything is strange, the country, the climate, laws, and customs. One ought to realize what it means to be an alien in a far distant land. More than this, the German in America is despised as alien, and he must often hear the nickname " Dutchman," at least until he learns to speak English fluently. It is horrible what the German immigrants must endure from the Americans, Irish, and English. . . Only in the places where the Germans are in the majority does the newly arrived immigrant find, after all the hardships of the journey, an endurable existence.[19]

The most important aspect of this situation is the attitudes of the native Americans and former immigrants in their definition and treatment of the new arrivals. Here was an extraneous group to which politicians, laymen, in fact everyone, could turn for an explanation of all evils, and all disturbing situations. Immigration from this time on has been indicted as a partial cause, at least, of every crisis situation in America. This condition is only an exemplification of the tendency in society when two things are found together, to say that one has caused the other. Immigration became identified with the abolition of slavery, political corruption, decrease in the native birth rate, problems of congestion, strike-breaking, protective tariffs, and all other aspects of economic life.

In these attitudes of fear, economic competition, pauperism, and criminality received the most attention, but there were also misgivings concerning the misuse of political power, growth of foreign colonies, a heterogeneous population, congestion in cities, Roman Catholicism, and dangers to American customs through social interaction. The attitudes of native Americans will be considered in terms of these problems. From the standpoint of those in the United States, immigration had become a real issue and would have been defined as a much greater problem had there not been a cessation of immigration during the economic de-

[19] Extract translated from Gottfried Menzel, *Die Vereinigten Staaten von Nordamerika mit besonderer Rücksicht auf deutsche Auswanderung dahin, nach eigener Anschauung beschrieben* (Berlin 1853), p. 348.

pression of 1847, and the fact that slavery and the Civil War came to attract more attention than the European migration to America.

(1) The attitudes of the period reveal the fact that economic competition had at last become an important aspect of the immigration problem. In the cities and towns, the foreigners were competing with Americans for places in the various manufacturing projects. The attitude before 1860 has been epitomized, in part, in the following statement by a writer of the period:

This unlimited and unrestricted admission of foreign emigrants is a serious injury to the native laboring population, socially, morally, religiously, and politically; socially, by overstocking the labor market and thus keeping wages down; morally and religiously, by unavoidable contact and intercourse; and politically, by consequence of want of employment and low wages, making them needy and dependent, whereby they become the easy prey or willing tools of designing and unprincipled politicians. And in this way the native population is deteriorated and made poor, needy, and subservient: and these realities produce want of self-respect, hopelessness, laxity in morals, recklessness, delinquencies, and crimes.[20]

Even at this early date, immigration was conceived as playing a part in the struggle between capital and labor.

Our manufacturers, ironmakers, machinists, miners, agriculturists, railway, canal, and other contractors, private families, hotel-keepers, and many others, have got into the way of expecting and seeking for cheap labor, through the supply of operatives, workmen, laborers, house-help, and various kinds of workers, kept up by the indiscriminate and unrestrained admission of emigrants.[21]

It was believed that manufacturers, interested in a high protective tariff on coal, iron, steel, machines, tools, and cotton and woolen goods, imported experienced operatives during this period from England who were willing to work for a lower wage. When an attempt was made to reduce the wages of the ironmakers and machinists, against which the workers rebelled, foreigners were induced to take their places and thus became responsible for a low wage scale.

[20] Extract from *Emigration, Emigrants, and Know-Nothings*, by a Foreigner (Philadelphia 1854), pp. 31–32.
[21] *Ibid.*, p. 33.

It is easy to understand that when one comes into direct competition with individuals considered inferior, fears and hatreds develop with great intensity. It is the nature of human nature, everywhere, to fear and hate those who threaten one's security, since one's occupation and other aspects of his environment are the subjective aspects of his life organization, a part of the individual. It was easier to fear and hate the immigrants in their close competitive relationship than it was the Americans responsible for their importation.

In many cases the immigrant was the successful one in competition since he could be employed at a lower wage and was used to a lower standard of living. This created a crisis situation for the native workers and led to the formation of a secret society for the protection of American mechanics. One clause in the resolution was an agreement to patronize one another in discrimination against the alien. Those who felt obliged to justify this procedure did so on the grounds that foreigners had secret societies, the members having pledged themselves to support one another in preference to Americans. So there were formalized efforts on the part of both groups to succeed in economic competition. These surreptitious organizations were indices that assimilation was not taking place. The immigrants were still conscious of themselves as a group set apart, and the native workers, by their attitudes, helped give them that definition.

(2) The attitudes concerning foreign paupers and criminals reveal another aspect of the thinking of Americans. Not all immigrants were successful in making economic adjustments. Many became paupers, others continued to be paupers as they were when they landed. If the immigrants were unsuccessful in competition, they were condemned as paupers; if they were successful, they were a dangerous group that seemed on the point of driving the native American out.

The problem of an economic adjustment was difficult for many immigrants because they had come in destitute circumstances that left them without resources on strange shores. Not only did they enter a new social situation, but in many cases were forced into occupations with which they had not had any experience. This condition along with the fact that many came as dependents, resulted in the objection to immigration because of pauperism.

In the cities the immigrants were looked upon as a criminal and pauper class. Since they lived in the areas of disorganization, they became identified with the pathological conditions of the area. However, many were paupers or criminals before they left Europe. The Mayor of New York for this period sent a message to the President of the United States concerning pauperism and crime in that city, as it had been increased by immigration. Most of the early legislation was directed toward the control of these two classes.

(3) Fear came to mark the thinking of a great many concerning the presence of the foreigner and his political participation. A writer of this period said:

We have now to resist the *momentous* evil that threatens us from *Foreign Conspiracy*. The Conspirators are in the *foreign importations*. Innocent and guilty are brought over together. We must of necessity suspect them all. That we are most seriously endangered, admits not of the slightest doubt; we are experiencing the natural reaction of European upon American principles, and it is infatuation, it is madness not to see it, not to guard against it. A subtle attack is making upon us by foreign powers. The proofs are as strong as the nature of the case allows.[22]

There was a feeling that the governments of Europe were anxious to destroy democracy as a means of self-preservation. American liberty was in great danger. There was enough blundering participation on the part of the immigrants to give the native citizens real reason for concern, as we shall see later in the chapter. The fear of the foreign group reached the place where orders were issued in both Massachusetts and Connecticut in 1855 to disband separate military organizations whether composed of German or Irish citizens. This move was regarded by Governor Gardner

[22] Extract from Samuel Finley Breese Morse, *Imminent Dangers to the Free Institutions of the United States through Foreign Immigration, and the Present State of the Naturalization Laws.* A series of numbers, originally published in the New York *Journal of Commerce* in 1825. By "An American." (New ed.; New York 1854), p. 25.

of Massachusetts as an attempt to Americanize America. A similar attitude was shown by Governor Minor of Connecticut. This was met by a threat to form independent companies and an appeal to the law on the part of the Irish of the two states. This is proof that assimilation was not coming to actualization. Assimilation includes the desires of both groups involved, Americans and Europeans; if one group exhibits attitudes of fear or reluctance, assimilation cannot be realized.

(4) The fear of the growth and ultimate strength of foreign colonies caused a great deal of concern. In a speech in 1849 designed to secure further restriction upon foreign immigrants, Hon. Garrett Davis of Kentucky pictured the danger of the coming of so many Germans who were establishing settlements where they could speak their own language and practice their European habits and thus pass on to their children German customs and traditions instead of American culture. According to the description there was danger of the Middle Western States becoming a German nation within a nation.

It is interesting to look back at the settlements in many of these states and see that the descendants of these immigrants now fill our colleges, or occupy places of importance, and many of them now evidence the same fear concerning the present influx from southeastern Europe.

(5) The heterogeneity of the population became important in the thinking of Americans when immigration was related to the many social problems and when the stream of immigration was large enough to attract attention through segregation. With the advent of a great many social problems there developed a fear of diverse units in the population and an attitude of " America for Americans." There was little realization that there did not exist at the time much that was distinctly American and that the best from these diverse cultures would form the basis of an American culture.

(6) Congestion in the cities, especially near the ports of debarkation, was a factor in keeping the matter of immigration always before the public. In the cities there was the greatest amount of poverty and crime and more political ac-

tivities by those of foreign birth than in the rural districts. Even the mere concentration apart from any pathological conditions became an obvious fact.

There are portions of New York, and of nearly every large city, where the population is as thoroughly Irish as in Dublin or Cork. There are also large tracts of these cities crowded with Germans. . . There is a German quarter and an Irish quarter, as well as French and American quarters in New Orleans. I found many of both races at Galveston, Texas. Nearly half of Cincinnati is German; and crossing a canal that divides the northern part of the city from the southern is popularly termed "going over the Rhine." It is much the same at Chicago and St. Louis. At Milwaukee, the Germans appeared to me to occupy nearly or quite a third of the city.[23]

(7) There were definite attitudes of fear concerning Roman Catholics. The cultural unit of religion, as we have seen, was the most important unit during the colonial period and maintained its place of significance down to the present time. England had spent a great deal in aiding European Protestants to reach the colonies, and this emphasized the breach between Catholicism and Protestantism.

There were some who did not entertain these fears, however. In discussing the Homestead Bill in the House of Representatives in 1852, A. G. Brown of Mississippi emphasized the fact that he did not fear the Jesuits who had been defined as a group whose purpose it was to destroy the Protestant faith in America. His attitude, however, was not shared by all governmental authorities and many other citizens.

(8) The situation of slavery and the impending Civil War, while eclipsing the problem of immigration, was in a sense responsible for objections to the coming of so many foreigners. The remonstrance on this basis came from states where slavery was an important institution. European migrants were settling largely in non-slave states, and as they became naturalized, the balance of voting power went to the states without slaves. In 1800 the population of the slave states was practically equal to the rest of the population, but the coming of immigrants to non-slave states greatly altered

[23] Thomas L. Nichols, M.D., *Forty Years of American Life* (London: John Maxwell & Co. 1864), II, 69.

this balance, and free labor was seen as a great danger to the institution of slavery. Most immigrants were opposed to slavery since there was little opportunity for redemptioners, indentured servants, and free European labor in those states where slavery was an accepted institution. The reactions of both the Southerners, and the immigrants were characterized by attitudes of self-defence.

(9) The attitudes concerning social interaction were other social facts to which immigrants had to adjust. Social distance between native Americans and immigrants is not a matter of recent times, as shown by the records of the early nineteenth century. In boarding-houses, the immigrant did not receive the same treatment as native Americans; he was looked upon with disdain even by the landlady. There was a great social distance between him and Americans of his own class. Unless there were some of his countrymen in the community, he had to associate with those who were not accepted, often with those of the Negro group, so it is reported; thus he further lowered himself in the opinions of those with whom he lived.

The same social distance was maintained between the native Americans and the Irish in many cases.

If ever two nationalities came into collision by meeting, it is the Irish and the American in the United States. Everywhere in the United States, the Irish-born part of the population is only tolerated by the native Americans as what has been termed " a serviceable nuisance "; it is a population of foreigners and out-casts, exceedingly valuable as a mass of labour which gives pro-ductiveness to capital in a country where the natives dislike work-ing for hire, but socially despised, and in so many ways ill-treated, that practically it does not enjoy that equality of rights which is the boast of the American democracy.[24]

Social interaction was considered undesirable with the Irish and the Germans in many instances. Both were com-ing in great numbers and both had units of culture around which sentiments and attitudes of opposition could easily be organized. The Irish, being Catholics, had a religious

[24] Extract from a letter to Lord John Russell, the Prime Minister, which was signed by W. H. Gregory, M.P.; M. J. O'Connell, M.P.; J. R. Godley; published in the London *Spectator*, XX, April 3, 1847, pp. 4–5.

variation in culture and the Germans a linguistic one.
Throughout the world wherever there have been cultural
conflicts these two units of culture have always been important.   The Americans then showed their ethnocentrism
concerning the Germans and the Irish and found the
language of the former and the religion of the latter outstanding symbols around which they could organize their
prejudices.   Both immigrant groups were self-conscious
about these units of culture, which fact aroused attitudes of
opposition in Americans.

These, then, are some of the reactions of native Americans that formed so important a part of the social order in
which the immigrants had to make adjustments.   Some of
the attitudes prevalent at this time found expression in legislative acts which reveal certain aspects of the problem of
immigration before 1860.   With little federal legislation as
a means of control, it devolved upon the various states to
cope with the situation and those having ports of debarkation
had laws for protection against undesirables.   The laws of
this period were largely restrictive and protective measures.
A head tax was levied by New York, the fees from which were
used to take care of destitute and sick immigrants at the
marine hospital.   The master of each ship had to report the
name, place of birth, last legal settlement, age, and occupation of all passengers.   New laws superseding the one of 1819
were passed by Congress in 1847 and 1855 to remedy the
shipping conditions, which contributed to the deplorable
state of the immigrants at the end of their transatlantic
journey.

The attitudes that we have been discussing were sponsored
so vigorously by some that they were crystallized into the
agenda of two different organizations: the Native American
Party and the " Know-Nothings."

The Native American Party became an active political organization about 1835.   Many nativist societies were formed
and a state convention was held in Louisiana in 1841; a national meeting of the organization convened in Philadelphia
in 1845, " for the purpose of devising a plan of concerted
political action in defence of American institutions against

foreign influence." [25]   As another writer of the time said:
" The object of this association is to give effect to the American sentiment of hostility to the Irish." [26]   There were anti-
Catholic riots in which a few Catholic churches and a con-
vent were destroyed.   The Nativists in their platform wanted
the naturalization laws repealed and the incumbent of all
offices to be native Americans.

The native American attitudes, which were symbolic of
the definition of immigration, placed most of our institutions in immediate danger.   To protect these institutions
the Know-Nothing Party had its inception about 1850 as a
secret organization.   The real name of the organization was
" The Supreme Order of the Star Spangled Banner."   The
name, " Know-Nothing Party," by which it was best known,
came from the fact that many of its members answered all
questions concerning it with a simple evasive statement, " I
don't know."   To gain its political objective it had to lose
its secretive aspect to the extent of nominating and endorsing
candidates.   The platform of the organization reveals its
true purpose and attitudes of fear.   There was a demand for
change in the existing naturalization laws, with a longer
period of residence for citizenship.   The society wanted the
state laws repealed that granted suffrage to unnaturalized
foreigners as well as a repeal of all Congressional acts providing land grants for unnaturalized foreigners and allow-
ing them to vote in the territories.   It was the plan of the
members of the party to have Americans rule America, but
after their national convention in which Millard Fillmore
was nominated, their power was on the wane with the attention of the people directed to slavery and the Civil War instead of to immigration.

Furthermore, not all native Americans were willing to
sponsor this method of dealing with the problem of immigration.   Actually, there did exist an immigration problem.
There has always been a problem and there will always be
a problem of immigration in any country where a people

[25] Extract from *Address of the Delegates of the Native American National Convention,
Assembled at Philadelphia, July 4th, 1845, to the Citizens of the United States,* p. 2.
[26] Extract from a letter to Lord John Russell, *op. cit.,* p. 4.

come with a culture whose unitary contents are unlike those of the culture that has been invaded, and this situation becomes more pronounced as there is an increase in the numbers of the minority group to a place where economic competition becomes important. We can be sure that one thing was accomplished by the Know-Nothings of this period. They helped by their activities and by their definition of immigrants to keep the immigrants aware of their social status, set apart as different, and thus greatly retarded the process of assimilation.

Now that we have had, through the attitudes of Americans, a cross-section of the situation into which the Europeans came, we can consider the adjustments made by the immigrants. Some of the adjustments were determined by the sentiments of fear in the United States and some of the native American attitudes were reactions to the accommodations made by the immigrants. It was difficult to tell which one had caused the other. At times the ethnocentrism of both groups became a sort of chauvinism, each being very self-conscious because of past experiences. America was a new country with newly developed rights to protect. The immigrants had come from a situation of oppression, seeking a place where they could carry out certain practices that had become sacred to them.

As has already been pointed out, the immigrant came with a cultural baggage made important to him through continual use and ethnocentrism, and settled in a situation where there was just as much ethnocentrism, supported by the strength of greater numbers. Add to this the fact that the character of human nature and the social process by which it develops make it impossible for the adult immigrant to become completely assimilated, and we can understand the adjustment problems of the European in America.

It is difficult to make a working classification of the types of adjustments made during the period, since the various methods overlap. (1) There was relative isolation in which the immigrants had their own institutions, language, press, and maintained their own habits and customs. (2) There were cases in which the immigrants were active participants in certain units of American culture, but preserved most of their Old World traits. (3) In relative isolation and also where there were open conflicts of cultures there was a move on the part of immigrants to organize, for it must be remembered that the foreigners were also apprehensive concerning the native Americans. Then (4), there were adjustments that were distinctly pathological; and last of all were the adjustments of the second generation in which there was an effort to live in two cultures, the result often being disorganization.

(1) Many of the immigrants went directly from the port of debarkation to the West, and their adjustment was merely isolation where no great break with their past experience was postulated. Though this caused a great deal of consternation regarding the formation of foreign colonies, it prevented the disorganization that was experienced by those who remained in the slums of the cities in the Atlantic states.

But complete isolation was no longer possible. Railroads, canals, and navigable streams had made America a potential economic unit. However, it was possible for Europeans to live in America much as they had in their native lands because of partial isolation and the attitudes of social distance evidenced by native Americans. Thus the adjustment was one of accommodation, largely in terms of European culture as it had to be modified in America. So living in a particular district did not mean that there had been complete integration into the community.

(2) There were adjustments, largely in terms of Old World customs, where the immigrants became active in certain units of culture without the background to comprehend the significance of the situation. This was most frequently in the political unit of the American social order, more through the solicitation of politicians than through the initiative of the newly-made citizens from Europe.

Politicians emphasized the " German vote " and the " Irish vote " and made these two nationalities self-conscious, thus pulling them farther into governmental activities than they were by experience prepared to go. The ambitious of the Know-Nothings helped to define them as an extraneous group. The *Citizen,* an Irish weekly edited in New York City by John Mitchell and the " Young Ireland " group, condemned the Irish votes as an anomaly and advised them not to vote in masses but for the best man; but this represented the thinking of a minority group. Others felt, however, that there should be an Irish vote.

At a charter election, held in the city of New York . . . the following hand-bill was published by the Irish organization, and extensively circulated, to wit:
Irishmen to your post, or you will lose America. By perseverance you may become its rulers. By negligence you will become its slaves. Your own country was lost by submitting to ambitious rulers. This beautiful country you gain by being firm and united. Vote the tickets Alexander Stewart, Alderman; Edward Flannigan, Assessor, both true Irishmen.
About the same time, at an election in the county of LaSalle, Illinois, a body of Irish immigrants, numbering about two thousand, brought forward and supported an Irishman for the office of sheriff, in opposition to an American of the same national politics, and of much longer residence in the country, and elected him, by upwards of one thousand majority.
In the town of Paterson, New Jersey, but a few years ago, an election was held, in which the foreigners elected thirty-three out of thirty-seven township officers.[27]

On some occasions there were election riots involving Irish and Germans; notable cases are those at Williamsburgh, Washington, and New Orleans. " During the fall of 1855, at an election held at one of the interior towns of Texas, the Germans marched in a body to the polls." [28] There were pre-election meetings held by Germans in various localities to nominate men of their own nationality or to get promises from other candidates. Previous to the election of a member of Congress in 1853 the German organization in Baltimore " addressed a series of questions to each of the candidates, and demanded of them written responses to the interrogatories. They were organized and determined to cast their votes *as a body of Germans,* for him who answered most satisfactorily." [29] They wanted to know if their organization

[27] Samuel C. Busey, *Immigration: Its Evils and Consequences* (New York 1856), pp. 24–25.
[28] *Ibid.*, p. 30.
[29] *Ibid.*, p. 25.

were approved by the candidate and if he would promise not to give preference to native-born American citizens once he were in office. There was a feeling on the part of many that these political adjustments were made largely through the activities of foreign and American demagogues.

These political adjustments on the part of a great many were the result of hurrying the process of Americanization by those who had political advantages to gain. A group, untutored in the political life of America, was led to believe that they were protecting themselves against native Americans. " Those emigrants who stop in the seaboard cities . . . rather than find work on the federal domain are a disturbing factor in the management of American institutions. These urban emigrants exercise the rights of citizenship only as the disciples of the political parties of which they become the tools. They take over the enthusiasms of party politics without having an insight into the social interests involved."[30]   Many, however, made perfectly normal adjustments in the political life, voting as other citizens did for the welfare of a particular area in which they lived. But the reactions of the native Americans were to the pathological aspects of the political situation, which is usually the case when behavior is on an emotional basis.

(3) We have seen that there were native American organizations to control the immigrant situation. Foreign groups availed themselves of the same privilege, some of the immigrant organizations existed before those of the Americans and some came to actualization later. It is doubtful if these various organizations ever accomplished anything more than the creation of a greater social distance between natives and foreigners, and the development of more nationalistic prejudice. It must be kept in mind that both groups were self-conscious and were reacting often to this fact rather than to a real situation.

The Germans who had settled in Texas had little social intercourse with the native planters. Their only contacts were through the economic process. They did not under-

---

[30] Extract translated from A. van der Straten-Ponthoz, *Recherches sur la situation des émigrants aux États-Unis de l'Amérique du Nord* (Bruxelles 1846), p. 30.

stand each other; their customs and habits were too divergent. Attitudes of curiosity, contempt, and fear became evident between these two groups on the frontier. It was discovered by each faction that they were in competition so far as economic interests were concerned. But little was said until there was an effort on the part of the Germans to organize in a political sense.

In 1854 the Germans were holding their annual musical festival in San Antonio, Texas. In conjunction with this occasion they held a political convention and published a platform revealing their attitudes concerning many American activities.

One of the resolutions discussed slavery, and declared it to be an evil which should be eventually removed.

The novel attitude of the Germans was disagreeable to the Americans, and this resolution, meddling with the question of slave-property, particularly offensive. An excitement sprung up, which for a month or more was kept within the limits of conversation, but broke out into newspaper clamor and open threats of violence, when, by a series of articles from a German source, it was discovered that the Germans were not unanimous in their opinions.

In fact, the time was unpropitious for such a political demonstration. " Americanism " was just beginning to show its strength in the East, and to extend its lodges and its barbarizing prejudices into Texas. This independent movement on the part of foreigners was a god-send to the new party. It gave it a tangible point of attack, and what with the cry of " foreign interference in politics," and " abolitionism in Texas," a universal howl from the American papers went up against the Germans.[31]

Organizations were formed by Germans in many centers. The German Social Democratic Association of Richmond, Virginia, described as being " an association existing in the center of the ' Old Dominion ' — the home of the presidents," had published a platform of reform. In discussing the *agenda* of a similar organization in Louisville, it was said:

All these demands are antagonistic to the fundamental principles and established usages of the government. The Bible is repudiated, the sanctity of an oath is rejected, the observance of

---

[31] Frederick Law Olmsted, *A Journey through Texas; or, A Saddle-Trip on the Southwestern Frontier* (New York: Mason Brothers 1857), pp. 435–436.

the Sabbath is enumerated among the evils which these Germans seek to correct. The presidency is to be abolished, all powers are to be vested exclusively in the masses, and the Constitution must give way to the whims and caprices of the people. All the safe-guards which protect the minority in the enjoyment of their rights and privileges are to be broken down, and every right, privilege, and immunity, all laws, the policy of the government, the institutions of the country, and its relations with other coun-tries, are to be dependent upon the will of an uncontrollable and licentious majority; the government is to become " a heterogene-ous, incoherent mass." [32]

The *Galveston Zeitung*, of August 19, 1855, the organ of the Germans of Texas, contained a manifesto to the Germans of that state to form guard companies, in all towns where the population was large enough, for the protection of the Ger-mans. This came after several clashes throughout the United States between Germans and natives.

The Irish had their own organizations as well, and many of them reflected their experiences of a good many genera-tions. With the Irish, religion had become identified with nationality, and America was predominantly Protestant. So the Irish were just as conscious of themselves as a religious group as they were as a nationality. They came to America with a most pronounced animosity for England and soon thought of America as an ideal place for operations in free-ing Ireland from English domination. To accomplish cer-tain nationalistic objectives several Irish organizations were developed.

" The Boston Hibernian Lyceum " was organized about 1833 and was composed of young men for mutual sympathy and mutual co-operation, in whatever may aid to qualify them to meet and discharge their responsibilities as the representatives of their native, as well as citizens of their adopted, country, as Irish-men and Americans.[33]

The Irish organization that attracted the most attention was the Irish Emigrant Aid Association. At the trial of Samuel Lumsden and eleven others in Cincinnati in 1856, it was said that certain documents showed " the existence of societies and organizations among the Irish population of

---

[32] Samuel C. Busey, *op. cit.*, p. 21.
[33] Extract from *The Catholic Diary* of March 14, 1835.

this country, the members of which are actuated by strong hostility to the government of Great Britain, and avow it as their purpose and desire to free their native land from British rule, and eventually to establish its independence. It is contended that in the furtherance of this design movements are in progress, with which these defendants are connected, which threaten to interrupt our peaceable relations with Great Britain, and which call loudly for the vigilant enforcement of the neutrality laws of the United States." [34]

(4) In a great many instances there were pathological adjustments made in America by immigrants. These adjustments involved pauperism, dependency, criminality, and insanity. As we observed in the discussion of the composition of the period, numerous immigrants belonged to these pathological classes before they left Europe; others were forced into certain of these categories by a long and perilous journey, while others through unfortunate distribution and experiences increased the class of social variants.

Many a German man who had his trade in the old world, has come here, and not knowing at once how to continue it has thankfully hearkened to the advice of his officious friends, and set up forthwith a beer-shop or drinking grocery; by which he has neither become a useful citizen, nor led his family in a way of safety — nay, has been himself perhaps the first victim. How many hundred such beer houses, kept mostly by Germans, there are at this time in our cities! . . . Every orderly German at the same time must suffer from it, in more than the reputation simply of his nation. Let any one only pass on Sundays by our German beer-shops. . . The taverns are full, but how is it with the churches? We have perhaps 30,000 Protestant Germans in Philadelphia alone. Of these not more than 3000 at most ordinarily attend church on Sundays. But where are the rest? Who can be foolish enough to expect much good from this state of things, as regards domestic life, social position, or public influence? However we may dislike all extreme principles and one-sided views, and though we may find in the relations of the foreigners themselves much to account for such evils, and excuse what can bear excuse, the case is still one of real anxiety, that calls for the most vigorous and decisive remedies, and that should stir the heart especially of every capable German to sorrowful feeling, and

[34] Extract from decision in case of United States v. Samuel Lumsden *et al.* (1856), *Bond's Reports*, I, 13.

engage him to the most earnest counter-action both in word and deed.[35]

A study of immigrants in New York City in 1858 showed that many of the undesirables remained in the city and became inadequates so far as adjustments were concerned. The statistics on pauperism, crime, delinquency, and insanity show a much higher rate for foreigners than for the native-born. Since these are adjustments to life just as is any other accommodation, they become important in our study. The census returns of 1850 show that $2,954,806 was expended for the support or partial support of 134,972 paupers. Over half (68,538) of these were of foreign birth. At that time there were only 2,244,625 in the United States of alien birth. This shows a very high rate of pauperism for Europeans in America; one out of every thirty-three being a pauper.

A description of the " Rag-Picking and Bone-Gathering Tenants" of New York in 1857 shows that the housing adjustment and living conditions were as bad as, or even worse than, the conditions that existed later in the slums as American cities increased in size.[36] The cholera in the Boston slums in 1849 involved to a large extent a foreign population; eighty-one per cent of the dead were foreigners.

Juvenile delinquency and juvenile vagrancy became at this time important as an adjustment on the part of the second generation. Most of these children were of Irish and German parentage. Of the fifteen hundred truant and vagabond children in Boston in 1850, slightly over ninety per cent were from foreign homes. Studies of this period show the same situation in the field of criminality. Convictions by the courts of several states in 1850 revealed that almost without exception the foreign convictions were more numerous than those of natives.

Insanity showed a higher rate with those of European birth than with the native citizens. In the Boston Lunatic Hospital

[35] W. J. Mann, "The Immigration," in *Mercersburg Review*, II (1850), 630.
[36] See *Report of the Select Committee Appointed to Examine into the Condition of Tenant-Houses in New York and Brooklyn* (New York State Assembly Document No. 205 (1857), pp. 20–22.

in 1839 nearly half were foreigners. Similar records appear for New York, Philadelphia, and other cities.

Mere figures mean very little when it comes to types of social adjustments. Pauperism, criminality, and other pathological adjustments are as much a matter of the situation as they are of the individuals involved, as we shall see later in discussing recent immigration, on which there are more available data. The immigrant comes with habits and customs which do not lead to facile adjustments in America. Lack of formal education and the limited experience of a peasant do not give him the flexibility that a new cultural situation requires. New situations are met by the most difficult way and the greatest expenditure of energy. Disappointments, anxiety, fears, the definitions given aliens, mean mental and physical sufferings.

We must remember that there are areas in cities where there is a high rate of poverty, delinquency, and crime, no matter who is living there. These sections usually contain the immigrants of the first generation. In these areas the rates of delinquency, crime, pauperism, etc., have been practically the same for all nationalities who have resided there.

In the matter of insanity for this period, an insane immigrant became a ward of the state and was sent at once to a hospital, while those of the native population who suffered mental ill health were often kept at home for sentimental and economic reasons, since the native Americans had to pay a fee for the use of institutions. An investigation through institutions for this period would not be a study of the proneness to insanity of the native Americans, since many insane individuals were not sent to institutions and most studies were made through institutions. Therefore, there is no basis for comparisons. Perhaps the rate of insanity was higher among immigrants, but no one knows.

(5) The conflict of cultures with the second generation became important at this early time and led to a certain amount of disorganization. The first generation was anxious to transmit their customs and habits to their children. The children were often anxious to lose their identity as Germans and Irish and to be known as Americans. Even

where they did not wish to lose their identity they had to live in two cultures. The fact that many of them could not speak English when they entered school meant that they were not adjusted in that situation. The German language being the cause of their difficulty, they wanted to learn English and were ashamed of the language of their parents. For a while they were not integrated into the school culture and were trying to get away from their adjustment at home. Their experience was similar to that of the immigrant who reaches the United States and must act immediately in terms of the American social order. The result in either case is a conflict of cultures, often causing disorganization and demoralization as both culture situations try to control the individual with diverse customs, different techniques, antagonistic interests, and divergent manners. Many of the second generation came to the attention of the public because of their inability to adjust in either the European or the American culture. This condition can be better demonstrated with the more recent arrivals.

There was a class, especially among the Germans and the English, that found adjustments difficult at this time. These were the educated immigrants. By training they were better equipped to make the transition had the situation into which they came been more propitious. The intellectual had acquired a broader world in which to live and realized to a certain extent that a change must take place, but they discovered that the transition must frequently be on a level below what their original adjustment to life had been. In America they often had to forego many of the cultural advantages they had enjoyed at home. They not only had to experience a change in economic and social standards, but had to curb many of their æsthetic likes and dislikes. The contrast between their cultural organizations and those of their contacts in America was greater than that suffered by the peasants.

This period presents the paradoxical situation in which each state had a desire for workers and settlers, but this desire was suppressed to a certain extent by a fear of consequences as there was a realization that certain evils were growing out of the influx of immigrants. The need of a larger population for the development of industries and the settlement of a great frontier was being met by a system that brought two cultures into conflict, the result of which is always a certain amount of social disorganization and personal demoralization on the part of the invading or minority group, and much ethnocentric consternation on the part of the native or majority group. However, we now look upon some of the descendants of these problem groups as native Americans and the founders of our social order.

READINGS

GENERAL

Fairchild, H. P., *Immigration.* 1926. Chapter V, pp. 93–107
Hall, Prescott F., *Immigration.* 1906
Johnson, S. C., *A History of Immigration from the United Kingdom to North America, 1763–1912.* 1913

COMPOSITION

Anderson, R. B., *The First Chapter of Norwegian Migration (1821–1840).* 1896
Faust, A. B., *The German Element in the United States.* 1909
Flom, George T., *Norwegian Immigration into the United States.* 1909
Hale, E. E., *Letters on Irish Immigration.* 1852
Janson, Florence E., *The Background of Swedish Immigration, 1840–1930.* 1931
Maguire, J. F., *The Irish in America.* 1868
Nelson, O. N., *History of the Scandinavians and Successful Scandinavians in the United States*

CAUSES

Abbott, Edith, *Historical Aspects of the Immigration Problem.* 1926. Pp. 85–146

JOURNEY

Abbott, Edith, *Immigration: Select Documents and Case Records.* 1924. Pp. 20–42

DISTRIBUTION

Faust, A. B., *The German Element in the United States.* 1909
Flom, George T., *Norwegian Immigration into the United States.* 1909

STATE REGULATION 1830–1860   113

Ford, H. J., *The Scotch-Irish in America.*   1915
Maguire, J. F., *The Irish in America.*   1868

SOCIAL INTERACTION AND ADJUSTMENT

Abbott, Edith, *Immigration: Select Documents and Case Records.*
     1924.   Pp. 110–164
—— *Historical Aspects of the Immigration Problem.*   1926.   Pp.
     252–325; 440–517; 566–638; 733–829
Anderson, R. B., *The First Chapter of Norwegian Migration
     (1821–1840).*   1896
Bowdle, S. E., *Influence of German Life and Thought on Ameri-
     can Civilization.*   1913
Dewees, F. P., *The Molly Maguires.*   1877
Faust, A. B., *The German Element in the United States.*   1909
Nelson, O. N., *History of the Scandinavians and Successful Scan-
     dinavians in the United States*
Park, Robert E., *The Immigrant Press and Its Control.*   1922
Rhodes, J. F., " The Molly Maguires in the Anthracite Region
     of Pennsylvania," *American Historical Review.*   XV, April
     1910.   547–61
Schrader, F. F., *The Germans in the Making of America.*   1924

CHAPTER VI
STATE REGULATION
1860–1882

INTRODUCTION

PREVIOUS TO 1860 there had been two crisis situations that meant a cessation in the volume of the stream of immigration to the United States — the Civil War and the industrial depression of 1857. This decrease in the number of European invaders came at a time when there was a need for laborers in all sections of the country. The abolition of slavery opened up the South to immigration, especially to agricultural laborers. The Liberal Homestead Act of 1862 made the West a desirable place to settle, consequently an enormous internal migration was soon under way. Not only did the western territories want people from the East, but they were eager for northern European immigrants as well, as evidenced by the activities of western states in many foreign countries. The exodus from eastern states, along with the great loss of life during the war, left many vacancies along the Atlantic seaboard. So the South, the East, and the West were in need of men.

While there was a demand for laborers, as shown by the legislation in 1864 to encourage immigration and the definite move on the part of certain states to direct immigration within their own boundaries, still there was some opposition to immigration; especially was there a great deal of consternation concerning the undesirable classes. The agitation for proper control resulted in a Supreme Court decision that eventually made immigration a matter of federal rather than of state regulation. Not only was the period from 1860 to 1882 the last period of state regulation, but it was also the last era when the immigrants from northwestern Europe constituted the greater part of the influx to the United States. Soon after 1882 the Slavic groups and Jews from eastern Europe and the Italians from southern Europe became the important ethnic elements in the European exodus to America.

COMPOSITION

GERMANY, Ireland, and England provided the greatest numbers in the migration of foreigners to the United States from 1860 to 1882. After 1865 the Germans were the most important element, with the Irish second. The Scandinavians came in considerable numbers for the first time in 1860 and by 1882 they contributed 13.4 per cent of those reaching the ports of debarkation in the United States. Some Mennonite communities from Russia also arrived during this period. There were, too, a great many from England, Scotland, Wales, and Switzerland — a population of immigrants still coming from northwestern Europe. The cultures represented in this migration from Europe were quite largely rural, with more mechanics, miners, and manufacturers coming from England and Germany than in the preceding periods of immigration. In the German contingent there were, also, a great many political refugees.

Emigration has been characterized by a greater number of males than females, and this period was not an exception. During the early years of this epoch there was often an excess of more than forty thousand men over the number of women. So noticeable was the surplus of males over females that European countries showed some concern over the loss of so many able-bodied workers. Despite the excess of males, the migration at this time came to include immigration by families especially with the Germans, British, and Scandinavians, the percentage being large enough to result in the establishment of many normal communities.

In 1862 only 72,183 Europeans reached the ports of the United States. This small number represented the diminution caused by the Civil War and the industrial depression of 1857, but by the end of the period the number had increased until 788,992 gained entrance at the various ports in 1882, the largest number that had ever come in one year. This number was not exceeded until the period of federal control in 1903 when southeastern Europe had become an important factor in the stream of immigration.

CAUSES

IN DISCUSSING the causes of immigration of 1881, near the end of the period of state regulation, it has been said: "This movement has been caused by deficient crops, old uneconomical methods, grinding poverty, overtaxation, military burdens, and social discontent." [1] This was more or less true of all the European countries, but in some regions there were other important factors as well.

The situation in Germany was not alone economic but political. ". . . the severe measures adopted in Germany against the socialists and communists and even against purely religious organizations such as the Separatists, the Mennonites, the Rappists, etc.," [2] were factors in the decision reached by many Germans to come to the United States.

In 1870, it was said that there were more than seventy thousand souls in the east end of London who must emigrate or die. The English government and charitable organizations sent many to the United States. A great many were mechanics who could be used in the new industries in America and who could make satisfactory economic adjustments at once. Poverty was a big factor in the emigration from Scotland at this time, especially in the Highlands. So around 1870 there was an increase in those arriving from Scotland. However, poverty was not so extreme here as in Ireland where there was no thought of a profit from agriculture. Many in Ireland chose emigration in preference to the poor-house.

---

[1] Edward Self, "Why They Come," *North American Review*, 134 (1882), 366.
[2] Extract translated from Alfred Legoyt, *L'émigration européenne; son importance ses causes, ses effets* (Paris 1861), p. xx.

The movement from the Scandinavian countries became important about 1866. The chief cause was economic. Minor causes were religious differences, required military service, and political oppression. The Dano-Prussian War of 1864 also became a factor in emigration. The people of Denmark suffered under the oppressive conditions forced upon them by Germany and some chose emigration as a means of escape. Many came to the United States, bringing their personal property with them, which was an aid in their initial adjustment.

" People emigrate from Switzerland today," said one of its citizens in 1844, " for neither religious nor political reasons, those two great and powerful causes of the emigrations of other centuries; an emigrant leaves the fatherland today in disgust because he cannot own there enough soil to live reasonably well, or at least in order not to die of hunger, and to live after some fashion." [3]

An outlet from these conditions was found in the United States. Following the Civil War there were places in industries for men in eastern states, and the West provided thousands of acres of free land. The Mississippi valley and states farther west were Eldoradoes for people interested in agriculture. Nearly all the textile industries employed Europeans of the first or second generation. Miners in the Pennsylvania coal region were English, Welsh, and Irish. Public construction on canals and railroads was done by the Irish, and the clothing trades utilized Germans in their work. So the situation in the United States offered an admirable escape from European conditions — offered, in fact, a solution to the predicament in which many Europeans found themselves. The Civil War had brought the United States to the attention of all areas of northwestern Europe in a way to reveal the mineral resources and the opportunities for agriculture. How attractive these conditions were to destitute Europeans is shown by the fact that thousands came even when the various European countries emphasized the lack of stability in our government as evidenced by internal strife. It

[3] Extract translated from Jules Duval, *Histoire de l'émigration européenne, asiatique et africaine au xix*^e *siècle: Ses causes, ses caractères, ses effets* (Paris 1862), p. 145.

was pointed out that heavy taxation must necessarily follow the war. Yet people continued to come.

Societies were organized to aid the immigrant and safeguard his welfare in both Europe and America. Protective
legislation was being worked out. Transportation prices
were lowered. Land in America was cheap. Wages were
higher than those in Europe. Gold had been discovered in
America. In fact, America offered a most desirable solution to problems in Europe. Europeans had already developed attitudes of dissatisfaction with their lots in their
native lands. Many of them were unhappy and restless and
had a vague desire to free themselves. When they saw their
condition in the light of the situation in America, their
vague longings became definite as they prepared to leave
their familiar though undesirable surroundings for a home in
a strange culture.

Efforts were made to attract immigrants to the western
states. Cultural factors so depressing in the European countries were displayed as utopian in the United States through
letters, published articles, and pamphlets. Immigrants were
aided, protected, and advised. Boards were organized and
agents appointed. State representatives were sent to Europe,
and pamphlets propagandizing the resources of the various
areas were circulated. While the western sections attracted
the most attention, similar efforts were made by eastern
and southern states, notably Maryland.

Another outlet from conditions in Europe was to be found
in better communication. Steam navigation and railroads
brought the western frontier of America closer to Europe.
Once emigration had been suggested as a means of escape
from European conditions, the process became a social con-
tagion. Emigration was said to have induced emigration.
Letters were sent back by successful settlers and were important in suggesting to many a way out of the predicament
of poverty and oppression in their native clime.

THE JOURNEY

By 1865 steamships had a wider use for the transportation
of immigrants than the sailing vessels. This meant shorter

periods of sailing and improved conditions on board obviating much suffering for the immigrants.

In 1856, of the passengers landed at Castle Garden, New York, 96.4 per cent were carried on sailing vessels, and 3.6 per cent on steamships. In 1873 the proportions were almost exactly reversed — 3.2 per cent on sailing vessels, and 96.8 per cent on steamships. The turn of the balance came between the years 1864 and 1865; in the first of these years the sailing vessel carried 55.7 per cent of the passengers, and in the second, 41.7 per cent. . . This change did more to alleviate the conditions of the steerage than anything which had transpired previously.[4]

Despite this great change in methods of transportation, many of the evils of the steerage remained. The improvements were only a matter of degree; few of the undesirable conditions were entirely done away with. Similar descriptions to those given for the periods already discussed could be given here.

DISTRIBUTION

PERHAPS it is not necessary to emphasize again the importance of distribution for adjustments on the part of immigrants. It is, however, a most significant matter. The immigrant thinks of all parts of America in terms of the locality in which he lives. His situation is America to him. The great mass of immigrants who availed themselves of the privileges of the Liberal Homestead Act had few problems of adjustment which were social in nature. They moved at once to the western states where they settled in colonies and there continued to live in terms of European culture where there was little reason for disorganization. The extent of the westward movement is shown by the amount of revenue secured from immigrants by the railways. " Mr. J. N. Abbott, agent of the Erie line, estimates the value of all emigrant inland tickets, sold in New York in 1881, at five million dollars certainly, and perhaps more." [5] So immigration became an important factor not only in the development of the West but in the development of transportation as well.

[4] From H. P. Fairchild, *Immigration*, pp. 94–95. By permission of The Macmillan Company, publishers.
[5] Edward Self, *op. cit.*, *North American Review*, 134 (1882), 350.

The abolition of slavery directed the attention of many to the South and casualties during the Civil War created a demand for laborers in the industrial cities and mining regions of the East. The Gold Rush in California made its appeal to many. Consequently all sections of the United States became potential destinations for immigrants. Cities were now developing and many immigrants were settling in New York, Chicago, Philadelphia, Brooklyn, Boston, Detroit, Lowell, Minneapolis, Milwaukee, New Orleans, and other cities. According to the census of 1880, over forty-five per cent of the Irish in the United States were in New York, Philadelphia, Brooklyn, and Boston. Nearly forty per cent of the Germans were in New York, Chicago, Philadelphia, and Brooklyn, while only about ten per cent of the Norwegians and seventeen per cent of the Swedish were in metropolitan centers.

SOCIAL INTERACTION AND ADJUSTMENT

IN MAKING adjustments, we have already observed that the adjustment with the first generation is likely to be one of accommodation, and with the second generation there may be disorganization as a form of accommodation or assimilation.

Where there was not segregation at first with the immigrant of this period there was usually disorganization. The more complete the segregation and isolation, with social interaction a gradual process, the more normal was the adjustment of accommodation. Especially was this true with a group. When the immigrant came alone and was thrown directly into the American cultural complex, he consciously took over the elements of the new culture in order to have a world in which to live. In a foreign colony there was a group inertia and the individuals already had a world in which to live, without creating one.

When the immigrants came as a unit from some village or rural community, there was a chance to discuss their former lives in Europe, so they continued to live, not in the physical world of their native abode but in terms of the mental organization they had concerning it, quite isolated from American influences. Their language, their ideas, their social definitions, were in terms of their earlier existence. They were in the same universe of discourse so they exchanged old memories and talked of old associations; culturally speaking, they were not in America.

Conversation and reflection tended to make old customs and traditions more sacred than they were before. The importance of their European culture increased in contrast with the American social order. The process of living became a conscious process and there was often the first realization that they had built up many sentiments around their old social milieu.

So the immigrants of the first generation, especially those in rural areas, made an accommodation by living in the culture they brought from Europe, but the members of the second generation found themselves trying to acquire two cultures and rebelling against both as they came into conflict with each other, so that the adjustments were often disorganization and demoralization. *A propos* of this is the statement written at this time:

> In the cities, observation justifies the opinion that the most dangerous class of young men, known as roughs, hoodlums, etc., is composed mainly of native-born sons of immigrants.[6]
> The breaking up of the homes and domestic life of multitudes of people; the adoption for a longer or shorter time of migratory habits; the difficulties which must be encountered in a strange land, perchance with a strange tongue; the fear of, and liability to, deception — all these experiences involve trials so formidable that it is not surprising that many succumb to temptation who would, under more favorable circumstances, have escaped contamination. Lives thus disordered cannot but tell unfavorably upon immigrants and their children; therefore it is to be expected that our criminals and persons dependent upon public charity will be largely of foreign birth, or, if native, of foreign parentage. Parents who, in their native villages in Europe, would have apprenticed their children to some honest trade, find it impracticable to do so here. The mere lack of apprenticeship does not always lead to crime; still, the connection between the two is very apparent.[7]

[6] Edward Self, "Evils Incident to Immigration," *North American Review*, 138 (1884), 86.
[7] *Ibid.*, pp. 84–85.

This is descriptive of the experiences of the immigrants in the cities rather than of those in rural communities.

As the adjustments for this period were analyzed, it was found that many factors became significant in the various processes of competition, conflict, accommodation, and assimilation. These may be enumerated as (1) The attitude of Americans concerning the various ethnic groups; (2) The degree of segregation and cultural isolation; (3) Language; (4) Status of the immigrants when they reach the United States, health, wealth, habits, age, and attitudes; (5) Occupation, distribution, and opportunity to continue the work for which the individual was trained; and (6) Marital status.

The adjustment of the immigrant of this period will be considered in terms of these factors. (1) The attitude toward the immigrant was vacillating at this time. The first federal legislation for the control of the volume of immigration was the act of July 4, 1864, and was designed to encourage emigration. This act validated contracts made in foreign countries for laborers, not to exceed a period of twelve months. The fluctuating nature of the attitudes at this time led to the repeal of this act in 1868. Later, under federal control, there was legislation against contract labor. The immigrant was needed and wanted, with reservations, yet he was feared and disliked in many cases. The apprehension concerning undesirables was to some extent offset by the need of the immigrant in industry and in the uninhabited regions. The attitudes of a great many Americans during the last part of the nineteenth century are recorded in the report of the Federal Investigating Committee in 1856. The conclusions reached were that immigration was the chief source of intemperance; that it filled our cities with a foreign convict and pauper population; that it furnished the United States with a juvenile vagrant class; that it was the source of ignorance, a danger to free institutions and liberty, and responsible for irreligion, immorality, and licentiousness. The findings, right or wrong, greatly influenced the thinking of the time. Many of these conditions actually existed, but there was little realization that the situation into which the immigrant came was just as important as the past experience or the nationalistic affiliation of the immigrant. It also shows that all that has been said recently about the immigrant from southeastern Europe was said, too, about those from northern and western Europe.

(2) In the Twenty-fourth Annual Report of the New York Association for the Improvement of the Condition of the Poor published in 1867, conditions were described in the following manner:

> So large are the aggregations of different foreign nationalities, that they no longer conform to our habits, opinions, and manners, but, on the contrary, create for themselves distinct communities, almost as impervious to American sentiments and influences, as are the inhabitants of Dublin or Hamburg. This principle or tendency of segregation extends to their private, social, and public life — which every new arrival augments in numbers and strength. They have their own theatres, recreations, amusements, military and national organizations; to a great extent their own schools, churches, and trade unions — their own newspapers and periodical literature. In further illustration of this tendency to sever themselves from everything American, we find that they have in this city seventy-three churches; they publish thirty-five newspapers and periodicals, in five different languages, and sustain several eleemosynary and philanthropic institutions, for the exclusive benefit of their own people. As these foreign masses, in short, have little intercourse with the native population, beyond the claims of business, and read few American papers, they are generally as ignorant of all that is peculiar to the institutions of the country, as if no such sources of information existed, or as if they still were subjects of a foreign power.[8]

These conditions demanded only an accommodation to the economic aspects of American life. The fact that the immigrants were censured for cultural isolation shows that there was not a realization that complete social intercourse would have led to maladjustments with a great many. Because of the nature of human nature, segregation was the desirable form of settlement for the immigrant. Forced cultural relationships that were unintelligible to a foreign population would have resulted in a superficial Americanization that would have made the problem of immigration more portentous than it really was.

[8] Extract from *Twenty-fourth Annual Report of the New York Association for the Improvement of the Condition of the Poor* (1867), pp. 41–42.

(3) The Germans and the Swiss were the only ones coming in large numbers where language was a very great handicap. Assimilation is a matter of attitudes and habits, and a failure to speak English often proved a barrier to understanding American attitudes and habits. There were communities where only German was spoken in daily social relationships. There were German regiments in the Union Army where very little English was spoken. There were German newspapers and schools and churches where only the German language was used. While the language technique often made some adjustments difficult because of the social definition given a strange language, and the inability to comprehend the content of customs and traditions, it did prove to be a strong cultural element in holding the Germans together and thus prevented disorganization. So a strange language had a dual function. It retarded the process of Americanization and made the Germans a self-conscious group, set apart as different; but it also helped them to maintain a certain amount of solidarity and social stability that prevented cultural disintegration before they were ready to comply with the dictates of a new social order.

(4) The status of the immigrants when they reached America was an important factor in their adjustments. Those who came in poverty or as paupers started the process of adjustment greatly handicapped. We must be careful to make a distinction between pauperism and poverty. The big difference is a matter of attitude. Poverty may not imply either intellectual or moral debasement, but crime and pauperism usually involve each of them to a greater or less degree. The attitude of pauperism hindered a normal social and economic adjustment for those who left Europe in this class.

The paupers or the criminals often brought with them attitudes that obviated a normal adjustment. Their habits like those of any individual continued and became the dominant and controlling forces in their lives. This is true with normal individuals, physicians, lawyers, farmers, as well as with criminals or paupers.

It is evident when viewed from the standpoint of age, that

poverty and pauperism could not have been so great a factor as was supposed. Most of the immigrants came during the productive period of life and at a time when there was work, so ready economic adjustments could be made. From the standpoint of wealth, the Germans were best equipped for making an adjustment. A report of the Commissioners of Emigration, December 15, 1854, showed that it was estimated by German authorities that the Germans brought about eleven million dollars to the United States annually.

In addition to the money brought by each immigrant there was other property, tools, jewelry, furniture, and wearing apparel. It was estimated that over $38,000,000 was transferred through the port of New York in 1869. Many in considering the economic value of the immigrant add the amount that the immigrant contributed each year through labor. A study of these facts along with pauperism helps to keep the problem of pauperism in better perspective.

The age of immigrants has a great deal to do with adjustment. Those past middle-age will probably never go beyond accommodation in the process of adjustment, while those younger will not find it so difficult to follow out the process and become thoroughly assimilated. In 1882 it was found that more than twenty per cent were under fifteen years of age. Seventy per cent were between fifteen and forty years of age. These ages were ideal for economic adjustments, but they included people who had well established habits and attitudes that had developed in a European culture. While these habits and attitudes meant assimilation in a peasant community in Europe, they only served to isolate the individual in the United States; yet on the other hand, these habits and attitudes gave them a world in which to live in terms of European culture and kept them from disorganization through cultural conflicts, especially where there was relative isolation on the western frontier and to some extent in the cities.

(5) The occupation of the immigrant and the chance he had to continue the occupation were important in his American adjustment. Germany and England were sending a great many mechanics at this time, but the vast majority of the

immigrants were agriculturalists. Those who remained in
the East had their occupation determined by location rather
than by their training and ability. In the West the immigrant could follow his hereditary occupation of agriculture.

In discussing the situation in the eastern states, one author has said:

Here we find the peasants of Ireland and Germany engaged,
painfully to themselves and often wastefully to their employers,
in all sorts of mechanical operations to which they have no traditional or acquired aptitude; while, on the other hand, not a few
of the skilled mechanics and cunning artificers of Europe, finding here no demand for their labor in the very special direction
in which alone they have been trained, or being excluded from
competition by trades-union regulations, or being disadvantaged
by their poverty, their strangeness, and their foreign speech, have
settled down by the mere force of circumstance, to breaking
stone for highways, to working on railroads, to menial service,
or to day-labour in any capacity. They are found in our mills,
earning a mean living by the side of utterly untaught and un-
trained laborers; or, they have joined their fortunes to those of
some ward-ring of politicians, and have become its bullies and
strikers . . .

Of those foreigners whose occupations have determined their
location, the most notable instances are the Welsh and the
Scandinavians.

Why should there be nearly four times as many Welsh in
Pennsylvania as in New York? Why four times as many in Ohio
as in Illinois? The reason is obvious. The Welsh are famous
miners and iron-makers. Their labour has not been wasted.
They have come out to this country under intelligent direction,
and have gone straight to the place where they are wanted.

Quite as striking has been the self-direction of the Swedish and
Norwegian immigrants. Four States, all west of Lake Michigan,
contain 94 per cent of all the Norwegians in the country, and
66 per cent of the Swedes; while of the remaining fractions, by
far the greater part is also found in other States and Territories,
within the same meridians. These immigrants have gone straight
across the country, a far greater journey than was required of the
Welsh, and have set at once about their chosen occupation, agriculture, in their chosen homes, Illinois, Wisconsin, Iowa, and
Minnesota, without loss of time, or injury to character by expo-
sure, unemployed and unprovided, to the temptations of city life.

Although the Scotch have not in the same way emphasized their
choice of locations, in which to pursue their chosen vocations,
being, indeed, scattered somewhat widely, we have the strongest

evidence that they have placed themselves to suit themselves (not merely been thrown ashore by a wave of immigration), in the fact that very few of the men of this country are employed as day-labourers.[9]

So, while many were maladjusted because their occupational habits could not function, necessitating the acquisition of others, many others continued their work lives much as they had in Europe.

If one can judge from the literature available on the subject of immigration for this period, the real problem of adjustment was to be found in the cities. Every criticism made concerning the recent immigrant who settles in the city was made about the immigrants from northern Europe. In the cities the foreign element came to the attention of the public since the urban colonies were not self-sufficient in the sense that they were in the rural areas.

It is to be expected that those who had meager resources when they arrived would be forced to accept work near the port of debarkation. It was said that the

. . . thriftless, the ignorant, and degraded, generally lodge, like driftwood, where they land, to fill our prisons, and burden our charities. As an indication of their lack of culture and low grade of civilization, official statistics show that of the persons over twenty-one years of age in this city, who cannot read and write, there are about twenty foreigners to one native. In other words, while there are but 1200 natives over twenty-one years of age who can neither read nor write, there are 40,580 of the foreign-born over that age who cannot read the English language. Is it, therefore, surprising that most of the social and political evils in the city, may be traced to the ignorance and debasement of our immigrant population?

It may be further remarked that the native-born, which comprise rather more than half the inhabitants, give about 23 per cent of our city indigence; the foreign-born, including those aided by the Commissioners of Emigration, amount to 77 per cent, which is nearly four imported paupers for one American. The statistics of crime exhibit results as marked and striking. Of the 68,873 persons arrested for offences against person and property, for the year ending October 31, 1865, 45,837 were foreigners; and of these 32,867 were Irish, and but 23,036 white and black,

[9] Francis A. Walker, "Our Foreign Population, II, What They Are Doing," *The Advance*, VIII (Chicago, December 10, 1874), 261–262.

all told, were natives. Of the whole number arrested, 13,576 could neither read nor write. Nor should the fact be overlooked, that many of the native-born paupers and criminals are the off-spring of foreigners, who were themselves paupers and criminals. Hence, much of our indigenous pauperism and crime is medi-ately traceable to foreign parentage, which, under our genial in-stitutions, produces and perpetuates this noxious and parasitic growth of unproductive humanity.[10]

It is well to remember that these reactions, in many cases, were to immigrants who were maladjusted in their native lands and not to immigrants in general. Even those who were willing to work found adjustments very difficult in cities, as did many native Americans. Criticisms of immi-gration have always been based on certain isolated facts; that is, certain pathological aspects have been considered apart from the entire immigrant situation. This does not mean that there has not been occasion for alarm and need for legislation to control the problems of immigration.

A good example of the coming together of a background and situation resulting in pernicious behavior is the case of the Molly Maguires in the anthracite coal regions of Pennsylvania. The Molly Maguires was a secret organiza-tion of Irish who made demands and proceeded with violence when they were not met. Murders were committed with impunity because the informer would have received the same type of treatment.

A request would be made for higher wages in some locality. When a brief period had elapsed without compliance with the demand, there would follow anonymous letters, made graphic by crude drawings of coffins, pistols, and other sym-bols. These letters were known as "coffin notices." Strikes were declared and those who refused to participate were greatly abused.

The Irish involved in this secret organization must be understood through the background experience in Ireland. There had been conflicts with landlords and agents in their native habitat. In that situation they had learned to mis-trust capital as an instrument of oppression. There was a

---

[10] Extract from *Twenty-fourth Annual Report of the New York Association for the Improvement of the Condition of the Poor* (1867), p. 39.

similar organization in Ireland but no direct connection between the two societies was discovered, although their activities and techniques were very much alike.

It can be said with some safety that a group has been assimilated when its members have lost their self-consciousness and are no longer spoken of as a certain nationality. This being the case it can be said that the Germans and the Irish were not thoroughly assimilated during this period. In the city elections there was still talk of a " German vote " and an " Irish vote," and candidates worked for such support by various means.

In spite of all the propaganda and objections to the various immigrant groups, the unprejudiced person came to the conclusion that a high grade European was reaching our shores by the end of the period in 1882.

The class of immigrants now reaching our shores is composed largely of thrifty, industrious, and able-bodied persons. There are some indigent, lazy, and worthless characters, like the Russian refugees, but in the main the immigrants form a very desirable addition to our population. Now, with such an in-pouring of labor as the last two years have witnessed, it cannot but be that we are greatly enlarging the basis of our industrial fabric and widening and extending very materially the limits of all departments of business. Yet the full effects of this beneficent stream of immigrants upon our internal commerce are not felt nor seen at once. It takes time. The immigrant, for instance, who takes to farming, probably does not make any very great progress on his farm during the first year of his arrival. He is a stranger to the land, the mode of conducting agriculture is in many respects different from that in vogue in his own country, and the capabilities of the soil, together with its adaptation for special crops, are unknown to him. In the second year he will do better than in the first, but it is not until the third or fourth year, doubtless, that he attains full results. It follows, therefore, that in the present immigration movement we are laying the foundations for great activity in the immediate future, and probably paving the way for business expansion on a greater scale than ever before.[11]

While the increase of many social problems was contemporaneous with the arrival of immigrants for this period, this increase also came with the growth of cities and the de-

[11] Extract from the *Commercial and Financial Chronicle*, **XXXV** (August 19, 1882), 201–202.

velopment of slums within the city. The development of the slum with all its problems must be explained by the process through which the city grows rather than by the presence of any particular ethnic group. As we shall see later, the growth of cities is accompanied by the development of areas of disorganization in which most of the social problems are concentrated irrespective of what nationality group happens to be in the area.

READINGS

GENERAL

Commons, John R., *Races and Immigrants in America.* 1920
Fairchild, Henry P., *Immigration.* Revised ed. 1926. Chapter IV, pp. 68–92
Jenks, J. W. and Louck, W., *The Immigration Problem.* 1914

COMPOSITION

Babcock, K. C., *The Scandinavian Element in the United States.* 1914
" Danes in the United States," *Literary Digest,* Feb. 22, 1919
Flom, G. T., *Norwegian Immigration to the United States.* 1909
Janson, Florence E., *The Background of Swedish Immigration, 1840–1930.* 1931
Johnson, S. C., *A History of Emigration from the United Kingdom to North America,* 1763–1912. 1913
" Kleng Peerson, Father of Norwegian Immigration to America," *Scandinavian Review,* July 1920
Maguire, J. T., *The Irish in America.* 1868
" Norwegians in the United States," *Literary Digest,* Feb. 8, 1919
Riis, Jacob, *Making of an American.* 1913
Rynning, O., *Norwegians in the United States.* 1917
" Swedes in the United States," *Literary Digest,* Jan. 25, 1919

CAUSES

Abbott, Edith, *Historical Aspects of the Immigration Problem.* 1926. Pp. 146–198

JOURNEY

Abbott, Edith, *Immigration: Select Documents and Case Records.* 1924. Pp. 42–58

DISTRIBUTION

Abbott, Edith, *Historical Aspects of the Immigration Problem.* 1926

Anderson, Rasmus B., *The First Norwegian Settlement in America Within the Present Century.* 1899
Brunner, Edmund de S., *Immigrant Farmers and Their Children.* 1929
Evjen, J. O., *Scandinavian Immigrants in New York, 1630–1674.* 1916
Haverstad, T. A., *Norwegian Farmers in the United States.* 1915

SOCIAL INTERACTION AND ADJUSTMENTS

"A Danish Home in America," *American-Scandinavian Review,* Oct. 1920
Abbott, Edith, *Historical Aspects of the Immigration Problem.* 1926. Pp. 328–405; 517–536; 638–694; 829–862
—— *Immigration: Select Documents and Case Records.* 1924
American-Scandinavian Review. Monthly. Published by the American-Scandinavian Foundation, N. Y.
Faust, A. B., *The German Element in the United States.* 1909
McMasters, J. B., " The Riotous Career of the Know-Nothings," *Forum,* 17: 524
Maguire, J. F., *The Irish in America.* 1868
Peterson, James A., *Hjalmar, or the Immigrant's Son.* 1922 (A story of early immigration to America)
Sundby-Hanses, H., *Norwegian Immigrant Contribution to America's Making.* 1921
Swedish Contributions to American National Life, 1638–1921. Comm. of the Swedish section of America's Making, N. Y. 1921

Part III. New Immigration

CHAPTER VII

INTRODUCTION TO THE PERIOD OF FEDERAL CONTROL

SUPREME COURT decisions ended the state regulation of immigration and by 1882 the federal government had assumed control. At this time the first comprehensive immigration law was passed, which in its accumulative form involved the policy of exclusion, selection, and deportation. Since the inception of this first important federal law there have been two methods of procedure. Regulation at first was through individual selection with legislation designed to exclude undesirables of all nationalities — individuals who were physically, mentally, or morally incapacitated for a normal adjustment. Through the passage of the literacy test, this classification of human deficiencies came to include an educational aspect as well.

Finally, through agitation, legislation was secured for restriction and group selection. While public opinion in 1882 favored selection in which undesirables would be kept out, still there were everywhere attitudes against restriction. Consequently its accomplishment had to be a process so that there might not be a reaction.

For twenty years before the World War the sentiment of Congress, in both Houses, grew steadily more and more restrictive. Most of the scientific students of the problem who attempted to approach the subject with an impartial mind, urged the necessity of restriction.[1]

[1] From H. P. Fairchild, *Immigration*, p. 434. By permission of The Macmillan Company, publishers.

The only immigration legislation by the federal government prior to 1882 had to do quite largely with the welfare of the immigrant, especially in trying to alleviate conditions in the steerage. On March 2, 1819, Congress enacted laws whereby the officer of each ship had to make a complete report of the number of passengers on board, giving in each case the name, age, sex, and occupation of the immigrant. This record for the year ending September 30, 1820, was the beginning of official statistics on immigrant arrivals. These laws also provided for better traveling conditions for immigrants which really never came to actualization, although there was further legislation in 1847, 1848, and 1855 to remedy the horrible conditions of over-crowding.

While federal legislation in its accumulative aspect has had to deal mainly with the immigrants from southern and eastern Europe, it had its inception as a means of individual selection of migrants coming from countries in the northern and western part of Europe. It is only a coincidence that immigration from Great Britain, Germany, and the Scandinavian countries should have reached their pinnacles in migrations to the United States in 1882 when the first comprehensive immigration law was passed. It is, also, a mere coincidence that the advent of the stream of immigration from southeastern Europe should have taken place at a time when a great deal of control legislation was being passed.

This last period of immigration has many factors to distinguish it from the early epochs of migration to the United States. (1) It has been under federal control rather than state regulation that the present immigration has reached the United States. (2) There has been a change in the composition and volume of the immigration stream. The significance of this lies in the fact that it meant the introduction of a new racial and cultural element at a time when there was a rapidly growing feeling that immigration should be restricted. The coming of this new element made a very convenient fact around which attitudes of restriction could be crystallized. We shall never know whether the same legislation would have been demanded and passed if the groups from northern and western Europe had continued to come with their culture which was basically the same as that in America. Certainly past attitudes toward the groups from northwestern Europe lead one to believe that the result would have been practically the same.

The change in composition is very important since it brought a European element whose cultural history was not so closely related to that of the United States as was that of Germany, the United Kingdom, and the Scandinavian countries. The waves of immigration from Italy and the Slavic countries included groups that were not directly ancestral to the early Americans. Not only were there differences in cultural patterns, but a greater number were coming. In 1882 the largest influx to reach the ports of the United States in one year totalled 788,992. The year 1882 was followed by a period of increasing and decreasing waves until there was a total migration into the United States of 1,285,349 foreigners in 1907.

(3) Conditions had changed in the United States and in northwestern Europe in a way to make emigration no longer so desirable for the countries that supplied America's early immigration. Through urbanization and industrialization, the United States now had many social problems: congestion, poverty, competition, and periods of unemployment. But, still more important, economic conditions had changed in Europe, especially in Germany where opportunities at home were almost as favorable as those in America. Laborers were given a wider range of activities and a chance to work under better conditions, thus producing a higher standard of living. There was state aid for those of old age and provisions for accidents and sickness through insurance. More healthful environment in which the laborers were to work was secured. Safety devices were introduced. All these improvements tended to decrease emigration.

(4) The change in the economic situation in the United States signalized by a transition from a rural to an industrial *régime* was also very important. There was no longer a great frontier that had to be reached by the construction of railroads, canals, and highways, through immigrant labor; a frontier when once reached offered great opportunities for

those interested in farming, which had been the activity of the majority of the immigrants in Europe. The ratio between men and land had greatly changed. It was an era of industrialization. Immigrants, therefore, went into the foundries, factories, sweatshops, and mines, with the result that there was the first great economic competition between the aliens and the native workingman. The America of today is not the America of the colonial period or of the nineteenth century, neither is the composition of the immigration stream the same. Consequently, there can be no comparison between old and new immigration since the two major factors have not been constant. At least, such a comparison would not have any scientific value.

(5) Another important factor for this period was the distribution of immigrants. The United States had changed from a primarily agricultural country to one equally industrial, the result of which was a concentration of populations in urban centers. Problems of adjustments with immigrants had always been more or less confined to cities, and this period operated to increase greatly this situation. This, as we shall see later, has had much to do with turning the attention of the people in America to the immigrant and thus helping to create by definition a problem of immigration.

There was a widening gap between the social situation in the United States to which the immigrant came and the one he had in his native habitat. The new immigrant left a simple, stable, peasant environment and located in a complex, disorganized, urban situation. Life was becoming more complex and adjustments more difficult even for native Americans. This whole matter will be dealt with under the chapter on distribution. While the old immigrant went to work on farms, roads, railways, and canals, the new immigrant has gone to industrial and mining cities to labor in factories, foundries, and at mining. This has thrown him more directly into economic competition with the native whites, a very significant fact for the adjustment of the immigrant. The old immigrant on the farm was not viewed as directly competing with his American neighbor. This is an extremely important point. Economic competition always tends to increase the feeling of nationalistic prejudice.

(6) Then, to complicate the situation further during the period of federal control came the World War of 1914, involving the United States directly in 1917. As already stated, a crisis situation such as this tends to make the inhabitants of every country cautiously aware and uneasy concerning its social values, and jealous of the welfare of its institutions. It creates or rather sharpens ethnocentrism in which every element of culture becomes sacred and needs protection. Along with other countries the United States became very self-conscious, and there arose an attitude of self-protection that aided legislation for group restriction in coming to actualization. It created a situation in which it was necessary to get support for a carefully worked-out immigration policy. The War revealed the fact that most immigrants had not been assimilated; they had not even had an opportunity, so complex is our social life in an urban environment.

(7) The large volume of immigration resulted in a fear that unlimited numbers might prove dangerous, so agitation for numerical restriction was instituted. There had already been legislation to control the influx so far as mental, moral, and physical incapacitations were concerned. There remained the educational aspect as a qualitative check, and the literacy test seemed to many to offer the solution.

It must be remembered that the objection at this time was not just an objection to immigration as such, but an objection to the migrants from southeastern Europe, who were culturally different and who in terms of common sense observation were racially inferior. The literacy test was considered most desirable, since it would discriminate in favor of the immigrants from northwestern Europe as those from the southeastern part had not had the educational privileges of the old immigrants. Few from the countries of the early sources of immigration would be affected by the passage of this measure.

" The literacy test, therefore, promised to combine the requirements of restriction, individual selection, and group selection." [2] It would be restrictive in nature and a matter of group selection since the rate of illiteracy was very high in southeastern Europe. It would be a matter of individual selection because admission was refused " all aliens over sixteen years of age, physically capable of reading, who cannot read the English language, or some other language or dialect, including Hebrew or Yiddish." [3] Thus the literacy test seemed an effective means of restricting the influx from southeastern Europe because of the high rate of illiteracy.

Many people of this period believed that the person who could not read nor write was in grave danger of becoming socially inadequate or a social variant. Perhaps the illiterate person would find it more difficult to understand our laws and our political and economic systems. However, the person who might be able to pass the reading test would not necessarily be able to analyze the social, political, or economic systems of the United States together with all their ramifications. Even native Americans who can read and write are unable to do so. Furthermore, ability to pass the literacy test is not necessarily a measure of superiority but of opportunity; nor is there any necessary relationship between knowledge of a formal nature and the character of an individual. Social variants are usually able to make ethical discriminations, but their behavior is not controlled by that fact.

The degree of literacy required to enter the United States would hardly be enough to help the immigrant put wise interpretations on the contents of our daily press. The immigrant who cannot read may even find his illiteracy an advantageous insulation from America's sensational press that might lead to misconceptions concerning Americanization.

After a struggle of twenty-five years the immigration law, embodying the literacy test, was passed. It followed a debate of ways and means which involved the creation of a Commission in 1906 to study the problem of immigration. The chief result of nearly four years of study and the expenditure of nearly a million dollars, was the recommendation for a restrictive law signalized by a literacy test. It was vetoed

[2] *Ibid.*, p. 385.   [3] *Ibid.*, p. 389.

four times and was finally passed over President Wilson's veto in February, 1917. Previous to this, President Wilson had vetoed it in 1915 and it had been vetoed by President Cleveland in 1897 and by President Taft in 1913. To each of these chief executives it was a break with a traditional policy, and it was further characterized by Wilson as a test of opportunity rather than a test of character in which restriction rather than selection was the aim of the law.

It was passed over President Wilson's veto in 1917 by both Houses. The act of which this was a part increased the head tax to $8 and added other social variants to the excluded classes. All this legislation proved futile in its effort to restrict numerically, as evidenced by the conditions following the World War when Europeans were anxious to get away from the crisis situation at home. Many Americans felt at this time that there should be a suspension of all immigration for a few years, but despite the popularity of this plan it was abandoned for the percentage quota system. It was merely an emergency gesture to meet a concrete situation, and was not regarded as a permanent plan.

Restriction came through the Quota Act of May 19, 1921, to be effective only one year, but was extended the following year to July 1, 1924. This act permitted the entrance into the United States in any fiscal year of any nationality only three per cent of the number of foreign-born of such nationality in the United States.

There were the usual exceptions which we need not consider here and only twenty per cent of the total eligible number might come in any one month. At first countries from northern and western Europe filled less than half their quotas, while those from southern and eastern Europe practically filled theirs. By 1924, however, northern and western Europe were sending their full numbers. In May, 1924, the new legislation provided that the annual quota of any nationality be only two per cent of the number of foreign-born individuals of such nationality resident in the continental United States as determined by the United States census of 1890. Countries from northern and western Europe were thus entitled to 84.11 per cent of the annual quota, while those of southern and eastern Europe could send 14.88 per cent.

This plan was to be effective until July 1, 1927, when the quota was no longer to be based on the census of 1890 but based on the national origins of the entire population coming from quota countries. The year 1920 was to form the basis for computation. It was found that there was a population of 89,332,158 from quota countries in the United States at that time. Since 150,000 were to be admitted from all quota countries each year, the number eligible from each country was determined by dividing 150,000 by 89,332,158 and multiplying this result by the number of inhabitants in continental United States for each country. While this plan was to have become effective on July 1, 1927, it did not really come to actualization until two years later.

There was a great deal of opposition to the plan from the Germans, since the quota of Germany was reduced from 51,227 to 25,957, also from the Irish Free State whose quota was cut from 28,567 to 17,853. Some other countries to suffer reductions were Sweden, Norway, Denmark, France, Switzerland, Roumania, Czecho-Slovakia, and Portugal. Great Britain and northern Ireland whose quotas went from 34,007 to 65,721 had the big increase. Italy, The Netherlands, Belgium, Austria, Poland, Russia, Hungary, Greece, and Jugo-Slavia were other countries that gained by the new plan of national origins.

Thus there came at last under federal control a policy in legislation that involved exclusion, selection, protection, and deportation. All undesirable classes of all races and nationalities are excluded. Immigrants are selected not only by elimination of undesirables but by numbers through the quota plan which gives the British Empire the greatest number. This plan is supposed to admit only an assimilable number. It provides for the deportation of all aliens who are not entitled by their adjustment to remain in the United States. It has been designed to give the immigrant protection from the time he leaves his native land until he has been in the United States long enough to make an adequate accommodation.

The effects of this great cultural invasion cannot be estimated. We are not far enough away from it even to predict the outcome. That the United States will be different because of this great influx does not need to be questioned. It has brought cultural elements with a new content which will be diffused with the same cultural elements in the United States if not in the first generation, then in the second or third generation. It is not possible to say exactly what will be the effect upon the United States, nor shall we ever know whether the situation would have been better or worse if the influx had come from the northern and western parts of Europe.

All we can say is that they are here in great numbers, that the first generation cannot be Americanized, that the second generation in the transitional areas of our cities shows every evidence of being disorganized. Those who get out of these disorganized areas make normal adjustments and good citizens. The recent immigrant represents a minority group in a transitional stage that must be a process of assimilation that will result in a few generations in Americanization, and this Americanization, once it is realized, will be the type of American pattern that is found where they live. If it is in the northern part of the United States, it will be northern Americanization. If it is in the Middle West, it will be Americanization peculiar to that region, since Americanization is a relative thing. A native-born person from an isolated region would not exhibit Americanization in an urban community if Americanization means adjustment — and what else could it mean?

Just what the effects are going to be, we do not know. No one knows. We do not even know what social changes will take place in the next fifty years, and the adjustment the immigrant will make will depend as much on the situation as on the immigrant. " Even in the case of the old immigration . . . the effects are largely in the future; in the case of the new immigration they are almost wholly so." [4] Had the United States not become industrial and consequently urban, perhaps there could be some predictions in terms of

[4] *Ibid.*, p. 167.

rural life. But changes in our social order have gone on as rapidly as the movement of immigration.

Since 1882 Europe has furnished the bulk of our immigration, so the influx is largely Caucasian and, at present, physical characteristics do not stand in the way of adjustments except with the Orientals. These will be considered in a separate chapter. The problem is one of cultural differences and is complicated by the fact that cultural conflicts are taking place at a time when America is in a transitional stage from a rural to an urban environment.

Legislation has covered practically every human ill and undesirable trait in its program of exclusion, so that fewer undesirables should be reaching our shores at the present time. Not only are laws more stringent, but transportation companies have been more careful since they are held directly responsible.

If scientific caution is to be exercised in the discussion of human behavior, then we do not have adequate data for saying what the effect of immigration will be. We shall never be able to say in specific terms. We have not the technique to separate the advantages from the disadvantages. We can give a picture of what has happened in the United States since it became an independent nation, but we cannot specifically allocate immigration in this development, nor shall we ever be able to say what would have happened in the United States without immigration. The United States has always been in a process of change and this change has involved immigrants. Perhaps immigration has expedited this change, or it may have hindered it. Doubtless it has done both. Adjustments made by the immigrants have been to a culture in constant transition and not to a static social order.

In discussing the effects of immigration, most people have tried to prove that there either should or should not be immigration. Most writers who have considered the matter have been interested in showing that there should not be. The procedure has been to select real or imaginary evils and draw conclusions on that basis. This is merely a reaction to isolated facts, only a part of a configuration. The other part of the picture is the values derived from immigration. An evaluation of immigration could not neglect this aspect without getting the problem out of perspective. No matter how many evils there may have been, immigration could not be evaluated scientifically without a comparison of the evils with the advantages. It is obvious that this cannot be done without exhaustive research and a consensus as to the advantages and disadvantages. Some would consider intermarriage desirable; others would see it as a means of the disappearance of the native stock. It is possible, however, to describe what takes place when a group brings its culture into a strange social order, in terms of some of the most significant sociological processes.

The true nature of the question of immigration and its place in American life will be discussed later under the problem of immigration, after the recent influx has been considered in all its aspects.

READINGS

Abbott, Edith, *Immigration: Select Documents and Case Records.* 1924. Pp. 181–251
Beals, Carleton, *Mexico: An Interpretation.* 1923
Bogardus, Emory S., " The Mexican Immigrant and the Quota," *Sociology and Research.* XII, pp. 371–378. 1928
Bouvé, Clement L., *Exclusion and Expulsion of Aliens.* 1912
Commons, John R., *Races and Immigrants in America.* 1920
Cook, A. E. and Hagerty, J. J., *Immigration Laws of the United States — Compiled and Explained.* 1929
Davis, James J., *Selective Immigration.* 1925
Fairchild, H. P., *Immigration.* Revised ed. 1926. Chapter VI, pp. 108–126; Chapter XVII, pp. 369–393; Chapter XX, pp. 434–472
Garis, Roy L., *Immigration Restriction.* 1927. Chapters III–VIII
Jenks, J. W. and Louck, W. J., *The Immigration Problem.* 1917
MacLean, Annie M., *Modern Immigration.* 1925
McLean, Robert, *That Mexican.* 1928
Ragsdale, Martha, *The National Origins Plan of Immigration Restriction.* 1928
Ross, E. A., *The Old World in the New.* 1914
" Should Quota Law be Applied to Mexico? " *Congressional Digest,* Vol. 7, No. 5, May 1928

Thomson, Charles A., " Restriction of Mexican Immigration,"
    Jour. of Applied Sociology. XI, pp. 574–578
Trevor, John B., *Immigration Act of 1924.* 1924
Whelpley, J. D., *The Problem of the Immigrant;* a brief discussion with a summary of conditions, laws, and regulations governing the movement of population to and from the British Empire, United States, France, Belgium, Switzerland, Germany, Italy, Austria-Hungary, Spain, Portugal, Netherlands, Denmark, Scandinavia, and Russia. 1905

CHAPTER VIII

COMPOSITION OF NEW IMMIGRATION

IMMIGRATION to the United States prior to 1882 had been from northwestern Europe and has been classed as "old" immigration as we have already observed. The "new" immigration comes from eastern and southern Europe and is composed quite largely of Slavs, Jews, and Italians. The countries included in this recent European exodus are "Austria-Hungary, Bulgaria, Roumania, Russia, Servia, Spain, Syria, and Turkey. This schedule refers only to European countries (with the exception of Syria and Turkey, which ethnically belong to Europe), without reference to non-European sources." [1] The "new" immigration comes from the Slavic and Mediterranean branches of the Caucasian race rather than from the Teutonic.

From the date of the passage of the act in 1819 to keep definite statistics on immigration, until 1883, about ninety-five per cent of the immigration was from northwestern Europe. By 1907 the new immigration from southern and eastern Europe constituted over eighty per cent of the movement from Europe for that year. It was about the year 1896 that the new immigration first exceeded the old immigration in numbers.

In regard to the volume of immigration, it was discovered that there was a counter current of departing aliens, which in some years was almost as great as the number of arrivals. For example, while more than 258,538 entered the United States in 1895, the net gain was only 41,871. The realiza-

---

[1] From H. P. Fairchild, *Immigration*, p. 133.

tion of the importance of this led to a provision in the immigration law in 1907 making it necessary to list all departing alien passengers for each ship leaving a port of the United States. Since 1908 there has been definite information concerning the net gain for each year.

In that year another important distinction is made, that between immigrant and nonimmigrant aliens on the inward passage, and emigrant and nonemigrant aliens on the outward passage. Immigrant aliens are those whose place of last permanent residence was in some foreign country, and who are coming here with the intention of residing permanently. Nonimmigrant aliens are of two classes: those whose place of last permanent residence was the United States, but who have been abroad for a short period of time, and those whose place of last permanent residence was in a foreign country, and who are coming to the United States without the intention of residing permanently, including aliens in transit. Departing aliens are classified in a corresponding way. Emigrant aliens are those whose place of last permanent residence was the United States, and who are going abroad with the intention of residing there permanently. Nonemigrant aliens are of two classes: those whose place of last permanent residence was the United States, and who are going abroad for a short visit only, and those whose place of last permanent residence was abroad, but who have been in the United States for a short time, including aliens in transit.[2]

The immigration for the period of federal control has been composed quite largely of unskilled peasants who have often had very little contact with city life even in their own country, yet they have come to an urban environment characterized by a strange culture. They have come from a situation where their religion and, as a matter of fact, all their customs and traditions were deeply rooted in nature. It has been a movement of simple people to a complex social life in a city, and to a strange physical, industrial environment.

The males have greatly outnumbered the females in the new immigration. With some groups the percentage of males is as high as 96 per cent, as in the case of the Bulgarians. The lowest percentage of males in the new immigration is among the Hebrews, who have only 56.7. In the old

[2] From H. P. Fairchild, *Immigration*, pp. 129–130. By permission of The Macmillan Company, publishers.

immigration the female population was actually greater with the Irish, where they constituted 52.8 per cent. A large male population means that the family life considered so important is entirely lacking in a great many cases. Normal social adjustments are often difficult. However, a preponderance of males tends to reduce poverty and facilitates economic adjustment.

The immigrant has reached the United States when he was in the productive age or approaching that age. The greatest numbers are in the age groups from fourteen to forty-four years. This means in most cases a ready economic adjustment where work is available, but a distinct barrier to social adjustment since they have come at an age when they were well established in terms of another culture. Coming at this age, their habits, attitudes, interests, and philosophies of life were adjustments to a European peasant culture quite foreign to that of the United States.

The ethnic composition, numbers, and age and sex distribution of an invading alien group are not the only important factors, especially when one is primarily interested in adjustments. Equally important are the life philosophies, the attitudes, the conception they have of themselves, that have been developed through the experience of the groups in forming their national characteristics.

A very significant difference is to be found between the old and the new immigration in reference to past experiences. While the people making up the old immigration suffered oppression, it was largely oppression at the hands of their own ethnic and nationalistic group. Theirs was not a struggle, therefore, for nationality, but for religious, political, social, or economic freedom. The Irish were the exception in the old immigration; they had suffered oppression at the hands of the English and had developed corresponding nationalistic attitudes. The German Palatinates were oppressed religiously by Germans, so their struggle was not for nationalistic freedom but for a chance to worship as they wished. But the new immigrant in most cases has a background experience of centuries of struggling for nationalistic freedom.

If one looks into the history of the groups making up the new immigration, he finds that group after group has been oppressed and has been involved in a struggle for national existence. They all have developed what Professor Miller has called the " oppression psychosis " which has resulted in an attitude of chauvinism regarding their customs, especially those of religion and language. This has not been felt in just this way by the peasants who have flocked to our shores, but conditions closely related to the oppression psychosis of the leaders have been felt by the peasant in the way of economic and cultural deprivation, resulting in a low standard of living and illiteracy. Often the real oppression psychosis of the peasant has developed after he has reached this country.

In the countries of central Europe from Finland on the north of Jugo-Slavia and Bulgaria on the south, there has been a struggle for national existence. This has led to self-consciousness and an exaggerated awareness of the group identity. The whole situation has been somewhat complicated by an extraneous group — the Jews who were not struggling for nationality but for an existence in these countries where nationality was the chief interest of many. These oppressed states treated the Jews much as they were being treated by the great powers of Europe, so that the Jews, though without a country, became very conscious of themselves as a class much persecuted, which made all that was Jewish more or less sacred to them.

Consequently the new immigration is made up of groups from countries that have an oppression psychosis. This is another label for human behavior which means very little until the conditions involved have been analyzed. A study of the past experiences will reveal the human nature aspect of the new immigration as well as the ethnic composition. This will be necessary for the discussion of adjustments later on, since, as already has been said, there are always two important aspects to an adjustment: the situation, and what the individuals bring into the situation in the way of attitudes, habits, customs, and traditions, especially the attitudes which are cross-sections of the experiences of a people.

Beginning with the most northern group, Finland has been dominated by Sweden and Russia. " For six and a half centuries the Finns were ruled by Sweden. . . At the University of Helsingfors, where twenty-five years ago all the work was done in Swedish, now a larger part is in Finnish, and the Finnish spirit is increasing by leaps and bounds. Seven and a half centuries of Swedish culture with no Finnish education has had no effect, except to stimulate the growth of Finnish national feeling." [3] Under Russia, the Finns had to endure foreign officials and have the Russian language forced on them in many cases; but there has been little assimilation, rather there has developed a growing appreciation of their own culture. Nearly the entire population of Finland has membership in the Evangelical Lutheran Church. There are more than 260,000 Finns in the United States, about half being native-born. The majority of these people have settled in the rural districts of mid-western states; this is unusual in recent immigration.

The language of the Esthonians, the Finns, and the Magyars shows a common origin for the three groups. Many years ago they invaded Europe from Asia. The Esths were under the Danish crown where they were in constant revolt. Then for nearly six hundred years they experienced a state of serfdom under the German landowners. Finally, Russia tried to denationalize and renationalize the Esths by harsh and repressive measures, but this treatment served only to strengthen a desire for nationalism. The number coming to the United States has been very small, only a few thousand. The religious affiliation in Esthonia is largely Lutheran. Esthonia has been an independent Republic since 1918.

South of Esthonia on the Baltic Sea is the small province of Latvia, the home of the Letts. In the Letts we have the first of the Slavic groups that have been controlled by the strong nations of Europe.

Each Slavic group has a strong developing Nationalism of its own coupled with the ponderously forming Pan-Slavic conscious-

[3] Herbert A. Miller, "Nationalism in Bohemia and Poland," *The North American Review*, 200 : 885 (December 1914).

ness. All the Slavic languages are closely related and serve as a symbol for a closer union of all the divisions.[4]

The Letts have struggled against the political domination of Russia and the cultural and economic domination of Germany, under a system of landlordism. In religion, they are mainly Lutherans and Roman Catholics. The number in the United States does not exceed 50,000.

The Lithuanians and the Letts are ethnically the same, being of Indo-European origin with a language somewhat like Sanskrit, but their experiences, culturally speaking, have not been the same. Through the marriage of rulers, there was a union of Poland and Lithuania in 1386. Despite the fact that Lithuania became somewhat dependent, it maintained its national character though there is evidence of cultural influence on the part of the Poles. As in many countries, the Lithuanian language was preserved in isolated rural districts by the peasants. From 1795 to 1918 when it gained its independence, Lithuania was under Prussia and Russia, with the latter anxious to annex Lithuania. The Germans and the Poles were the landlords for many centuries and the Lithuanians were the laborers and serfs. But there still remained a smoldering Lithuanian spirit that was easily revived. Besides the domination of the Polish and the German aristocracy they had to contend with the political domination from Russia. There are about 300,000 Lithuanians in the United States.

Poland, one of the larger nations of central Europe, has been divided under the influence and domination of Germany, Russia, and Austria. The Poles belong to the Slavic group. Their situation has been greatly complicated by the presence of a large Jewish element that was not accepted, partly because the Jews were not Catholics, and partly because of their dominance in economic activities.

Poland, perhaps, offers the most highly developed example of Nationalism. It was never a conspicuous country, but over a hundred years ago it was free. Germany, Austria, and Russia divided it, and, completely ignoring sociological laws, have tried to absorb it. Never was there another so persistent and deliberate

[4] *Ibid.*, p. 880.

effort to wipe out national individuality, but if there ever was a case of imperial indigestion, Poland has caused three chronic attacks. Bismarck's foolish policy of forbidding the Polish language and forcing German in its place, and Russia's similar policy with Russian, can be called a basic cause for the present European turmoil, because it has made the preservation of language a religion, and martyrdom for it a glorification. The Poles think that their love for the church is piety, while in reality they are good Catholics because their religion is Poland, and Catholicism is a Polish protest against Orthodox Russia and Protestant Prussia.[5]

Consequently the Poles have come to America with well developed, ethnocentric attitudes concerning their religion and language.

The situation in Poland was more complex because of the presence of the nobility. The nobles exercised little political influence so far as Germany, Austria, and Russia were concerned, but they were in a position to keep alive an interest in Polish nationalism. Their activities under the advantages of an economic and cultural superiority were directed always toward a united Poland and freedom from the three great powers of Europe. Though there was a great cultural abyss between the aristocracy and the ignorant peasants, there was transmitted to the latter a feeling of dissatisfaction with foreign domination.

The Poles are largely Roman Catholics, though Christianity with the peasants has been colored somewhat by the continuance of pagan beliefs. There is a Jewish population in Poland of about 3,000,000. There are more than 2,000,000 Poles in the United States.

East of Poland is Ukraine whose population is chiefly Slavic, frequently spoken of as the "Little Russians." It is one of the most densely populated regions in Russia and has sent nearly 100,000 emigrants to the United States. Eighty per cent of the people are engaged in agriculture, but the country is in a transitional stage toward industrialization.

The people of Ukraine left the Polish-Lithuanian empire to escape oppression from the Polish and Lithuanian

[5] *Ibid.*, pp. 883–884.

princes. After this movement they were known as Cossacks.
They became a part of Russia in 1793. In 1917 a Republic
was proclaimed, but trouble with the Bolsheviks lasted until
1920. Their religious affiliations are divided among the
Greek, Catholic, Eastern Orthodox, Roman Catholic, and
Protestant religions.

The Ukrainians who are in Galicia are known as Ruthenes.
" It may be said at once that there is no group, or fraction
of a group, of Ruthenes, which does not cherish for the
Poles a hatred so fierce that by the side of it the bitterest
protest of the Russian Ukrainians against Russian rule appears tame and insignificant." [6] There are about 100,000
Ukrainians in the United States, nearly half that number
being native-born.

Russia is north of Ukraine and east of Poland, Lithuania,
Latvia, Esthonia, and Finland. It has been a powerful nation in that it has exercised political domination over all
these bordering countries mentioned above. Despite this
position of political power, the Russian peasant before the
World War " was probably the most ignorant and degraded
and was only beginning to learn to emigrate." [7] Russia has
had a Jewish population of about 3,000,000 and the Jews
constituted by far the greatest number emigrating from
Russia. Since the War a great many " White Russians "
have come who are not of the peasant class.

Before the War about 92 per cent of the Russians coming
to the United States were peasants. Most of them were
old enough to have been well oriented in terms of Russian
culture in a way to make cultural adjustments in America
difficult. They have come from a situation where there was
an unequal distribution of land in a country where the
peasant is very much attached to the soil.

The Greek Orthodox faith is the chief religion, though
some Russians have emigrated because they wanted to break
with the church. The peasant feared the government and
disliked the five years of military service.

---

[6] Ralph Butler, *The New Eastern Europe* (London: Longmans, Green & Co.
1919), p. 135.
[7] H. P. Fairchild, *op. cit.*, p. 143.

He was the victim of religious intolerance, social inequality, economic discrimination, political despotism, and compulsory ignorance. While all these conditions made life uncomfortable, poverty was the most potent force in stimulating emigration.[8]

In discussing Russian immigration, Jerome Davis has said:

There were three chief groups: the political refugees, or revolutionists, the unorthodox who sought religious freedom, and the vast majority who came to make money and then return home, or at least to escape the poverty and injustice of Russia.[9]

South and west of Poland is Czecho-Slovakia. This Slavic country is populated by the Czechs or Bohemians, and the Slovaks. Though an independent republic since 1918, it has been subjected to the domination of the Germans, the German-Austrians, and the Magyars. The Bohemians are located in the western part of the province and the Slovaks are in the eastern section. The Czechs have struggled for nationality with the Germans and Austrians; the Slovaks have been controlled and dominated by the Hungarians or Magyars. In discussing the Bohemians, Miss Balch said:

The struggle with the Germans is in a sense the master-thread in their whole history, and this contact, even though inimical, has meant interpenetration and rapprochement. No other Slavic nationality is more self-conscious and patriotic, not to say chauvinistic, in its feeling, and at the same time none begins to be so permeated with the general European culture and so advanced economically.[10]

Despite the European influence on the Czech culture, the Bohemian still hates the Germans for their domination.

The Czechs were under the oppressive influence of Austria as well as Germany. It was in this domination that the "free-thinking" in Bohemia had its origin as a reaction against Catholic Austria, which had used the clerical party to make its control more complete.

The Bohemians are simply one illustration of a fact that has not been sufficiently taken into consideration, namely, that every immigrant group comes here equipped with distinctive attitudes

---

[8] Jerome Davis, *The Russian Immigrant* (New York: The Macmillan Company 1922), p. 209.
[9] *Ibid.*, p. 210.
[10] Emily Greene Balch, *Our Slavic Fellow Citizens* (New York: Charities Publication Committee 1910), p. 78.

and habits of mind, only through the understanding of which can the unusual things about them be explained. There are several outstanding facts in Bohemian history which are reflected in every Bohemian community in the United States. The most interesting social manifestation among the Bohemians has been that of " free-thinking," so called.[11]

More than half a million Czechs have migrated to the United States.

The Slovaks who make up the eastern part of the Czecho-Slovakian Republic have had their experiences of oppression not with the Germans but rather with the Hungarians. They are peasants who live almost entirely upon the land, utilizing primitive methods of agriculture. The Slovaks did not have the same religious experiences as the Bohemians so they have not evidenced the same religious reactions. They are largely Roman Catholics, with Lutherans an important minority. The Slovaks have become self-conscious over the fact that the Czechs have been accredited with a culture superior to their own; then, too, they suffered from oppressive measures when the Magyars tried to denationalize them. These two facts have led to a collective sensitiveness.

The Slovaks have suffered greatly from the efforts of the Magyars to wipe out their nationality. They have been forbidden the use of their own language, and have had priests imposed upon them who did not speak their tongue. . . Because of the methods pursued by the Magyars, which prohibited the Slovaks from getting any education in their own language, they show a very much larger percentage of illiteracy than the Bohemians, though many of the most prominent leaders in Bohemian life have been Slovaks who came to Bohemia for education.[12]

There are nearly seven hundred thousand Slovaks in the United States.

The dualism between Austria and Hungary resulted in many difficulties. Certain factions in Hungary were hostile to the union from the outset. There were dissensions in the army and riots and patriotic demonstrations by students. Agrarian Hungary thought industrial Austria was using its country as a colonial market for manufactured goods. No

[11] H. A. Miller, "The Bulwark of Freedom," II. *The Survey*, 41 : 117 (November 2, 1918).
[12] *Ibid.*, pp. 118–119.

Hungarian official had an important place on the Austro-Hungarian general staff. At first there was not a language difficulty since Latin was the official language. Finally schools were established so that anyone might have a secondary education in his mother tongue. This only helped to accentuate the ethnocentrism in Hungary. These minority groups in Hungary wished always to break in some way the Magyar supremacy. There was much interest in a move to shift the dualism to a triarchy in which there would be a third state, a slavonic state. The coming of the World War found the dualism in parliamentary strife.

The Austrians come from the western part of Austria-Hungary, south of Germany and the western part of Czecho-Slovakia. The majority of the inhabitants of Austria speak German and almost all are Roman Catholics. Their culture has been mainly German and their attitudes have been colored by their close proximity to Germany and the hatred for the Magyars.

Although there is a mixed population in Hungary, the Magyar speech predominates. More than half of the population are Roman Catholics, about 27 per cent are Protestants, and the rest are Greek Catholics and Jews. The Magyars were in Hungary as early as the ninth century. The Hungarians had been under Turkish rule in the sixteenth and seventeenth centuries. After 1849 German became the official language, but it was replaced by the Magyar in 1867. Magyars are known in English as Hungarians. Although they are only a part, about half, of the population of Hungary, Magyar is the official language.

While struggling for equal rights in Austria-Hungary, the Magyars made their presence felt by trying to Magyarize the nationalities around them, utilizing force, as dominant nations often do, to accomplish their purpose. This served effectively to arouse the spirit of nationalism with the heterogeneous population of Slovaks, Ruthenians, Croatians, Germans, Roumanians, and Jews. A great number of them migrated to America to escape this situation and brought with them attitudes of oppression. Though the Magyars hated the Germans and Austrians they have co-operated with them in oppressive measures because they have alienated all the Slavic groups. More than 3,000,000 Austrians and nearly 500,000 Hungarians are found in the United States.

The Roumanians, occupying an area south of the Ukrainians and east of Hungary, have had to accommodate themselves to political and economic domination for many centuries. Not only has Roumania suffered under the oppression of an attempted Magyarization, but it was once controlled by Italy and Turkey. As a matter of fact the Roumanians who have come to the United States are largely from Hungary rather than from Roumania.

The present population of Roumania is made up of approximately 70 per cent of pure Roumanian blood and origin; other important elements in the population are Magyars, Germans, Jews, Turks, Bulgars, Poles, Ukrainians, and gypsies. In early days there was a close contact with the Romans and many of them are descendants of the Roman invaders. The Magyar group, numbering about 1,500,000, represent a dissenting political minority encouraged by their countrymen in Hungary. The German settlements in Roumania are and have been more or less independent, with their own institutions and local government. The Jews are city dwellers, where, in contrast with the Germans, they have had few civil and legal rights though their status is better now than before the War.

A large proportion of the population of Roumania is engaged in agriculture. Before the War Roumania was characterized by large estates and absentee landlordism, but partial expropriation of large estates has placed much of the land in the hands of the peasants, who have been handicapped by lack of capital. An unsatisfactory distribution of the land after the emancipation of the peasants finally led to a revolt in 1907 against Jewish middlemen and large landowners.

Roumania has been at times involved in the Balkan struggles and was with the Allies during the World War. The constant struggle of the Roumanians for nationality has left its impress on their adjustments to life. In their religious life they are mainly members of the Eastern Orthodox church, but some of them are affiliated with the Greek Catholic, Roman Catholic, and Protestant churches. There are more than 800,000 Jews in Roumania.

Bulgaria is a Balkan kingdom south of Roumania and east of Jugo-Slavia. More than 80 per cent of the population of the country are Bulgarians. Other important elements are the Turks, the Jews, and the Slavs. The Bulgarians were originally a Slavonian tribe. They belong quite largely to the Orthodox Bulgarian church for which there was a tremendous struggle; there are also some Roman Catholics and a few Protestants. As with Roumania, an early Roman influence is to be observed.

The Bulgarians have been involved in many conflicts with their Balkan neighbors. For five centuries their territory was annexed by Turkey which resulted in a " dark epoch in Bulgarian history." In the eighteenth century they suffered greatly as the Turkish armies passed through Bulgaria during the war with Austria. There were also Russian invasions early in the nineteenth century. At one time Bulgaria was subject to Serbia and very early it was ravaged by the Magyars.

The Bulgarians are chiefly an agricultural people with farms too small to be an adequate economic unit. The dormant national spirit, which has become important in eastern European countries, in Bulgaria was aroused by a literary revival. Language provides an excellent symbol around which attitudes can be organized. This revival led to a revolt against Greek domination in the literary field, Greek having been the language of the upper classes. There are fewer than 15,000 Bulgarians in the United States.

The Jugo-Slavs, or southern Slavs, include the Serbs, Croatians, Slovenes, and the Montenegrins. Croatia-Slavonia had been a part of the Austro-Hungarian empire until 1918. This brought all the southern Slavs together.. The Serbs constitute the largest element but have not made the economic and cultural development that the Croatians have made. The Slovenes are predominantly Catholics and highly westernized.

The Serbs, Croats and Slovenes constitute over 80 per cent of the population. Other important groups are German, Magyar, Albanian, Roumanian, and there are quite a number speaking a Slav language other than Serbo-Croat or Slovene. Most of the inhabitants are engaged in rural pursuits.

Even after the World War there were great internal political struggles which might have been more serious had it not been for the realization that Italy and Hungary had not yet forgotten the War, and protection was assured only through a union of the southern Slavs. Many of the Serbian immigrants came to the United States from Austria-Hungary where they grew tired of being treated as aliens and inferiors. It has not been easy for the Jugo-Slavs to create an independent state because of the long traditional antagonisms based on religion and other factors, though that has been accomplished at last. The Croats and Slovenes are Roman Catholics; the Serbs are affiliated with the Serbian branch of the Eastern Orthodox church. This has been an important cause of much of the dissension in Jugo-Slavia. There are a great many more Slovenians and Croatians in the United States than there are Serbians. While there are only about 50,000 of the latter, there are over 140,000 Croatians and more than 200,000 Slovenians.

Albania is on the west coast of the Balkan peninsula between Jugo-Slavia and Greece. The majority of Albanians are a mountain people who have been isolated from the outside world and to a certain extent from one another. Turkish rule left its influence. About 70 per cent of them are Moslems, while some are Roman Catholics and a group in the south belong to the Albanian Eastern Orthodox church. These religious groups have been in constant conflict with one another.

At various times parts of Albania have been under the control of Italians, Greeks, French, Turks, Bulgarians, Jugo-Slavs, etc., but it became an independent Republic in 1925. The ethnocentrism of the Albanians has been greatly sharpened because of their isolation, though throughout their history there have been periods in which they have had to suffer the domination of other countries. There are only about 7000 Albanians in the United States.

Thus far we have had a discussion of groups that have struggled against domination in an effort to preserve their nationalities, with language and religion important culture elements in the struggle.

Most of the national groupings have been so stimulated to self-accentuation by imperialistic oppression, that they no longer represent normal mental attitudes, but what might be called oppressed-nationality psychoses. Dividing and ruling by force have created antagonisms and inhibitions which constitute a heritage of all the new nations of Europe, and thus are congenital in the psychological make-up of the majority of our immigrants.

Forcible methods of assimilation were directed first against language and then against religion, so that the resulting inhibitions constitute " balked dispositions " or distinct psychoses that are very deep-seated. The instinct for freedom is universal; when it is inhibited it breaks out in diverse and exaggerated forms. By reason of suggestion the form such expression takes will be comparatively uniform through a given group. It may be chauvinism, which is the focussing of attention on the supreme significance of the national values. It is a positive resistance to the suppression of group individuality, which is far more important to most human beings than person individuality.

Had it been possible, Austria-Hungary would have forced the eight non-German nationalities of the empire to speak only German; but the result of her attempt was the complete dissolution of the empire. Under such a condition, preservation of language becomes the highest duty of the group. Certainly one of the contributing causes of the present disorganization of Europe was the oppression-psychosis instituted by Bismarck when he forbade the Poles in Posen the use of their own language.

Religion is the other most obvious symbol of national unity. Religious expression in some form is normal and universal; but when the religious organization is built up to supply a fighting machinery it tends to become abnormal, and it acquires strength in direct proportion to the efforts made to crush the nationality of its members. Among the Poles the strength of clerical organization has been stimulated by the ruthless methods of protestant Prussia and orthodox Russia. On the other hand, freethinking Bohemia is explained by the alliance of the church with Vienna, the oppressor of Bohemian nationality; as the religious indifference of the Italians is explained by the struggle of the Vatican for temporal power. The synagogue is strong where

Christians oppress Jews. Protestant England has controlled Catholic Ireland by force until to many people the terms Irish and Catholic are synonyms. Where economic and political exploitation has been aided by the church, the technique of devotion which normally related itself to religion is often carried over in a new adherence to socialism.

An oppressed people never gives up its struggle for its language and its religion. Under conditions of freedom these are only means to a fuller life; under oppression they become the objects of life. The freeing of oppressed nations was one of the objects of the war. The restoration of normal national psychoses is one of the necessities of peace.[13]

We have accepted immigrants from middle Europe and in directing their adjustments in the United States we have to take into consideration their cultural experiences which date back many generations. Any accommodations that they make must be in terms of their past relationships. They have brought from Europe traditions replete with attitudes concerning the treatment of their language, religion, and other units of culture. " It was compulsion to learn German, Russian, and Magyar that created the attitudes that underlie some of the most complex problems in Europe at the present time." [14] Knowing the nature of human nature, we must expect that the first generation of immigrants will not want to learn English if it means giving up their own language around which so many sentiments have developed. Americanization is not resisted where there is no compulsion; it is taken on unconsciously so far as it is possible for human nature to change.

The American-born of Slavic parents usually have a very different attitude. Experiences with English-speaking children at school and on the playground prevent the development of attitudes of reverence for the language of their parents. The definition given a foreign language in the United States leads to their trying to avoid the vernacular of their homes. Consequently there is a distinct difference, culturally speaking, in the composition of the Slavs born in the United States and those from Europe. While they

[13] H. A. Miller, "Treatment of Immigrant Heritages," *Proceedings of the National Conference of Social Work* (Chicago: 1919), pp. 733–734.
[14] *Ibid.*, p. 736.

have the same biological inheritance, their human nature is quite dissimilar.

In considering the composition of immigration, it is very important to know the historical experiences of any particular group. Adjustments cannot be directed wisely unless this is the case. Those who have been active in Americanization work without understanding the mental organization of those from middle Europe as a result of their experiences of oppression, have proceeded along lines that would arouse antagonisms for things American. If learning English is considered an educational process for making better adjustments, the attitude of immigrants is one of co-operation. If they feel that it is another oppressive gesture to make them forget their own language, their attitude will be very different. It is the nature of human nature, as it has developed under oppression, that is responsible for these reactions. Racial affiliation is not a determining factor.

Greece, unlike many of the countries of southern and eastern Europe, is inhabited quite largely by its own countrymen. By 1924 most of the Greeks in Asia Minor had been ejected and returned to live in Greece. This influx, involving many who were destitute, became a great burden, making emigration almost a necessity, though the situation was somewhat relieved by outside aid. Turkey has been the great enemy of Greece but there have been conflicts also with Serbia, Bulgaria, and Albania. In most of these struggles, the great powers took a hand — at least in the final settlement.

Greece is primarily an agricultural country and is always threatened with overpopulation. There is little of political, religious, or social conditions that would lead to migration, yet emigration is a tradition of long standing in Greece. The cause for migration is largely economic. The Greeks utilize primitive methods in agriculture; their standard of living is very poor. Home and village industry is prevalent.

Not only have economic conditions led to emigration from Greece, but hostilities with Roumania and Bulgaria have led many to come to the United States who formerly went to these two countries. The Greeks in America have provided money for a great many. The ethnocentrism of the Greeks is based on ancient traditions with a feeling that the world is greatly indebted to them for past contributions. There has been a high proportion of males in Greek immigration who readily become self-sufficient and soon establish themselves in America with the Greek Orthodox Church and the coffee-house as the centers of their lives. Practically all Greeks belong to the Eastern Orthodox Church. There are more than 200,000 in the United States.

Italian immigration has come to the United States from northern and southern Italy, the latter furnishing by far the greater number. Those from southern Italy have had fewer contacts and a lower economic status. For these reasons they have greater problems of adjustment in a foreign clime. Add to this the fact that many of them do not expect to remain in a foreign country and that most of them are unskilled agriculturists living in a strange city, and one has the explanation for their lack of accommodation.

The southern Italians have come quite largely from Basilicata, Calabria, and Sicily. Those from the north are chiefly from Venetia, Lombardy, and Piedmont. Especially in southern Italy emigration has been a necessity. Although there has been an increase in the population, there has been no increase in the amount of food produced.

Italy has not recently been dominated by foreign powers as have the countries of eastern Europe, but an internal situation has kept the people in subjugation. The agricultural system under absentee landlordism and contract cultivation with a brief tenure has made economic security impossible. This situation has not only kept the southern Italians maladjusted in their own country but has not equipped them for adjustments in a foreign land. Despite this experience in their native land, most of them have expected to return. With this attitude there was little chance for more than an accommodation in America. The majority of Italians are Roman Catholics. There are more than 3,000,000 in the United States, more than half of them being native-born.

The Portuguese that have emigrated to the United States

are peasants. In many cases they are superstitious and illiterate. The majority of them are Roman Catholics. While most authorities regard the Portuguese as a rather homogeneous group, from an ethnic standpoint they are the descendants of many groups. Predominantly Kelt-Iberian, there is some Moorish and Negro blood. The Bravas from the Cape Verde Islands have been classed as "colored" by the federal census since 1915.

The Portuguese have come from Portugal and from the Azores, Madeira, and the Cape Verde Islands, a greater number being from the Islands. The excess of males over females is not so great as with many other nationalities. These peasants are predominantly unskilled laborers. They have settled chiefly in California and in the New England states; in the former they are farmers while in the eastern states they are in the textile industries.

The Jews in America have come from most of the European countries, with Germany, Poland, and Russia furnishing the greatest numbers. The Jewish situation is, in a sense, unique. The social definition that they have faced since their dispersion in 70 A.D. in every part of Europe has been such that they have always been forced to think of themselves as different. This social definition — this attitude of anti-Semitism — grew with certain important events beginning with the crucifixion of Christ. The Crusades, the fact that the Jews became the money lenders of the Middle Ages when such activity was connected with sin by the Christian Church, and finally the emphasis placed on nationalism by the countries of Europe — all contributed to this growing attitude. An important factor, also, was the increasing self-consciousness of the Jews, in which they defined themselves as different, a people who had sacred customs and traditions to protect.

The attitude of anti-Semitism has existed so long that it is at present, and for many centuries has been so well rationalized as to be almost a duty in the gentile world. No doubt certain units of human nature with the Jews had a different content at the time of their dispersion following the Roman conquest of Palestine, but the ever-present social definition of the Jews has made them different, because they were forced into cultural isolation.

The self-consciousness of the Jews led to segregation first in the voluntary ghetto of Europe and then in the compulsory ghetto. This forced process of isolation, following the Crusades, was accompanied by many persecutions and embarrassments for the Jews. The Church passed decrees forbidding intimate relationships between Jews and gentiles. In some instances the Jews were expelled from their ghettos. They were excluded from many spheres of life. They were humiliated by being forced to wear a badge that would identify them as Jews. They were often insulted in the streets. In this predicament the Jews turned to the emperors and popes for protection.

Generally the Jews also had to buy the right to live in a community in which they had not as yet lived. This was known as the right of *Judaeos tenere* or *Judaeos habere*. This right of keeping or holding Jews that the emperor was free to sell to local authorities or individuals, much as a city nowadays sells a streetcar franchise, implied, of course, that the status of the Jew was a precarious one. They were not citizens — not even men — in the eyes of the law, but rather were taxable property.[15]

These were the conditions under which the Jews lived during the Middle Ages. Late in the eighteenth century there was some evidence of a changing attitude in western and central Europe, especially in France. Even then, they were in a special category.

The Jews were still aliens . . . in the countries in which they had lived for centuries. They were barred from landownership, from many occupations, from the universities and schools, from participation in civil and political affairs, and from the ordinary rights of citizenship. Furthermore, they were restricted in choosing their domicile, and were subjected to special taxation. In some countries their private lives were circumscribed even as regards dress, speech, and worship. They were subject to arbitrary expulsion, and exposed to insult and violence on the part of the populace, without rights of redress.[16]

[15] Louis Wirth, *The Ghetto* (Chicago: The University of Chicago Press 1928), p. 17.
[16] *Ibid.*, p. 111.

It was discovered that the formal abolition of the ghetto did not mean that the ghetto would disappear. Many of the Jews did not want to endanger the customs and traditions that were so intimately connected with their social heritage. There was a realization that the " persistence of traditional Jewish life seems to depend upon the favorable soil of the ghetto, upon exclusion from the disintegrating and corroding influences of other cultural areas." [17]

Then modern anti-Semitism finds its explanation in part in the struggle for nationalism discussed in the preceding pages in relation to the countries of eastern Europe. In Poland, Russia, and Roumania there were pogroms and denial of participation of Jews in many important spheres of life. This fact has led to the migration of many Jews to America where they have accommodated themselves to American life through the settlement in ghettos in most of our cities of any size.

In dealing with the Jewish immigrant, we have a person whose human nature has been shaped by isolation, first voluntary, then forced — human nature which seeks isolation because it was cradled in the isolation of the ghetto; there it finds a warmth that the world outside the ghetto does not offer. The Jew is what he is because of the rigid customs of the ghetto and the explicit laws and rationalized attitudes outside the ghetto. In this process the Jew became extremely self-conscious and in many cases has overcompensated for this feeling of oppression when he has had contacts with the gentile world. There are approximately 4,268,000 Jews in the United States.

Three rather important groups from Asia must be included in recent immigration. These are the Armenians, the Syrians, and the Persians. The Armenians are from a small mountainous country north of Turkey and Persia where it borders on the Black Sea. The language spoken by the Armenians is Indo-European, though there has been an infiltration of many Persian words. Most Armenians are members of the Armenian National Apostolic church. The fact that they are Christians living near Moslem neighbors

[17] *Ibid.*, p. 286.

has resulted in many conflict situations for them. They have been able, however, to maintain their religion and nationality but have suffered greatly under Turkish rule. Armenia has been a republic since 1920. There are more than 75,000 Armenians in the United States, most of them being refugees who were anxious to get away from the despotism of Turkey. They are to be found in greatest numbers on the two seaboards.

The Syrians have come from the small country at the eastern end of the Mediterranean and are of the Semitic branch of the Caucasian race. Syria has had an important place in world history. Here originated the alphabet from which our own was derived. Early, by nature of its position, the country played a leading rôle in the economic organization between the East and the West. Syria was taken by the Mohammedans in the seventh century and Arabic became the common language. Before this time all Syrians were Christians but most of them are now Mohammedans. Those coming to the United States are largely Christians who have emigrated to escape religious persecutions. The Turks invaded the country in the sixteenth century and many other alien groups have played an important rôle in Syria. There is a great nationalistic spirit in this little country which surges toward the establishment of an independent kingdom. There are more than 100,000 Syrians in the United States, nearly half of this number being native-born.

The Persians are an Asiatic group. Their native country is mountainous in nature and they are chiefly a rural people. Those who have come to the United States are quite largely Assyrians, Christian Persians. Religious intolerance and persecutions have made them extremely egocentric concerning their religion. The church has become the center of the community established in America. The emigrants from Persia are mostly males who are without a trade or a profession. There are not many in the United States; the largest colony is in Chicago which numbers more than 3000. In this settlement the majority have come from the province of Urmia, though some are from Hindustan and the Transcaucasus.

Two groups that have been important in recent immigration to the United States are from North America: the French-Canadians and the Mexicans. The Mexicans are a transient population, often entering and leaving the United States many times in one year. Most of these immigrants come from the states of the central plateau (*mesa central*) and from the northern plateau (*mesa del norte*). The greatest numbers have gone to Texas, California, New Mexico, and Arizona, where they work in the cotton, sugar beet, and corn fields. They are employed also in the orchards, on the railroads, and in the mines. Most of them are unskilled workers; some are tenant farmers.

Mexican immigrants are largely Roman Catholics but, as with many peasants, some pagan practices are found in their modes of worship. The darkest-skinned individuals meet about the same restrictions in the United States as do the Negroes. Many are illiterate and evade the literacy test by crossing the border illegally at an unguarded point. Americanization usually takes place only in respect to material culture. Very few become American citizens. It is hard to determine the number in the United States since many return to Mexico for the winter and come to this country for the summer and autumn months. Official estimations place the number around 900,000.

The French-Canadians have come in great numbers to the textile and paper mills in the eastern part of the United States. While they have been in Canada since the early days of settlement, they are still French-Canadians so far as language, religion, laws, and customs are concerned. The most cherished units of their culture are language and religion. The French-Canadians have resisted assimilation in Canada and are almost as successful in this respect in the United States. They are not French, they are French-Canadians who have had few contacts with France and its recent development. The French-Canadians are Roman Catholics.

Here, as among the Poles and the Irish, loyalty to the Church is identified with loyalty to the nationality; and religion and nationality, especially the preservation of the language, are the dominant interests of the French-Canadians in the United States and the most persistent themes for discussion in the French-Canadian press.[18]

No group is more conscious of its struggle to maintain its identity than are the French-Canadians.

When the French-Canadian speaks of the problem of his people, he refers to the ever-present danger of losing himself in the English-speaking world. When the English person speaks of it, he refers to the tenacity with which the French-Canadian resists assimilation.[19]

This feeling becomes intensified in the United States because the migrants become employees of non-French firms, and find themselves under a government and in a school system that are not based on French traditions. Their loyalty to their French-Canadian heritage does not always preclude their loyalty to the adopted country. Over 900,000 French-Canadians are in the United States, more than half of them having been born in this country.

The French-Canadians have been drawn toward New England for a long time. The upper counties of New York, Vermont, New Hampshire, and Maine are full of farmers and woodsmen of French-Canadian extraction. The factories of Massachusetts use entire French-Canadian families. Like other immigrants they live in colonies, surrounded by their own institutions. But they are much closer to their native land than are other immigrants. In times of unemployment it is an easy matter for them to return to the land in Quebec. Visits from relatives and other contacts with the homeland keep quick their sense of solidarity. New Englanders, of both the Puritan and the Irish stocks, regard them as being singularly unassimilable immigrants.[20]

In discussing the composition of recent immigration, too much emphasis cannot be placed on the human nature that has developed in each group through many vicissitudes of experiences in a foreign clime. This human nature is an adjustment to the experiences that they have had, and is the mental organization that has to be utilized in any process of adjustment in the United States. Any accommodation that

---

[18] Robert E. Park, *The Immigrant Press and Its Control* (1922), p. 260. Reprinted by permission of The Carnegie Foundation of New York.
[19] From an unpublished manuscript by Everett C. Hughes, Professor of Sociology, McGill University, Montreal.
[20] *Ibid.*

is made will be in relation to these historical experiences, and the result in each instance will be human nature that is European- or Asiatic-American, and not just American.

The groups making up the new immigration have struggled for nationalism in nearly every case before they reached the United States. The chief aspects of a national feeling are usually language and religion. In coming into a strange culture, it is natural for them to become more conscious of their nationalities than they were in their native countries. Nationalistic ideas and organizations have flourished in America. Numbers tend to strengthen and emphasize the difference between their nationalities and the social nature and cultural order found in America. They become conscious of themselves as having a culture that must be conserved. While they do not try to force their culture on Americans they expect to maintain it for themselves. Unconsciously, however, they become Bohemian-American or Finnish-American and think that they are still Bohemian or Finnish. This is the situation unless they are coerced into accepting American culture; then they rebel, as they have for many generations.

We have seen that all groups under normal conditions tend to overestimate their own values. With a history of oppression as a background, and in a strange land where the immigrants see American culture at its worst in the slums of our cities, there is likely to be an increased interest in their own social values. Despite this fact American ideas and practices gradually filter in unnoticed until the members of the second generation refuse to accept the heritages of their parents. Where the immigrants have been exploited or mistreated, there is a distinct barrier to the adjustment process. In struggling to maintain their culture, they are unwittingly fighting against social disorganization.

READINGS

Alvarado, S. M., " Mexican Immigration to the United States,"
    National Conference of Social Work, 1920.   479–80
Baerlein, Henry, *The Birth of Yugoslavia.*   1923
Balch, Emily Greene, *Our Slavic Fellow Citizens.*   1910.   Chapters I–XIII, pp. 3–252

Beals, Carlton, " Mexican as He Is," *North American Review,* 214: 538-46

Belcourt, N. A., " French-Canadians Outside of Quebec," *Annals of Amer. Acad.,* 107: 13-24. May 1923

Bernheimer, C. S., *The Russian Jew in the United States.* 1905

Bloch, Louis, " Facts About Mexican Immigration Before and Since the Quota Restriction Laws," *Jour. of Amer. Statistical Assoc.* March 1929

Brunner, Edmund de S., *Immigrant Farmers and Their Children.* 1929

Burgess, Thomas, *The Greeks in America.* 1913

Butler, Ralph, *The New Eastern Europe.* 1919

Callcott, A., " The Mexican Peon in Texas," *Survey,* 44: 437-38. 1920

Capek, Thomas, *The Czechs in America.* 1919

" Caravan of Sorrow," *Living Age,* 332: 87-92. 1927

Chicanot, E. L., " French Canadian Exodus," *Canad. Forum,* 10: 9-10, Oct. 1929

Congressional Hearings, " Immigration from Countries of the Western Hemisphere," Before the Committee on Immigration and Naturalization, House of Representatives. On H. R. 6465, 10955, 11687, Feb. 21 to April 5, 1928. Government Printing Office. 1928

—— " Restriction of Western Hemisphere Immigration," Before the Committee on Immigration, U.S. Senate; on S. 1296, 1437, 3019; Feb. 1, 27-29, March 1, 5, 1928

Cotter, Arthur, *The Finns.* 1923

Dako, C. A., *Albania the Master Key of the Near East.* 1919

Davis, Jerome, *The Russian Immigrant.* 1922

—— *The Russians and Ruthenians in America.* 1922

Dexter, R. C., " Fifty-fifty Americans," *World's Work,* 48: 366-71, August 1924

Esquivel, S. I., " The Immigrant from Mexico," *Outlook,* 125: 131. 1920

Fairchild, Henry P., *Immigration.* Revised ed. 1926. Chapter VII, pp. 127-146

—— *Greek Immigration to the United States.* 1911

—— *Immigrant Backgrounds.* 1927

Fergussons, Erna, " New Mexico's Mexicans," *Century,* CXVI: 437-44. 1928

Galarza, Ernest, " Life in the United States for Mexican People; Out of the Experience of a Mexican," *National Conf. of Social Work,* 1929. 399-404

Garth, Thomas R., " The Intelligence of Mexican School Children," *School and Society,* 27:791-94. 1928

—— " The Industrial Psychology of the Immigrant Mexican," *Industrial Psychology.* 1926. 183-87

Handman, Max S., " The Mexican Immigrant in Texas," *Southwestern Polit. and Social Science Quarterly*, 7: 33–41. 1926

Harby, L. C., " Mexican Texan Types and Contrasts," *Harper's*, 81: 229–246. 1890

Hendrick, Burton J., " The Jews in America," *World's Work*, 45: 144–161

Johnson, Alvin S, " Mexico in San Antonio," *New Republic*, 7: 190–191. 1916

Joseph, Samuel, *Jewish Immigration to the United States from 1881 to 1910.* 1914

" Jugo-Slavs in the United States," *Literary Digest*, June 7, 1919

King, E. S., " My Mexican Neighbors," *Survey*, 37: 624–6. 1917

Kirkpatrick, Clifford, *Intelligence and Immigration.* 1926

McClure, Archibald, *Leadership of New America.* 1916

McLean, Robert N., " Mexican Workers in the United States," *National Conf. of Social Work*, 1929. 531–8

Marston, H. D., " Mexican Traits," *Survey*, 44: 562–64. 1920

" Mexican Invaders of El Paso," *Survey*, 36: 380–82. 1916

Miller, Herbert A., *Races, Nations and Classes.* 1924. Chapters VII, VIII

Miller, Kenneth D., *The Czecho-Slovaks in America.* 1922

" Our Albanian Population," *Literary Digest*, October 18, 1919

Park, Robert E. and Miller, H. A., *Old World Traits Transplanted.* 1921

Pehotsky, Bessie O., *The Slavic Immigrant Woman.* 1925

Peters, Madison C., *The Jews in America.* 1905

Philipson, David, *The Jews in America.* 1909

Radisavljevich, P. R., *Who Are the Slavs?* 1919

Reade, A., *Finland and the Finns.* 1917

Redfield, Robert, *A Plan for a Study of Tepoztlan, Mexico.* 1928

Reuter, E. B., *Population Problems.* 1923. Chapters VII–XXI

Roberts, Peter, " Bulgarians in America," *Survey*, Nov. 23, 1913

Rose, Philip M., *The Italians in America.* 1922

" Roumanians in the United States," *Literary Digest*, August 10, 1918

Ruhl, Arthur, *The New Masters of the Baltic.* 1921

Santiago, Hazel D., " Mexican Influence in Southern California," *Sociology and Social Research*, XVI: Sept.-Oct. 1931

Schevill, Ferdinand, *History of the Balkan Peninsula.* 1922

Souders, D. A., *The Magyars in America.* 1922

Survey, June 11, 1921. Czechoslovakian number

The Mexican Mind: A Study of National Psychology. 1922

Thomas, W. I. and Znaniecki, F., *The Polish Peasant in Europe and America.* 1918

Thompson, Charles A., " Mexicans — An Interpretation," *National Conf. of Social Work*, 1928: 499–503

Thompson, Wallace, *The People of Mexico, Who They Are and How They Live.* 1921

" Ukrainians in America," *Literary Digest,* Nov. 15, 1919

Vasconcelos, José and Gamio, Manuel, *Aspects of Mexican Civilization.* 1926

Vlach, J. J., *Our Bohemian Population*

Warne, F. J., *The Slav Invasion and the Mine Workers.* 1904

Wirth, Louis, *The Ghetto.* 1928

Xenides, J. P., *The Greeks in America.* 1922

CHAPTER IX
CAUSES OF NEW IMMIGRATION

FOR EACH PERIOD of immigration it has been advisable to distinguish between the conditions in the country of the source of emigration and the conditions in the United States. The factors that prevent an adequate adjustment in the native habitat are the real causes while the propitious-appearing situation in America merely offers a solution that is a way out of the unsatisfactory situation. It is true that the industrial opportunities in the United States tended by contrast to accentuate the undesirable economic conditions in the peasant areas of eastern and southern Europe, nevertheless the real reasons for migrating were the meager opportunities for economic security in the native lands of the emigrants. Furthermore, the propaganda of steamship companies through agents and the activities of other immigrants are not causes. These factors are only a technique which contrasts the European conditions with those in the United States and thus suggests a way out for the peasant who has suffered so long under an oppressive political and economic situation. The industrial opportunities in the United States provided the occasion for emigration, but they were not the causes.

Although the early immigrant migrated for political, religious, and social, as well as economic reasons, the recent immigrant has come chiefly from an economic cause; but in each case the economic condition is closely related to a political situation of long standing. In some instances the economic cause is directly or indirectly related to religious or social experiences.

Despite this relationship between economic and social factors, the recent immigrants were not consciously coming to the United States for cultural and educational advantages or religious opportunities, but to increase their economic status. This fact is important when it comes to the matter of adjustments. If an immigrant comes primarily for economic reasons, he often expects to return as soon as he has accumulated enough wealth to make a satisfactory adjustment in his own country. Consequently he is not interested in the political and cultural processes in the United States. This means that his adjustments in America will be largely in terms of the economic process.

The economic situation in Finland is closely related to the political domination of Sweden and Russia. The Esthonian economic life was for many years virtually a serfdom under the Germans, Danes, and Russians. The Letts suffered under Russian political domination and the landlordism imposed by Germany. The Lithuanians were retarded through their union with Poland and the relation of subordination to Germany and Russia.

In Poland the cause of emigration was not just the existing conditions but a changed attitude involving new economic desires. There was a time when the economic wishes of the Polish peasant included only the idea of living. Even an agricultural servant had a " living instead of a regular wage." But there has been a change in this respect. Economic advancement rather than living has become the object of work. The new desire to accumulate wealth is really an interest in the ownership of a great amount of land, since social status is determined in this way.

For centuries the peasant did not own the land he farmed, so that the ownership of land became the " main condition of the social standing of the family. Without land, the family can still keep its internal solidarity, but it cannot act as a unit with regard to the rest of the community; it ceases to count as a social power. Its members become socially and economically dependent upon strangers, and often scatter about the country or abroad; the family ceases to play any part in the affairs of the commune; its young generation can hardly be taken into account in matters of marriage; it cannot give large ceremonial receptions, etc. The greater the amount of land, the greater the possibility of social expression." [1]

The land-hunger became so great that peasant families went in great numbers to South as well as to North America.

There was a real fever of emigration. Whole villages moved at once, and this emigration, in 1911–12, was centered in the most isolated and backward part of the country, in the eastern parts of the provinces of Siedlce and Lublin, and precisely where the tendency to advance had still the elementary form of land-hunger.

A phenomenon essentially different from this emigration of colonists with their families in search of land is the emigration of single individuals in search of work. . . Of course there are many in the community — and their number increases every year — who cannot hope to advance if they stay in the country. Most of them, indeed, can live as hired laborers, servants, or proprietors of small pieces of land, and earning some money in addition by outside work. Their living is on the average even better than that of their fathers and grandfathers under similar conditions, but they are no longer satisfied with such an existence; they want a better future, " if not for ourselves, at least for our children," as they express it. This is the essential change of attitude which accounts for the simultaneous appearance and enormous development both of emigration and of land-hunger. Moreover, emigration to cities, from this standpoint, belongs to the same category as emigration abroad. When a peasant emigrates, it is usually with the desire to earn ready money and return home and buy land. He goes where he can find a ready market for work involving no technical or intellectual preparation, and he is at first satisfied with the wages he can secure for his unskilled labor. [2]

This desire for economic advancement as it is related to the desire for national unity is the chief reason for emigration to America on the part of the Polish peasant.

The Ukrainian and the Russian peasants have come to the United States for economic and political reasons, very similar to those found in Poland. The Ukrainians suffered under Polish landowners and political domination from Russia. In Russia the peasants are as much attached to the land as those

[1] W. I. Thomas and F. Znaniecki, *The Polish Peasant in Europe and America* (N. Y. 1918) by permission of and special arrangement with Alfred A. Knopf, Inc., authorized publishers. I, 162.

[2] *Ibid.*, I, 191–192. By permission.

in Poland and they have emigrated to make money so that they may return and increase their social and economic status through the purchase of land.

The Russian peasant left Europe when his country was in a transition from domestic economy to modern economic life, but the system of agriculture was still primitive, of the medieval type. Although the Emancipation Act of Alexander II terminated the serfdom of the peasant, still he did not receive enough land in many instances for his needs and to meet the heavy taxation demanded by the government. When eastern Europe, including Russia, entered the slow process of economic transition, the Russian peasant was still a serf in his attitudes.

In Czecho-Slovakia the Bohemians and Slovaks have been under the domination of Germans and Magyars. The Slovaks have utilized very primitive methods of agriculture and, with the struggle for national freedom, have developed an interest in economic advancement which has led to emigration. The Bohemians or Czechs have left their native land for economic and political reasons. Rather the cause has been economic, greatly complicated by political and religious conditions under German control. The Slovaks with antiquated methods of agriculture have left their native land to better their economic status.

The conditions in Austria-Hungary leading to a desire for emigration were quite largely economic, political, and social. The great race diversity resulting in political inequality made conditions deplorable because it was responsible in no small way for the great economic inequality. Not only was there racial diversification, but there was also social variation expressing itself in nobility and peasantry. It was the latter class that migrated to get away from situations to which it could not make satisfactory adjustments. The system of landlordism and antiquated methods of agriculture with high taxes, meant for the peasant and the farm servant a great deal of poverty and inequality, and its accompanying factor — illiteracy.

In addition to the undesirable factors already mentioned, there was a hard term of military service for the protection of the more favored groups. With little or no tradition for migration, peasants even in isolated regions found conditions so deplorable that they were ready to cut loose from age-long moorings and leave behind those of the primary group so important to the peasant.

The Roumanian peasants have come to the United States for economic and political reasons. Many of them were living in Hungary and have migrated for the same reasons given under the discussion of Austria-Hungary. Throughout eastern Europe land is the thing most desired by the peasants and, with the emancipation of the Roumanian peasant, this desire was greatly increased. This fact was demonstrated by the revolt in 1907 when there was an unsatisfactory distribution of land.

The Bulgarians have turned to America for economic reasons and to escape military service which to them has been very oppressive. A large proportion of the Bulgarians own their own land but the farms are too small, with poor agricultural methods, to make them an adequate economic unit for a family. With high taxes to contend with, the Bulgarians have been forced to emigrate because of their poor economic adjustment.

The Jugo-Slavs, including the Serbs, Croatians, and Slovenes, are a rural people who have been under the subjection of Austria-Hungary. They have come to the United States for economic reasons chiefly, from regions where there has been Austrian domination. To them this domination has been the explanation of their retarded economic status.

Albania has not sent a large number of immigrants to the United States. Many of them have come from Jugo-Slavia. The mountainous nature of Albania, leading to isolation, has not resulted in agricultural progress, making the economic conditions the real cause of migrations.

In all of the Slavic countries there has been a desire to get away from conditions of oppression described in the preceding chapter. In each case the repressive measures have been closely related to the economic situation. While the economic factors were the immediate reasons for emigration, these factors go back into the more fundamental political oppressions and nationalistic ambitions.

Greece is primarily a rural country, with very primitive methods of agriculture. There has been for some time over-population in Greece, with this situation being relieved by emigration. Europe no longer offers a solution for the economic condition of the Greeks, so they come to America.

In Italy the causes are largely economic and political, both conditions being closely related. The economic factor is outstanding as evidenced by the fact that many who come from Italy expect to return. Immigrants who run away from political and religious situations, usually go to stay, since a brief absence from their native habitat would not alter these factors, but often a brief period away from an inadequate economic status may mean earnings great enough to return and live in complete adjustment in their own culture, obviating the necessity of a complete adjustment in a strange situation.

When we consider the matter of production along with a population increase we can see that the economic cause is a great one in Italy.

After 1871, while the population was increasing by a quarter, the production of olive oil remained stationary; that of wine, rising at first, became stationary after about 1885. After 1884, the production of wheat, which occupies the greatest acreage in Italian agriculture, rose about 20 per cent, partly under the stimulus since 1888 of a high protective tariff. But the excess of importations of wheat over exportations rose until in recent years it has amounted to a quarter of the home production. Indian corn, of which a quantity one-half as great as that of wheat is annually produced, has been unvaried in amount since 1884, but an importation a fifth as great as the home production has meanwhile grown up. After 1870, a large increase took place in the production of oranges and lemons, but the prices declined by 65–70 per cent. Similar great declines have ruled, since before 1880, in the prices of many other important agricultural products, while the production has in general either remained stationary or declined, and the imports have risen.[3]

[3] Robert F. Foerster, *The Italian Emigration of Our Times* (Cambridge: Harvard University Press 1919), p. 50.

In discussing southern Italy, Foerster points out that the rainfall is very slight, making the range of products exceedingly small. The air and soil are both dry, partly through deforestation. The aftermath of deforestation was landslides; streams left their courses; there were costly repairs after rains; soil would not retain its moisture; malaria was a scourge through the presence of stagnant water, and there were frequent earthquakes to destroy crops and property as well as the morale of the people.[4]

With the abolition of feudalism in the early part of the nineteenth century and the secularization of church lands during the middle of the same century, the land was to go to the communes for division among the people. However, much of the land came into the hands of a few wealthy proprietors. The peasants lost a large part of what they received because they were unable to pay the taxes. Consequently agriculture in southern Italy is under a system of absenteeism with a middleman who sublets to those who actually till the soil. Modern methods of agriculture have not been adopted and, with a brief tenure, most farming efforts produce less than is needed for the necessities of life.

Land tax has been heavy and unequal. This falls as a burden on the small landowner and the tenant pays a tax upon his agricultural income. Taxes on commodities are high; on salt the tax is almost as much as the price of the commodity. There are duties on transactions that curtail business. There is a tax on dairy and draft animals. National debts, the army and navy all claim much of the tax receipts.

The conditions of the hired laborer are even worse.

Half of the cultivators of Basilicata, two-thirds of those of Calabria and Sicily, are hired laborers. They are a passive element in the agricultural economy, determining little, the victims of much; socially despised, a residuum of the population. Whether engaged by the year or the day they are the most miserable group of all; and they are particularly wretched when engaged by the day, which is the usual course with three out of four of them. It is by the proprietors and the tenants of the medium-sized and large estates that they are chiefly employed.

[4] *Ibid.*, pp. 51–63.

At the time of the *Inchiesta Agraria* their wages, still paid largely in kind, ran from 250 to 400 lire in the year, say one or one and a half per working day, with an extra lira daily in the harvest period, and as little as half a lira per day in the slack season. . . According to a recent study, a usual wage in upper Basilicata is 1.50 lire and food or — following a spreading practice — 2.20 lire without food; but January and February are almost without work, and employment during the rest of the year is inconstant. In interior Sicily, 1.80 lire per day may be earned for 150–200 lire per year is not supplemented by rations; on the coast the situation is better.[5]

More favorable conditions exist in the north but all the undesirable features of the south prevail in a lesser degree. There have been larger wages and more employment resulting in a higher standard of living.

A better clergy, a religion less suffused with superstition than in the South, have allowed the growth of a more liberal spirit. And the school system is better — though gravely defective still, and constituting one of the most vexatious problems of the entire region.[6]

The Jews have been reaching America for a great many years and in most cases they have come for the same reasons. However, we are interested primarily in the recent influx from eastern Europe. The Spanish Jews coming in the seventeenth century were often refugees whose old homes in western Europe had been expropriated. The greatest number of German Jews came around 1848 after the political revolution in Europe.

Recent Jewish immigration has arrived in greatest numbers from Russia, Roumania, Austria-Hungary, and Poland, so we need only consider the causes in relation to these states. It is in these countries that the greatest concentration of Jews in Europe is to be found and in each the Jews have played an important rôle in the economic life.

In attempting to understand the foreign situation of the Jews, we must not lose sight of the fact that eastern Europe has been passing through a social and economic transition, and that the Jews were used as scapegoats to explain much of the disorganization and demoralization that accompanied

[5] *Ibid.*, p. 85. [6] *Ibid.*, p. 121.

the change that was taking place. The Jews became the victims of this social-economic transition not alone because of the traditional attitude concerning Jews throughout Europe, but because they occupied a position in eastern Europe that set them apart as different. They therefore became a center of attack in a crisis situation when some object was needed around which the emotional attitudes of the time could be organized.

Originally, the Jews were not Slavs and they were identified with a different religion quite foreign to that of the rest of Europe. They constituted the most important element in the commercial and industrial activities, where they virtually had a monopoly. The Jews were essentially an urban population in countries where the chief nationality groups were almost entirely rural. This tended to give them a higher cultural and educational status than other groups and made them the largest part of the middle class.

Being separated from the masses by a lack of nationality, different religion, and occupations, they were soon controlled by a special set of laws, and confined to a definite area known as the Pale. In Russia and Poland the laws relating to Jews multiplied until they included " more than a thousand articles, regulating their religious and communal life, economic activities and occupations, military service, property rights, education, *etc.,* and imposing special taxes over and above those borne by all other Russian subjects. The direct consequence of these laws was to mark the status of the Jews as the lowest in the Empire, placing them in the position of aliens as to rights and citizens as to obligations." [7]

The Jews were confined to the Pale and with the laws of 1882 they were restricted to certain areas within the Pale. They were forced to leave the villages and settle in towns, severing their contact with the peasantry. Through these laws an effort was made to 'end the ownership of land by Jews in rural districts or anywhere outside the Pale. Further laws were designed to bar them from educational and professional institutions. There was no interest in as-

[7] Samuel Joseph, "Jewish Immigration to the United States," *Columbia University Studies in History, Economics, and Public Law,* LIX, 57 (1914).

similating the Jew. His Russification was a thing to be avoided.

When laws failed to separate the Jews from the Russian people, pogroms characterized by " murder, outrage, and pillage " were resorted to.

Beginning as a movement to suppress the Jews in their economic and cultural activities, and to separate them as far as possible from their Russian neighbors, the anti-Jewish program became in its final form the expulsion and extermination of the Jews from Russia.[8]

The situation in Roumania was similar. In certain sections all non-Christians were denied civil and political rights. The Jews were regarded as aliens and, therefore, could have their activities circumscribed by specific laws.

The Jews were forbidden to buy the products of the soil, to acquire real property; non-resident Jews were debarred unless they could prove an occupation and show the possession of property. Definite restrictions as to occupation, residence in the villages, the ownership, in villages, of houses, land, vineyards, *etc.*, existed. As vagabonds they could be expelled from the country by administrative decree. Thus was their legal status fixed.[9]

Although the Jews could not become citizens, they had to pay taxes and were held for military services. They were often excluded from educational opportunities and certain professions.

Until the middle of the nineteenth century, the legal position of the Jews in Austria-Hungary differed from that of their brethren in Russia and Roumania only in degree. Prohibited the free exercise of their religion, the right to hold real property, and to enter certain occupations, and burdened by special Jewish taxes, the Jews remained a class apart and governed in all their activities by special laws. Their legal emancipation, begun in 1848, was definitely established by the promulgation in each division of the Empire of the Fundamental Law of 1867, declaring that religion should not be a ground for discrimination in civil and political rights.[10]

The legal status of the Jews was theoretically secure, but there was a great deal of antagonism for Jews through Austria-Hungary and especially in Galicia. But the situation

[8] *Ibid.*, p. 68.   [9] *Ibid.*, p. 69.   [10] *Ibid.*, p. 77.

was not one of expulsion and extermination as it was in Russia and Roumania.

These, then, were the reasons that so many Jews left eastern Europe for the United States and other countries. The volume of Jewish immigration increased with each new crisis situation in Europe, which shows how closely the movement was related to the economic and social persecutions of the Jews. The situation in Russia will illustrate this condition. There was an increase in the stream of Jewish immigrants in 1882 following the pogroms of 1880 and 1882. When the educational restrictions were instituted in 1887 there was another large movement to the United States. The expulsion of the Jews from Moscow in the early nineties was another occasion for a new and increased influx.

Another rise began in 1899. Economic depression, revolutionary terrorism, and anti-Jewish propaganda paved the way for a great inpouring of Russian Jews to the United States. The Kishineff massacre of 1903 sent thousands of Jews in veritable flight to the United States, a fact which is reflected in an immigration of 77,544 Russian Jews in 1904, the greatest number up to this year. With the beginning of the Russo-Japanese War, the outbreak of the revolution, and, above all, of the Jewish massacres, the immigration rose in 1905 to 92,388. In 1906 a year of *pogroms,* it reached the number of 125,234, the highest in the entire period — and in 1907, 114,932, the second largest immigration.[11]

The direct causes of immigration from eastern Europe, then, were the economic and social transitions which, like all changes, were signalized by a great deal of disorganization. There was a further general cause, the oppression suffered by those struggling for nationalism.

The Portuguese in America are peasants who migrated for economic reasons. In their native land they were mostly small tenant farmers or were employed on large estates under a system of landlordism. Wages or earnings from small farms meant living on a mere subsistence level. Exploitation by absentee owners, heavy taxation, and high custom duties have prevented any improvement in conditions.

In the small Asiatic countries from which immigrants have

[11] *Ibid.*, pp. 100–101.

come, the causes of migration have not been entirely different from those in Europe. The Armenian immigrants have left their Christian kingdom situated in a Moslem world to escape the despotism of Turkey and thus preserve their religious heritage. Many of them are refugees. This main cause of emigration does not entirely overshadow the fact that low wages and other economic conditions have led to the migration of a great many in recent times. The Syrians have emigrated to escape religious persecutions and to better their economic status. Religious intolerance and persecutions have caused the migration of the Christian Persians to the United States.

With the two North American groups the causes of migration are largely economic; especially is this true with the French-Canadians. While there is a conflict of cultures in Canada, there is no opposition to the language, religion, and other cultural elements maintained and cherished by the French-Canadians, so they are not an oppressed group. They have come to the United States because their home situation did not offer economic opportunities found in the United States.

The causes of emigration from Mexico are slightly more complex, yet the economic factor is the most significant. Mexicans come to this country because they have to endure deplorable working situations and low wages at home. In some regions conditions for farming are difficult. Land is owned by big proprietors. Many have shown their distaste for this situation by emigration; others have interested themselves in revolutionary movements. For some, revolutionary activities have been an added cause for migration. Although only a few have left Mexico because of political disturbances, many have remained in the United States to escape the conflict; especially is this true when the rebellion has been colored by religious implications.

To be meticulous in the discussion of the causes of emigration we should have to examine the conditions in various regions of each country, since isolation, both geographical and cultural, results in certain differences. There are, however, causes that are general for a country or even for a whole section of Europe, that can be considered in a study of this sort.

READINGS

Balch, Emily G., *Our Slavic Fellow Citizens.* 1910

Butler, Ralph, *The New Eastern Europe.* 1919

Fairchild, H. P., *Greek Immigration to the United States.* 1911

—— *Immigration.* Revised ed. 1926. Chapter VIII, pp. 147–165

Foerster, Robert F., *The Italian Emigration of Our Times.* 1919. Chapters III–VII, pp. 47–126

Gruening, Ernest, *Mexico and its Heritage.* 1928

Joseph, Samuel, " Jewish Immigration to the United States." 1914. *Columbia University Studies,* LIX

Miller, Herbert A., *Races, Nations and Classes.* 1924. Chapters IV–IX, pp. 32–104

—— " The Rising National Individualism," *Publications of the American Sociological Society,* VIII. 1913

Ross, Edward A., *The Social Revolution in Mexico,* 1923

Thomas, W. I. and Znaniecki, F., *The Polish Peasant in Europe and America.* 1918. Volumes I, II, III

" Unhappy Mexico — Our Duty," *Outlook,* 133: 527–30. 1916

CHAPTER X

THE JOURNEY — NEW IMMIGRATION

THAT THE journey is a definite attitudinal experience for the immigrant has already been pointed out in previous chapters. Immigrants coming from the central and eastern part of Europe have a long hard trip before they reach even the port of embarkation. This part of the journey as well as the period at the port includes examinations and experiences often very important to the migrant in developing certain attitudes concerning life outside his native abode.

All European countries have laws which place restrictions upon the emigration of certain classes so that examinations and investigations are necessary. Add to this the fact that the United States restricts a great number and it will be seen that a rigid examination before the emigrant leaves his own country is essential. Most of the legislation connected with the migration has been designed for the protection of the emigrant through proper information before he leaves his native land. Some governments maintain national information offices; others have bureaus, institutions, and associations privately directed. Helpful data are disseminated through publications so that prospective emigrants may know something of the conditions of foreign countries. They are supervised in their contacts at the port of embarkation and in their relationships with all agencies.

In many cases there is a long journey before the emigrant reaches the port of embarkation; this is a contributing factor to the condition in which the migrant reaches the United States. The following is descriptive of the experiences of many from central and eastern Europe:

Emigrants travelling by rail are subject to conditions which are no better than those which prevail at sea.

Everyone has seen troops of continental emigrants travelling in old carriages, in which young and old, men, women, and children are crowded together, with their luggage, clothing, and tools of all kinds.

They travel slowly, from station to station, and from country to country, in filth and misery; frozen in winter, and suffocated in summer, without proper nourishment, medical attendance, or guidance.

After a long journey, they arrive at the port of embarkation, or at their destination, in a deplorable condition. They then have to submit to long and wearisome formalities before they can sail, and they must undergo the fatigue of the sea voyage before they can reach their employment.

Such was the situation before the war. Since then it has become still worse. The trains are slower, and the carriages more dilapidated than ever. Food is even more difficult to obtain, and the customs formalities take still longer.[1]

In Italy, the General Emigration Office is the central authority dealing with everything concerning emigration affairs. The Office, placed under the Ministry for Foreign Affairs, is composed of a Commissioner-General and three Commissioners. A central office is maintained, and, apart from that, officials are placed in different parts of the kingdom and in foreign countries. The Office, under the direction and political responsibility of the Ministry of Foreign Affairs, organises the emigration services of the kingdom for the grant of licenses to transport agents, fixing the price of journey tickets, maintaining organisation in the ports of embarkation, the grant of permits to recruit workers for European countries, etc.; ensures the protection of emigrants on board ship; prepares international agreements on emigration and labour; is responsible for giving aid and protection to emigrants in foreign countries; and supervises aid institutions, both public and private.

Apart from the General Emigration Office and the auxiliary services dependent upon it, there are other offices and societies, both public and private, which give emigrants the information and assistance of which they stand in need. . . Some of these institutions organise special instruction and evening classes in order to prepare the emigrants for the new conditions under which they will be placed. The curriculum of these classes varies according to the place to which emigrants are going, the trade or profession in which they will be engaged, the economic and social conditions of the different countries of

[1] Extract from *Report of the International Emigration Commission* (International Labour Office, Geneva, Switzerland, August 21, 1921), p. 123.

immigration, and the intellectual standard of the intending emigrants.

Before starting, emigrants have to undergo a medical examination and are vaccinated, and their luggage is disinfected. At Naples, the principal port of emigration in Italy, there is a hostel where emigrants receive medical attention and where they are vaccinated, where they undergo a period of isolation (if necessary), are submitted to a bacteriological examination, and other medical precautions that may be found necessary are taken. Arrangements are being made for similar hostels in other Italian ports, always under the control of the Emigration Office.[2]

In some places there are hotels at the port of embarkation where migrants are housed and examined. In other places a final examination is held on the steamship before it sails so that the unfit are turned back before they have started the ocean voyage. More care was necessary after 1897 when trachoma was classified by the United States Public Health Department as a dangerous, contagious disease found to be very prevalent with some nationalities. Further precautions were taken by steamship companies when the Immigration Act of 1903 provided for a fine of one hundred dollars for a steamship company conveying a person afflicted with a contagious disease that could have been discovered before the emigrant embarked for America.

The United States Quarantine Law makes it possible for consular officers to participate in most cases in the examinations at the port of embarkation. Not only do they examine the emigrants but they inspect the ships, their crews, and their cargoes. At the important Italian ports the medical examination of steerage passengers is virtually in the hands of the United States Public Health officials. In Belgium the United States officials have little or nothing to do with examinations. Between these two extremes the American consular officials have certain functions at the various ports.

The ocean voyage is the next experience for the migrant on his way to the United States. When compared with earlier periods there has been much improvement in transport conditions, especially before the World War. During

[2] Extract from International Labour Office, *Emigration and Immigration: Legislation and Treaties* (Geneva 1922), pp. 54–55.

the War, however, many ships were allowed to get into an unsanitary condition. Legislation has been designed to care for this matter through rigid inspections.

The vessels have to be re-inspected before each voyage, in order to discover whether they fulfil the special conditions necessary for that particular voyage. The following points in particular are investigated: (1) food to be supplied to the emigrants and the stocks on board; (2) accommodation, air space, separation of men's and women's quarters, arrangement of bunks; (3) the hygienic arrangements, organisation of medical, sanitary, and pharmaceutical services, organisation of sick bays, etc.; (4) security of vessels and passengers, life-saving apparatus, life-boats, cargo; (5) the supervision and protection of emigrants, especially women and children, against abuses and dangers to which they are exposed.[3]

It is rather difficult to control the shipping situation since there is a great variation between laws of various countries, even on the matter of space. When immigrants on one boat may have come from several countries, it is difficult to follow definite regulations. Uniform legislation would make possible very much better sanitary conditions in every case.

In the investigation made by the United States Immigration Commission in 1911, the woman selected to travel in steerage of the old type found conditions very bad. In a summary statement of her report she said:

During these twelve days in the steerage I lived in a disorder and in surroundings that offended every sense. Only the fresh breeze from the sea overcame the sickening odors. The vile language of the men, the screams of the women defending themselves, the crying of children, wretched because of their surroundings, and practically every sound that reached the ear irritated beyond endurance. There was no sight before which the eye did not prefer to close. Everything was dirty, sticky, and disagreeable to the touch. Every impression was offensive. Worse than this was the general air of immorality. For fifteen hours each day I witnessed all around me this improper, indecent, and forced mingling of men and women who were total strangers and often did not understand one word of the same language.[4]

[3] Extract from *Report of the International Emigration Commission* (International Labour Office, Geneva, August 21, 1921), p. 120.
[4] Extract from "Steerage Conditions," *Reports of U. S. Immigration Commission*, XXXVII, p. 23 (1911).

Another inspection by a woman disguised as an immigrant showed much the same steerage conditions, but the third class passage was not so bad.

> The third class on the —— proved to be an idealized steerage. The passengers were treated with care and consideration. There was every attempt to give satisfaction. Where cabins were for any reason unsatisfactory, a new arrangement was attempted and made wherever possible. All actual human needs were supplied, with cleanliness, order, and decency. The third class was confined to the stern of the vessel.[5]

A quite different story is told about the steerage conditions.

> The steerage passenger certainly gets but very little besides his passage. Practically no consideration is had for him as regards either space, food, service, or conveniences. One of ten rules on the walls announces that the passengers are responsible for the order and cleanliness of the steerage. The difference in cost between passage in the third class and the steerage is about $7.50; the difference between accommodations is everything, and the third class does no more than provide decently for the simplest human physical needs. The white napkins are the only nonessential that might be omitted. Every other provision is essential to decency, propriety, health, and the preservation of self-respect. To travel in anything worse than what is offered in the third class is to arrive at the journey's end with a mind unfit for healthy, wholesome impressions and with a body weakened and unfit for the hardships that are involved in the beginning of life in a new land.[6]

Then comes the experience of the emigrants at Ellis Island where the United States government exercises its first official control. The examinations at the ports of embarkation are merely a matter of courtesy on the part of foreign states. Varying reports are to be had of conditions on the Island. The number received each year has been too great to permit a proper handling of all cases. While Ellis Island is not the only immigrant station, it is the largest and best equipped and receives a large percentage of those coming as immigrants to the United States.

About January 1, 1892, this station was used for the first time for immigration purposes. The main buildings, of frame construction, were destroyed by fire on June 15, 1897, after which

[5] *Ibid.*, p. 35.   [6] *Ibid.*, pp. 38–39.

work was resumed at the Barge Office and continued there until the semifireproof new buildings were ready for occupancy in December, 1899. Since then, until inspection was inaugurated in European countries, practically all arriving aliens other than first and second class have been brought here for examination.

The original island covered an area of 3.3 acres. It has been added to from time to time and at present has an area of approximately 21 acres.

Not inappropriately, some of the fill originally used to enlarge the island came from foreign countries as ballast in ships built before water ballast tanks were adopted. The Government during the World War permitted dumping at designated places about the island.

There are now 27 buildings, including hospitals and power houses. The quarters occupied by detained aliens consist of large, light, well-ventilated rooms with floors and dados of Dutch or white glazed tile. A covered porch is available for recreation in stormy weather, while in pleasant weather a playground supplied with equipment for games and entertainment for both children and adults, is provided. Dormitories are also of white tile, and each person is allotted a white enameled single bed with woven-wire spring, good quality mattress, pillow, blankets, and clean linen. Bathrooms have built-in porcelain tubs as well as showers. Two well-equipped laundries are in operation daily.

The hospital, operated by the United States Public Health Service, is equipped with modern apparatus required for the approved methods of treatment. It is rated by the American Medical Association as a class A hospital. . .

As may be readily inferred from what has been previously said, Ellis Island, due to diminished immigration, presents something of an economic problem. The buildings are larger than needful to accommodate present-day immigration. The overhead generally in the maintenance of this tremendous plant is a heavy item of expenditure. However, so many practical difficulties would be encountered in any attempted change of base, such action would be of questionable expediency and wisdom. Ellis Island as it is to-day is the best equipped and operated immigration station in the world.[7]

When a shipload of immigrants reaches the port, it is visited at once by quarantine officials. The cabin passengers who pass the initial inspection are landed at once; the steerage passengers go to Ellis Island and are under the supervision of the officers of the Immigration Bureau. One part

[7] Extract from *Annual Report of the Commissioner General of Immigration* 1928, pp. 27–28.

of this immigrant station contains hospital facilities. Another section includes accommodations for sleeping and eating. Here also are the rooms for inspection, ticket offices, and the quarters for officials.

Ellis Island has had at times a large staff of more than six hundred persons for the giving of examinations designed to comply with immigration legislation. The regular procedure includes a medical examination by United States Public Health doctors and officials from the Marine Hospital. Then non-physical tests through questions are given to comply with other postulates in the statutes for the control of immigration. If the applicant passes these two examinations he is allowed to enter the United States.

If he has failed in these examinations, he still has the privilege of appearing before a special board of inquiry. A member of the board who does not agree with the findings may make an appeal for the alien in some instances or the alien may do it for himself. The appeals go to the Secretary of Commerce and Labor who has the power to give a final decision.

There have been many complaints registered against the situation at Ellis Island and no doubt there have been reasons for accusations concerning unfair treatment. However, the examination at this port of entrance is not a simple process. During rush periods thousands are cared for in a day, most of whom cannot understand nor speak English, which makes them appear very stupid. What is routine and seems simple to the officials is unintelligible and seems complex to the immigrant. If there is any place where an official needs to understand human nature, it is at the various ports of debarkation, since human nature manifests itself daily in terms of all the diverse cultures and individual differences of the many immigrants. Officials at the various ports of debarkation have their likes and dislikes and their racial prejudices just as others have. Their social heritage, in many instances, would lead them to believe that they are dealing with an inferior species. From this belief have come many cases of unfair treatment.

At Ellis Island hardships are endured every day. Families

are separated.   There are cases of detention and deportation, some for trivial reasons but most of them in accordance with legislation.   Many are sent home under the contract labor law which has never functioned properly because of its terminology.   During detention, segregation is not on the basis of tastes; every migrant is treated as an immigrant, which to many means that they are all alike.

The Immigration Commissioner is doing his best with the available equipment, according to those who are in a position to know.   Even though this is true it does not obviate the fact that the immigrant has his first contact with the government of the United States through the officials at the port of debarkation.   One's reception in any social situation is important for further adjustments in that situation. Unfortunate experiences at the port of entrance have led to attitudes of suspicion and distrust.   The significance of this is seen when we realize that attitudes are the most important factors in the process of accommodation in the United States.

In 1922 the Advisory Committee of the United States Bureau of Immigration made the following recommendations which show certain respects in which conditions needed to be improved at Ellis Island:

An official director of information should be appointed to take entire charge of the welfare work at Ellis Island, such official to be under the immediate direction of the commissioner of immigration of New York.

That interpreters speaking several languages and trained in social work be appointed to serve immigrants pending their inspection and during such time as they are not permitted direct communication with their friends.

That a plan be developed for the systematic exchange of allowed information between immigrants who are detained and their waiting friends.

That women and young children be provided with separate and considerably improved night quarters and that a trained dietitian be placed in charge of the feeding of the children.

That detained immigrants be provided with better laundry facilities.

That the representatives of private welfare organizations who are authorized to carry on work at the station be allowed, under the direction and supervision of the Federal director of information, to aid in general welfare service for immigrants after they have been duly examined.

That three separate religious services, Protestant, Jewish, and Catholic, be held on Sundays " with occasional services for other groups when needed."

That when aliens are excluded and deported an explanation of the reason for such action should be given to them and also, when practicable, to their interested relatives and friends.

That there shall be some welfare workers on duty at all hours.

That official interpreters meet arriving immigrants when embarking on the barges taking such aliens from the vessel to Ellis Island and that an information service be made available to them while they are detained at the Island. Heretofore immigrants have been without service of this kind until their examination was completed, and frequently they have been held apart from the public for several weeks pending their examination by a special board of inquiry.

That pending medical examination immigrants be taken to large and comfortable reception rooms in the main immigration building instead of being held on the barges.

That milk and crackers be served to all women and children at meals in the dining room and between meals and at bedtime in the detention quarters. Previously, only the small children had been provided with such food.

That the large room on the ground floor of the main building which is being used as a money exchange and railway ticket office be converted into a day room for detained women with children, such room to be provided with conveniences for the care of the children and to have easy access to an outdoor recreation place fitted up as a playground. That other commodious outside rooms near large porches with a view of the bay be made available as day rooms for other detained immigrants. That a large outside room be made into a dormitory for women and children, so that they will not have to occupy the general dormitories.[8]

Although conditions have changed somewhat since these recommendations were made in 1922, they reveal the situation as it has been during the arrival of a large percentage of the immigrants from eastern and southern Europe. The attitudes developed at Ellis Island by those who are already in the United States are the attitudes that concern us here.

[8] Mary T. Waggaman, "Immigrant Aid: Legislative safeguards, and activities of Bureau of Immigration," U. S. Bureau of Labor Statistics, *Monthly Labor Review*, XVI (February 1923), pp. 30–31.

The problems of the journey have never been solved despite the great amount of legislation in the United States as well as in the countries sending immigrants. Special classes of individuals who make their livings by evading laws and exploiting immigrants have been the instigators of many irregularities. Immigrants have never been properly protected during the voyage and many have reached America with an apprehensive feeling which has been a cogent part of their mental organization — an essential factor in the process of adjustment.

With laws in operation excluding all undesirable classes, many aliens have looked for ways of making an illegal entry. In a report made by Inspector Braun in 1907, he shows the methods used by a party of two hundred and fifty Syrians to enter the United States through Mexico.

These Syrians had made a rather roundabout trip to reach the United States. It was, however, not the fascination of a longer sea voyage which induced them to do this, nor was it cheaper for them; it was necessity with some; aforethought with others. The steamship agents at Beirut, Naples, Marseille, or Havre, from which points they had intended to embark on shorter, more direct routes, coming directly to New York, Boston, or Philadelphia, had rejected " some " as afflicted with trachoma, while the " others " were advised by steamship subagents or runners to go via Mexico, as by that route their entry was " easier "; they being told that on the Mexico-American border the examination would be less strict, or that they might evade the examination entirely. . . Of the 250 Syrians I met on the steamer 20 per cent were desirous to reach New London, Conn., and a like number were heading for Fort Wayne, Ind., which cities seem to be the central points from which Syrian " merchants " start on their itineraries in pursuit of their vocation. On their arrival in Vera Cruz none of them were subjected to any examination such as would be required by our laws, and the majority of them reached or will reach the United States by the famous, or rather infamous underground system of smuggling themselves or being smuggled into the territory of the United States. The fact is, only few perhaps three or four of the 250, remained in Vera Cruz, about a score of them in Mexico City, while the balance moved northward toward the American border. Among these 250 Syrians found some who had heretofore attempted to enter the United States via eastern ports, but were deported as afflicted with trachoma, yet within a few days after their arrival in Mexico they were on their road to Indiana, Connecticut, or other points.[9]

In a recent investigation by Assistant Secretary of Labor, Murray W. Garsson, the extent of the practice of illegal entries was revealed. Immigrants are being brought in by smuggling and by trickery. When they are smuggled into the United States their status is rather insecure since they may be discovered at any time without documentary evidence concerning their right to be in this country. If an entrance has been made through trickery, credentials have been forged which give the appearance of authenticity.

Surreptitious entries are made possible through the ingenious activities of "racketeers" who have skilful officers in the large foreign and American cities. While they have aided criminals and other undesirables in their illegal migration, they have also helped many law-abiding persons, many of whom did not know that they were coming in violation of any law. This latter group of immigrants have suffered at the hand of racketeers, often having to make periodic payments which consume most of their earnings in the United States. The protection of these individuals has become a problem of equal importance with the detection and deportation of aliens who have no legal right to be in this country.

The Mexicans and the French-Canadians have not had the same experiences as those from Europe and Asia. They have had to contend with the immigration laws in their native countries, however, as well as those in the United States. Difficulties relative to the journey have centered around admissions at the points of entry into the United States.

For the Mexican the journey has been most important since it has often seemed expedient to him to enter the United States in an illegal manner. This has been done because passing through official channels

. . . entails a great deal of bother and delay, and also expense (for besides the money of the head-tax and *visé* there are the living expenses of the days spent in waiting), and since many laborers, furthermore, are not able to pass the literacy tests of the

[9] Extract from *Annual Report of the Commissioner General of Immigration* 1907, p. 73.

American authorities, a great number of them enter illegally into American territory. It is relatively easy and quite common to smuggle or be smuggled across the border, and there are many people who make a profession of this. The number of illegal entries has recently been materially reduced by the growing effectiveness of the border patrol.

There are several ways of doing this. One of the most frequent in Ciudad Juarez is to take the immigrants to little towns near the official port of entry, which are as a rule scarcely watched. These towns are San Ignacio, San Augustin, Guadalupe, and La Colorada. Here, especially at La Colorada, the border line is little more than a barbed-wire fence, which is easily passed. La Colorada is full of saloons, cheap dance halls, and gambling dens, where come many cowboys and adventurers from the American side, to drink, gamble, and cut loose generally. Many of these go to the line in cars, leave the cars at the fence, and jump over into Mexico. This is very easy and not very risky, since there are few officials on the watch, and those few there merely to prevent contraband of munitions or valuable goods. Busses loaded with laborers leave Ciudad Juarez daily for La Colorada, not far away. The trip costs three Mexican *pesos*. These men jump the fence, usually at night, and get work on nearby ranches. Their employers, taking advantage of their risky position, as a rule pay very low wages and treat them almost like slaves.

There are many other ways of crossing, most of them engineered by professional smugglers, called " coyotes," who hang around the *plaza,* hotels, restaurants, and even offices where the laborers must go, and suggest that at a lower price — from five to ten dollars — and less trouble, they can go over the border. Sometimes they take them in automobiles across the shallow places in the river, or in carts and trucks. Others are taken in boats, and some even swim across, a dangerous thing to do because the river is treacherous.

The smugglers, or " coyotes," who manage the illegal crossing of the immigrants work as individuals and also in gangs. These people know their ground thoroughly, and the habits of both American and Mexican authorities, and sometimes they even have an arrangement with some district official; therefore they are generally successful in taking their human cargo over. They charge as a rule from five to ten dollars apiece, and more if there is baggage or in unusual cases. Sometimes instead of taking the person over they sell or rent a forged head-tax receipt and passport. Such a receipt costs from two to five dollars, and often it is not sold outright for this price, but merely rented, to be returned once the immigrant using it is safely in American territory. The passports generally belong to people in the United States, who " rent " their document to the smugglers, and they in turn to the immigrants. When the smugglers form a gang, they have men on both sides, either in the offices or along the banks of the river — depending on their system — and they employ a set of signals to avoid an armed clash with the authorities, which nevertheless sometimes occurs.

The smugglers are at times employed by big commercial, industrial, or agricultural enterprises in the border states and even in the interior of the United States, which have need of Mexican labor. When labor is scarce, they pay to the smuggler so much for each laborer imported, and when labor is plentiful, they maintain the smuggler on a salary basis. Most of the immigrants are under contract before they cross, although this is against the American laws, and therefore they are instructed to say that they are going in search of labor. Soliciting labor from one side to the other is likewise against the Mexican laws, but this goes on under cover. Just on the other side of the river are stationed the offices of the contractors, or *enganchistas,* who either make or clinch the bargain. From these offices men are sent to ranches, railroads, factories, or wherever labor is needed and has been asked for. The contractors get, generally, from fifty cents to a dollar for each man they supply. Sometimes the enterprises themselves smuggle their own labor over, but as a rule they prefer to " contract " for it; married men are preferred to single.

There are a great many abuses and many ways in which the immigrants are exploited. From the beginning they are absolutely in the hands of the contractor, and even more so if they have been smuggled by him. One of the most common abuses is the " camp store," the concession for which is sold to the contractor, who makes enough out of the store — living expenses and traveling expenses of the laborers, charged to them according to his own will — to repay him well for the trouble. Immigrants contracted for and taken to their place of work are often overcharged greatly for food and incidental expenses on the road, and in the camp. Since the wages of the men are kept in the hands of the contractor until the debt to him is paid, generally for the first two or three weeks the laborer gets nothing, and sometimes it results that he is in debt to the contractor at the end of that time.

In spite of American and Mexican laws, the smuggling agents are numerous, for the demand for labor pays them well, and even when caught and fined they do not suffer greatly because, since the fine is about a hundred *pesos,* and since a " coyote " sometimes earns that much in one day, two or even more such fines a month can well be borne.[10]

[10] Manuel Gamio, *Mexican Immigration to the United States* (Chicago: University of Chicago Press 1930), pp. 205–207.

When emigrants from Mexico go through official channels the following procedure is necessary:

As soon as they arrive in Ciudad Juarez (this information, secured there, nevertheless holds good for the other ports of entry on the Rio Grande border) they go to some little hotel or boarding-house, and then to the Mexican Migration Office. Since many arrive daily, each one is given a number and waits his turn, sometimes three or four days. Bringing to the Mexican office the documents, photographs, etc., required, the immigrant is given a passport, which he takes to the American consular authorities for a *visé*. This takes a varying time, sometimes even several days. After this he goes to the offices on the international bridge, where he is examined and questioned again, is given literacy tests, and asked how much money he has. Here he pays his head-tax (eight dollars), after which he is given a medical examination and bathed, sometimes with gasoline, while his clothing is disinfected. Women go through the same process. The total cost, head-tax plus *visé*, is eighteen dollars. On both sides of the border there are "coyotes" who for five dollars arrange that the documents be obtained very quickly. The American officials speak Spanish to the immigrants, but often very coarsely and roughly; to this the immigrants as a rule submit quietly, sometimes smilingly.

While waiting for the documents to be put in shape, the immigrants stay in poor hotels and boarding-houses. At this time they change from their peasant's white-cotton clothing or whatever other garment they are wearing into the overalls and jumpers of the laborer. They also buy and wear shoes, instead of the Mexican sandals or *huaraches*. They generally arrive in Ciudad Juarez in groups of three or four, and sometimes stay together even after they have crossed, managing to go to work for the same enterprise. The hotels and boarding-houses where they stay are near the railroad station in Ciudad Juarez. The regular price in these places is fifty cents, Mexican gold, for each person. Four or five individuals generally share one room, and in this case they make a discount to perhaps thirty cents a day; for this reason sometimes as many as ten share one room. They have wide beds, in which two or even three men sleep at once. There is, of course, no bath. Throughout this period of wait, they spend their spare time singing, playing cards, etc., and some even learn to read in those few days, in order to pass the American literacy test. They eat in the markets and cheap restaurants, for about twenty-five *centavos* a meal. Here, also, they begin to change their money, and this often places them in the hands of unscrupulous speculators, who charge high rates both ways. Near by are many photographers, who make a specialty of passport photographs, and professional letter-writers.[11]

READINGS

Abbott, Edith, *Immigration: Select Documents and Case Records.*
    1924
Brandenburg, Broughton, *Imported Americans.* 1904. Chapters
    IX–XXI, pp. 119–296
Fairchild, H. P., *Immigration.* Revised ed. 1926. Chapters
    IX–XI, pp. 166–212
Gamio, Manuel, *Mexican Immigration to the United States.* 1930
Gwin, J. B., " Immigration Along Our Southwest Border," *Annals
    of Amer. Acad.,* 93: 126–30. 1921
—— " Back and Forth to Mexico," *Survey,* 39: 9–10. 1917
Raley, Helen, " Guardians of Our Border," *Sunset,* 57: 30–31, 62
Reports of the International Emigration Commission
Reports of the United States Immigration Commission
Roberts, Peter, *The New Immigration.* 1912. Chapters I–III

[11] *Ibid.,* pp. 204–205.

CHAPTER XI
DISTRIBUTION OF NEW IMMIGRATION

WE HAVE already seen that the problem of adjustment in a strange culture is contingent upon the area of settlement. This was true as early as the colonial period. In recent times regional differences are even greater, especially between urban and rural communities. The northwestern Europeans came to the United States with a rural culture and located quite largely in isolated rural districts, so the transition from one situation to another, with some exceptions, was not one of great contrasts.

The new immigrants from Europe, incumbents of a peasant culture, have had to settle here with their simple arcadian background, in a strange, complex urban environment. Not only have they invaded a strange social organization, but they have entered a city environment with a rural culture, the latter fact in itself a great transition, even within one's own country. So our immigration problem since 1882 is what it is not alone because southern and eastern Europeans have migrated to America, but also because of the situation in which they have to live. The demand for their services has come from industrial and mining communities where there have developed alien settlements in the slums, the only sections of the cities where there is little or no effort made to keep the immigrants out. Outside of the slum the new arrivals do not find a welcome. All other residential communities resist the coming of a new group that has an inferior status. Consequently the immigrants of the first generation have had to live in the slums.

This has been true of all groups that have gone to industrial centers whether they were from northwestern Europe or the more recent arrivals from southeastern Europe.

For all new groups with one or more of the following characteristics — an alien culture, a low economic status, and a different race — this point of arrival naturally tends to be in or near the central business district. A commercial district, a business street, or a rooming house area puts up notoriously slight resistance to the intrusion of a new group.[1]

Since the recent immigrants of all nationalities have located chiefly in urban communities, and since they have settled almost entirely in the disorganized areas of American cities, the discussion in this chapter will center about the social situation of the slum. Dr. E. W. Burgess has produced an ideal construction of a city by which it is possible to describe and understand the area in which the immigrant finds his home in America.[2] No city quite conforms to this ideal scheme, but it has a graphic value. An adaptation of this plan portrayed by the use of concentric circles appears on page 202.

For our purposes here it will be necessary to characterize only the zone in transition, since this is where the immigrant lives. While wave after wave of different nationalities has passed through the transitional area in every city, the slum has not been produced by the immigrant, nor has he chosen the slum as a place to live. He is there through the ecological process of segregation in the city.

This zone of transition has not been created by any nationality. It is a result of growth in any particular city. Industrialization brought a rapid expansion in cities, but growth could not be by mere accumulation or accretion on the periphery of the city. The central business section would naturally expand, since it is what its name implies, the " headquarters " area of the city. The function of the central busi-

[1] Ernest W. Burgess, "Residential Segregation in American Cities," *The American Negro, Annals of the American Academy* of Political and Social Science Vol. CXXXX (November 1928), p. 109.
[2] See Ernest W. Burgess, "The Growth of the City: An Introduction to a Research Project," *The City.* Edited by E. W. Burgess *et al.* (Chicago: University of Chicago Press 1925), p. 51.

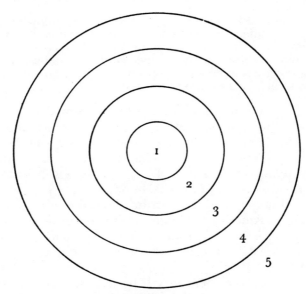

PLAN OF THE CITY

1. Central business district
2. Zone in transition
3. Zone of workingmen's homes
4. Residential area
5. Commuters' zone

(Chart after Burgess. See Ernest W. Burgess, *The City*, page 51.)

CHARACTERIZATION OF THE ZONES OF THE CITY

I. Central Business District
II. Zone in Transition
  A. Immigrant Areas (Slums)
    1. Jewish Ghetto
    2. Little Sicily
    3. Little Italy
    4. Chinatown
    5. Little Poland, etc.
  B. Black Belt (Negro slum)
  C. Slum
    1. Physical characteristics
      a. Tenements
      b. Basement apartments
      c. Cheap movies
    2. Problems
      a. Poverty
      b. Conflicting social definitions
      c. Crime and delinquency
      d. Vice
    3. Adjustment types
      a. Social misfits
      b. Economic failures
      c. Dregs of society
      d. Social parasites
  D. Rooming House Areas
    1. Types of adjustments
      a. Homeless men
      b. Childless homes
      c. Anti-social sects
      d. Fakers
      e. Quack doctors
    2. Types of relationships
      a. Secondary and impersonal
      b. Clandestine

      c. Anonymous
      d. Mobility
      e. Individualistic philosophy
    3. Special areas
      a. Latin quarter (Bohemia)
  E. Bright Light Areas
    1. Cabarets
    2. Dance Halls
    3. Pawnshops
  F. Underworld
    1. Adjustment types
      a. Vice
      b. Crime
      c. Delinquency
      d. Gambling
      e. Alcoholism
      f. Drug addiction
      g. Suicides
    2. Organizations
      a. Gangs
III. Zone of Workingmen's Homes
  A. Area of second settlement for immigrants (Escape from foreign culture)
  B. Area of cultural conflicts
IV. Residential Zone (exclusive)
  A. Area of third settlement for immigrants
  B. Hotels and apartments
V. Commuters' Zone
  A. Area of third settlement for immigrants
  B. Single homes

These areas in the Transitional Zone all tend to overlap. Many of the characteristics given only for one area will be found in all the others. The purpose of the chart and the descriptive data is to characterize the Transitional Zone and thus give a graphic picture of the area in which the immigrant lives.

---

ness district is to serve not only the city proper but the great metropolitan area as well. As the city expands, its central business becomes functionally related to an ever-widening hinterland. This being true, the " headquarters " area of a great metropolitan center must have more room.

Skyscrapers with their great capacity fail to take care of this expansion. Consequently the central business has to invade the encircling area, the zone in transition. Such is the case with each zone, but it is the zone of transition that interests us here since it is this region in the city that receives the newly arrived immigrant.

This region encircling the central business district is the slum of the city. Once it contained some of the best homes; some of the largest churches of the city still stand there, but many of them serve a new function, having been turned into business houses. As the central business district invades the surrounding zone, it creates a slum. Property owners refuse to make repairs on the dwellings in this area since they will soon be sold for some commercial enterprise. Deterioration is the result. Community pride and community controls disappear and an area of physical disorganization and social disintegration is produced.

The slum is a mosaic of cultural areas, a number of sections being immigrant colonies, Little Poland, Little Italy, the Jewish Ghetto, and Chinatown. Besides the immigrant areas, one finds in this transitional zone all that is connected with social disorganization. Drab tenement buildings form the architectural structures of the region. In these ramshackle buildings there live not only the immigrants of the first generation, but there remains a remnant of each nationality that has once occupied that area. The present Europeans in these areas have been preceded by several other nationalities, often the Irish, German, and Scandinavian groups. It is this " sediment " of marooned families and individuals that helps give the slum its distinctive nature. Each group has left its stragglers who were unable or unwilling to leave with a new invasion. So the slum is not only an area of first settlement for immigrants, but a place of segregation for the residue of society. In addition to the immigrant residual, there are to be found there most of the social variant types and social misfits: the hobo, the radical, the unconventional, and the eccentric, as well as the parasitic classes connected with vice, gambling, sale of " dope," etc.

The radical individuals not only live in or near the slum, but their public meetings are held in these areas. In these places one finds anarchists, socialists, proletarians, communists, syndicalists, I.W.W.'s, and those who associate with them. Near the slum or within its boundaries are also people who like to experiment with life and break with conventional patterns. Mr. Zorbaugh has called them "egocentric poseurs, neurotics, rebels against the conventions of Main Street or the gossip of the foreign community, seekers of atmosphere, dabblers in the occult, dilettantes in the arts, or parties to drab lapses from a moral code which the city has not yet destroyed." [3]

Completing the mosaic of cultural areas in the transitional zone along with the foreign colonies are the underworld regions, rooming-house districts, [4] and the bright-light areas. It is hard to tell where one begins and the other leaves off. In the underworld there is a concentration of vice, crime, and drug addiction. The rooming-house district shelters a mobile population, the hobo, the criminal, childless families, and misfits of all types. "The rooming-house is a place of anonymous relationships. One knows no one, and is known by no one. One comes and goes as one wishes, does very much as one pleases, and as long as one disturbs no one else, no questions are asked." [5] The bright-light areas harbor amusement centers, cabarets, night clubs, and restaurants with "atmosphere." They are places where conventional individuals are thrilled by an evening in the unconventional life of the city. They provide a place where people can congregate and do things that they would not do in the more censorious communities in which they live.

The very nature of the transitional zone makes it an area without the ordinary informal social controls. There are not any community traditions or public opinion. Situations are defined by individuals rather than by groups. Conventional standards are non-existent, so far as the community is concerned. Mores tend to lose their potency. "The life of the slum is lived almost entirely without the conventional world. Practically its only contacts with the conventional world are through the social agency and the law." [6]

[3] Harvey Warren Zorbaugh, *The Gold Coast and the Slum* (Chicago: The University of Chicago Press 1929), p. 92.
[4] For a description of rooming-house areas read Nels Anderson, *The Hobo* (Chicago: University of Chicago Press 1923), Part I, pp. 3–40. H. W. Zorbaugh, *op. cit.*, pp. 69–86.
[5] H. W. Zorbaugh, *op. cit.*, p. 75.   [6] *Ibid.*, p. 152.

In these areas in transition, where the immigrant must live, many of the traditional institutions, once powerful techniques of social control, are no longer influential. The home, the church, and the school play circumscribed rôles in these areas. While the immigrant establishes his own institutions, the change in these American institutions is one of the indices of the disorganization in these areas.

In the followng statements Professor H. W. Zorbaugh has shown how these institutions have failed in a disorganized region in Chicago by contrasting them with their traditional village rôle.

In the town or village the status of the church was defined in the mores of the community. Sects might compete with one another; but the church played a definite rôle in community life. Significant family events — christenings, marriages, burials — centered about the church. The church took a leading part in community celebrations, and was looked to in time of crisis. The church was intimately identified with the life of the locality, and was the visible symbol about which centered a great part of the community's ritual and tradition. The church plays a very different rôle in the life of the local areas of the Near North Side, the rôle varying with the degree of " community " remaining to those areas.[7]

Professor Zorbaugh found that very few of the churches had any direct relationship to the group life of the area. Having realized this fact, most of the churches are trying to accommodate themselves to the area with a new technique, emphasizing the fact that the church did not change with the transition in the life of the community, especially in the rooming-house area.

The rooming-house district is a district of many church spires, relics of the day when this was a fashionable residence community. But it is a district of dying and abandoned churches. Without exception, these churches are supported by members who now live far outside the community, but cling to the old church out of sentiment for the days that were. A few of these churches have withdrawn into themselves, content to let the life of the city rumble faintly by without their doors. But others are attempting to reach down into the life of the area.[8]

[7] *Ibid.*, p. 183.   [8] *Ibid.*, p. 185.

Little need be said of the relationship of the school to the local life of the Near North Side; there is none. The schools, centrally directed and standardized, are interested in turning out " Americans " at so many per year, not in making adaptations to the problems and needs of a Little Sicily, a gang world, or a life in furnished rooms. The attitude of the Board of Education practically killed the school community center movement. As we have seen in the case of Little Sicily, the school rather creates local problems than adjusts or controls them. . .

Like the church and the school, the family, considered as an institution, functions far differently in an area like the Near North Side than in the town or village community. The maps showing the distribution of desertion and divorce over the Near North Side and the distribution of juvenile delinquency are indicative of the extent of family disorganization. Over large areas, like the rooming-house district, the family as an institution does not exist. In practically every immigrant group, as in Little Sicily, the family is going to pieces in the conflict with an alien culture. The fact that there is no occupational continuity and tradition within the family, that the child tends to follow a different trade from that of his father, and is taken into a world of different values, materially contributes to this conflict and disintegration. The map of United Charities cases indicates that the family is failing, also, in those areas of the Near North Side to function as an economic unit.[9]

Where traditional institutions are no longer important, there is always a weakening of the mores as a means of social control.

An adequate social organization serves two functions in society. It implies institutions — such as the family, church, school, commercial and industrial organizations, recreational facilities — sufficient to care for the varied interests of the people who live in the society or community; and it implies customs, traditions, ideals, and purposes of sufficient homogeneity throughout the group, and built up about the institutions, to control the individuals and cause them to find adequate outlet for their needs and energies in the existing institutions.[10]

In the areas where the immigrants must live, this is not the case except as they establish their own social milieu.

The studies made in cities have been quite largely studies

[9] *Ibid.*, pp. 187–189.
[10] Ruth Shonle Cavan, *Suicide* (Chicago: University of Chicago Press 1928), p. 100.

of this transitional zone, since it contains most of the outstanding city problems and has as well a large alien population. It is interesting to see what these studies have revealed concerning the environment into which the recent immigrants have come. It has been found to be an area of social variants who are involved in crime, delinquency, vice, poverty, desertion, suicides, drug addiction, and general disorganization and demoralization.

In the study of 1313 gangs in the city of Chicago, Dr. Thrasher discovered that this area surrounding the central business district included great sections of the three chief gang areas: "The North Side Jungles," "The West Side Wilderness," and "The South Side Badlands." In each section the invasion of business and industry has created regions within these areas of transition which provide a habitat for the activities of gangs — railroads, canals, uninhabited areas around warehouses, factories, and lumber yards, which make possible the activities of gangs.[11]

Not only is this transitional area the habitat of gangs, but it includes the activities of gangs, crime, delinquency, and truancy. In a consideration of the home addresses of school truants and delinquents in the city of Chicago, Mr. Clifford R. Shaw and his associates discovered by the use of the spot map:

. . . that school truancy, juvenile delinquency, and adult crime rather than being distributed uniformly throughout the city of Chicago are largely concentrated in certain areas. The highest rates are found in the area adjacent to the central business districts and the large industrial centers, while the lowest rates occur in the outlying residential communities.

The areas in which the greatest concentrations and highest rates are found have many characteristics which differentiate them from the outlying residential communities. As indicated previously, these areas are in a process of transition from residence to business and industry and are characterized by physical deterioration, decreasing population, and the disintegration of the conventional neighborhood culture and organization.[12]

[11] See Frederic M. Thrasher, *The Gang* (Chicago: University of Chicago Press 1927), Chapter I.
[12] Clifford R. Shaw *et al*, *Delinquency Areas* (Chicago: University of Chicago Press 1929), p. 204.

Not only is the rate of truancy, delinquency, and crime higher in areas of first settlement for immigrants, but the rate of recidivism is higher. That is, in these areas individuals have shown a tendency to become not only delinquents and truants but to become repeaters in these patterns of behavior.

In a study of seven American cities for the National Commission on Law Observance and Enforcement, it was found that delinquency and crime tended to be concentrated in the transitional zone where the immigrants are forced to live. This study eliminated nationality as an important factor in delinquency when it was discovered that the rates of delinquency remained about the same no matter what ethnic group was living in this area of physical deterioration.

It has been pointed out . . . that there has been a succession of nationalities in the areas of the first settlement near the central business district and the important industrial centers in Chicago, and that while this change was taking place there were few significant changes in the relative rates of delinquents in the same areas. In other words, the composition of the population changed; the relative rates of delinquents remained unchanged. It was found also that as the older immigrant group moved out of the areas of first settlement there was a decrease in the percentage of these nationalities among the cases in the juvenile court. This fact, which suggests that the high rate of delinquents in these national groups was at least in part due to residence in these areas of high rates, is substantiated by the fact that the rates of delinquents are much lower in the areas of second and third immigrant settlement.[13]

Vice is found in its most flagrant form in the disorganized areas near which the immigrants of the first generation find their homes. Although the vice resorts are not in the immigrant settlements, they are in the underworld regions adjacent to them.

The underworlds of vice and crime have usually been inseparable. The distribution of crime throughout the urban community portrays, in the main, the location of commercialized

[13] Clifford R. Shaw and Henry D. McKay, "Social Factors in Juvenile Delinquency," *Report on the Causes of Crime* (Washington: National Commission on Law Observance and Enforcement 1931), Vol. II, p. 98.

vice. A spot map of felony cases, giving the place of the crime and the address of the criminal, which were reviewed by the Chicago Crime Commission during 1921, describes about the same territorial distribution for crime as the spot map of the cases dealt with by the Committee of Fifteen of Chicago in 1922 does for vice. On analysis it appears that both crime and vice depend upon mobility and collections of people; both forms of activity are legally and morally isolated and consequently must hide in the disorganized neighborhoods in order to thrive. It is also interesting to note that commercialized vice exists in the same general regions of the city characterized by the distribution of the cases of poverty, divorce, desertion, suicide, abandoned infants. Indeed, these problems, considered ecologically, indicate the areas of greatest social disorganization within the city.[14]

The area of deterioration encircling the central business district furnishes the native habitat for the brothel type of prostitution. All the conditions favorable to the existence of this flagrant, highly organized form of commercialized vice are to be found there. In the slums the vice emporia not only find very accessible locations, but also experience practically no organized resistance from the decaying neighborhoods adjacent. And, furthermore, they are located in a region where the pattern of vice is an inevitable expression or product of great mobility and vast social disorganization.

The rooming-house sections and, to some extent, the tenement districts harbor an unorganized form of prostitution. The free-lance, clandestine prostitutes, unattached to brothels, resort frequently to furnished rooms as a place to live and " bring tricks." The landlords or landladies either demand high rents from them or require a special room tax on each service. Because of the great anonymity in these rooming-house areas the activities of these prostitutes go on relatively unnoticed and consequently undisturbed. Here again the location is one of proximity to the demand, for it is a matter of common observation that the rooming-house and lodging-house areas quarter the hordes of homeless men in the community.[15]

The area of deterioration, with its anonymity and lack of community control, has provided an excellent rendezvous for drug peddlers and those who use " dope." In some of the immigrant areas, Negro districts, and regions adjacent to them, drugs can be secured with little danger of detection except during special raids.

[14] Walter C. Reckless, "The Distribution of Commercialized Vice in the City: A Sociological Analysis," *The Urban Community*, edited by Ernest W. Burgess, pp. 199–200.   [15] *Ibid.*, pp. 196–197.

The personal statement of a drug addict shows the disorganized area of the city to be a place where "dope" can be secured and used.

> I found a peddler and got two dollars worth. He told me where I could get it in large quantities down in the "Bottoms." The Bottoms were the slums of the town where dope can be bought and where the dope fiends hang out. No one cares down there who you are but they would knock you over for a nickel.
> In the morning I went down into the Bottoms and soon met a man that I recognized as a dope fiend by his looks. I can tell them as soon as I see them. He was a peddler but didn't have any with him, but he directed me to a place where I could get it. I went to the address he gave me and found an old tumbledown shack that didn't seem to be occupied. I made myself known by asking: "Have you any stuff?" [16]

In a study of suicides, Dr. Cavan found the area of disorganization to contain many sections where there are high rates of suicide. Though suicide rates were high with the immigrants, it was found that "The foreign communities, instead of coinciding with the areas of high suicide rates, surround these areas, which are for the most part made up of native-born whites." [17] So the immigrant areas are contiguous to regions where there are enough social disorganization and personal demoralization to lead to high rates of suicide.

To reveal more conclusively the disorganization of the transitional zone, Dr. Cavan discovered some important correlations. Suicide areas correspond closely to areas with high divorce rates.[18] Pawnshops, an indication of an uncertain economic status, show a close relationship. "It is not without significance that forty-four of the fifty-four pawnshops listed in the classified telephone directory for January, 1925, are within the areas of high suicide rates." [19] The other indications of personal and social disorganization found by Dr. Cavan in the transitional zone in Chicago where immigrants live were murders, deaths due to alcoholism and use

---

[16] From "A Sociological Study of Drug Addiction," unpublished manuscript by author.
[17] Ruth Shonle Cavan, *op. cit.*, p. 88.   [19] *Ibid.*, p. 95.
[18] *Ibid.*, p. 93.

of drugs. She found here, also, " houses, hotels, and cabarets catering to those in search of promiscuous sex relations." [20]

The zone in transition which is the "port of first entry " for the immigrant is not only an area of truancy, delinquency, crime, vice, drug addiction, and other forms of disorganization mentioned here, but it is the poverty belt of the city. Organized charities exist for the purpose of helping the people of this region. The foreign peasant becomes more involved in poverty and crime than in any other two types of social disorganization. In the poverty belt, destitution has been about the same for every nationality. While the industrial organization paying low wages to unskilled workers and demanding a great "reserve army" of workers, is responsible for poverty, the group occupying the region is identified with poverty and considered as being prone to social inadequacies because they are inferior.

The importance of living in a poverty belt and being identified with it is seen in the social definition of poverty. There is prevalent in the thinking of a great many a tendency to find a relationship between poverty and ability to make economic adjustments. Some authors have made a definite correlation between native capacity, degeneracy, and poverty. Since the three have been found together, it is easy to reach the conclusion that the presence of poverty connotes a lack of capacity for better adjustments. Many feel that the immigrants in all cases are where they belong and should not be advanced.

Being unskilled workers and living in the poverty belt, the peasants from southern and eastern Europe have been identified with all that accompanies poverty: common labor, low wages, bad housing, and vice. Once in this situation the traditional thinking tends. to keep them there. With this association of poverty and inferiority in the common definition of American opinion, it is strange that so many of the second generation are able to leave the area. Not only do they have to struggle against the demoralizing influences of the poverty belt but also against the attitude that identifies them with the situation.

[20] *Ibid.*, pp. 98–100.

It is only natural that there should develop slum attitudes and slum patterns of behavior in which the conventional mores of the other urban areas tend to lose their sanction.

The slum is a confused social world to those who grow up in it. This is due on the one hand to what we have referred to as the cosmopolitan nature of the slum, its lack of common social definitions, and its many conflicting definitions that arise out of its various cultures.[21]

The ethnocentrism of the immigrants along with other forces leads to the establishment of colonies which isolate them from many of these conditions. The immigrant segregates himself as best he can in these disorganized areas in American cities. His language, for which he is condemned, helps to insulate him from the influences of the slum. Fortunately he is denied free participation in American life since his contacts would be with factors in disorganized areas. He does not become Americanized. The nature of human nature protects him in this respect. To him America is quite largely interpreted through the social situation in which he lives. Americanization to him means assimilation in the slum cultural complex, and he is much disturbed when he sees his children becoming members of gangs and a part of the disorganized social situation, thus losing their national characteristics.

The immigrant colonies in American cities prevent the immigrant from becoming a greater problem than he really is. It is in the foreign settlement that he has any social life at all and the segregation for which he is criticized prevents his disorganization and demoralization. When people talk of Americanization, they are thinking of the conventional aspects of life; but the immigrant does not come into contact with the conventional aspects of American life.

In the colony he meets with sympathy, understanding, and encouragement. There he finds his fellow-countrymen who understand his habits and standards and share his life-experience and viewpoint. In the colony he has status, plays a rôle in a group. In the life of the colony's streets and cafés, in its church

[21] H. W. Zorbaugh, *op. cit.*, p. 153.

and benevolent societies, he finds response and security. In the colony he finds that he can live, be somebody, satisfy his wishes — all of which is impossible in the strange world outside.[22]

When immigration is being considered, the matter of foreign colonies is nearly always emphasized without a realization of the fact that segregation is and always has been a tendency in urban life. All city dwellers live in segregated areas, with wealth, occupations, interests, etc., furnishing the basis for separate districts. The aristocratic section represents the process of segregation as well as do the immigrant colonies. The latter attract more attention since they are located in the slums; but from the standpoint of the ecological process in city life both are produced in the same way and have the same social significance.

The fact that the immigrants from the same village or the same province can settle together and speak their own language, sing their own songs, eat their native food, greatly facilitates their adjustment. This fact along with their ethnocentrism is the most significant force in the immigration situation. Without segregation, cultural isolation, and ethnocentrism, the immigrant would be demoralized and without a world in which to live. Konrad Bercovici has shown the manner in which they settle in our cities and thus protect themselves from disorganization.

A map of Europe superposed upon the map of New York could prove that the different foreign sections of the city live in the same proximity to one another in Europe: the Spanish near the French, the French near the Germans, the Germans near the Austrians, the Russians and the Rumanians near the Hungarians, and the Greeks behind the Italians. People of western Europe live in the western side of the city. People of eastern Europe live in the eastern side of the city. Northerners live in the northern part of the city and southerners in the southern part. Those who have lived on the other side near the sea or a river have the tendency here to live as near the sea or the river as possible. The English, islanders, living on the other side of the Hudson as if the river were the channel that separates them from the rest of Europe.

A reformation of the same grouping takes place every time the city expands. If the Italians move further up Harlem, the Greeks

[22] *Ibid.*, p. 141.

follow them, the Spanish join them, with the French always lagging behind and the Germans expanding eastward. And yet these people hate one another as only neighbors can hate one another.[23]

While the immigrant must live in the transitional zone of industrial cities, he has been protected at least partially by transplanting his own culture to these areas of disorganization. A description of some of these areas shows how complete this isolation tends to be.

Until 1914 the Sicilian colony in Chicago was an absolutely foreign community. The immigrants were mostly from villages near Palermo, though nearly all of the Sicilian provinces are represented. The most important of the village groups are those from Alta Villa Milicia, Bagheria Vicari, Cimmina, Termini-Imarezi, Monreali, and the city of Palermo. These groups retained their identity, living together as far as possible, intermarrying and celebrating the traditional feasts. Immigrants who settled in Louisiana came up to join their village colony. Those who had been leaders in Sicily retained their power here and, having greater force and intelligence, made contracts with local politicians, police officials, labor agents, and real estate dealers, and became the go-betweens for their colony and the outside-world labor agents. . .

In the entire district there was no food for sale that was not distinctly foreign; it was impossible to buy butter, American cheese, sweet potatoes, pumpkin, green corn, etc., but in season artichokes, cactus fruit (*fichi d'India*), pomegranates, cocozella, and various herbs and greens never sold in other parts of town were plentiful. There were no bookstores. Italian newspapers had a limited circulation, and the Chicago daily papers were sold at only two transfer points on the edge of the district.[24]

The Greek colony of Lowell is probably the most exclusive and distinctively Greek settlement, of any considerable size, in the United States. It centers around a stretch of Market Street about a quarter of a mile long, a district of old two- and three-story wooden buildings, many of them apparently contemporaneous with the founding of the city. In this quarter practically every store is a Greek one and every dwelling house is inhabited by Greeks. As in Chicago, if anything still more so here, the conditions of Greek life are reproduced with the greatest fidelity pos-

[23] Konrad Bercovici, *Around the World in New York* (New York: The Century Company 1924), pp. 20–21.

[24] Robert E. Park and Herbert A. Miller, *Old World Traits Transplanted*, 1921, pp. 151–152. Reprinted by permission of the Carnegie Corporation of New York.

sible. There are the same queer little grocery stores, the same dingy restaurants, the same close, smoky coffee-houses, with here, as in Greece, at all hours of the day, a crowd of big, lazy, able-bodied men, loafing, smoking, and playing cards, while some poor child toils eight or ten hours a day to support them. The self-sufficient nature of this colony will be evidenced by the following list of Greek business houses and business and professional men: seven restaurants, twenty coffee-houses, twelve barber-shops, two drug stores, six fruit stores, eight shoe-shine parlors, one dry goods store, four ticket agencies, seven bakeries, four candy stores, twenty-two grocery stores, five coal and wood dealers, eight truck-men, one pool room, one flavoring extract factory, one wholesale meat dealer, four physicians, one Orthodox priest, two Protestant ministers, three milkmen, five farms (owned in partnerships of four or five men to each farm), two hundred farm laborers, ten real estate owners, one real estate broker, two bankers, three teachers. The large number of coffee-houses is an impressive witness of the transplantation of Greek customs to this country.[25]

This is much the manner in which immigrants of all nationalities have settled in the United States since the colonial period. The chief difference is the fact that recent immigrants have had to go to cities to establish their colonies. The immigrant of the first generation is able to remain in this situation through segregation and to continue the intimate type of relationship in which his life organization developed. Every aspect of his life is more or less controlled by this closed community, except his economic and political contacts with the outside world. The members of the second generation, however, are not so successful in finding isolation in terms of the European culture of their parents. They are forced to make contacts outside.

The immigrant generation, feeling little other pressure than the necessity of learning the minimum of the English language required to get along economically, shuts itself off in a Little Sicily or a ghetto and lives to itself. The American-born generation, however, is not able to live to itself. The law requires it to attend American schools; and in many other ways it is precipitated into American cultural life. It finds itself living in two social worlds, social worlds which define the same situation in very different ways. At once cultural conflicts arise; perhaps merely vague bewilderment and unrest, but often definite prob-

[25] Henry P. Fairchild, *Greek Immigration to the United States* (New Haven: Yale University Press 1911), pp. 134–135.

lems of personal behavior. In the normal native community, we have said, the family and the community meet these problems for the child. But the foreign family and community are not able to do this completely or successfully. Their attempts as likely as not but serve to mark the child as a delinquent in the eyes of the *American law*. The child, consciously if vaguely, feels this inadequacy of the family and community in helping him to make his adjustments; nor can he find in the Old World life of the colony satisfaction for his wishes as defined by his contact with American life.[26]

The American-born in the families of immigrants come in contact with the disorganized life of the slum in their early adjustments outside the immigrant community. Then they find themselves reacting to a much larger world, utilizing the behavior patterns peculiar to urban life. The parents continue to think in terms of the peasant community in Europe where they developed their social natures. The immigrant community touches only minor aspects of the personalities of the second generation, so it does not demand their loyalities.

This receding of the community from the actual daily life of the individual means a weakening of the immediate and spontaneous social restraints and a new form of social control by means of law. But although the law with its public sanctions may bind the individual more strongly, it binds much less of him. A large sphere of behavior is thus freed from immediate restraint, and in this the individual is allowed an opportunity for differentiation and specialization.[27]

Becoming a part of cultures outside the immigrant colony there is not only a " pluralistic social universe " for the individual, but there is also a dual situation. In the colony there is a great contrast with the world outside.

The social behavior pattern of the city life is characterized from the formal individual point of view, that is, from the point of view of behavior process, by a numerical preponderance of unrestrained over restrained; individualistic over conformative; rational over emotional; formal, objective over personal, intimate; self-assertive over self-effacing behavior.[28]

[26] H. W. Zorbaugh, *op. cit.*, p. 154.
[27] Nicholas J. Spykman, "A Social Philosophy of the City," *The Urban Community*, p. 56.
[28] *Ibid.*, p. 59.

The immigrant of the second generation does not want to be a part of the European cultural situation brought by his parents, and he finds it difficult to become an intimate part of any situation. He is associated with many situations but not actually a part of them in a stabilizing sense.

Although the first generation of immigrants manages to protect itself from the social disorganization of the slum, the second generation is not so successful. If the children of immigrants do not become a part of the underworld through their early adjustments in gang life, they usually move out to the area of second settlement. If they fail economically, they remain in the slum and become a part of the residue that has been left there by the preceding waves of population movements.

READINGS

Abbott, Grace, " Bulgarians in Chicago," *Survey,* Jan. 8, 1909
—— " Bulgarians in Granite City, Ill.," *Survey,* Feb. 1, 1913
—— " Study of the Greeks in Chicago," *American Journal of Sociology,* Nov. 1909
—— *The Immigrant and Coal Mining Communities of Illinois.* 1920
—— *The Immigrant and the Community.* 1917
Addams, Jane, *A New Conscience and an Ancient Evil.* 1912
—— *The Spirit of Youth and the City Streets.* 1909
—— *Twenty Years of Hull House.* 1910
Almy, Frederic, " Huddled Poles of Buffalo," *Survey,* Feb. 14, 1916
Anderson, Nels, *The Hobo.* 1923. Part I, pp. 3–60.
—— " The Slum Endures," *Survey,* 57. 1927
Anderson, Nels and Lindeman, E. C., *Urban Sociology.* 1928. Chapter IV, pp. 67–93; Chapter XV, pp. 306–332
Anthony, Robert W., *A Study of the Jews in Greater New York.* 1921
Babson, H., " The Finns in Lanesville, Mass." *Sociological Monograph No.* 13, Vol. IV, Oct. 1919. University of Southern California
Balch, Emily G., *Our Slavic Fellow Citizens.* 1910. Chapter XIII, pp. 253–281; Chapter XV, pp. 317–348
Bassett, E. M., " Distribution of Population in Cities," *American City,* XIII, July 1915, pp. 7–8
Bercovici, Konrad, *Around the World in New York.* 1924

—— " The Greatest Jewish City in the World," *Nation,* Sept. 12, 1923
Burgess, E. W., *The Urban Community.* 1926
Burgess, Thomas, *The Greeks in America.* 1913
Camblon, Ruth, " Mexicans in Chicago," *Family,* 7: 207–211. 1926
Capek, Thomas, *The Czech Community in New York.* 1921
Cavan, Ruth Shonle, *Suicide.* 1928. Chapter V, pp. 77–105
Cohen, Israel, " The Jewish Community," *The Sociological Review,* III, pp. 216–218. 1910
Cole, W. J., " Immigrant Races in Massachusetts: The Greeks." *Mass. Bureau of Immigration.* 1919
Daniels, John, *America Via the Neighborhood.* 1920
Davis, Michael M., *Immigrant Health and the Community.* 1921
Drachsler, Julius, *Intermarriage in New York City.* 1919
Goldenweiser, E. A., " Immigrants in Cities," *Survey,* Jan. 7, 1911
Hammond, L. J. and Gray, C. H., " The Relation of the Foreign Population to the Mortality and Morbidity Rate of Philadelphia," *Bull. Amer. Acad. of Med.,* XIV: 113–129. 1913
Handbook-Bibliography on Foreign Language Group, compiled by Amy B. Green and Frederic A. Gould. 1925. (Lists the chief centers of immigrant groups)
Handman, Max S., " The Mexican Immigrant in Texas," *Southwestern Polit. and Social Science Quarterly,* 7: 33–41. 1926
Hapgood, Hutchins, *The Spirit of the Ghetto: Studies of the Jewish Quarter in New York.* 1902
Hedges, Leroy, " Slavs on Southern Farms," *Senate Doc. No.* 575
Holdsworth, J. T., *Economic Survey of Pittsburgh.* 1912
Hughes, E., " Chicago Housing Conditions," *American Journal of Sociology,* Nov. 1914
Hunter, Robert, *Tenement Conditions in Chicago.*
" Jewish Community of New York City," *The Jewish Communal Register of New York City,* 1917–18
Jones, Anita E., " Mexican Colonies in Chicago," *Social Service Review,* II, pp. 579–597. 1928
Kellogg, Paul V., *The Pittsburgh District.* 1914
Kenngott, George F., *The Record of a City: A Social Survey of Lowell, Massachusetts.* 1912
Kobrin, Leon, *A Lithuanian Village.* 1920
" Little Mexico in Northern Cities," *World's Work,* 48: 466. 1924
McKenzie, R. D., *The Neighborhood: A Study of Local Life in Columbus, Ohio.* 1923
Odencrantz, L. C. and Potter, Z. L., *Industrial Conditions in Springfield.* 1915
Park, Robert E., " The Immigrant Community and the Immigrant Press," *American Review,* III, March-April 1923
—— *The Immigrant Press and Its Control.* 1922. Chapter IX

Park, Robert E. and Burgess, E. W., *The City*. 1925. Chapter II, pp. 47–62

Park, Robert E. and Miller, H. A., *Old World Traits Transplanted*. 1921

Riis, Jacob, *How the Other Half Lives*. 1922

Roberts, Peter, *Anthracite Coal Communities*. 1904

" Russians in Los Angeles," *University of California Monograph No. 17*

Shaw, Clifford R., *The Natural History of a Delinquent Career*. 1931. Chapter II, pp. 13–25

Shaw, C. R., *et al*, *Delinquency Areas*. 1929

Shaw, C. R. and McKay, Henry D., " Social Factors in Juvenile Delinquency," *Report on the Causes of Crime, National Commission on Law Observance and Enforcement*. 1931

Simkhovitch, Mary K., *The City Worker's World in America*. 1917

Sinclair, Upton, *The Jungle*. 1906

Sombart, Werner, *The Jews and Modern Capitalism;* translated from the German by M. Epstein. 1913

Steffens, Lincoln, *The Shame of the Cities*. 1907

Strong, Josiah, *The Twentieth Century City*. 1898

Sullenger, T. Earl, " Mexican Population of Omaha," *Journal of Applied Sociology*, 88: 289–293. 1924

Taylor, Graham R., *Satellite Cities: A Study of Industrial Suburbs*. 1915

Thomas, W. I. and Znaniecki, F., *The Polish Peasant in Europe and America*. 1918. Vol. V

Thrasher, F. M., *The Gang*. 1927. Chapter I, pp. 5–25; Chapters VIII–IX, pp. 132–158; Chapter XII, pp. 191–220

Tibbitts, Clark, " A Study of Chicago Settlement of the Jews in the United States," *Social Forces*, VI, 430–437

United States Bureau of Census, A Century of Population Growth. 1909. (VII, VIII, X)

Weber, A. F., *The Growth of Cities in the Nineteenth Century*. 1899

Wilcox, W. F., " The Distribution of Immigrants in the United States," *Quarterly Journal of Economics*, 20: 523. 1906

Wirth, Louis, *The Ghetto*. 1928. Chapters VIII–XI, pp. 131–263

Woods, R. A., *Americans in Process: A Settlement Study, North- and West-End Boston*. 1902

—— *City Wilderness*. 1889

Woolston, H., " The Urban Habit of Mind," *American Journal of Sociology*. XVII

Zorbaugh, Harvey W., *The Gold Coast and the Slum*. 1929

CHAPTER XII

SOCIAL INTERACTION AND ADJUSTMENTS

THE TREMENDOUS migration from a foreign culture entails a problem of immigration for the United States, as we have seen, because of the character of human nature and the social process by which it develops. When habits, attitudes, desires, interests, and a philosophy of life have already developed in relation to one cultural complex which indicates a complete adjustment in that social organization, these human factors usually lead to maladjustment in another cultural situation. Especially is this true when there is a language difference, in which words are really symbolic of certain social values, and represent the attitudes and interests of the individual.

So what the individual brings with him in the way of personality organization, and the strange, disorganized social situation into which he takes his human nature in the United States, are the two general factors that create the inevitable problem of immigration that has increased in importance as the social milieu in America has become more industrial, increasingly urban, and more complex.

The northern and western Europeans found the transition somewhat less difficult than the recent immigrants, since they came at a time when American culture was similar to the social organization of northwestern Europe, differing only as it had been modified in America. Furthermore, they came with a rural culture and settled in a rural community. Adjustment did not involve so many elements of culture as at present when a people from a simple rural environment settles in a complex urban situation.

Practically all of the immigrants coming to the United States have been peasants representing a relatively simple social organization. Primary groups, the family and the neighborhood, have been potent functioning units of control. The life organization of the individual has been shaped by the social organization of these groups. For generations there has been cultural isolation for the peasant so there have been no cultural conflicts, and therefore no choice of patterns of behavior, since the accessible cultural patterns have been too few and carefully defined. There has always been conformity with little social disorganization and little personal demoralization, with each individual perfectly accommodated to the only social situation he knows at all.

There is a tremendous difference between the environment of the European peasant in his native land and in urban America. In Europe his situation was dominated by flora and fauna; here he lives in a world of machines. In his original habitat, customs and traditions were controlling forces; here they tend to break down. In rural Europe his attitudes, beliefs, ideas, and fears were tied up with nature; here they fail to find their counterpart in an industrial environment. His subjective personality does not find its objective aspect in reality. This new life becomes a conscious process.

In the relatively simple social organization of a primary group [such as a peasant community [1]] the individual life organization is largely, or completely, a replica of the inclusive social organization. The culture patterns are limited in number and rigidly defined, and the accommodation of the individual to them is complete and relatively perfect. There is no individual choice of work, no choice of metaphysical belief, no variation from the conventionalized sex patterns, and little opportunity in any direction for choice in accordance with individual inclination. The individual conforms to the relatively fixed group patterns. . .

But in any complex culture situation [urban life in America [2]] that permits of any degree of choice on the part of the group members, individual differences appear. The culture patterns are numerous and competing; frequently they are conflicting and contradictory. Within this system the individual life organization of each member of the group is based on the elements he

[1] Inserted by author.   [2] Inserted by author.

selects or which are selected for him. He engages in a certain type of work to the exclusion of other types; he subscribes to some one of the various contradictory types of religious philosophy; he chooses one from among a variety of types of sex and family life; he selects certain forms of hedonistic activities and rejects or neglects others; and so for all the elements that go to make up his personal life organization.[3]

This in brief shows how significant is the problem of assimilating the immigrant into American culture.

The problem of assimilating the native-born is a very real one; it is the problem of the education of children in the homes and of adolescents in the schools. But the assimilation of adult migrants, finding for them places in the communal organization, is a more serious problem: it is the problem of adult education, which we have just in recent years begun to consider with any real sense of its importance.[4]

The children of American rural parents may accommodate themselves fairly well to city life but their parents will be unhappy, and their adjustment to American city life is better than that of the immigrant only because there is not a language handicap.

It is more than difficult for the native population to keep pace with the rapid changes in society without a certain amount of disorganization. There is not a definite technique for helping people make adjustments, since we do not know enough about human nature and the social process by which it develops to make the transition from one cultural situation to another less a crisis situation. Our knowledge does not keep up with the changes that are taking place. We have what Dr. Ogburn has called a " cultural lag," [5] in which we do not have a cultural technique to keep pace with material progress.

The adjustment process of the immigrants has been somewhat complicated by the fact that they have not all reached the United States at the same time. Each year there have

[3] Edward Byron Reuter, *The American Race Problem* (New York: Thomas Y. Crowell Co. 1927), pp. 93–94.
[4] Robert E. Park, "The Urban Community as a Special Pattern and a Moral Order," *The Urban Community*, p. 7.
[5] See William Fielding Ogburn, *Social Change* (New York: The Viking Press, Inc. 1923), Part IV, pp. 200–268.

been arrivals bringing with them unadulterated traditions and customs from Europe that serve to retard any change in the pattern of the group. True, they were known as "green-horns" by those who preceded them, but they have exercised their influence. Another retarding power is the fact that the recent immigrant, in many instances, has not expected to stay in America. His lack of adjustment in his native land was economic. He expected to come to the United States and save what is required to make this economic adjustment in Europe a satisfactory one. Consequently he is interested in an adjustment of accommodation in America and not one of assimilation.

Important among the accommodations made by immigrants in the United States are the cultural and economic adjustments which have a bearing on their life organizations and determine the type of citizens they are going to be. In reality these two adjustments are closely related, but they are separated here for the purpose of convenience in analysis. The economic adjustment includes occupations, wages, standard of living, housing, vagrancy, poverty, and pauperism. The cultural adjustment includes crime, delinquency, insanity, and vice, as well as the normal adjustments such as institutions established by the immigrant. These must be thought of as adjustments to a social situation, that is to experiences in the United States, as they are interpreted in terms of the background of experiences of the immigrant. Some of these adjustments are pathological but they are accommodations to a social situation just as normal adjustments are.

In considering economic adjustments we find that a very large percentage of the immigrants from southern and eastern Europe are common laborers or have no definite occupation, and belong, therefore, to the unskilled class. This has made it possible for them to find a place in our industrial organization. In each case the recent arrivals have entered an industry at the very lowest level, doing the undesirable work of the plant.

In one respect the vocational adjustment of the newcomer has tended to follow a certain pattern. The established tradition has been that newcomers start at the bottom with unskilled work, no matter what their qualifications for better jobs might be. Nearly every race thus pays the price of immigration by the suffering of the first generation. The second and the third descendants usually overcome the handicaps of language and education, and graduate out of their original lowly status. Then as a new group of immigrants or a new race descends upon the country, they, too, are introduced into the American scheme by starting their cycle of adjustment. The history of American racial relations in industry may be read as a succession of attempted substitutions of one racial group for another. Thus we find that the hardest, dirtiest, and poorest-paying work has been passed over to the " freshmen " who have been so insistent upon entering the American institution.[6]

The wages and the standard of living of any group are a reaction to past experiences and the present situation. Many of the immigrants are employed at a wage rate below what has been regarded by charity organizations as sufficient to maintain a proper standard of living, but it has been higher than they have known in some cases in Europe. The earnings of the father are often supplemented by the earnings of other members of the family, a plan that is characteristic of the rural situation in Europe, especially with those groups having the larger family organization, such as the Polish peasant.

One of the objections used against immigration has been that immigrants work for less money and maintain a lower standard of living than Americans. However, Americans working on the same industrial level receive about the same wage and those in the transitional zone of large cities evidence about the same standard of living. If a comparison is made between the immigrants of the third zone in the city, that is the area of workingmen's homes, and the native citizens of that area there is little difference between the two groups. In making comparisons there should be as many common denominators as possible, occupational levels, residential localities, etc. Quite naturally the newly arrived immigrant will suffer in contrast with the skilled worker, experienced in some industry and living in a better section

[6] Herman Feldman, *Racial Factors in American Industry* (New York: Harper & Brothers 1931), p. 137.

of the city. A fair comparison would be in terms of the wages received by each group at its advent into an industry at its lowest level, and the standard of living at that time.

. . . A more general consequence of having foreign groups do our most disagreeable types of work is the creation of a belief that these occupations are preferred by some of our foreign citizens, or are activities for which they are best fitted. The traditions thus arise which tend to make it more difficult for members of some nationalities to raise themselves in the industrial world. The racial minority follows the occupation at which its members have " made good " or earned a satisfactory livelihood in the past; and the employers, having had experience with them in that capacity and not in others, sometimes assume that that work is the only kind they can do.[7]

The wages and standard of living for immigrants have often been too low for their good or for the welfare of those in direct competition with them. We must remember, however, that the various industries and not the immigrants determine the wage rate, and in many cases wages have been lower when native Americans, mountaineers, and other isolated groups have been secured as industrial workers. The fact of low wages and an inadequate standard of living lies much deeper than immigration itself, but since the two are found together it has been easy to say that one has caused the other. Numerous strikes show that the recent arrival from Europe has not always accepted meager remuneration in a passive manner.

The housing condition of the immigrant in America is a slum pattern that is followed of necessity by anyone living in the poverty belt. The immigrant settles in that area of our large cities where property is held for speculative purposes. Consequently no improvements are made. There have been attacks upon slum conditions but still the slum exists through the process by which the city grows. The slum is the product of city growth and change; it is an area out of control of conventional mores, where there are not organized attitudes concerning patterns of behavior, and where unassimilated people, immigrants, Negroes, and social variants can live — in fact, the only place they can live. It is an area

[7] *Ibid.*, pp. 138–139.

of high land values and low rent, and low rent is absolutely essential to the low wage of the immigrant. To change the housing adjustments of the first generation of immigrants or the recent arrivals would mean changing the major processes in city growth. Certainly the situation is out of the hands of the immigrants and others who live in the slum.

Obviously, workers who are employed for the least desirable work on the least desirable terms are also likely to be subjected to the least desirable surrounding conditions. In the smaller communities the immigrant has had to live quite close to the mill or mine. In our large cities the immigrants huddle into slums which have long served as an exposition of depravity and have reinforced people's notions as to the inferiority of foreigners.[8]

Evidence that housing adjustment in the slum is not peculiar to the immigrant is the fact that the second generation and often the most ambitious and progressive of the first generation move out. Only the unsuccessful, a certain residue of each group, remain. A cross-section of the slum reveals marooned individuals, families, and small groups of every nationality that has inhabited this area of transition: natives, Germans, Irish, Scandinavians, Italians, Poles, Negroes, Mexicans, etc.

It is interesting to see the housing adjustment of just one group in one of our American cities where one finds areas of first, second, and third settlements. Dr. Wirth has shown this succession with the Jews in Chicago. He says:

One of the important adjustments that any immigrant group has to make, it has been observed, is that of finding a suitable habitat corresponding to the habits and attitudes of the individuals. This adjustment to the areas of a large city tends to take the form of distinct areas of settlement. When he first arrives, the immigrant settles in the slum, which is called the area of first settlement. But if the immigrant himself continues to live in this area for his whole lifetime, his children seldom do. In a fast-growing city a neighborhood has a life of no more than one generation. It changes its local color with the turnover of its inhabitants.[9]

---

[8] *Ibid.*, p. 140.
[9] Louis Wirth, *The Ghetto* (Chicago: The University of Chicago Press, 1928), p. 246.

The area of second settlement may suffice for a while, but in many cases there is a movement to an area of third settlement by the second generation and in some cases it has included the first generation.

The latest avenue of escape from the ghetto is represented by the rapid influx of Jews into the apartment and residential hotels of the city, particularly of Hyde Park and the North Shore. So popular have these hotels become with the Jewish population that a " Jewish Hotel Row," as it is called by real estate men of the district, is rapidly springing up. Many of these hotels, while not advertising Kosher food, are nevertheless catering to the traditional tastes of the Jews. The middle-class business men among the Jews moved into these hotels originally, not merely because their wives wanted to be free from household duties, nor merely because they had reached a station in life where they could afford the luxuries of hotel life, but rather because they wished to be taken for successful business or professional men — not merely successful Jews.[10]

So the housing condition of the immigrants, with a few rooms to each household and a great number in each room, including boarders, is an adjustment to a social situation produced by the rapid growth of cities. Congestion and general conditions are worse with the southeastern Europeans, Negroes, and Mexicans, since they were the last to invade these areas. Any comparison made regarding housing should be made between people of the same situation, that is, on the same economic, educational, and cultural levels.

Economic adjustments in America have been influenced greatly by the fact that the immigrant has been exploited in the United States especially by the earlier arrivals of the same nationality. The main methods of exploitation are exercised through certain economic institutions, chief of which are the padrone system, the contract labor system, the system of peonage, the sweatshop system, the immigrant bank, and in some cases through social institutions founded for the protection of immigrants. Many of these practices are disappearing, but will be discussed here because they were important in the early part of the period of federal control.

[10] *Ibid.*, pp. 257–258.

The word "padrone" is the Italian expression for master or boss, which in America refers to the person who makes contacts with American life for recent arrivals from his own country. Such a person is able, because of the ignorance of his victims, to hold them in bondage by planning their activities day after day, dictating where they shall live, where they shall work, and seeing that they have little chance to learn English. Board, lodging, and a small salary are provided by the boss.

The system was introduced by the Italians chiefly for railroad labor, but it was adopted by Greeks, Turks, Macedonians, and Bulgarians. It has flourished as a means of exploitation in those trades where unskilled laborers can be used in great numbers with the investment of very little capital.

Through the contract labor system the American employer is able to reach the foreign worker. Between the capitalist and the alien laborer, the immigrant who has already accommodated himself to American life plays a leading rôle. At one time these agents went abroad to secure workers, but more recently the method of securing aliens is through a representative in Europe. The importer often advances the passage money and secures men who are willing to work a year for a few hundred dollars. Some men are engaged after they reach the United States.

Since there is a contract labor law, the whole system is in violation of that legislation. The immigrant is coached regarding the method he is to follow so that he may not become involved. This is necessary in every case, since the law, if strictly adhered to, would exclude anyone who had been promised work in America.

The peonage system is similar to that of contract labor. This system is based upon indebtedness of the immigrant to an employer or master. While it attracted enough attention to precipitate an investigation, the Immigration Commission "found no general system of peonage anywhere." It did find, however, cases in every state except Oklahoma and Connecticut that "would constitute peonage as the Supreme Court defined it." To quote from this study:

There has probably existed in Maine the most complete system of peonage in the entire country. In late years the natives who formerly supplied the labor for the logging concerns in that State have been engaged in the paper mills, and the lumber companies have been compelled to import laborers, largely foreigners, from other States. Boston is the chief labor market for the Maine forests. The employment agents misrepresent conditions in the woods, and frequently tell the laborers that the camps will be but a few miles from some town where they can go from time to time for recreation and enjoyment. Arriving at the outskirts of civilization the laborers are driven in wagons a short distance into the forests and then have to walk sometimes 60 or 70 miles into the interior, the roads being impassable for vehicles. The men will then be kept in the heart of the forest for months throughout the winter, living in a most rugged fashion and with no recreation whatever. A great many of them have rebelled against this treatment, and they have left their employers by the score. The lumbermen having advanced transportation and supplies have appealed to the legislature for protection.[11]

A bill was passed in 1907 which required a worker to fulfill his agreement. This law has been used to force laborers to work against their will; many of them were imprisoned who refused to continue to work.

Since the immigrant has come to the United States for economic reasons, he is greatly interested in saving money. His ethnocentrism, fear of strange situations, and ignorance of American ways have led to doubt concerning the reliability of American banks. Consequently, he trusts someone from his own country, a saloon-keeper, merchant, steamship agent, real estate dealer, his landlord, or his boss. Poor bookkeeping and dishonesty result in a great deal of loss for many of the laborers.

These immigrant banks are convenient for the alien worker because he can deposit his money after working hours or on Sunday. He does not have to speak the English language, and trusts his native countryman, even though he may have a bad reputation, in preference to an American. This whole system shows that little progress has been made in assimilation. These unchartered banks become meeting places for those of a certain nationality and the banker

[11] Extract from *Reports of the United States Immigration Commission*, II (1911), pp. 446–447.

often assists his clients in many ways and thus wins their confidence.

The immigrant banker is often called upon to perform many other services. Not infrequently as saloon-keeper or licensed labor agent he secures work for his patrons, and as grocer keeps them supplied with provisions. Even when not actually a labor bureau, the banker's place of business is in a number of instances practically a labor headquarters, where the idle men congregate and where agents or contractors in need of laborers come to secure them. In forwarding mail, in writing letters for the illiterate, and in many other ways, the banker performs necessary and efficient service. He cashes pay checks, and acts as interpreter, intermediary, and, in some cases, legal adviser. As notary public he prepares legal documents for his patrons and assists them in the disposition or management of their property.

The immigrant banker does not, of course, extend such accommodations without compensation. Even if there is not immediate remuneration, such services lead to ultimate gain. By the methods described the banker obtains a distinct hold over his " clients," as they are usually termed, and is in a position to turn their needs to his own advantage.[12]

In many cases these immigrant bankers have placed these deposits out at interest or have utilized them in their own business or purchased real estate. In some instances, adequate records are not kept of the amounts received. Loss of savings makes adjustments in America very much more difficult. With some, the money is left for transmission abroad to pay the passage of a family to the United States or to support a family in Europe. Even though the loss has been through the activities of a fellow countryman it results in certain attitudes concerning America, for the unfortunate victim feels that such an experience could not have taken place in his native land.

The sweatshop system provides work in the home, largely in the clothing industry, for women and children as well as men, who work for long hours at a low wage, under the unsanitary conditions of a slum tenement. Ignorance of American ways makes this type of occupation possible with those who cannot communicate enough with others to make a better occupational adjustment. Loss of health under such

[12] *Ibid.*, pp. 431–432.

conditions seriously handicaps the immigrant for the necessary adjustments.

Immigrant or home aid societies or similar institutions exist as benevolent organizations to make the adjustment of the immigrant easier. This position of trust has granted the privilege of entering the work to some individuals who are interested primarily in private gain.

However, many of the institutions have done an admirable piece of work in caring for the helpless immigrants at the port of debarkation when they had not been met by relatives or friends, or when they lacked sufficient funds to reach their destination. This service has been needed especially with women and girls traveling alone.

On the other hand, some of the homes were operated for private gain, and were unsanitary. The immigrants were exploited and little care was taken in the placement of girls, some of whom went to houses of immoral character. The immigrant is at the mercy of others and in the majority of cases has every reason not to be interested in Americanization.

Not a few of the recent immigrants have gained impressions regarding America and laws in the United States through experiences in courts. Exploitations have been carried out through unscrupulous, ignorant interpreters and shyster lawyers.

In many States the police judges and justices of the peace have been accused of the grossest abuse of their power in cases where immigrants are concerned, so that the worst possible lesson has been learned by the immigrant in his first conscious contact with American law.[13]

One experience may lead to a disrespect for law. Often the immigrant is induced by an interpreter to file a complaint for wages, for injury, or fraud, so that the interpreter and some lawyer may receive money from the immigrant for their services, in which the work of the uneducated and dishonest interpreter leads to injustice for the client. Such an experience may determine the future of this individual

---

[13] Extract from *Report of the Massachusetts Commission on Immigration* (1914), p. 107.

and his family in the United States, engendering in them a disrespect for all American institutions.

Experiences in securing work through employment agencies have been factors in immigrant adjustments to conditions in the United States. An official investigation showed the seriousness of exploitations in the matter of occupations.

The different phases of exploitation practiced in the West may be separated under the following heads: (I) charging exorbitant fees and commissions; (II) discharging the men from their work that they must pay for reinstatement, or that the labor agents may collect more fees for finding them other work, or being obliged to "square" themselves with foremen; (III) sending men to places where jobs do not exist; (IV) interpreters' dishonesty; (V) the furnishing of poor food at a high price by contracting supply companies; (VI) transportation dishonesty; the charging of fares where men are entitled to ride free.[14]

The immigrant who is trying to adjust himself to the strange conditions is easily exploited. He cannot speak our language and is ignorant of our customs, habits, and laws. After such experiences as those discussed above he is not a "good" American; he is afraid to do those things that would make him an American.

Occupations, housing, wages, and standards of living, as we have seen, are all adjustments to life. These adjustments are not the same in the second and third generations, consequently they are not accommodations that are peculiar to any particular nationality; they are merely adjustments to situations by individuals who are not in a position to choose. Furthermore, we must keep constantly in mind the fact that the personality organization of the immigrant makes all these adjustments more difficult for him in a strange culture.

While these adjustments have been considered in their economic aspect, they have greatly influenced the cultural adjustments of the immigrant. Some of the more strictly social accommodations will now be considered, but they, too, have an economic aspect.

Many of the adjustments in America are through institu-

[14] Extract from "Immigrants in Industries," *Reports of the United States Immigration Commission*, XVIII (1911), p. 428.

tions: the press, churches, schools, national societies, and theaters.

The nationalistic tendencies of the immigrants find their natural expression and strongest stimulus in the national societies, the Church, and the foreign-language press — the institutions most closely connected with the preservation of the racial languages. In these the immigrant feels the home ties most strongly; they keep him in touch with the political struggle at home and even give him opportunities to take part in it. Both consciously and unconsciously they might be expected to center the immigrants' interests and activities in Europe and so keep him apart from American life.[15]

This, however, is not disconcerting to one who realizes that the transition from one culture must be in terms of the background of the individuals and that it must be a process. Contacts with the culture in which one's human nature developed tend to keep him adjusted until he is organized in terms of a new social milieu. Those of the second generation are more interested in American newspapers and American life, and those of later generations live entirely, with few exceptions, in the cultural complex of the United States.

The immigrant press, though printed in a foreign language and partly designed to prevent assimilation, often leads to a genuine interest in things American because it publishes news regarding activities in the United States.

Nationalistic editors seek to use this monopoly to keep their readers' interest and activity focused on the home country. But under the terms of its existence the press is apt to aid rather than prevent the drift toward the American community.[16]

Here for the first time, with few exceptions, the European peasants find newspapers written about things that interest them, in the languages they speak. Here for the first time the reading habit is established among them. The newspaper brings them into contact with the current thought and the current events of their community, primarily the race group, with its interests merging on one side into the homeland and on the other into the larger American community. Gradually, and largely through

[15] Robert E. Park, *The Immigrant Press and Its Control* 1922. Reprinted by permission of the Carnegie Corporation of New York, pp. 50–51.
[16] *Ibid.*, p. 79.

the efforts of the Socialist press, the reading habit establishes the thinking habit. The net result has been to raise the intellectual level of the immigrant body.[17]

The fact that the number of immigrant papers tends to decrease is one of the indices that eventually each group develops an interest in American life that is more potent than its interest in European social relationships. In 1895 there were 789 German papers in the United States. In 1929 there were 219. In 1884 there were 53 Scandinavian papers in the United States. The number increased until there were 149 in 1909, and decreased until there were only 83 in 1929. The Italians had only five papers in 1886 but 130 in 1929. This is the case with the more recent immigrants who still think in terms of Europe. The Hebrews did not have a single paper in 1888 but printed 41 in 1929. Polish papers increased in number from three in 1884 to 90 in 1929.

If space permitted, one could show the process of assimilation through the changes in the immigrant press. " From the contents of the press it is possible to estimate the extent to which the immigrant peoples have actually taken root in the United States and accommodated themselves to the forms, conditions, and concrete purposes of American life." [18] The press is a form of adjustment, but its presence means that this adjustment is an accommodation rather than assimilation. An interest in a foreign land combined with an interest in America can mean a trend toward international-mindedness which might be an asset in the realization of world peace. A German immigrant interested in Germany and America would not want to see the two countries at war with each other. This situation, however, has been defined as a danger to the United States.

" The Church has proved an effective medium for either the assimilation of peoples or their isolation, according to the purposes of the clergy." [19] It has at least been a bond that has united immigrants in America. In the areas of American cities where immigrants have settled, the churches of the former group that occupied the region have not remained long in operation. The growth of the city, with

[17] *Ibid.*   [18] *Ibid.*, p. 307.   [19] *Ibid.*, p. 52.

earlier residents moving out of the transitional zone, has created not only slums but unchurched areas as well. Apparently these churches did not have the technique or the organization to meet and deal with the problems peculiar to the new population brought in by the rapid change in our modern city life. Consequently many church doors were closed; in some cases the buildings were torn down to make room for approaching business.

This condition is shown by the following statement:

One of the most evident tendencies of Protestantism in New York City has been the movement of the churches uptown, or out of town, following the movement of the rich or well-to-do people. In fact, the Protestant churches for over a century have been in a constant flight away from the common people. Where poor people, or foreigners, or Jews moved in, the Protestant churches moved out. Apparently they were afraid of foreigners, afraid of the poor, afraid of the Jews, afraid of the Catholics.[20]

No matter what may have been the reason for this failure on the part of American churches, the significant fact is that the immigrants have had to provide their own churches which of course they wanted to do. This has prevented the disorganization that would have resulted had it been otherwise.

The most powerful bond which unites immigrants of the same nationality in a foreign country is that represented by religion and the Church. Pious people, like the Poles, Slovaks, Lithuanians, and others, carry with them to the land across the sea their own profound religious sentiment. In their churches they feel at home. The church is a little corner of the distant fatherland. It is thus in America that religion has become the most powerful source of resistance against Americanization (assimilation).[21]

The person who does not understand human nature and who is interested only in Americanization sees the foreign church as an alien institution that will prevent assimilation. However, it is a stabilizing influence that prevents social disorganization and keeps the question of immigration from being a greater problem than it is.

[20] Roy S. Baker, *The Spiritual Unrest* (New York: F. A. Stokes Company 1910), p. 69.
[21] A. Kaupas, "L'Église et les Lituaniens aux États-Unis d'Amérique," in *Annales des Nationalitiés*, II, 233, 1913.

In many instances these religious institutions have been for centuries the center of the social life of a group. Dr. Wirth has shown that the Jewish ghetto has grown up around the synagogue.

The dominant position held by the synagogue in Jewish life is to be accounted for on the basis of the function of religion in that life and the synagogue as an expression of that function. Whatever else they may have been, the Jews were certainly and primarily a group of people held together by common religious traditions and practices. This bond, which found expression through the synagogue, as the center of religious life, colored the whole of their existence.[22]

The synagogue had three traditional functions. It was of course, first of all, a *Beth Hattefilah,* a " house of prayer," in the widest sense of that term. Here not only was the scene of the routine services and ritual, but here too gathered the Jews for those more spontaneous prayers in time of crises, when death threatened a member of the community, or when enemies assailed the gates of the ghetto, or when disease or pestilence swept the country, or when their political fate was in the balance.

The synagogue was also a *Beth Hammidrash,* a " house of study." The association between school and synagogue in the Jewish community has always been close. Before and after the services the Jews studied in the synagogue, read, and argued about the " Law " and the commentaries of the rabbis. The rabbis were generally not only the religious but also the intellectual leaders of the community, and learning has always been a primary duty and a mark of distinction for every Jew. Here, at the synagogue, moreover, was the meeting place for strangers, who brought news from the world without, and here one gathered such knowledge of conditions of affairs in foreign lands from wandering students, scholars, and merchants as the medieval world afforded. In the synagogue centered those currents of thought that gave the Jewish medieval life some of its distinctiveness, in strange contrast to the intellectual stagnation in the world outside.

The synagogue was, finally, a *Beth Hakkeneseth,* a " house of assembly." In the synagogue centered all those activities that were vital in the life of the community and held it together. The synagogue was the administrative center of the ghetto and at the same time the community center. Most of the public announcements that concerned the entire community were made there, and through the synagogue the secular authorities were able to reach

[22] Louis Wirth, *op. cit.*, pp. 52–53.

the Jews. Here taxes were assessed and such functions as were left to the Jewish community itself by their civil or ecclesiastical overlords, such as local regulations, passed and proclaimed. The synagogue officers had important judicial functions which they sometimes exercised with the assistance of the secular ' government. In the synagogue centered the educational, the philanthropic, and much of the recreational life of the community. The synagogue organization remained for several centuries a highly integrated and undifferentiated unit, and thus strengthened its hold on the community.[23]

This shows the close relationship of the synagogue to every aspect of Jewish life and its value to Jews in new places of settlement. The religious institutions of the immigrants are of much greater worth to them than any American institution forced upon them. The Social Settlement which has had considerable success, is the only notable exception. Even it has succeeded best where the cultural background of the immigrant has been respected. The value of foreign institutions may not be important for later generations, but for the initial adjustment, familiar institutions do not have any equals.

With many groups religion has become identified with national unity. Emigration to Amerca has given them their first religious freedom. We are extravagant in our praise of the qualities in the Pilgrim Fathers who came to America for freedom of worship. The motives of the recent immigrants in establishing their religious institutions are similar to those of the early settlers, yet we condemn rather than praise them. Culture and human nature are composed of the same number of units with each nationality and play the same functions and have the same emotional values. Attachment to religion on the part of recent immigrants is identically the same social phenomenon as the attachment of the Pilgrim Fathers to their religion.

Most immigrant groups coming to America have established their own schools in certain localities. These church or parochial schools are an institutionalized method of adjusting to a strange cultural situation. They have played a rôle in social accommodations for immigrants despite the

[23] *Ibid.*, pp. 53–55.

fact that they have caused a great deal of concern for Americans because they use a foreign language and have often maintained low educational standards.

The rôle of the school in the adjustment of immigrants has been shown by Drs. Thomas and Znaniecki in their discussion of the Polish peasant.

Good or bad, the parochial school is a social product of the immigrant group and satisfies important needs of the latter. The most essential point is neither the religious character of the parochial school, nor even the fact that it serves to preserve in the young generation the language and cultural traditions of the old country; it is the function of the parochial school as a factor of the social unity of the immigrant colony and of its continuity through successive generations. The school is a new, concrete, institutional bond between the immigrants. Its first effect is to bring them territorially together, for it has been noticed that proximity to the school — where the children must go every day — is considered even more desirable than proximity to the church. Further, the education of the children is an interest common to all members, just as the religious interest, and this community is fostered by the participation of the parents in all school celebrations and festivities. But even more important than this unification of the old generation is the bond which the parish school creates between the old and the young generation. Whereas children who go to public school become completely estranged from their parents, if these are immigrants, the parish school, in spite of the fact that its program of studies is in many respects similar to that of the public school, in a large measure prevents this estrangement, not only because it makes the children acquainted with their parents' religion, language, and national history but also because it inculcates respect for these traditional values and for the nation from which they came. Moreover the school is not only a common bond between all the members of the old generation but is also considered by the young generation as their own institution, thus fostering their interest in the affairs of the Polish-American colony. The parochial school is a necessary expression of the tendency of the immigrant community to self-preservation and self-development.[24]

Schools are maintained by immigrants so that they may preserve their native language — their means of communication.

[24] William I. Thomas and Florian Znaniecki, *The Polish Peasant in Europe and America* (N. Y. 1918) by permission of and special arrangement with Alfred A. Knopf, Inc., authorized publishers, V, 50–51.

Each national group expresses its group consciousness in varying degrees of effort to preserve its language by providing more or less adequate instruction for the children in the mother tongue. Generally there are very strong traditional and historical reasons for devotion to the language. Often the immigrant comes from countries where attempts have been made to substitute the language of foreign rulers for the mother tongue with the result that the preservation of the language has become a matter of patriotism.[25]

The recent immigrant groups that have placed a great deal of emphasis on parochial and foreign language schools are Bohemians, Croatians, Hungarians, Jews, Lithuanians, Poles, Russians, Ruthenians, Roumanians, Serbians, Slovaks, and Slovenians. Most of these will be recognized as groups that have been oppressed and have struggled to maintain their language and religion in Europe and have come to America for freedom. Some of them have come from countries in Europe other than their own, so that they are learning in America to read their own language for the first time. This is true in the case of many Roumanians and Slovaks. The Hungarians or Magyars, though not a subject group, reach America with a language ethnocentrism because of their anti-German feeling and their disdain for the Slavs.

Many immigrant children go to parochial and other language schools, but thousands are in our public schools. Since we have accepted the immigrants from southeastern Europe, it is unfortunate that the teachers in our public schools have not been required to learn something of the cultural history of these migrants. In school adjustments the immigrant child must first of all use his cultural background just as the American child reflects his home in his first school adjustments. Consequently the teacher must understand human nature and the cultural experiences of her pupils. This is just as important as knowledge concerning certain school subjects. The school is perhaps the greatest medium of Americanization and the process of Americanization must utilize first of all the cultural natures that already exist.

[25] Herbert A. Miller, *The School and the Immigrant* (The Survey Committee of the Cleveland Foundation 1916), p. 37.

The provincial self-satisfaction which many teachers feel in their Americanism does not help them make good Americans out of their foreign pupils. They seem to fear sometimes that if any affection for foreign traditions and ideals is retained, the child is likely to be less American in his sympathies. Nothing could be farther from the truth. There is the closest relation between the central ideal of Americanism — freedom and liberty — and the principal motive underlying the abandonment of his native land by the immigrant.[26]

Too often the Americanization of the school has resulted in social disorganization because the teacher has not understood the cultural history and characteristics of the different national groups. This situation in the school is only a part of a larger situation, a failure to realize that adjustments made by immigrants in the United States must be in terms of their past experiences and that many of their cultural traits must be preserved for a time to prevent social disorganization. The same criticism can be made about schools maintained by immigrants. The teachers do not understand the social order in the United States well enough to prepare the pupils for a normal adjustment in American life; instead they try to insulate them from American culture.

Immigration is not a simple problem. It is complex in all of its ramifications. The second generation can be assimilated and its first contact with American life is through the school. What happens in that situation depends on how efficiently the teacher uses what the child brings into the school in the way of human nature, since the child must react in terms of that human nature.

The object of the teacher should be to see her group from the inside as it sees itself. In this way not only will sympathetic relations be established, but human values recognized which cannot be comprehended when seen from the outside.[27]

The immigrants in America have evidenced a great nationalistic spirit as a means of adjustment in this country and as a plan for aiding their own native lands. These motives have resulted in the development of many organizations that have helped in economic and social accommoda-

[26] *Ibid.*, p. 55.　　　　　　　　[27] *Ibid.*, p. 71.

tions in America as well as serving as a mooring to the culture of their native lands.

These organizations are not, in fact, pure heritages, but the products of the immigrants' efforts to adapt their heritages to American conditions.[28]

A number of elements enter into the nationalistic sentiments of the immigrant: (1) the idealization of home conditions, natural in one who is absent; (2) the desire to aid the struggle for self-determination going on at home; (3) the desire to gain recognition at home, preparatory to a return; (4) the wish to improve his status in the eyes of the American public by improving the status of the national group; (5) the feeling of non-participation in American life which leads to the attempt to create here a situation in which he can participate.[29]

These mutual aid and benefit societies as well as the nationalistic organizations are useful as objects around which the immigrant can organize his interests and sentiments and thus have a cultural habitat. There is no doubt that these organizations at the outset fostered a greater loyalty for some peasant community and for some foreign country than they did for the slums of an American city and the United States. The character of human nature makes it impossible for the reaction to be otherwise. While the interest in these organizations at the beginning may be alien, since they deal with foreign affairs, it would not be possible for the societies to exist long without some relationship to the needs of the immigrant in the United States — so they became a means of adjustment. The greater number of organizations the immigrant is connected with, the more numerous will be his contacts with some aspect of American life in an effort to make these organizations a success.

The first arrivals of any group in America find themselves in a situation where their language, customs, and habits are very different from those around them. This contrast leads to a consciousness of their own cultural character and the development of sentiments concerning it with little or no desire to participate in American life. There is little that exists in these new environs that can be associated with the

[28] Robert E. Park and Herbert A. Miller, *Old World Traits Transplanted*, 1921. Reprinted by permission of the Carnegie Corporation of New York, p. 120.
[29] *Ibid.*, p. 112.

peasant life in Europe, so the immigrants create fraternal organizations and other institutions to care for their needs. Those who come later accept what they find in an immigrant-American community with few questions just as each individual tends to accept his social heritage.

Local societies and lodges become units that are eventually welded together in a nationalistic organization. " Thus the Sons of Italy, the most powerful Italian organization in the United States, which has a membership of 125,000, and 887 lodges in 24 states, is a congeries of benefit and insurance societies." [30] The purpose of the order is to unite all Italians in America for mutual aid in all difficulties and keep alive an interest in Italy and the Italian language.

The Polish National Alliance, the Polish Roman Catholic Union, and the Alliance of Polish Socialists are names of organizations that have played an important part in the adjustments of the Poles in the United States.[31] The first named of these organizations was interested in Poland and America. The second was interested only in the Polish-American community. The last has been interested in the return to Poland of all Poles to participate in the struggle for independence. Success has attended the activities of these organizations when they have worked for the benefit of the Polish-American society in America.

Thus during the war the Polish National Alliance did as much as any purely American institution in fostering the recruiting of volunteers and the sale of Liberty bonds and war stamps; but its efforts did not remain unrewarded, for it earned special recognition from the United States government, had its existence guaranteed (while the German National Alliance lost its charter), obtained freedom from censorship for its organs, helped to gain for Poles who were former Austrian or German subjects exemption from the laws concerning alien enemies, etc.[32]

The Mexican in his native village has not shown a pronounced penchant for organizations but as an immigrant he has turned to societies as a means of adjustment. Most important are "The Honorary Commission," "The Blue

[30] Robert E. Park and Herbert A. Miller, *op. cit.*, pp. 132–133.
[31] See W. I. Thomas and F. Znaniecki, *op. cit.*, V, 110–162.
[32] *Ibid.*, pp. 119–120.

Cross," "The Spanish-American Alliance," and the "Woodmen of the World." The object of most of these, as well as other organizations, is mutual aid and protection in a strange social milieu. "The Spanish-American Alliance" had a political motive back of its establishment, but now it is quite largely a fraternal society.

While many immigrant organizations were much interested in the welfare of the native lands of their members, they became stabilizing institutions operating to aid the transition from one cultural situation to another. With all nationalities they helped make the adjustment in the United States a process of accommodation rather than an abrupt, disorganizing change. The fact that the adjustment could be a process has greatly lessened the problem of immigration.

The immigrant has been able to reproduce and recall some of his past life through theatricals as well as enjoy aspects of American life that excite his humor and thus to some extent rationalize his maladjustment.

Dramatic organizations are frequent in immigrant groups. There are many amateur performances advertised for the benefit of churches, lodges, and schools. Some of the Socialist Finns, Jews, and Lithuanians have good amateur companies which give several performances a year.

Most of the immigrant groups have vaudeville performances of their own in the big cities. They get a great deal of fun out of the puns of the comedians and the half-foreign, half-American patter which is just like the conversations of the street.

The Jews, Ukrainians, Poles, Hungarians, French, Germans, Italians, and Japanese all have one or more professional companies in the United States, most of which are located in New York, Chicago, and San Francisco. With the exception of the Jews, these companies all give plays imported from the old country. The Jews have a group of contemporaneous playwrights whose plays deal with American life. For example, Ossip Dimoff, who has only recently come from Russia, had a play at the Madison Square Garden Theater in the winter of 1920, called "The Bronx Express," which is a very clever satire on Americanization.[33]

Institutional adjustments to American life vary somewhat with the differences in the cultural experience of each group in America. With the Greeks the coffee-house has been an

[33] Robert E. Park, *The Immigrant Press*, pp. 129–130.

important factor. In describing the Greek community in New York, Professor Fairchild has said:

> The coffee-houses are as exact a reproduction of those in Greece — with the exception of the outdoor features — as one could hope to find. There are the same small tables, the same familiar lithographs of the " Death of Patroclus," " The Vengeance of Achilles," " Byron Taking the Oath of Allegiance," and " King George of Greece." There is the same vile atmosphere and the same crowd of big, able-bodied loafers with apparently nothing to do all day but smoke, drink, play cards, and talk. And as in Greece, the proprietors and waiters are often in their shirt sleeves and collarless, with a decidedly unkempt appearance in general.[34]

These represent the more or less unconscious adjustments that may be considered as normal accommodations. Too much emphasis cannot be placed on the value of these institutions in preventing complete disorganization. They have given the immigrant a chance for a mooring in terms of his own social heritage and life patterns while he made a transition to the status of a European- or Asiatic-American. An attempt to understand the nature and rôle of these institutions instead of condemning the immigrant for their existence would reveal the possibility of the way in which institutionalized group activities could be incorporated into American life. The immigrant institutions exist to satisfy needs that are common to people everywhere. In satisfying needs, institutions must do so in terms of human nature that already exists. American institutions meet needs in terms of human nature as it has developed in the United States. They would be of little value if they did not. European institutions care for the needs of the immigrant in terms of the human nature that he brings with him. They care for his economic, cultural, and religious life. They are of inestimable worth to the immigrant at the outset.

Despite the fact that the recent immigrant has availed himself of institutional aids, there have been many pathological adjustments. Crime, delinquency, pauperism, vice, and insanity are all adjustments to life. One of the chief objections to unrestricted immigration from the colonial period on has been the increase of pauperism. Pauperism

[34] H. P. Fairchild, *Greek Immigration to the United States*, p. 149.

has always been high, and will always be high with the immigrant group, no matter what its nationality may be, since immigrants live in the poverty belt of our great cities. It has decreased in rate, however, due to legislation. If one is to make a comparison between native whites and foreign whites as to pauperism, as many have done, this comparison would have to be more than a statistical one. Most studies have been on the basis of the number of each group in the total population. In 1910 about 15 per cent of the total population were foreign while nearly 40 per cent of the paupers in the United States came from the foreign group. On the other hand, nearly 75 per cent of the general population were native whites, but this group furnished only about 53 per cent of the paupers. These figures show a higher rate for the alien, but like many statistical reports, they indicate only the existing conditions and not the causes.

Before we could say that the foreign whites are more prone to pauperism than the native whites, we should have to know what percentage of each group lives in the poverty belt, where there is pauperism and poverty no matter what the nationality may be. There would have to be data on the percentage of each group in low-paid occupations and in industries where there are accidents and diseases closely connected with their work, which lead to pauperism. We must remember that the new arrivals always enter an industry at the level where the wages are the lowest. Furthermore, the recent migrant with his language handicap, unadjusted to our economic and cultural life, is more likely to be the victim of want and demoralization. This, however, does not obviate the fact of a high rate of pauperism with the immigrant from southeastern Europe, but we must realize that it is closely related to the social situation in which he lives. There is legislation to keep out all who are likely to become dependent. There has always been a high rate of pauperism in the poverty belt or area of transition in our large cities. There are complete areas, outside the poverty belt, where native whites live, in which there would not be a single case of pauperism. On the other hand, pauperism with native whites within the poverty belt is probably just as high or higher than with the immigrant. The following quotation reveals the fact that nationality is not the chief factor in poverty:

It is interesting to see how each city has its special problem. For instance, in Buffalo 32 per cent of all the cases were foreign-born Poles, and in Chicago 20 per cent were of the same class. In Hartford 15.1 per cent of the cases were foreign-born Irish, in Lynn 10.7 per cent were foreign-born Canadians (other than French), and 19.3 per cent foreign-born Irish. In Milwaukee 33.3 per cent were Germans, in Newport 22.2 per cent were Irish, in Orange 26.4 per cent Irish, in Rochester 14.6 per cent south Italian, in San Francisco 23.7 per cent were "other races." By way of comparison, it is interesting to note that in Washington 56.9 per cent of the cases were native-born Negroes of native father.[35]

Proneness to any social inadequacy should be measured in a situation where an individual is culturally adjusted and not where he finds himself totally unaccommodated. The tendency of the Poles to social inadequacy, pauperism, immorality, delinquency, etc., should be measured in Poland where they are culturally adjusted, and not in America where they are culturally unadjusted and where they live in a social situation in which there is a very high rate of social variance. So it is with every group. A group of Americans of the peasant class would probably show the same degree of social inadequacy in Italy, Poland, or any European country, as the immigrants show here. The French-Canadian peasant finds adjustments in Montreal or any other city difficult and the mountaineer or rural dweller in the United States finds it difficult to adjust his habits to urban life in America.

This is in no sense a defense of immigration, because America does have a tremendous immigration problem. Anyone understanding human nature and the process by which it develops, and its close relationship to the cultural complex in which it is produced, would expect a great deal of social inadequacy and the production of a great many social variants. Cultural conflicts always result in disor-

---

[35] From H. P. Fairchild, *Immigration*, p. 313. By permission of The Macmillan Company, publishers.

ganization and demoralization. This means that any alien group in the first generation will not be Americans, culturally speaking. This means that many of the second generation will be social variants, delinquents, etc., since they are trying to live in two cultures and are not stabilized in either. This does not mean, however, that the third and fourth generations in a new situation will not make good American citizens.

It is true that the immigrants are a picked group in respect to age. A very large percentage of them come to the United States during the age of greatest productivity and a very large percentage of them are males. However, they live in the poverty belt, they are employed in occupations where there is a great reserve army of workers who are used only part of the year and then at a very low wage. The employer of cheap labor is in part responsible for pauperism. There is little evidence that there is anything inherently wrong with the immigrant when he fails to make an economic adjustment, especially when we realize that he has come primarily for financial gain. There is something wrong, however, with our industrial system and the organization in society that creates a poverty belt. Paupers or those likely to become paupers are refused admission; so pauperism turns out to be an adjustment to the social situation in the United States rather than the result of an influx of dependents from Europe. Most of the cases of pauperism among immigrants are due, so we are told, to lack of employment, low wages and small earnings, death and disability.

Legislation has been passed to prevent the admittance to the United States of any person who shows a history that may lead to insanity. Despite this precaution a great many who have gained entrance have become insane. Too little is known about insanity to be very sure about its causes. No doubt there is a social element that is important. While insanity is not caused by critical situations, any crisis might precipitate insanity.

There is a high ratio of insanity among foreign-born, but this fact alone does not form any basis for conclusions regarding the proneness to insanity on the part of eastern and southern Europeans who have reached the United States in recent years. If the social factor is as important as recent opinion would make it, then one would predict a high rate of insanity among immigrants who face a great problem of adjustment and who have their habitual means of control greatly disturbed.

If insanity in many cases is due to biased reactions to certain aspects of life, then the immigrant is in a position to develop a psychopathic personality or certain types of insanity. In a situation where there is a conflict of cultures, and a realization that he is not accepted, there is a good opportunity to develop paranoiac attitudes or the withdrawal attitudes in relation to an unfriendly environment. Any mental organization leading to insanity is strengthened by similar attitudes of the group in which the immigrant lives.

It is a startling fact, by no means recognized, that there exist definite conditions of mental disease within the individual which are directly corroborated and sustained by those composing the individual's milieu. It may be shown that this circumstance has arisen because of the emotional sympathy or unconscious congeniality between the patient's family or friends and the false impressions existing within him. Naturally this unconscious bond renders them incompetent to challenge collectively these isolated states of disorder as they exist within the single individual. It is quite unrecognized that within the walls of numerous homes, known to us only in their superficial aspect, there exist definite conditions of insanity that are maintained only because of the subtle existence of this collective social protection.[36]

There is no doubt in the minds of those familiar with the immigrant that he has false impressions concerning life in America. He has experiences that lead him to believe that he is being persecuted or discriminated against because he does not have the status in an American locality that he had in a peasant community in Europe. In most cases he is treated as an alien but he tends to dwell on the fact and it becomes greatly magnified in his mind because others of his nationality feel as he does about it. He is in an excellent position to develop attitudes of persecution or a desire to

[36] Trigant Burrow, "Insanity a Social Problem," *American Journal of Sociology*, 32 : 83. 1927.

withdraw from the hardships of life. These attitudes become "mental systematizations" that are regarded in society as insanity.

The mental systematizations thus formed derive unconscious mental and social adhesions in the economic, political, industrial, and religious world by which they also are surrounded.[37]

The author of these statements goes on to say: "It is the position of this essay that an individual discord is but the symptom of a social discord. To reckon constructively with the pathological conditions of the insane is to reckon with these expressions as an integral part of our common social system. An organismic study of insanity, sex aberration, and crime gives evidence that these conditions are symptomatic of a dissociation within the single individual that is in reality due to a disorganization within the body social as a whole."[38] In the slums of industrial cities immigrants are often forced into conflict situations despite their isolation and the presence of their European institutions and their fellow countrymen. Cases of insanity in the United States might never have developed in a peasant community in Europe.

Crime and delinquency in any nationality or race are adjustments to a social situation. They are complex social patterns and cannot be passed on through the biological process. The criminal and the delinquent are produced by identically the same social process as the non-delinquent, and where one finds a delinquent he finds a delinquent social situation. The immigrant who invades our shores goes immediately to the delinquency belt of American industrial cities. The relative tendency of any nationalistic group toward criminality should be measured in a social situation to which it is adjusted, since social variants are produced in cultural conflicts and not where one is controlled by a definite cultural pattern. Furthermore, the tendency toward crime of any group that lives in the crime belt should not be compared with the tendency of any other group that lives in a non-delinquent area. The study by The Behavior Research Fund of Chicago under the direction of Mr. Clifford R. Shaw, shows that the rate of delinquency for all nationalis-

[37] *Ibid.*, p. 81.   [38] *Ibid.*, p. 87.

tic groups was practically the same while residence was confined to delinquent areas or the transitional zone of the city.

It is the native-born children of immigrants, those of the second generation, who are involved in delinquency and crime. They find an adjustment most difficult since they are enmeshed more directly in conflicting cultures than those of the first generation. They are supposed to conform to one culture at home and another at school, with the result that they do not have a world in which to live but have to vacillate between two cultures. This means that they create a social order apart from these two situations which may become a gang world.

It is the individuals of the second generation who find adjustments difficult until they have reached the age where they can emancipate themselves from conflicting controls and choose the cultural complex in which they wish to develop their life organizations. Their choice will depend in each case on their experiences, that is, on the way they have defined objects, institutions, and situations. The experience of an individual of the second generation may lead eventually to a social type in terms of American culture or European culture or the two combined. The experience may lead to a social type that involves behavior that is law-abiding or there may be a rebellion against the European culture of his home and the American culture of his school and he may choose the gang, eventually becoming a social variant.

These immigrant children do not have the same chance to develop a life organization in relation to one cultural complex as is the usual case in society. Instead, part of the day, at home, they attempt to build a life organization in relation to a peasant European or Asiatic culture, and an American culture at school, and another type of American culture as they play in the streets and alleys of the slum. The scheme of behavior imparted at school gets the children into trouble at home, and the European or Asiatic patterns of the home set them off as different at school.

The individuals of the second generation in an American city find themselves in a unique situation. Their parents had a chance to develop life organizations in terms of only one culture and have in most cases been able to bring enough of this culture to the United States to remain adjusted personalities. The children of immigrants find themselves confronted with the insuperable task of trying to develop human nature, or a life organization, in two conflicting social situations, each demanding a different content for each unit of human nature. While the acquisition of their world and the development of human nature with the parents was a more or less unconscious process, with those of the second generation it is a difficult, conscious process. As Drs. Thomas and Znaniecki have said:

. . . There is a large proportion of immigrant children — particularly in large cities — whose home and community conditions are such that their behavior is never socially regulated, no life-organization worthy of the name is ever imposed upon them.[39]
    We must realize that in Polish peasant life [might be any peasant group [40]] the educatory rôle of the marriage-group was something entirely different, much richer in content and better ordered than it is here. The marriage-group was an integral part of the wider social milieu and shared its stock of traditions and schemes of behavior. The children were early made to participate in all the activities of the parents — economic, hedonistic, social, religious — and thus unreflectively absorbed and imitated their entire life-organization. Further, the parents gradually, without effort or reflection, introduced the children into the accumulated body of traditions of the community and into the present active life of the latter and thus prepared them to supplement later from the principles and examples offered by the community whatever deficiencies there might have been in their early education. The parents did not need to be expert educators nor even to be conscious of their moral standards and planfully follow an educational system. All they had to do was to act themselves in accordance with the morality of their social milieu and to mediate between the traditions and social opinion of the community and the consciousness of their children.
    All this is radically changed in America. The children no longer take part in the activities of their parents. They go to school or run the streets while the parents work, or play in their own separate milieux. There is still some community of interests and occupation left between the girl and her mother but the boy has very little in common with his father. Education by action is no longer possible. And even if the boy had any opportunities

---

[39] W. I. Thomas and F. Znaniecki, *op. cit.*, V, 295.
[40] Inserted by author.

of participating in his father's activities he would not gain much by it for these activities have little social meaning left in them — unless, of course, the father is one of the active builders of the Polish-American social system. Furthermore, the marriage-group is no longer the medium through which the child is introduced into the social life of his wider milieu. On the contrary, not only are his contacts with this milieu for the most part direct and independent of the selective control of his elders but he is often called to mediate between his parents and American institutions whose real meaning he may not understand any better than they, but with which he has a better superficial acquaintance. Any authority which the parents might claim as bearers of the social traditions of the wider milieu is thus definitely undermined.[41]

The immigrant of the first generation is struggling to maintain his old life organization and to preserve the culture he acquired, over a period of half his life, against great odds, the greatest of which is the effort on the part of his children to become American and thus get out of the culture that is sacred to their parents. The second generation is struggling to become organized in terms of a fluctuating environment which means disorganization and demoralization in many cases. The first generation tries to pull its children back into a European culture. Failing, in desperation the parents often make a futile attempt to get into the world of the second generation and die unhappy because they are conscious of being in a different social order from their children.

In their effort to hold the second generation, the older immigrants work against the natural trends in society instead of working in terms of trends. Parents of native Americans do the same thing so that the second generation, whether they have alien or native-born parents, become disorganized through the attitudes of their parents. This is not the only explanation of disorganization with the younger generation, but it is one explanation. Parents find it impossible because of the attitudes and habits that they have developed to enter the world of the child and the youth of the next generation. Unable to do this, they cannot become a part of social trends and direct them, rather they work against them, and the result is disorganization. The immigrant father and mother

[41] W. I. Thomas and F. Znaniecki, *op. cit.*, V, 311–312

are greatly handicapped because they do not live in American culture at all.

The immigrant coming to America was born into customs that were so old that they were no longer questioned. For the first generation these customs have become doctrines of welfare and a guide to correct living. Then in America their children question the desirability of such standards and customs. As the second generation becomes disorganized, the immigrant parents think of the American culture as something pernicious, and Americans think of the disorganization as evidence that the immigrants are undesirable. Neither see it as a matter of a conflict of cultures which inevitably leads to disorganization. The people who reach these conclusions, whether American or foreign, do not understand human nature and the process by which it develops. They do not realize the crisis situation that results for the younger generation who find it difficult to acquire a world in which to live.

The immigrant of the second generation has to play rôles and pose because he has to behave in several cultures. He is too American to be appreciated at home, and too Italian, too Polish, or too Jewish to be accepted away from home. His struggle for status keeps his attention on himself and makes him self-conscious, awkward, often boisterous and ill at ease.

Another important adjustment in America that has led to a certain amount of disorganization is the effort on the part of individual Europeans to lose their identity as members of a certain nationality. This may happen because of a prejudice concerning a certain group, or for business reasons.

But this effort usually fails because the individual cannot completely lose the marks of identity with his native group; he is betrayed by some sign — his speech or gestures, or sentiments. He consequently finds himself out of his old society without being completely in a new one and in a painful position — without recognition from any group whatever. We find, therefore, that the men who begin by deserting their groups end by attempting to improve the status of these groups — seeking to make them something with which a man may be proud to identify himself. The fact that the individual will not be respected unless his group is respected becomes thus, perhaps, the most sincere source of the nationalistic movements in America. To this extent the nationalistic movements represent an effort to participate in American life.[42]

The following quotation concerns a rather extreme case of an individual who failed in an effort to make an adjustment to American life by trying to lose his identity. Although this is typical of a great many experiences, there are many instances where individuals were more successful.

During my long residence in New York I have observed the following changes in one man: He arrived a bearded talmudical scholar in 1910. Rabbi Glockman was then less than thirty years old. He had a wife and four children, two sons and two daughters. The oldest was twelve years old, which meant that the father had married at eighteen. A year later Rabbi Glockman was still teaching Hebrew in a little afterschool *Cheder* where the Jewish children were sent by their parents so as not to forget that they were Jews. The school was on Division Street, way down on the East Side. Two years later, with beard a little trimmed, Mr. Glockman owned a Kosher delicatessen store on Second Avenue near Tenth Street. The place closed on Friday evening and remained closed till Saturday after prayers. Mr. Glockman was the president of a congregation. Four years later Mr. Glockman was the partner in a shirt-waist factory where they worked on the Sabbath. The beard was completely gone. They lived in the Bronx. Six years later Mr. Glockman smoked on the Sabbath, ate " unclean " food, and was denounced in a strike as the worst exploiter. He employed only Italian labor, and had changed his name to Bell, George Bell, and had moved from the Bronx to Morristown, because there were no Jews there. Eight years later his daughter had married a Gentile. But then the railroad strike broke out. The great Morristown plan, by which the wealthiest commuters manned the trains, entered into vogue. Mr. Bell came to the station every morning with his overalls under his arms, ready to take his place as a scab — to help the country. But Mr. T. and Mr. D. and Mr. F., who were at the head, would not have the Jew with them in the cab. He had to ride as a passenger. They would not even give him the privilege of acting as conductor. Today Mr. Bell is again Solomon Glockman. He lives in Harlem, in the heart of the Jewish district, is a member of the congregation, and a fanatical Zionist.

[42] Robert E. Park and Herbert A. Miller, *op. cit.*, pp. 143–144. The authors of this statement were concerned with the Jews but they might have had any group in mind.

Even the beard was allowed to grow back, a little trimmed, to its full length. Until the daughter divorced her husband and married a Jew she was not allowed to enter her parents' home.[43]

In certain cases this attempt to lose national identity assumes the form of a group movement out of the area of original settlement. This adjustment, however, is contingent upon a successful economic accommodation and is, therefore, more often found with the Jews than with any other group. Usually the immigrants move in such great numbers that they find that they have only established an area of second settlement, a little less European than the area of first settlement. The chief change is in occupation and a disintegration of the traditional institutions that held them together at the outset in their American homes. They no longer settle by villages as they lived in Europe or Asia. Customs and traditions are weakened. Primary group organizations are not so important. In this area of second settlement, members find themselves trying to live in two cultural worlds. Failing to realize the satisfaction that they thought would come from leaving the slums, they move again as soon as they are financially able to do so.

There are other adjustments that have been made in certain instances, but those above seem to be the most important. It is these cultural adjustments that create for the United States or any other country a problem of immigration. " The transition from one culture to another, and from one personality to another, is a process that requires not only time but demands the co-operation of both groups." [44] It is common knowledge that the co-operation of neither the Americans nor the immigrants is secured. Ethnocentrism is too great with both groups. There are exceptions in both instances, but the number is not great enough to make any considerable difference. In most cases, the immigrant who tries to enter American life meets many difficulties. " He stands on the map of two worlds, not at home in either. His self is divided between the world that he has deserted and the world that will have none of him." [45]

[43] Konrad Bercovici, "The Greatest Jewish City in the World," *Nation* (September 12, 1923), p. 259.
[44] Louis Wirth, *op. cit.*, p. 263.   [45] *Ibid.*, p. 265.

READINGS

Abbott, Edith, *Immigration: Select Documents and Case Records.*
1924. Pp. 252–801.
Abbott, Grace, *The Immigrant and the Community.* 1917
Andreyko, G., *Ukrainians and Their Part in the Making of America*
Antin, Mary, *The Promised Land.* 1912
Balch, Emily Greene, *Our Slavic Fellow Citizens.* 1910. Chapter XIV, pp. 282–316; Chapters XVI–XVIII, pp. 349–425
Bamford, Edwin F., " Mexican Casual Labor Problem in the Southwest," *Journal of Applied Sociology,* VIII: 363–71. 1924
Batten, James H., " The Mexican Immigration Problem," *Pan-Pacific Progress,* VIII: 39, 52. 1928
Bell, P. L., *Mexican West Coast and Lower California.* 1923
Berkson, I. B., *Theories of Americanization, A Critical Study with Special Reference to the Jewish Group.* 1920
Bierstedt, Edward H., *Aspects of Americanization.* 1922
Bloch, Louis, " Report on the Mexican Labor Situation in Imperial Valley, 1926," *22nd Biennial Report, Bureau of Labor Statistics,* Calif. 1925–26
Bogardus, E. S., *Essentials of Americanization.* 1920. Second ed.
—— " Second Generation Mexicans," *Sociology and Social Research,* XIII: 276–83. 1929
—— " The Mexican Immigrant," *Journal of Applied Sociology,* XI: 470–88. 1927
Breckenridge, S. P., *New Homes for Old.* 1921
Bridges, Horace J., *On Becoming an American.* 1919
Brooks, C. A., *Christian Americanization.* 1919
Bryan, Samuel, " Mexican Immigrants in the United States," *Survey,* 28: 726–30. 1912
Burgess, Thomas, *Foreign Born Americans.* 1920
—— " On the American Side of the Rio Grande," *Missionary Rev.,* 50: 689–92
Butler, Fred Clayton, *Community Americanization; a Handbook for Workers.* 1920
—— *State Americanization; the Part of the State in the Education and Assimilation of the Immigrant.* 1920
Capek, Thomas and Capek, Thomas, Jr., *The Czechs and Slovaks in American Banking.* 1920
Claghorn, Kate H., *The Immigrant's Day in Court.* 1923
Clark, F. E., *New Homes of New Americans.* 1913
Cohen, Abraham, *The Rise of David Levinsky.* 1912
Cohen, George, *The Jews in the Making of America.* 1924
Cohen, Rose, *Out of the Shadows.* 1918

Congressional Hearings, "Seasonal Agricultural Laborers from Mexico," before the Committee on Immigration and Naturalization, *House of Representatives.* On H.R. 6741, 7559, 9036. Jan. 28, 1929; Feb. 2, 9, 11, 23, 1926

Daniels, John, *America Via the Neighborhood.* 1920

—— "Americanizing 80,000 Poles," *Survey,* 24: 372–85. 1910

—— "Spirit of Poles in America," *Survey,* 40: 720–21. 1918

Davis, Michael M., *Immigrant Health and the Community.* 1921

Davis, Philip, *Immigration and Americanization.* 1920

Drachler, J., *Democracy and Assimilation.* 1920

Fairchild, Henry P., *Immigration.* 1926. Revised ed. Chapters XI–XVI, pp. 213–368; Chapters XVIII–XIX, pp. 394–433

—— *The Melting-Pot Mistake.* 1926

Feldman, Herman, *Racial Factors in American Industry.* 1931

Foerster, Robert F., "The Problems Involved in Immigration from Latin America and the West Indies to the United States," *U.S. Dept. of Labor.* 1926

Fry, C. Luther, *The New and Old Immigrant on the Land.* 1922

Garis, Roy L., *Immigration Restriction.* 1927

Gavit, John P., *Americans by Choice.* 1922

Gosnell, H. F., "Non-Naturalization: A Study in Political Assimilation," *The American Journal of Sociology,* May 1928

Groves, Ernest R., *Social Problems and Education.* 1925

Gwin, J. B., "Social Problems of Our Mexican Population," *National Conf. of Social Work,* 1926: 327–32

Hall, P. F., *Immigration.* 1906

Hasanovitz, E., *One of Them.* 1918

Holdsworth, J. T., *Economic Survey of Pittsburgh.* 1912

Hourwich, Isaac A., *Immigration and Labor.* 1922

Husband, Joseph, *Americans by Adoption.* 1920

Jerome, Harry, *Migration and Business Cycles.* 1926

Kendall, Joseph L., "Progress Above Expectation in the Fundamental Subjects at a School for Mexican Children," *Educational Research Bull.,* Los Angeles. 1925

Krueger, E. T. and Reckless, W. C., *Social Psychology.* 1931. Chapter XIII, pp. 386–437

Lasker, Bruno, *Jewish Experiences in America.* 1930

—— *Race Attitudes in Children.* 1929

Leiserson, William M., *Adjusting Immigrant to Industry.* 1924

Lescohier, Don S., "The Vital Problem in Mexican Immigration," *National Conf. of Social Work,* 1927: 547–54

Lewisohn, Ludwig, *Up Stream.* 1922

Lofstedt, Christine, "The Mexican Population of Pasadena, California," *Journal of Applied Sociology,* VII: 260–68

Mangano, A., *Sons of Italy.* 1917

Mariano, John H., *The Italian Immigrant and Our Courts.* 1925

May, Carl L., " Our Anti-Social Mexican Class," *Los Angeles County Employee,* 2: 12–13, 22. 1929

McCall, S. W., *The Patriotism of the American Jews.* 1913

McClure, Archibald, *Leadership of the New Americans.* 1916

McCombs, V. M., *From Over the Border.* 1925

McLean, R. N., " Rubbing Shoulders on the Border," *Survey,* LII: 184–85; 201–4

—— *That Mexican.* 1928

" Mexican Rights in the United States," *Nation,* 115: 51–3. 1922

Miller, Herbert A., *Races, Nations and Classes.* 1924

—— *The School and the Immigrant.* 1916

Morgenthau, Henry, *All in a Life-time.* 1923

Niemi, Clemens, *Americanization of the Finnish People.* 1921

Odencranz, Louise, *Italian Women in Industry.* 1919

Panunzio, C. M., *The Soul of an Immigrant.* 1921

—— *Immigration Crossroads.* 1927

Park, Robert E., " Behind Masks," *Survey,* May 1926

—— " Human Migration and the Marginal Man," *American Journal of Sociology,* May 1928

—— *The Immigrant Press and Its Control.* 1922

Park, R. E. and Miller, H. A., *Old World Traits Transplanted.* 1921. Chapters VI–IX.

Patri, Angelo, *A Schoolmaster in the Great City.* 1917

Pupin, Michael, *From Immigrant to Inventor.* 1923

Ravage, M. E., *An American in the Making.* 1917

Report on Crime and the Foreign Born. National Commission of Law Observance and Enforcement, No. 10, June 24, 1931

" Results of Admission of Mexican Laborers, Under Departmental Orders, for Employment in Agricultural Pursuits," *Monthly Labor Review,* 11: 1095–97. 1920

Riis, Jacob A., *Making of an American.* 1901

Roberts, Peter, *The New Immigration.* 1912. Chapters IV–XXIII

Sartorio, E. G., *Social and Religious Life of Italians in America.* 1918

Shaw, Clifford R., *The Jack Roller.* 1930

Shontz, Orfa J., " The Land of ' Poco Tiempo,' " *Family,* VIII: 74–9. 1927

Simpich, F., " The Little Brown Brother Treks North," *Independent,* 116: 237–39. 1926

Slayden, J. L., " Some Observations on Mexican Immigration," *Annals of Amer. Acad.,* 93: 121–26. 1921

Smith, William C., " Changing Personality Traits of Second Generation Orientals in America," *American Journal of Sociology,* May 1928

Speek, Peter A., *A Strike in the Land.* 1921

Steiner, Edward A., *Against the Current.* 1910

—— *Confessions of a Hyphenated American.* 1916
—— *From Alien to Citizen.* 1904
—— *Introducing the American Spirit.* 1915
—— *On the Trail of the Immigrant.* 1906
—— *The Immigrant Tide.* 1909
Stella, Antonio, *Some Aspects of Italian Immigration to the United States.* 1924
Stern, E. G., *My Mother and I.* 1917
Stowell, J. S., " The Danger of Unrestricted Mexican Immigration," *Current History,* 28: 763–68. 1928
—— *The Near-Side of the Mexican Question.* 1921
Streightoff, F. H., *The Standard of Living Among the Industrial People of America.* 1911
Talbot, Winthrop, *Americanization.* 1920
Taylor, Paul S., " Mexican Labor in the United States: ' Imperial Valley,' " *University of California Publications.* 1928
" The Padrone System and Padrone Banks," *Bull., Dept. of Labor,* March 1897
Thomas, W. I. and Znaniecki, F., *The Polish Peasant in Europe and America.* 1918. Vol. III
Thompson, F. V., *The Schooling of the Immigrant.* 1918
Tobenkin, Elias, *Witte Arrives.* 1916
Walker, Helen W., " Mexican Immigrants as Laborers," *Sociology and Social Research,* XIII: 55–62. 1928
—— " Mexican Immigrants and Citizenship." *Sociology and Social Research,* XIII: 450–56. 1929
Wirth, Louis, *The Ghetto.* 1928. Chapters I–VII, pp. 1-130; Chapters XII–XIV, pp. 241–91
Zangwill, Israel, *The Melting Pot.* 1909

Part IV. The Orientals

CHAPTER XIII

INTRODUCTION TO ORIENTAL IMMIGRATION

THE ORIENTALS are discussed separately because they are of a different race and they are the bearers of an extremely diverse culture from that found in the United States. In both respects the contrast is greater than with the Europeans. These, however, are not the most important reasons. The Orientals are considered by themselves because they have been defined and made a group apart through the attitudes of Americans and by specific legislation in this country.

The Japanese and the Chinese have come to the United States with a different type of mental life from that found in this country. Their development has taken place in a social organization where the institutions and social values are of the East. They have a different conception of God, marriage, the home, and the state. The production of these differences has been going on for centuries, with the East isolated from the West, until the economic, political, cultural, and religious organizations are not the same though they serve a purpose similar to those found in the United States.

Through legislation the Chinese and Japanese have been excluded on the basis that they are ineligible to citizenship. This decision was reached through the enactment of the immigration law of 1924. Before this date the Chinese laborers had been excluded by the law of 1882 and the migration of Japanese of the same class had been controlled by the Gentlemen's Agreement in which it became incumbent upon the Japanese government to regulate the emigration of Japanese workingmen.

The Act of 1924 includes seven different classes of aliens, ineligible to citizenship, who are admitted to the United States. These classes are considered in two categories: non-immigrants and nonquota immigrants. The first category includes government officials, their families, etc.; temporary visitors; continuous through transits; and treaty merchants. The second category includes returning domiciled residents; ministers and professors, their wives and children; and students.

Other Asiatics were excluded in 1917 by the " geographical delimitation clause " in the legislation of that year. This clause reads:

Unless otherwise provided for by existing treaties, persons who are natives of islands not possessed by the United States adjacent to the continent of Asia, situate south of the twentieth parallel latitude north, west of the one hundred and sixtieth meridian of longitude east from Greenwich, and north of the tenth parallel of latitude south, or who are natives of any country, province, or dependency situated on the continent of Asia west of the one hundred and tenth meridian of longitude east from Greenwich and east of the fiftieth meridian of longitude east from Greenwich and south of the fiftieth parallel latitude north, except that portion of said territory situate between the fiftieth and the sixty-fourth meridian of longitude east from Greenwich and the twenty-fourth and thirty-eighth parallels of latitude north, and no alien now in any way excluded from, or prevented from entering, the United States shall be admitted to the United States. The provision next fore-going, however, shall not apply to persons of the following status or occupations: Government officers, ministers or religious teachers, missionaries, lawyers, physicians, chemists, civil engineers, teachers, students, authors, artists, merchants, and travelers for curiosity or pleasure, nor to their legal wives or foreign-born children who fail to maintain in the United States a status or occupation placing them within the excepted classes shall be deemed to be in the United States contrary to law, and shall be subject to deportation as provided in section nineteen of this act.

The countries in this barred zone are India, Siam, Indo-China, Afghanistan, parts of Russian Turkestan and Arabia, New Guinea, Borneo, Sumatra, Java, Celebes, and other lesser islands. This eliminated the East Indians who had begun to attract a great deal of attention and opposition on the Pacific Coast.

With the exclusion of immigration from Oriental countries, the problem connected with the groups at the present time has to do with the adjustments of those already in the United States, some of whom are alien and some are citizens. The Constitution grants citizenship to anyone born in this country or to children of citizens of the United States born in other countries.

The whole question of Oriental migration must be considered in the light of the entire immigration situation in the United States. The period of mass migrations has come to an end, for both Europeans and Asiatics. Even if it were not over, aggregate movement would not solve any population problems for the Orient; it has never relieved the conditions of over-population for any country. It has given America a cheap labor supply for industrial developments and a hardy people for conquering an intractable frontier, but countries furnishing this man-power have not solved their problem of over-population through emigration. They realize now that it cannot be done in that way. The trend at present, though it is slow, is for each country to regulate the extent of its own population. It is more retarded in the Eastern world than it is in the Western, but even there students of the situation have already reached that conclusion. No nation today expects to send its people in great numbers to the United States. Wholesale emigration belongs to the days of our early development from a pioneer country to a recognized State. Consequently our problem of immigration has to do with the unassimilated groups in the United States and especially with the marginal individuals of the second generation.

Along with the Chinese and the Japanese, the Hindus and the Filipinos are being included in this section. Ethnically, the Hindus do not belong with the Orientals, but they have been placed in the same category by the attitudes in the United States.

READINGS

Andrews, S., " The Gods of Wo Lee," *Atlantic Monthly,* 25, 1870
—— " Wo Lee and his Kinsfolk," *Atlantic Monthly,* 25, 1879
Bahr, A. W., *Old Chinese Porcelain and Works of Art in China.* 1911
Burgess, J. S., " Cultural Synthesis in China," *Sociology and Social Research,* Nov. and Dec. 1929
Bushell, S. W., *Chinese Art.* 1904
Cheng, S. G., *Modern China: A Political Study*
Crocker, W. R., *The Japanese Population Problem.* 1931
Crow, Carl, *Japan and America: A Contrast.* 1916
DeGroot, J. J. M., *The Religion of the Chinese.* 1910
Douglas, Paul H. and Director, Aaron, *The Problem of Unemployment.* 1931
Fairchild, Henry P., *Immigrant Backgrounds.* 1927
Gamble, Sidney and Burgess, J. S., *Peking, A Social Survey.* 1921
Giles, H. A., *History of Chinese Literature.* 1923. (New ed.)
—— *The Civilization of China.* 1911
Gregory, J. W., *The Menace of Color*
Gulick, S. L., *America and the Orient.* 1916
Hahn, C. C., " Asiatic Civilization in Transition," *Sociology and Social Research,* July–Aug. 1929
Hodgkin, Henry T., *China in the Family of Nations.* 1923
Holcombe, Chester, *The Real Chinese Question.* 1900
" Inferiority of the Caucasian Race," *Independent,* Feb. 1909
Kawakami, K. K., *Asia at the Door.* 1914
King, F. H., *Farmers of Forty Centuries.* 1911
Kulp, Daniel H., *Country Life in Southern China*
Kuo, Ping Wen, *Chinese System of Public Education.* 1915
Lee, Mabel Ping-Hua, *The Economic History of China.* 1921
Lee, Yan Phou, *When I Was a Boy in China.* 1887
Leong, T. K. and Tao, L. K., *Village and Town Life in China.* 1924
Lew, T. T., *China Today Through Chinese Eyes*
Lewis, O., " Transplanted Sections of the Orient," *Overland,* n.s. 1. 1883
Littleton, L. A., " Chinese Mythology in San Francisco," *Overland,* n.s. 1. 1883
Liu, John, " Social Relationships of Chinese Villagers," *Sociology and Social Research,* March and April 1930
Ozaki, Y., " Misunderstood Japan," *North American Review,* V. 171, pp. 566–575. 1900
Richardson, A. D., " The Celestials at Home and Abroad," *Blackwood's Edinburgh Magazine,* 72, 1852
Ross, E. A., *The Changing Chinese.* 1911

Russell, Bertrand, *The Problem of China.* 1922
Smith, A. H., *Chinese Characteristics*
Smith, William C., " The Second Generation Oriental American," *Jour. of Applied Sociology,* Oct. 1925
Tyau, M. T. L., *China Awakened.* 1922
Waley, Arthur, *An Introduction to the Study of Chinese Painting.* 1923
Wing, Yung, *My Life in China and America.* 1909

CHAPTER XIV

THE CHINESE

INTRODUCTION

A BRIEF HISTORY of legislative acts concerning the Chinese and the Japanese will be an excellent frame of reference for the consideration of the Oriental question, since these laws reveal the attitudes of Americans concerning Asiatics. These attitudes constitute the dynamic aspect of the social situation in which the two groups from the Orient have had to make their adjustments.

The Chinese first reached the Pacific shores of the United States during pioneer days, when the interests and the philosophies of the inhabitants of that region were individualistic rather than nationalistic. There was little national or racial consciousness. Everyone, no matter what his ethnic affiliation might be, was looked upon as a settler, a newcomer on the western coast. There was competition at this time because material gain was the chief motive, but the competition was between individuals rather than between groups. During the days of the Gold Rush there was little opposition to the Chinese since there seemed to be a definite place for them in activities which were not of primary interest to the Caucasians.

In the first few years the Chinaman was welcomed, praised, and considered almost indispensable; for in those days race antipathy was subordinated to industrial necessity, and in a heterogeneous community where every Caucasian expected to be a miner or a speculator, the reticent, industrious, adaptable Chinese could find room and something more than toleration. They were highly valued as general laborers, carpenters and cooks; the restaurants established by them in San Francisco and in the mines were well kept and extensively patronized; they took to pieces the old vessels that lay abandoned in the channel of the Golden Gate; they cleared and drained the rich tule lands, which the white miners were too busy to undertake. Governor McDougal recommended in 1852 a system of land grants to induce the further immigration and settlement of the Chinese — " one of the most worthy of our newly adopted citizens." The editor of the Pacific News remarked upon their industry, quietness, cheerfulness and the cleanliness of their personal habits. (Whatever the white man scorned to do the Chinaman took up; whatever white men did, the Chinese could learn to do; he was a gap-filler, doing what no one else would do, or what remained undone, adapting himself to the white man's tastes, and slipping away, unprotestingly, to other tasks when the white man wanted his job.[1])

The cleanliness, unobtrusiveness and industry of the Chinese was often commented upon. As cooks and laundrymen they supplied the places of women domestics. The few women in California at that period were not of a class to fill these needs, and on the basis of these virtues a permanent place in society was predicted for the Chinamen. James A. Carson, a pioneer, declared that they were the best immigrants in California — sober, industrious, and inoffensive. He thought that thousands of them were ready to become citizens if protection was afforded them, and that no better class of men could be chosen to develop the agricultural resources of the country.[2]

Even in the mining districts they were tolerated at first because they in no way interfered with the ambitions of white miners who could sell worked-out claims to the Chinese and then pre-empt new and more promising sites. It was in the mining regions, however, that a change in attitude from tolerance to hostility concerning the Chinese took place. In keeping with the policy of the Know-Nothing Party of the East, there was a growing opinion that California and its gold mines should be for Americans alone. The antipathy that evidenced itself first of all concerning all foreigners gradually transferred itself to only those who were not regarded as white. South Americans, natives of the Mediterranean countries, Malays, in fact all who had dark skins, became objects of prejudice in the economic competition of

[1] Mary Roberts Coolidge, *Chinese Immigration* (New York: Henry Holt and Company 1909), pp. 21–22.
[2] *Ibid.*, pp. 23–24.

the mining regions. The Foreign Miners License tax was directed first of all toward the Spanish-Americans and when they were driven out, the attack centered on the Chinese, since they were the only nonwhite group left in any great numbers.

Once attention had been directed to the Chinese they were no longer considered docile, subservient laborers. People became emotional and highly suggestible, making propaganda effective. Anything derogatory said about the Chinese was readily believed by many. " Governor Bigler charged them with being Contract coolies, avaricious, ignorant of moral obligations, incapable of being assimilated and dangerous to the welfare of the state." [3] He found many Americans who were in the right state of mind to believe what he said.

Just at this time the *Daily Alta California*, the most influential paper in the State, which had been warmly pro-Chinese, went over to the Bigler party owing to a change of editors. The series of anti-Chinese editorials published in the spring of 1853 did much to inflame the people. They charged the Chinese with being debased and servile coolies, inferior to the Negroes morally and mentally — more clannish, dangerous, deceitful and vicious — and immeasurably lower than the Indians; with living upon rats and lizards and shell-fish where flour, beef and bacon abounded. The editor even declared that they made neither good servants nor laborers, though he did acknowledge that there were many who made intelligent citizens and that much of the prejudice against them was due to the jealous greed of the miners.[4]

A special Committee on Chinese Immigration, in a report to the California State Senate in 1877, said:

During their entire settlement in California they have never adapted themselves to our habits, mode of dress, or our educational system, have never learned the sanctity of an oath, never desired to become citizens, or to perform the duties of citizenship, never discovered the difference between right and wrong, never ceased the worship of their idol gods, or advanced a step beyond the traditions of their native hive. Impregnable to all the influences of our Anglo-Saxon life, they remain the same stolid Asiatics that have floated on the rivers and slaved in the fields of China for thirty centuries of time.

[3] *Ibid.*, p. 31.   [4] *Ibid.*, pp. 57–58.

In this report the Chinese were attacked for prostitution, criminality, economic competition, coolie slavery, and the inability to be Christianized. These accusations became the rationalized basis for the collection of revenue from the Chinese. Later, on the same grounds, the eagerness for revenue was replaced by a desire for exclusion.

The exclusion movement became important only with the rising tide of national and racial consciousness. Its first basis was economic but there finally came a demand for restriction and exclusion for cultural and biological reasons. First there was local agitation on the Pacific Coast where nearly all the Chinese lived, but it finally reached national proportions. The exclusion movement was under way as soon as economic competition was discovered.

In an effort to curb the activities of the Chinese, secure revenue from them, and finally exclude them, many municipal, state, and federal laws were passed. In San Francisco there was a laundry tax of $5 per quarter for laundries not using vehicles, which included most of the Chinese laundries. Vegetable hucksters had to pay $10 if they went on foot and only $2 if they drove a wagon. The "queue ordinance" required that anyone convicted of crime should have his hair cut. This meant that when a Chinese was involved, he lost his queue, to him a shameful disgrace. Only the Chinese were held accountable in the "cubic air ordinance" which prohibited the renting of a room that did not have a capacity of five hundred cubic feet for each occupant.

The State of California also enacted considerable legislation designed to control the activities of the Chinese. In 1850 all foreigners were made the incumbents of a miners' tax, which was changed from time to time but was declared void by the amendments to the Federal Constitution in 1870. Reports show that most of this tax was paid by the Chinese. In 1855 a legislative act imposed a tax of $55 on every Chinese immigrant. Three years later in a more drastic piece of legislation all persons of the Chinese or Mongolian races were forbidden to land at any port of the United States unless driven ashore in a storm. In 1861 all Mongolians over the age of eighteen years had to pay a monthly tax of $2.50 unless they had paid the Foreign Miners License tax or were engaged in the production of rice, sugar, tea, or coffee. All these acts were later declared unconstitutional.

The anti-Chinese movement, long a political factor on the Coast, finally became a national issue. Some important treaties and Congressional legislation have been significant in determining the status of the Chinese in the United States. The first treaty which defined our political relationships with China was negotiated by Caleb Cushing in 1844. It made no provision for the residential or commercial rights of the Chinese in the United States. The Reed Treaty four years later neglected this aspect also, which shows that the Chinese were in no way circumscribed at this time so far as the federal government was concerned. In 1868 the Burlingame Treaty recognized the right of migration between the two countries but naturalization was not made possible. Many expected that this treaty would settle the racial problem on the Pacific Coast but they had not been able to predict the great economic depression that came with its corollary of unemployment. Local agitation and legislation, augmented by political leaders, soon attracted national attention. Congress met the situation by appointing a committee to investigate conditions. Recommendations were submitted, asking for a restriction of Asiatics for the protection of the Pacific states. The investigation had included little more than hearing anti-Chinese testimonies designed to secure exclusion.

This agitation resulted in the treaty of 1880 which gave the government of the United States the power to regulate, limit, or suspend the coming to or residence in this country of Chinese laborers. Despite this agreement, the Chinese continued to arrive in increasing numbers until 1882, when 35,579 entered this country. Steamship companies were partly responsible for the migration of so many since they found the transportation of steerage passengers to be a profitable business, consequently they advertised throughout China the opportunities in the United States.

In order to carry out certain phases of the treaty, the legislative act of 1882 was passed. Many objections had been raised concerning the Orientals which finally led to their exclusion. These criticisms have been summed up as follows: " (1) Social — they were said to be unassimilable, with strange and repellent manners, customs, and ideals; (2) economic — they were cheap labor, with a low standard of living, able and willing to work for less than a white man's wage; (3) moral — they engaged in opium-smoking, incessant gambling, and other vices; (4) political — if their numbers were not checked, they would soon overrun and control the whole Pacific Coast. These objections were cited, with varying emphasis upon one or another of them, throughout the whole campaign. There was some truth in them, but the truth was often concealed in a mass of exaggeration or falsehood. The desire of most Californians that Chinese immigration be restricted was a proper one, but the measures taken by the local officials and by many of the citizens were, in many cases, absolutely indefensible. The story of the mistreatment of the Chinese in California and other Western States is a discreditable page in American history." [5]

This legislation suspended the coming of all Chinese laborers for ten years and provided for the deportation of those who arrived in violation of this law. Ship masters were made responsible if they brought laborers, being subject to a fine of not more than $500 and a probable year's imprisonment. This legislation, however, did not take care of the situation on the Pacific Coast where there was much unemployment. In 1885 there were many demonstrations against the Chinese in which some were killed and others were injured and driven from their homes.

A further treaty was drawn in 1888 which prohibited the coming of Chinese laborers for twenty years. This was not ratified by China, so a Congressional act was passed, excluding this class. In 1894 a new treaty was signed in which Chinese laborers were excluded except under certain conditions. In 1904, the expiration of the treaty, China refused its continuance, so the exclusion of Chinese laborers was taken care of by Congressional legislation. This law is still in force.

[5] Payson J. Treat, *Japan and the United States, 1853–1921* (Boston: Houghton Mifflin Company 1921), p. 252.

In 1924 all immigration was suspended for those who were ineligible to citizenship, and this included the Chinese.

The United States has two methods of exclusion for the Chinese. The law of 1882 with subsequent amendments prohibits the immigration of Chinese laborers and the Act of 1924 excludes all aliens ineligible to citizenship. The aim of these laws was to do away with the competition between American laborers and laborers from Asiatic countries. They have achieved that purpose. There are fewer Chinese in the United States than in 1870, and they are no longer concentrated so completely in certain communities in western states.

COMPOSITION

CHINESE immigration to the United States has been composed almost entirely of laborers, small farmers, and merchants. From the outset there has always been a predominance of males over females. This is a significant fact for the process of adjustment. Economic accommodations are made easy because a male population possesses a high degree of mobility, but where there is a disproportionment of sexes social adjustments are difficult to make according to the traditional standards of normalcy. A predominance of males always means a lack of family life as well as a lack of the stabilizing influences of such an organization.

Legislation concerning immigration from China has tended to change the composition since the coming of the earliest arrivals. The law of 1882 excluded Chinese laborers on the basis of race. The Act of 1924 excluded all aliens ineligible to citizenship. Since only " free white persons " and "aliens of African nativity or African descent" are eligible to citizenship through naturalization, the Chinese were excluded. Certain classes of Chinese have been admitted as nonimmigrants since the Exclusion Law. These are (1) teachers and ministers, (2) students, (3) travelers for curiosity or pleasure, (4) merchants and their lawful wives and minor children, (5) government officials, their families, attendants, servants, and employees, (6) Chinese previously lawfully and permanently admitted to the United

States returning from temporary visits abroad, (7) Chinese in continuous transit, (8) Chinese persons shown to have been born in the United States, and the children of such Chinese-American citizens, (9) Chinese citizens lawfully admitted to the United States who later go in transit from one part of the United States to another, through foreign contiguous territory, (10) a *bona fide* seaman.

This legislation reduced the stream of incoming Orientals but also checked the outward flow. Following the enactment of 1924, there was a noticeable decrease in the number of nonimmigrants as well as the number of immigrants. The phase of this law that has caused the most concern to Chinese is the fact that Chinese-American citizens cannot bring their alien wives to America while alien merchants are granted this privilege. Citizens, however, can bring the children born to these alien wives, since the children are American citizens by the act of February 10, 1855.

Many absurdities arise in connection with this type of " American citizen " who applies for admission to the country of his allegiance. Frequently, such " citizens " come to the United States for the first time as mature individuals without the slightest knowledge of American institutions, customs, or language. During the last two months, three brothers, Chinese, age 21, 35, and 39 arrived at the port of Seattle claiming admission on the grounds of citizenship. None of the three could speak a word of the English language or had the slightest idea of the country to which he was coming as a full fledged citizen. On the other hand, many Chinese, and Japanese too, have come to the United States as small children and have been reared here to manhood and womanhood but being foreign-born, they are not granted the privilege of becoming citizens.[6]

In his report of 1916, the Commissioner General of Immigration wrote as follows:

Under the naturalization laws of this country, it makes no difference how long a person of the Mongolian race may have lived here nor how devoted he is to our country and its institutions — how thoroughly Americanized in the substantial sense he may have become — he must remain a foreigner; he cannot become a citizen. Yet a person of the Mongolian race who is so fortunate

[6] Roderick D. McKenzie, *Oriental Exclusion* (New York: The Institute of Pacific Relations 1927), p. 69.

as to be born here is vested by the "accident of birth" with American citizenship; and no matter how thoroughly foreign he may be in his ideas, ideals, and aspirations . . . and even though he demonstrates his foreign inclination by going to the native country of his parents and marrying and establishing a home there and there begets children and rears them to maturity . . . the children of such a person, born and reared abroad and having not the least idea of what American citizenship means, may at any time, either before or after attaining their majority, come to the United States, be freely admitted at our ports (irrespective of their moral, mental, or physical condition) and on the very day of landing claim and exercise all the rights, immunities, and privileges of American citizenship; and moreover, such a person's foreign-born children may also in turn assert American citizenship. Citizenship in this country should rest upon substantial elements, not upon mere technicalities.

The peculiarities of the laws have led to some unusual family groupings in the United States. "First there is the case of the wife and part of the family in the Orient and the husband with the rest of the family in America. Next the wife and husband are in America while some of the children are marooned in the Orient. A third, and less common, condition is for the children to be in America while the parents are in the Orient." [7]

These abnormal situations are created by legislative acts and the Constitution of the United States. The Constitution states that all persons born in the United States and "subject to the jurisdiction thereof are citizens of the United States and of the state wherein they reside." The Act of 1855 reads: "All children born out of the limits and jurisdiction of the United States whose fathers were or may be at the time citizens thereof, are declared to be citizens of the United States."

Alien Chinese merchants can come to the United States for the purpose of establishing a business. This right was granted under the treaty of 1880. The Immigration Act of 1924 substantiated this arrangement by admitting "an alien entitled to enter the United States solely to carry on trade under and in pursuance of a present existing treaty of commerce and navigation." With the Chinese the term "mer-

[7] *Ibid.*, p. 92.

chant " was defined to include those in domestic as well as international trade. The law of 1924 had a diminishing effect on the number of merchants coming to the United States from China.

CAUSES

THE CHINESE have left their native land to come to the United States for economic reasons. The dimensions of a farm in China are not great enough to make it a sufficient economic unit. In the northern region the average size of a farm is about four acres, in south China about one and a half acres. Crop failures under these conditions meant famines and suffering. The Taiping rebellion of 1850 disorganized the lives of those who made their homes in the southeastern provinces. Later the introduction of Western industrial methods paralyzed the traditional habits of the people and made them dissatisfied. Even their great attachment to family and village was not enough to compensate for the disorganization.

As in Europe, propaganda from the masters of foreign vessels concerning the advantages in America found the Chinese eager to try anything that would relieve their situation. The discovery of gold in California offered an attractive solution to the problem of poverty among the Chinese peasants. The early migrants returned to their native villages with glowing accounts of the " Golden Hills " in the United States; thus others were induced to come.

THE JOURNEY

THE MOST important aspect of the journey for the Chinese includes the problem of proving their status so that they may be admitted at the port of debarkation. Since all Chinese have been excluded from the United States with the exception of nonimmigrants and nonquota immigrants, a large part of the question at the place of entry has to do with those returning from a visit abroad. Chinese families in America are broken by the tradition that the wife should remain with her husband's parents, and by the exclusion laws, so that many who visit China go for family reasons. More than half of the Chinese aliens admitted in recent years were residents who had been abroad. Return certificates have to be secured before they depart for the Orient. To secure these certificates, since the Immigration Act of 1924, the migrant must show that he had entered this country originally by legal procedure and for permanent residence; the length of his intended visit abroad must also be stated.

Immigration legislation did not change the desires of the Chinese laborers; they still wanted to come to the United States and thus escape the economic distress in their native land. Since the exclusion laws permitted the coming of nonimmigrants and nonquota immigrants, those who were denied admittance often tried a surreptitious entry by masquerading as belonging to one of these admissible classes. Individuals were coached for the process of passing through the immigration office. Questions and answers had to be memorized. All changes in entrance procedure were ascertained by the coach who was well paid. Coolies have come as merchants. Prostitutes have tried to enter as the wives of American citizens. Many who came as students changed their status once they were in America and became laborers or merchants.

The Commissioner General of Immigration in his annual report of 1905 described the possibilities of illegal entry on the part of Chinese:

There is no Chinese steerage passenger so destitute that money practically without limit is not available to pay for his entrance. He can command legal advice of the most expensive counselors; he can secure witnesses to testify to anything; he can carry his case through all the tribunals up to the Supreme Court of the United States. His youth, his obvious ignorance, his equally conspicuous poverty, his lack of friends or relatives known to him in this country, his lack of knowledge even of the occupation to which he will apply himself if landed — all combined do not deprive him of the benefit of ample funds from some source to secure his admission in some way, if possible.[8]

It is not possible to estimate how many have been smuggled through the immigration office, but a large enough

---

[8] Extract from *Annual Report of Commissioner General of Immigration* 1905, pp. 79–80.

number have been caught to create an attitude of distrust on the part of immigration officials. Under these conditions it becomes incumbent upon each Chinese to show that he is not trying to enter the United States by fraudulent means. Harsh treatment has been the result in certain cases. Innocent persons have been returned to China. Many have been detained for long periods; students and merchants have been held and deported because of some error in passports or certificates. Even Chinese-American citizens have experienced the same difficulty because of the attitude at the port of embarkation developed through handling contraband cases.

A serious feature of the exclusion acts is the failure of the United States to set up machinery for the satisfactory movement of exempted persons. Not only do Chinese merchants, in particular, transfer their business connections to Vancouver, London, and Paris because of the indignities to which they are frequently subjected at our ports, but also American-born Orientals are subjected to what amounts to a virtual inquisition when they wish to return home after a prolonged absence. To the United States Immigration Service, in its unwillingness to recognize the passports of our own State Department, a result partly due to a rather voluminous record of fraudulent certificates, is added the United States Customs Service as a third branch of the government, which usually requires affidavits both in Asia and America.[9]

At the time that the first exclusion law was passed only simple experiments had been made even at Atlantic ports in excluding undesirable aliens; and there was no body of trained officers and interpreters and no bureaucratic machinery with which to enforce the new law on the Pacific Coast. The work of putting in operation a statute new in principle and, as it proved, badly drawn, was thrust upon the heads of departments wholly without experience and already fully occupied with other duties. Even the money necessary to enforce the law was not forthcoming, for Congress appropriated only meagre sums for Chinese exclusion during the first six years.[10]

Those who were seeking entrance to the United States by illegal means sought other gates of entry as soon as it became difficult to get through the Immigration Office. The Canadian and Mexican borders became the most used routes

[9] Eliot Grinnell Mears, *Resident Orientals on the American Pacific Coast* (New York: Institute of Pacific Relations 1927), p. 127.
[10] Mary R. Coolidge, *op. cit.*, p. 278.

for the "bootlegging" of Chinese immigrants. Following the Exclusion Act of 1882, Chinese laborers, by paying a head tax, could still go to Canada until 1923. This placed them closer to the United States. In many places the boundary line between the two countries is practically uninhabited and people can walk across almost any time.

The entire northern boundary of our nation, from the Lake of the Woods to the Pacific Coast, is a gigantic wilderness. The prairie, the plains of the western provinces, and the thick-clustered mountains of British Columbia are repeated in our Minnesota, North Dakota, Montana, Idaho, and Washington. Geologically and naturally there is no difference between the countries, the boundary line is an arbitrary mark. At intervals of a mile apart this otherwise intangible division is established by means of surveyors' "monuments" that are imbedded in the earth and stand slightly above it, each marked "B.A." on one side and "U.S.A." on the other. There are few settlements on the line — almost none — and the whole region is practically known to men only as they cross it by the water-course in canoes, or the far-apart trails of the great grass plateaus, and of the valleys between the mountains. There is no part over which a China-man may not pass into our country without fear of hindrance; there are scarcely any parts of it where he may not walk boldly across it at high noon. Indeed, the same is measurably the case all along our northern boundary — even upon the St. Lawrence north of our state, where smuggling has always been a means of livelihood whenever varying tariffs made it remunerative.[11]

But not all have come in by this easy method. Many have been smuggled across. The Commissioner of Immigration has said:

In my last annual report, reference was made to information which had been received from various sources indicating that those interested in the unlawful traffic of smuggling Chinese into the United States were planning intensive campaigns for the introduction of Chinese into our country by "underground methods." This had particular application to operations along the seacoast of Maine, which were then under investigation, it having been learned from a reliable source that smugglers were operating from St. John, New Brunswick, the practice being to move the Chinese to the boundary by automobile and thence proceed by boat to various points along the coast. Owing to the fact that

[11] J. Ralph, "The Chinese Leak," *Harper's Magazine*, 82 (1891), p. 520.

all the officers in the district concerned were required to work long hours in connection with their routine duties of inspection, it was only as a result of great sacrifice on their part that the various clues were followed and the final apprehension of the guilty parties brought about, there having been taken into custody at the same time eight contraband Chinese. Our officers likewise seized the motor boat in which the Chinese were being transported. This boat, which is said to have been built at a cost of $1500, has now been turned over to our service for patrol duty. The breaking up of this gang of notorious Chinese smugglers was most fortunate, and no doubt will have a salutary effect upon others in the vicinity who heretofore have been engaged in like unlawful operations.[12]

Before 1921 Chinese laborers could enter Mexico and then cross the border into the United States. This border line is just as easy to cross as the one between Canada and the United States.

The border towns on the Mexican side are generally filled with large numbers of Chinese obviously waiting only for a favorable opportunity to enter this country. They do not seek work at these towns, and remain there idle, in Chinese lodging houses and restaurants, until a safe avenue of entrance to this country is opened. It is impossible to police effectively the entire stretch of that long frontier. The port of Ensenada in Lower California, about 40 miles below San Diego, was formerly a point where they disembarked in numbers, the border being conveniently near. Now Guaymas, inside the Gulf of California (with a direct railroad line to Nogales in Arizona), Mazatlan, and San Blas, farther down the Mexican coast, are the points where the sea transit often ends, whatever the asserted destination. While with Chihuahua, Saltillo, the City of Mexico, and other interior points as ostensible destinations, Chinese going by rail transit are unloaded at the first convenient station across the Mexican border, so that along the lines of travel, as at Eagle Pass, El Paso, and Nogales, there is a concentration, in the Mexican villages near the line, of Chinese awaiting an opportunity to enter this country. The Chinamen themselves generally have no knowledge where they are going, and various unmistakable indications show that their only conception is that ultimately they will be landed in the United States by the various mysterious agencies who seem to guarantee this result.[13]

[12] Extract from *Annual Report of Commissioner General of Immigration* 1920, p. 419.
[13] Extract from United States Senate, *Chinese Exclusion, Testimony taken before the Committee on Immigration* 1902, pp. 216–217.

Some Chinese laborers have been smuggled in from the West Indian Islands but it is hard to determine the number. The Bureau of Immigration report of 1920 places the following facts before us:

> Briefly, it may be stated that the bureau's investigators found that there are now in Cuba some 30,000 young Chinese aliens, many of whom have proceeded there in the past two or three years because of the known facility with which admission to that country could be obtained and with the fixed purpose in mind of later, as opportunity might seem to offer, making their way to nearby inaccessible and unguarded points on the Florida coast, and entering surreptitiously; that these Chinese in Cuba, for the most part, are unemployed, are not seeking employment, and, in fact, there is no employment there for them; that, notwithstanding these conditions, young Chinese in relatively large numbers are still proceeding to Cuba, with no fixed intention of remaining there; that a not inconsiderable number of persons resident in Havana are engaged in the smuggling of aliens of all classes, narcotics, and whisky to points on the Florida coast, and even to points on our coast line more distant, as far north as New York and west as far as New Orleans; that a considerable number of power launches, of good speed and capable of carrying from 20 to 40 or 50 aliens, are available at all times in Havana and neighboring harbors; that Chinese aliens are willing to pay anywhere from $500 to $1000 to be smuggled across and into the United States, and aliens of other nationalities from $100 to $200; that a well organized ring, or rings, for the smuggling in of Chinese exists, with ramifications throughout this country and extending to Cuba; and that, as a matter of fact, the smuggling of aliens from Cuba is virtually rampant.[14]

Chinese have been smuggled into this country by every means of transportation: automobiles, boats, airplanes, etc. Many escape detection, and this has led to the stopping of Chinese in America who must prove their right to be in the country by a legal certificate. Whole Chinese quarters, in Cleveland, Chicago, Boston, Philadelphia, New York, and other cities have been raided for the purposes of locating those who have entered the United States illegally, but this practice has been discontinued.

There have been instances where Chinese sailors have entered this country illegally.

[14] Bureau of Immigration, *1922 Report*, pp. 15–16.

At one time there were from three to five thousand such sea-men (Chinese) in the port of New York alone, having been discharged from vessels on which their arrival occurred while such vessels were laid up awaiting an improvement in shipping conditions. The presence of so many idle and in many cases destitute Chinese seamen in New York at one time was a matter of grave concern not only to the bureau but to the local state and city authorities. Now that, according to reports, many of these Chinese have drifted into employment in neighboring manufac-turing plants the problem has become even more acute. . . While these Chinese are proper subjects for deportation, both under our Chinese exclusion laws and our general immigration act, it would cost probably as much as half a million dollars to deport them, and the funds are not available.[15]

DISTRIBUTION

AT FIRST the Chinese population in this country was concen-trated on the Pacific Coast, but now they are found in every state in the Union. As late as 1870, 99 per cent of the Chi-nese gainfully employed were west of the Rocky Mountains. While the greatest numbers are found in California, the dis-tribution is such that it no longer attracts so much attention.

Following the agitation for exclusion and the objections to Chinese in certain occupations, they left the rural districts. Now they are largely an urban population segregated in Chinatowns throughout the United States. These isolated communities serve the same purpose as do the other foreign colonies in our large industrial cities. They are cultural areas where the Chinese can live in accordance with their traditional customs, and thus accommodate themselves to American life.

San Francisco has not only the largest but one of the most important Chinatowns in the United States. The first colony had its origin during the Gold Rush, but was de-stroyed by the earthquake in 1906. Like other immigrant settlements, it was in the slum with the worst sort of tene-ments and basement apartments. The new Chinatown was constructed on the site of the old and has many shops that cater to tourists who are anxious to see the Orient as it exists in America.

[15] Extract from *Annual Report of the Commissioner General of Immigration* 1922, p. 12.

In Chicago there has been a Chinatown of importance since 1880. Its location is partly in the old "red-light" district. While this section has been improved by the Chinese it is closely associated with some of the most deteriorated areas in the city. In New York, Chinatown is near the Bowery, in an area where buildings are old and dilapidated. These are some of the most outstanding Chinese settlements, but every city of any size on the Pacific Coast has its Chinatown — Oakland, Los Angeles, Seattle, Portland, etc. They are found also in many mid-western and eastern cities.

It is well known that as soon as the Chinese Exclusion Law stopped the flow of immigrants, the domiciled population began to scatter, forming little "China towns" in all the large cities of the country. The percentage of the total Chinese population resident in California dropped from approximately 100 per cent in 1860 to 46.7 per cent in 1920. When the flow of newcomers was stopped the domiciled Chinese business men were forced to look to Americans for customers and this necessitated a wider distribution throughout the country as the forms of business in which the Chinese participated were of a rather limited variety.[16]

Chinatown as a segregated cultural area has an important function to play in the lives of the immigrants who come there to live. It provides a setting for transplanting some of the Oriental institutions and customs into a strange Occidental environment. Located near the central business districts of most large cities, these cultural areas are places of accommodation where the Chinese can live in accordance with their traditional customs, thus avoiding the disorganization that results from having to make an abrupt cultural transition.

SOCIAL INTERACTION AND ADJUSTMENTS

WHEN the Chinese first reached the Pacific shores of the United States they were probably as well adjusted as any foreign group that has come to America. They were well oriented because they found a place in the social and economic situation of the pioneer days in California. They were valuable since they did work that white miners did not wish to do, and were unobtrusive in their adjustments, espe-

16 R. D. McKenzie, *op. cit.*, p. 169.

cially in their economic accommodations, which were the important ones during the Gold Rush. In their cultural life they lived apart and followed their Oriental customs and traditions. For that early period, they had made an ideal accommodation, since they were desired by the whites and in turn they needed the Americans so that they might be employed at all times. This mutualism which existed as a form of accommodation was a part of a frontier situation.

But as a region passes from a pioneer to a settled condition, the human material that was once of value becomes a source of annoyance and trouble. The entire Caucasian fringe of the Pacific is studded with pockets of Asiatic peoples whose ancestors were induced to come to supply a pioneer demand for unskilled labor. But as these pioneer conditions gradually pass into established settlements, anti-Oriental sentiment emerges, finding expression in restrictive legislation, local and national. Moreover, the immigration once artificially stimulated tends to develop a spontaneous flow which does not readily respond to changes in demand or sentiment. This is especially true of labor that is transported a great distance. The ebb and flow of labor to nearby sources of employment is much more sensitive to changes in demand.[17]

As we have seen, the people newly established on the Pacific Coast had not objected to the presence of the Chinese so long as the white settlers were successful in mining activities or hoped to be successful. Not until there was some evidence of failure, some demonstration of unemployment or competition with the immigrants from the Orient did antagonism become any more than an individual affair. It took some crisis situation to inculcate race prejudice in groups with similar interests; they saw themselves as having certain definite rights to protect. The boom in California, with its prosperity and promise of wealth, was not marked by a crisis, but the aftermath was characterized by elements similar to those found following any unusual happening.

Nothing like a crisis happened in California before 1870. During those pioneer days the demand of labor was always greater than the supply. White labor was absorbed in more remunerative fields than those in which the Chinese were engaged, and the small amount of white labor in proportion to the work to be

<hr/>

[17] *Ibid.*, p. 12.

done left a vacuum which the Chinese only partly filled. . . In 1869 about ten thousand Chinese, and between two and three thousand whites, were discharged upon the completion of the Pacific railroads, and many of them wandered back to the Pacific Coast. With them also came a stream of white immigrants from the Eastern states who found in the newly completed railways an easy means of getting to the other end of the continent. In 1868 and 1869 there came into the state of California 59,000 white immigrants — a number more than double the net increase of the ten years previous. This heavy immigration precipitated the inevitable fall of wages, which had remained extraordinarily high as a consequence of isolation and the conditions of pioneer mining. . . By the winter of 1870–71 there were three men — two white and one yellow — for every job in San Francisco. This was the first period of crisis.

The second crisis came about 1876. The effects of a general panic which started in New York City in 1873 began about this time to reach California. Depression had set in there later than in the other states. Meanwhile, in the three years 1873, 1874, and 1875, approximately 150,000 immigrants from the East had entered the state. The flood of Chinese immigrants reached the high water mark in 1876, when the officials reported 22,943 arrivals. Consequently, when the crisis came in 1876, the usual number of unemployed always to be found in San Francisco was augmented many fold. It was estimated that in 1876–77 there were in San Francisco 10,000 men out of employment.[18]

After this, whenever a depression occurred in any of the western states, it was not difficult for agitators to direct attention to the Chinese. Their presence became the accepted explanation for all economic suffering, especially if Chinese could be found at work when whites were unemployed.

In a crisis situation there must always be some object, symbol, or slogan around which a group can organize its attitudes. Rarely has a group in a critical situation been able to react to a total situation which at this time was a period of general depression with myriad factors involved. In these complexities the Chinese had a part. Many of them were at work while thousands of whites were unemployed. They became at once undesirable aliens who were crowding out the native workers. They became the objects around

---

[18] Ching Chao Wu, *Chinatowns: A Study of Symbiosis and Assimilation* 1928, pp. 56–58. (Doctoral dissertation at present deposited in the University of Chicago Library.)

which sentiments could be organized. The Chinese, instead of other immigrant peoples, were selected as a cause of all suffering since they were not whites, and furthermore were representatives of a culture more at variance with American social organizations than were the cultures brought from Europe. Their differences were no longer a matter for curiosity, but causes for derision. Their dissimilarities in color, customs, dress, language, and religion all became cynosures in the labor agitation that grew in intensity with the rise of the Workingmen's Party in 1877.

The matter of reacting to only one aspect of a total situation is not a new phenomenon, as we shall see later in the chapter on *The Problem of Immigration*. In any crowd or group situation, attention is seldom directed toward more than a part of the entire combination of circumstances. It is in this way that most prejudices are developed. While the Chinese were competitors in certain trades, and while most leading statesmen saw the need for their restriction, the Chinese were not the chief factor in the situation on the Pacific Coast. Misery and unemployment would have continued even if they had all been deported.

Agitation against the Chinese started with laborers, the group in direct economic competition with the Orientals. Labor organizations connected with various industries in which Chinese were employed led the movement for exclusion. These organizations soon united to form the Workingmen's Party. During any racial disturbance hoodlums usually have a chance to give vent to their attitudes concerning life and this proved to be no exception. The Chinese suffered greatly at the hands of the idlers in the coast cities. Anti-Chinese agitation became so widespread that politicians were not able to ignore the Chinese if they expected to win the votes of the workingmen. It proved to be the easiest way for a politician, little known, to gain popularity and support. While the attack was led by the Workingmen's Party, both the Republican and Democratic Parties included anti-Chinese planks in their platforms as early as 1876. These elements in society were supported by some of the newspapers on the Pacific Coast which became important organs in disseminating anti-Chinese attitudes. Meetings, parades, and demonstrations became valuable means of influencing public opinion. Out of this agitation came the Los Angeles massacre of 1871 and the Sand-lot riot of 1877, as well as other disturbances.

The Chinese had to make an adjustment to this situation and they have been able to do so, as shown by the following statement made by Dr. Robert E. Park after his experiences in the Race Relations Survey on the Pacific Coast:

> In spite of the bitter antagonism that once existed toward the Chinese, the attitude of the Pacific coast is now generally amiable, even indulgent; and this in spite of the nuisance of their tong wars and other racial eccentricities.[19]

Now we shall turn to a more detailed discussion of the manner in which the accommodation was made. At first, although most of the Chinese entered occupational fields with which they were unfamiliar in China, their occupational adjustments were very satisfactory even so far as Americans were concerned. The Orientals did the work that the white miners did not wish to do and when a few Chinese turned to mining, they worked the less desirable mines and little economic friction resulted. Following the rush of mining days and the completion of transcontinental railways, when there was much unemployment, the Chinese on the Pacific Coast were discovered to be in many occupations with the white laborers. The focus of attention on this fact by politicians and labor organizations led to a gradual withdrawal on the part of Chinese from employment where they were in direct competition with citizens and prospective citizens of the United States. They are no longer an important factor in manufacturing, mining, railroad construction, domestic service, or farming; rather they are becoming an urban population after experimenting in many occupational fields.

They tried this and that, finding more hostility here and less conflict there. In some occupations they found that the white laborers were quite numerous, and that their presence caused animosity at times. In other occupations the competition was

[19] Robert E. Park, "Our Racial Frontier on the Pacific," *Survey*, 56 (1926), p. 196.

not so keen, and they remained unmolested for a long time. Through a long process of adjustment, the Chinese are now, with proper numbers, in those occupations where they supplement the whites, but do not compete with them. Something approaching commensalism is brought about. The relations of the two races have become symbiotic rather than social. They live side by side, but they live on the whole in different worlds.[20]

. . . The Chinese have gradually withdrawn from most of the competitive occupations. They are no longer engaged in agriculture, in the logging camps, or in the mines. They participate, to a very limited extent, in types of business in which Americans compete. Their sphere in business is confined almost exclusively to transactions with their own people or to supplying wants in the American community uncatered to by whites. To be sure, much of the Chinese business is of the parasitic type, such as gambling, dealing in narcotics, smuggling, and the like. Although detrimental to the white community, these occupations do not give rise to competition with whites to any considerable extent, and when they do, the competition is of such a nature that the white competitor cannot enlist the sympathy of the American people to assist him in combating his Oriental rival.

. . . The tendency of the Chinese with reference to place distribution has been such as to provoke a minimum of irritation among the whites. Along with their pronounced tendency during the past twenty years to distribute themselves throughout all the states of the Union, there has also been a correspondingly marked tendency on their part to segregate in the hearts of a few of the very large cities of the country. These two tendencies make for place relations least provocative of irritation. The total Chinese population of the country is so widely distributed that it does not appear menacing in any particular spot. On the other hand, the fact that the Chinese are segregated near the centers of the larger cities gives them an impersonal relationship in our communal structure, and permits them to live with less enforced contact with the American people. Instead of being considered as a disturbing element in our communal life, the Chinatown, in some cities at least, is looked upon as a commercial asset — a sort of human zoo — which becomes a point of attraction for tourists.[21]

This, then, has been the way in which the Chinese have finally adjusted themselves in America.

The Chinatowns with their Oriental customs and tradi-

[20] Ching Chao Wu, *op. cit.*, p. 93.
[21] R. D. McKenzie, "The Oriental Invasion," *Journal of Applied Sociology*, 10 (1925), pp. 125–126.

tions, for which Chinese have been condemned, have been the real mediums of adjustment in the United States.

> Chinatown . . . affords a milieu where the Chinese feel comfortable and safe. No one will stare at him, make fun of him, nor mistreat him there. Here he may eat with chop-sticks instead of knife and fork, drink tea instead of cold water, wear comfortable dress instead of stiff collar and unmanageable tie, talk and swear in Cantonese dialect and indulge in a cup of Wu Chah Pi or a game of Fan Tan. . .
>
> It is only in Chinatown that a Chinese immigrant has society, friends, and relatives who share his dreams and hopes, his hardships and adventures. Here he can tell a joke and make everybody laugh with him; here he may hear folk tales told and retold, which create the illusion that Chinatown is really China.[22]

Like other immigrant groups in the United States, the Chinese have their own organizations for the regulation of their daily lives. Most important in the adjustment process are district associations, known in this country as the " Six Companies." These district associations are to be found in the large cities of China where they exist as social centers. The membership of an association in this country is often made up of people who come from the same region in China, but in other cases members may be from several districts. These associations exist for mutual protection and aid. The officers give advice and assistance and are able to settle most of the difficulties that may arise between members.

In addition to these district associations, there are guilds which protect the individual in a particular commercial activity, in his relationships with other Chinese in the same business. This assures an adequate economic adjustment for all.

The Chinese have transplanted their temples which are found in many Chinatowns. These are particularly valued by the older generation, who can turn to the idols or gods in a critical period. Of equal importance to the immigrant generation is the cemetery where offerings are made at the tombs in the spring and autumn. Protestant churches and missions play an active rôle among the Chinese, especially in an educational way. The Y.M.C.A. has held a prominent

[22] Ching Chao Wu, *op. cit.*, pp. 157–158.

place, also. Many adult Chinese enlist the aid of these organizations in learning English.

Theaters and the press are other institutional means for making adjustments in the United States. The dramatic productions of the Chinese are lengthy affairs, but the people are accustomed to this. Newspapers are usually sponsored by some nationalistic organization and keep the Chinese in America well informed concerning political activities in their native land. Many of these nationalistic organizations are secret societies which had their inception in China during some political crisis. The restaurants and stores are the social centers of Chinatown.

Language schools in the Chinatowns have prevented a break between the immigrant generation and those born in the United States who attend the American schools. They have provided a means for understanding the traditions, customs, and ideas of the parents with whom the children must live, and have prevented in no small degree a conflict of cultures in its most disorganizing and demoralizing form.

One of the most outstanding instances of the tendency toward Americanization is the establishment of the Chinese-American Citizen Alliance. Unlike the nationalistic organizations, it is interested in political life in the United States. Its main purpose is to protect the Chinese against discriminating legislation and to maintain a high status for the Chinese in America, in their relationships outside of Chinatown.

An interesting phase of the life in an American Chinatown is the annual celebration of numerous festivals significant in the social heritage of the Chinese. The Double Ten, or the National Holiday of China on October tenth, is just as important as the fourth of July in America. The New Year festival is second in value only to the observance of the National Holiday. Other celebrations of importance are the Festival of Lanterns; Visiting of Tombs; the Double Seven; the Festival of All Souls; the Festival of the Full Moon; the Winter Solstice Festival; and the Children's Festival. While these are not fully appreciated by Americans, they play a stabilizing rôle in the life of the Chinese although they emphasize the fact that the habitués of Chinatown are Oriental and far removed from assimilation into Occidental culture. These festivals, however, have their share in promoting adjustments for the Chinese; at least they are a means of prevention of disorganization.

One thing that has hindered the adjustment of the Chinese in the United States is the lack of family life and the great disparity between the sexes. When we consider the important rôle that the family plays in China, this fact becomes more significant. It is in the mores of the Orient that every normal man shall marry and raise a family. There is no greater calamity in life than to fail in this respect; success is more or less contingent upon the prescribed marital union.

Chinese laborers have not been able to bring their wives to the United States since the Exclusion Act of 1882. Those who are citizens have been denied this privilege since 1924. While there have been strenuous objections to this legislation, the fact still remains that Chinese immigration included a very small percentage of women even when there were no legal restrictions. Considering the attitudes regarding marriage this would be hard to understand if one did not know that a married woman has been selected by her parents-in-law and belongs to them as much as or more than she does to her husband. Economic factors and the treatment at the port of debarkation have also been instrumental in keeping the Chinese women in their native land.

Many Chinese men living alone in the United States are married but their families are in China. This, however, does not permit the establishment of a normal family life and does not help make Chinatown a normal community. There is little likelihood that this condition will change. The Chinese population in this country will remain predominantly a male population, denied the advantages that accrue through the presence of children in American schools where the process of Americanization is greatly aided even for parents.

The lack of a familial accommodation in America is somewhat compensated for by the clan organization characteristic of Chinese society. People of the same surname in China have a common ancestral hall and live in the same locality. This is carried out to a certain degree in the United States. The clan organization is a protective and a philanthropic association. The transplantation of the clan to America gives each person a chance to enjoy some privileges similar at least to those derived from the family.

Like all other immigrant groups the Chinese have had some individuals who have made social pathological adjustments. As we have seen, the Chinese have been driven out of many legitimate occupations and have, as an accommodation to this fact, entered parasitic occupations instead. In the matter of crime, the Chinese have been guilty of many offenses against public decency and good morals. This category includes gambling, vagrancy, and vice. They have also been found as violators of the narcotic and smuggling laws. Despite their participation in these anti-social activities, they are not considered a criminal group, since their offenses do not include white Americans to any great extent. They can commit crimes against themselves and other nonwhite groups without being regarded by officials as a dangerous class — an interesting commentary on American ethnocentrism.[23]

The Chinese adjustment in the United States that has attracted the most attention is the one made through the tong organizations. Daily papers have found the activities of the tongs interesting and colorful news. The presence of these societies in Chinatown has labeled the Chinese as undesirables much as the " Black Hand " activities of the Italians operated in singling them out as dangerous immigrants. In describing a tong, Dr. Wu said:

A tong is an organization to accommodate the gambling and vice interests in a hostile environment. It protects and helps its members who are engaged in these and other illegal businesses such as smuggling. At first its members consisted of " unprincipled " persons. As its influence increases, merchants join it for business' sake, and honest persons also become its members in order to be free from the annoyance of the rough element of the tongs.[24]

[23] See *Report on Crime and the Foreign Born*, National Commission on Law Observance and Enforcement, No. 10, June 24, 1931.

[24] Ching Chao Wu, *op. cit.*, p. 210.

It is true that any organization reveals the interests, attitudes, and to a certain extent the character of the people who constitute its membership. Most important of all, it reveals the historical experiences of a group and their conception of how situations should be met as a result of their experiences. Two things must be considered in relation to an organization: the experiences of the people who make up the organization and the manner in which they interpret the situation in which the organization is to function.

The tongs in the United States have a close relationship to many activities of the Chinese population which is predominantly male. Protection for gambling and vice has been an important function of the tongs. Dr. Wu has explained the relationship to these two activities:

> Gambling is deeply rooted in the folkways of the Cantonese, and most Chinese peasants learned to gamble before they came to this country. . .
> These peasants, when they landed at San Francisco, brought with them their gambling habits just as inevitably as the Puritans brought with them their rules of Sunday observance. The desire to gamble was further stimulated by the gambling atmosphere then existing in San Francisco. San Francisco was at this time a frontier town, a " man's town." It has remained more or less a frontier town for the Chinese to this day.[25]

When laws were passed prohibiting gambling, the Chinese carried it on in a clandestine fashion. To do this they realized that there would have to be protection much as is found in the underworld of American cities among native-born and with other nationalities. Tongs were organized to make gambling safe after the fashion of large gambling syndicates. In the same manner protection has been secured for vice. Chinatown has a male population with a paucity of family life. As a result of this abnormal situation vice became an organized business that turned to tongs for protection. The greatest enemies of this parasitic business were the Christian missions organized to free the women brought from China for immoral purposes.[26]

Since the passage of the Chinese Exclusion Law in 1882, and the bill of 1909 prohibiting the importation of opium,

[25] *Ibid.*, pp. 191–192.   [26] *Ibid.*, Chapter X, pp. 190–211.

it is said that the tongs have been active in smuggling into the United States both immigrants and opium. Not only have they been involved in "bootlegging" opium, but they have sold their services for the protection of opium dens.

To be a tong member, one is protected in conducting illegal and immoral business. This fact differentiates a tong from other benevolent protective societies such as district association or family society. The latter protect their members if they stay within the bounds of law and morality. The Young Wo district association, for example, definitely states in its constitution that "difficulty brought upon men by their own vices and follies will not receive attention. Thievery and receiving of stolen goods will not be protected; nor will troubles in bawdy-houses, nor those in gambling houses, nor debts to such . . . nor smuggling, nor any violation of American laws." [27]

The presence of tongs in Chinatowns of America has been revealed largely through tong wars. When hostilities cannot be settled by arbitration, then a war follows. These conflicts are usually over territorial rights in some city which involve a monopoly of profits from gambling and vice. These wars have brought the Chinese into disrepute in the United States.

We have seen that an individual of the immigrant generation cannot be assimilated. Coming as an adult from a culture unlike that found in America, he remains in large part under the influence of his early experiences. He may acquire some of the behavior patterns of Americans but these are always mere accommodations to an unavoidable situation. The adjustments of those of the second generation are not in terms of the Chinese culture alone, since they are forced, sooner or later, to live in two social worlds. It is the Oriental of the second generation who will find a problem of adjustment in the United States.

In the traditional Chinese family there is no doubt as to the position of each member. The father's supreme authority in the group is accepted; the children accept a rôle of subordination. In the United States the children of Chinese immigrants do not remain wholly within the Oriental culture. In the schools and on the playgrounds they assimilate,

[27] *Ibid.*, pp. 207–208.

consciously or unconsciously, American ideas and patterns
of behavior which result in conflicts within the family;
thus the customary alignments in the marital group are
challenged.

Despite the fact that those of the second generation do
absorb American ideas from their environment, they do not
escape the influence of their homes wherein they spent their
pre-school days when the foundations were laid for their social natures. The Chinese ideas which were early instilled
are unwittingly influenced during the contacts of the children with American life even though these children may, in
extreme cases, be ashamed of their homes. These facts keep
them from being entirely assimilated in the culture in the
United States and thus their acceptance outside their homes
will probably not be complete.

Another factor that prevents complete assimilation on the
part of many American-born Chinese is the definition given
them by Americans because of their color. This racial characteristic singles them out as different and they are regarded
as foreigners for this reason. It is difficult for them to think
of themselves as Americans when they are constantly defined
as aliens. They are discriminated against in the same manner as are the foreign-born. There is a tendency to cate-
gorize all individuals of an ethnic or racial group. Though a
Chinese may be Occidental in culture, he is an Oriental to
most people.

This definition often results in the American-born of Chinese parentage losing their interest in being American. This
we observed to be the case with many European immigrants
also. When Chinese discover that they are not accepted as
Americans they become more interested in things Oriental
and withdraw from American social life. The matter of re-
treating from American life is not easy since there is not a
familiar place to which the individual of the second generation can retire. He is not entirely within the Chinese culture. He would not feel absolutely at home in an American
Chinatown and he would be a greater cultural stranger in
the Orient. Usually he speaks English better than he does
Chinese. His mental organization of ideas and ideals is

American but his appearance is Oriental.
ing makes him a misfit in Chinatown ar
pearance prevents a ready acceptance in A

The conflict that often exists in such
in the following statement:

For many years I struggled between the tv
doing things, the way my parents brought i.. ..p,
that I became acquainted with in college. I really feel that I
have had the chance to know the best in conservative Chinese and
in American life, but for a long time I tried to decide which of the
two was better and which I should follow. But now I try to think
of it as little as possible, I do what seems to me sensible, and
think about the conflict only when some situation arises that
forces me to think about it.[28]

In this situation there is often produced an atomized individual who is not controlled by the conventionalized behavior of either culture. It is in this group that pathological
adjustments are frequently found.

[28] *Ibid.*, p. 329.

READINGS

GENERAL

Coolidge, Mary Roberts, *Chinese Immigration.* 1909
—— " Chinese Labor Competition on the Pacific Coast,'' *Annals,*
34, 1909
Department of Labor, *Treaty, Laws, and Rules Governing the
Admission of Chinese.* 1926
George, H., " The Kearney Agitation in California," *Popular Sci-
ence Monthly,* 17, 1880
McKenzie, Roderick D., *Oriental Exclusion.* 1927
O'Meara, J., " San Francisco in Early Days," *Overland,* n.s. 1,
1883
—— " The Chinese in Early Days," *Overland,* n.s. 3, 1884
Richardson, A. D., " John," *Atlantic Monthly,* 24, 1869
" The Celestials at Home and Abroad," *Blackwood's Edinburgh
Magazine,* 72, 1852
Wu, Ching Chao, *Chinatowns: A Study of Symbiosis and As-
similation.* 1928

COMPOSITION

Davis, J. J., " A Century of Immigration," *Monthly Labor Review,* 18, 1924

. S., " Chinese Workmen in America," *Independent,* 75, 1913
odenough, F. L., " Racial Differences in the Intelligence of School Children," *J. Exp. Psy.,* 9, 1926
Graham, V. T., " The Intelligence of Chinese Children in San Francisco," *J. Comp. Psy.,* 6, 1926
Maitland, W., " The Chinaman in California and South Africa," *Contemporary Rev.,* 88, 1905
Murdoch, K., " Study of Differences Found between Races in Intellect and in Morality," *School and Society,* 22, 1925
Roberts, S. H., *Population Problems of the Pacific.* 1927
Sandiford, P. and Kerr, R., " Intelligence of Chinese and Japanese Children," *J. Educ. Psy.,* 17, 1926
Young, K. T., " The Intelligence of Chinese Children in San Francisco and Vicinity," *J. App. Psy.,* 5, 1921
Wu, Ching Chao, *Chinatowns: A Study of Symbiosis and Assimilation.* 1928

THE JOURNEY

Davis, J. J., " Bootleg Immigrants," *Review of Reviews,* 67, 1923
Foster, J. W., " The Chinese Boycott," *Atlantic Monthly,* 97, 1906
Hao, F. C., " My Reception in America," *Outlook,* 86, 1907
" In Chinatown and in China," *Nation,* 121, 1925
Ralph, J., " The Chinese Leak," *Harper's Magazine,* 82, 1891
Wu, Ching Chao, *Chinatowns: A Study of Symbiosis and Assimilation.* 1928

DISTRIBUTION

Asbury, H., " Doyers Street," *American Mercury,* 8, 1926
Clark, H., " Chinese in New York City," *Century,* n.s. 31, 1896
Foo, Wong Chin, " Chinese in New York," *Cosmopolitan,* 5, 1888
White, F. W., " Last Days of Chinatown in New York," *Harper's Weekly,* 51, 1907
Wu, Ching Chao, *Chinatowns: A Study of Symbiosis and Assimilation.* 1928

SOCIAL INTERACTION AND ADJUSTMENTS

A Half Chinese, " Persecution and Oppression of Me," *Independent,* 71, 1911
Andrews, S., " The Gods of Wo Lee," *Atlantic Monthly,* 25, 1870
—— " Wo Lee and His Kinsfolk," *Atlantic Monthly,* 25, 1879
Asbury, H., " Doyers Street," *American Mercury,* 8, 1926
Bennett, J. E., " Chinese Tong Wars in San Francisco," *Harper's Weekly,* 44, 1900
Block, E. B., " Fighting the Opium Ring," *Overland,* n.s. 58, 1911
Chew, Lee, " The Biography of a Chinaman," *Independent,* 55, 1903
" Chinese Highbinders," *Current Literature,* 27, 1900

Clark, F. S., " Seats down Front," *Sunset,* 54, 1925
Connor, J. F., " A Western View of the Chinese in the United States," *Chautauquan,* 32, 1901
Davis, J. J., " Bootleg Immigrants," *Review of Reviews,* 67, 1923
Drachsler, J., *Intermarriage in New York City*
Dyer, F. J., " Rebuilding Chinatown," *World Today,* 8, 1905
Fairchild, Henry P., *The Melting Pot Mistake*
Far, Sui Sin, " Her Chinese Husband," *Independent,* 69, 1910
—— " Leaves from the Mental Portfolio of an Eurasian," *Independent,* 66, 1909
Fitch, G. H., " In a Chinese Theatre," *Century,* n.s. 2, 1882
Fong, W. N., " Chinese Labor Unions in America," *Chautauquan,* 23, 1906
—— " The Chinese Six Companies," *Overland,* n.s. 23, 1894
Foo, Wong Chin, " Chinese in New York," *Cosmopolitan,* 5, 1888
Goldenweiser, A., " Race and Culture in the Modern World," *Jour. Soc. Forces,* 3, 1924
Gregory, J. W., *The Menace of Color*
Hayes, A. A., " A Symposium on the Chinese Question," *Scribner's,* 17, 1879
Jones, I., " Cathay on the Coast," *American Mercury,* 8, 1926
Leighton, C. C., *Life at Puget Sound*
Lewis, O., " Transplanted Section of the Orient," *Overland,* n.s. 70, 1917
Literary Digest, 83, Dec. 13, 1924, 56, 1918
Littleton, L. A., " Chinese Mythology in San Francisco," *Overland,* n.s. 1, 1883
Loomis, A. W., " The Six Chinese Companies," *Overland,* 1, 1868
McDowell, H. B., " The Chinese Theatre," *Century,* n.s. 7, 1884
McKenzie, R. D., " The Oriental Finds a Job," *Survey Graphic,* 9, 1926
—— " The Oriental Invasion," *Journal of Applied Sociology,* 10, 1925–26
MacNair, H. F., *The Chinese Abroad.* 1925
Maitland, W., " The Chinaman in California and South Africa," *Contemporary Review,* 88, 1905
Masters, F. J., " High-binders," *Chautauquan,* 14, 1892
—— " The Chinese Drama," *Chautauquan,* 21, 1895
Mears, E. G., *Resident Orientals on the American Pacific Coast.* 1927
Miller, J. F., " Certain Phases of the Chinese Question," *Overland,* 7, 1866
Moravsky, M., " Those Wicked Chinamen," *Outlook,* 131, 1922
M. T. F., *My Chinese Marriage*
Pang S., " Chinese in America," *Forum,* 32, 1902
Park, Robert E., " Behind Our Masks," *Survey Graphic,* 9, 1926

Park, Robert E., "Human Migration and the Marginal Man," *Am. Jour. Soc.*, 33, 1928
—— "Our Racial Frontier on the Pacific," *Survey Graphic*, 9, 1926
—— *The Immigrant Press and Its Control*, 1922
Park, R. E. and Miller, H. A., *Old World Traits Transplanted.* 1921
Reinsch, P. S., "The Attitude of the Chinese Towards Americans," *Annals*, 95, 1921
Report on Crime and the Foreign Born, National Commission on Law Observance and Enforcement, No. 10, June 24, 1931
Ritchie, R. W., "The Wars of the Tongs," *Harper's Weekly*, 54, 1910
Roberts, S. H., *Population Problems of the Pacific.* 1927
Schaffaner, H., "The Old Chinese Quarter," *Living Age*, 254, 1907
Seward, G. F., *Chinese Immigration*
Shaler, *The Neighbor.* 1904
Shewin, H., "Observation on the Chinese Labor," *Overland*, n.s. 7, 1886
Smith, W. C., "The Second Generation Oriental American," *Jour. of Applied Sociology*, 10, 1925
Stellman, L. J., "Chinese Reform in San Francisco," *World Today*, 20, 1911
Sterry, N., "Housing Conditions in Chinatown, Los Angeles," *Jour. of Applied Sociology*, 7, 1922
—— "Social Attitudes of Chinese Immigrants," *Jour. of Applied Sociology*, 7, 1923
Stoy, E. H., "Chinatown and the Curse that Makes it a Plaguespot in the Nation," *Arena*, 38, 1907
Taylor, W., "The Chinese Quarter of New York City," *Munsey*, 6, 1892
Tow, J. S., *The Real Chinese in America*
Trumbull, M. R., "Race Relations on the Pacific Coast," *Review of Nations*, No. 4, 1927
Washington, B. T., "The Race Problem in Arizona," *Independent*, 71, 1911
White, F. W., "Last Days of Chinatown in New York," *Harper's Weekly*, 51, 1907
Wilson, T. B., "Old Chinatown," *Overland*, n.s. 58, 1911
Wu, Ching Chao, *Chinatowns: A Study of Symbiosis and Assimilation.* 1928

CHAPTER XV

THE JAPANESE

THE JAPANESE migration to the United States had its inception much later than emigration from China. In fact, it had its origin about the time that the Chinese movement had ceased. It was not until 1885 that emigration was legalized by the Japanese government; even then the natives of Japan could not repudiate their allegiance to the Mikado by becoming citizens of another country. By 1896 an Emigrants' Protection Law had been passed by the Japanese parliament and companies were organized to aid immigrants in their relationships to this law; in some instances these companies were officially connected with labor contractors in the United States.

Like their Chinese predecessors the first Japanese immigrants were encouraged to come to America to meet the demand for unskilled labor, a demand accentuated by the sudden cessation of Chinese immigration. But the America which the Japanese entered was quite different from that to which the first Chinese had come some forty years before. During the intervening period the population of the Pacific coast had increased many fold; all the main railroad lines had been constructed; large cities had emerged, creating a demand for agricultural products and building materials. The early Japanese immigrants, therefore, especially those who came to the Pacific Northwest, passed their pioneer days in America working in gangs clearing land, doing unskilled work around saw mills and logging camps and seasonal work in the Alaska canneries.[1]

While the Japanese were received at first as a valuable labor supply, it was not long before racial consciousness began

[1] R. D. McKenzie, "The Oriental Finds a Job," *Survey*, 56 (1926), pp. 152–153.

to evidence itself in economic and cultural relationships with the Japanese. Anti-Japanese attitudes have had about the same history as have the sentiments of antagonism against the Chinese. First there was agitation on the Coast where there was a concentration of these Orientals, but the movement against them soon attracted wide attention and became national in its scope. The opposition to the presence of Japanese did not begin until 1900 and not then because of great numbers since there were fewer than twenty-five thousand in the United States at the beginning of the twentieth century. These, however, were concentrated in a few communities along the Pacific Coast, and it was here that the agitation for exclusion had its inception.[2]

In 1894, long before the protests against Japanese immigration were voiced, a treaty had been signed by Japan and the United States. This gave the citizens of either government the right to enter, travel, or reside in any part of the territory belonging to the other country, providing such did not conflict with any regulations already in existence within these countries. This was superseded by the treaty of February 21, 1911, which permitted the Japanese to come only for the purpose of trade. The former treaty had not so limited the stream of migration.

During the bubonic plague in San Francisco in 1900 only the Japanese and Chinese quarters were quarantined. This led to the formation of the "Japanese Association of America" for the protection of Japanese interests. The same year the San Francisco Labor Council held a mass meeting in which a resolution was passed asking that the Chinese exclusion laws be extended to include the Japanese and Korean laborers.

This was the first move toward making the Japanese question a political issue and it came at a time when the governmental situation in San Francisco was corrupt because of the type of municipal officials. The Labor Party was in power and the Japanese were the competitors of the laboring man.

[2] For an adequate and scholarly treatment of the development of the anti-Japanese sentiment, see R. L. Buell, "The Development of the Anti-Japanese Agitation in the United States," *Political Science Quarterly*, Vols. 37 and 38, Dec. 1922, and Dec. 1923.

The political leaders were anxious to divert public attention from their own misdemeanors, so endeavored to bring to the notice of the populace the "new Oriental peril." The Japanese government acted at once and amended the Emigration Law of 1896 in an effort to control the migration of laborers. For the first time the Gentlemen's Agreement became a factor in the regulation of immigration in 1900. While the nature of the Gentlemen's Agreement was kept a secret at this time, its contents were revealed in a note from Ambassador Hanihara to Secretary Hughes, dated April 10, 1924, which reads as follows:

One object of the Gentlemen's Agreement is . . . to stop the emigration to the United States of all Japanese laborers other than those excepted in the Agreement, which is embodied in a series of long and detailed correspondence between the two Governments, publication of which is not believed to serve any good purpose, but the essential terms and practice of which may be summed up as follows:

(1) The Japanese Government will not issue passports good for the Continental United States to laborers, skilled or unskilled, except those previously domiciled in the United States, or parents, wives, or children under twenty years of age of such persons. The form of the passport is so designed as to omit no safeguard against forgery, and its issuance is governed by various rules of detail in order to prevent fraud.

(2) Passports are to be issued by a limited number of specially authorized officials only, under close supervision of the Foreign Office, which has the supreme control of the matter and is equipped with the necessary staff for the administration of it. These officials shall make thorough investigation when application for passports is made by students, merchants, tourists, or the like, to ascertain whether the applicant is likely to become a laborer, and shall enforce the requirement that such person shall either be supplied with adequate means to insure the permanence of his status as such or that surety be given therefor. In case of any doubt as to whether such applicant is or is not entitled to a passport, the matter shall be referred to the Foreign Office for decision.

Passports to laborers previously domiciled in the United States will be issued only upon production of certificate from Japanese Consular officers in the United States, and passports to the parents, wives, and children of such laborers will be issued only upon production of such consular certificate and of duly certified copy of official registry of members of such laborer's family in

Japan. Utmost circumspection is exercised to guard against fraud.

(3) Issuance of passports to so-called " picture brides " has been stopped by the Japanese Government since March 1, 1920, although it had not been prohibited under the terms of the Gentlemen's Agreement.

(4) Monthly statistics covering incoming and outgoing Japanese are exchanged between the American and Japanese Governments.

(5) Although the Gentlemen's Agreement is not applicable to the Hawaiian Islands, measures restricting issuance of passports for the Islands are being enforced in substantially the same manner as those for the Continental United States.

(6) The Japanese Government are further exercising strict control over emigration of Japanese laborers to foreign territories contiguous to the United States in order to prevent their surreptitious entry into the United States.[3]

The context of this letter suggests that the political situation was not the only reason for agitation. Laborers kept coming despite the Gentlemen's Agreement. The powerful emigration companies were able to secure passports from the local officials so that laborers continued to go to the United States and Hawaii, greatly alarming the citizens on the Pacific Coast where most of them settled.

Many other happenings in the United States and Japan focussed attention on this recent Oriental invasion. The Japanese had appeared in an unfavorable light because of their demands following the Russo-Japanese War. There was consternation lest there might be an epidemic of emigration to escape the economic hardships following this conflict. The Japanese were making progress in their financial ventures in California, no longer being just laborers; they were in direct competition with white Americans. At this time there were a great many rumors concerning the dangers of Japanese immigration. The press became an important factor in anti-Japanese movements. Union labor became active and through the Labor Council of San Francisco urged a boycott on Japanese as well as on all whites who employed Japanese. In response to this agitation the Japanese government

---

[3] Extract from Ambassador Hanihara's Note respecting the "Gentlemen's Agreement" to Secretary Charles E. Hughes, reprinted in Raymond L. Buell, *Japanese Immigration* (World Peace Foundation Pamphlets 1924), pp. 359–360.

limited the number of workers who might emigrate to Hawaii to five hundred per ship, and finally suspended all emigration to Hawaii for a period.

By this time the Exclusionists were thoroughly aroused and were not satisfied with this move on the part of the Japanese government. The Exclusion League became active in a political sense and drafted the following platform asking

(1) that the Chinese exclusion laws be extended so as to exclude all classes of Japanese and Koreans, except those exempted by the terms of the Chinese Act, from the United States and its insular territories; (2) that the members of the League should pledge themselves not to employ nor patronize Japanese nor to patronize any person or firm employing Japanese or dealing in products coming from such firms; (3) that the action of the School Board in adopting a policy segregating Japanese from white children be approved; (4) that a propaganda campaign calling the attention of the President and Congress to this "menace" be undertaken; (5) that all labor and civic organizations in California be asked to contribute a fixed assessment to the cause.[4]

President Roosevelt urged a non-discriminatory policy and was far from favoring Japanese exclusion. Many leading citizens and organizations opposed the plan of activities of the League but certain events were occurring that spurred on its members. Following the earthquake of 1906 when they moved to many sections of the city formerly occupied only by whites, the segregation of the Japanese was broken up. A crime wave followed in the wake of the great disaster. Japanese restaurants were burned. Stores were burglarized and a few Japanese were killed.

In the political campaign of 1906 anti-Japanese propaganda was popular; both parties declared for exclusion. The California legislature contributed its share to the agitation against the Japanese by considering many anti-Japanese bills. The School Board of San Francisco ordered all Japanese children to attend the Oriental school in Chinatown. While this order was not carried out, it was not settled without a conference with the President in Washington.

[4] Raymond L. Buell, "Anti-Japanese Agitation in the United States," *Political Science Quarterly*, 37 (1922), p. 618.

The solution agreed upon was: (1) that the School Board would rescind its resolution ordering Japanese children to attend the Oriental School; (2) that the President would prevent Japanese in Hawaii, Canada, and Mexico from entering the United States on passports issued by Japan only to those destinations; (3) that the President would undertake to restrict Japanese emigration coming directly to the United States from Japan, by diplomatic means; (4) that the federal government would withdraw the suits instituted to test the constitutionality of the California school law.[5]

In all this agitation the Japanese government protested the action of the School Board but finally confirmed the Gentlemen's Agreement and assumed the responsibility of restricting emigration to the United States.

It had required seven years to bring about the prohibition of Japanese immigration. The first step had been taken in 1900 when Japan voluntarily prohibited the emigration of laborers to the United States. Upon the failure of this voluntary restriction, President Roosevelt took the second step, in March, 1907, when he prohibited the emigration of Japanese from Hawaii, Mexico, and Canada without proper passports. The third step came in December, 1907, when Japan entered into a Gentlemen's Agreement with Canada, which affected materially the United States, because it made smuggling over the Canadian border less probable. The fourth step came when an informal agreement to prohibit emigration to the United States was reached — an agreement which carried out and strengthened the restraints imposed in 1901, and which also prohibited, at least temporarily, emigration from Japan to Hawaii. Thus by 1908 the emigration of Japanese laborers to the United States, to Canada, and Hawaii had been severely restricted. As a result the San Francisco school controversy came to an end, and the agitation which had accompanied it temporarily died down.[6]

The agitation on the part of labor organizations resulted in a movement of many Japanese from the cities on the Pacific Coast to the rural districts where there had been little opposition to their presence. As greater numbers settled in the agricultural areas the attitudes of the white farmers changed and the most recent protests against Japanese settlements have come from the rural Americans.

The Exclusion League of California had never been satis-

[5] *Ibid.*, p. 631.   [6] *Ibid.*, p. 636.

fied with the Gentlemen's Agreement because Japanese immigrants continued to arrive. The state legislature had cherished the same feeling. Furthermore, both organizations thought that there was a problem with the resident Japanese on the Pacific Coast that could not be touched by the Gentlemen's Agreement. Each time the legislature convened, many anti-Japanese measures were introduced. Since the Japanese were going to the rural districts, the majority of these bills dealt with the right of land ownership by aliens. A land measure was finally passed but the Japanese were able to evade it with little difficulty. They could not buy more land, but were allowed to keep what they already had. The period of tenure on land that was leased could not exceed three years, but this was not especially effective since they could renew the lease when it had expired.

The means taken by the Japanese to evade the law and acquire title to real property were: (1) by dummy corporations in which the majority of the stock was held by American citizens (who might be Japanese children born here) but paid for and controlled by Japanese, themselves ineligible to own land; (2) by trusteeships, where Japanese paid American citizens to purchase land and hold it for them or for their children; (3) by guardianships, in which the Japanese parents, as guardians of their American-born children, purchased land in their name, but used it for themselves. The amount of land thus acquired by the Japanese was not very large. In the nine counties of Southern California only 518 acres of farm land and 47 city lots were acquired in the name of Japanese children in the seven years following 1913. Nevertheless, the Anti-Japanese League exhorted against the shocking immorality of the Japanese who stooped to such practices. But they failed to recognize that the evasions had been brought about by American lawyers, and that Americans themselves utilize every possible means of side-stepping laws affecting their own interests.[7]

Following the World War, anti-Japanese legislation was dropped by the California Senate at the request of Secretary Lansing who was in Paris at the Peace Conference. But the Hearst papers and anti-Japanese politicians did not subside. In 1919 the old Exclusion League became active again and asked that all Japanese immigrants be excluded, and that citi-

7 *Ibid.*, pp. 65–66.

zenship be denied all children born in the United States whose parents were ineligible to citizenship.

The Hearst papers, the Exclusion League, and the American Legion were now the active organizations working for Japanese exclusion. The War had made everyone more or less primarily interested in the welfare of his own country. It had aroused a great deal of ethnocentrism throughout the whole world. Politicians found Japanese exclusion a valuable issue for furthering their own interests. They were successful in having the land law changed through the ballot whereby aliens not eligible for citizenship could not lease agricultural lands. It was further designed to remove all possibilities of evasions that had been practiced by the Japanese in relation to an earlier land law. But the federal courts made it possible for them to use the lands as long as the white owners were willing to have them do so.

In the legislation of 1917 which included the " geographical delimitation clause," the Japanese discovered a statement that they considered had been placed there further to exclude the Japanese. The sentence reads as follows: " No alien now in any way excluded from, or prevented from entering, the United States shall be admitted to the United States." Certain classes of Japanese had been excluded under the Gentlemen's Agreement, and this statement was interpreted as excluding them by law.

The next gesture of importance which involved the Japanese was the Immigration Act of 1924 which excluded aliens ineligible to citizenship. Previous to this year the Japanese had to qualify under the Gentlemen's Agreement to enter the United States and the Japanese government was responsible for its enforcement. Under the exclusion law, the problems of administration were transferred to the United States. The Gentlemen's Agreement admitted all non-laborers and their relatives as well as laborers who were visiting abroad. The exclusion law denied admittance to all aliens ineligible to citizenship, except the following classes: (1) government officials; (2) merchants and tourists, in this country " temporarily"; (3) immigrants returning from a temporary visit abroad; (4) *bona fide* ministers and professors, their wives, and children under eighteen; (5) *bona fide* students at least fifteen years of age.

In Japan, governmental representatives, organization leaders, press correspondents, and other prominent citizens protested vehemently against this exclusion law. Anti-American demonstrations were carried out in some cities. A boycott of American products was attempted. Societies posted placards reading: "Hate Everything American." Propaganda was disseminated against the work of American missionaries.

In the United States there was not a unanimity of opinion. Most people favored the exclusion of Asiatic immigration, but many regarded the Gentlemen's Agreement as adequate for this purpose. Some were convinced that the Agreement was a failure and a third group thought further diplomatic procedure, supplanting the Agreement, would have been the logical means of excluding Asiatic immigrants who could not become citizens. The press in many centers characterized the action of Congress as an affront to Japan. The Hearst papers supported the Congressional achievement. Many organizations passed resolutions criticizing the abrogation of the Gentlemen's Agreement by the passage of an exclusion law. It, however, is the present means of regulating Japanese immigration.

COMPOSITION

IMMIGRATION to the United States, irrespective of its source, has usually been of a rural population, and the Japanese have not been an exception. Many Japanese agricultural workers have gone to Hawaii and have eventually entered this country. Most of those arriving from Hawaii were contract laborers who had gone there to work on the sugar plantations. Those who came directly from Japan were of a more desirable class.

In discussing the farmers from the southern part of Japan, Mr. Yoshida said:

This class consists of those who are engaged in agricultural pursuits, either as tenants or as farm laborers. They belong to the lower classes of the Japanese community, if not to the lowest

of all. They are the real corner-stone of the nation, but they are
poor. In this class of emigrants the most conservative, uneducated and innocent persons can be found. The greater number
of them being quite ignorant of foreign conditions, they are usually cared for and transported by the so-called " emigration companies." Farm laborers whose daily wages are an average of only
thirty-two sen (sixteen cents) , have hardly an opportunity to accumulate money to escape from their own group. The sole motive of this emigration is simply " to make money," and nothing
more.[8]

There have been, of course, many Japanese from other
classes in the migration to the United States. Though not
immigrants in a strict sense of the word, students from Japan
have been handled by immigration authorities and are, therefore, an important part of the immigration problem. Some
who were not students have reached the United States by
claiming this status. Under the régime of the Gentlemen's
Agreement the Japanese government was responsible for
regulating the admission of this class. During that period
the student could alter his plans and remain in America as
long as he desired, but this situation was changed to some
extent by the law of 1924.

At present a student must have adequate resources to support himself in this country. He must have been accepted
by an accredited university before he can leave Japan. His
attendance at school, once he has been admitted, must be
regular, and he has to leave the country at the expiration of
his period of study.

The Japanese population shows a better balance between
the sexes than does the Chinese. This aids materially in the
establishment of homes, better social life, and more stability
in settled occupations. Many of those who were not married
before they left Japan have returned to be married and have
brought their wives with them to America. In some cases
they have secured " picture brides " without making the trip
to the Orient.

" Picture brides " were Japanese women married by proxy
in their own country to Japanese men in the United States;

[8] Yosaburo Yoshida, "Sources and Causes of Japanese Emigration," *Annals of
the Amer. Acad.* 34 (1909), p. 165.

they were then given passports so that they might join their husbands in America. This greatly increased the Japanese population in the United States since they usually became the mothers of large families, the children of whom are American citizens; many are living in Japan and elsewhere but they are still citizens of this country. The citizenship of American-born Japanese is taken care of by the Constitution of the United States.

The Immigration Act of 1924 has materially affected the composition of the Japanese population in the United States since it excludes all aliens ineligible to citizenship with certain exempt classes. Domiciled Japanese can no longer bring their wives, minor children, and aged parents from Japan. This act also limited the admission of Japanese merchants to those only who are engaged in international trade. Domestic merchants are excluded. The Department of Labor has allowed the managers of international trade the privilege of bringing a staff including stenographers and servants.

The United States has had an influx of Japanese agriculturists, merchants, and students, but by far the greatest number of Japanese immigrants were farmers in their native land and have entered that field in this country.

CAUSES

THE CAUSES significant in Japanese immigration are economic. The ratio between the number in the population and the amount of land is an important factor.

The average holding of land owned by one farmer is only 9 tan 8 se. The annual yield from such a small piece of land, less than three acres, even under the most perfect system of utilization, is absolutely insufficient to support a family according to modern standards of comfort. Under such an economic condition the peasant class, which constitutes the bulk of the Japanese emigration to the United States, are spending their days.[9]

The agricultural conditions with the farmer in Japan are similar to those described in European countries where the peasant has labored for years under a system of landlordism. Regarding the Japanese situation, Mr. Yoshida has said:

[9] *Ibid.*, p. 160.

The competition among the working classes in a country where the area of land is limited, where no national labor organization exists, where no labor legislation operates, results in vast millions of struggling creatures spending their daily lives under the economic pressure of landlords and capitalists in a hopeless and stricken condition.[10]

The importance of small holdings is magnified in a country that is largely agricultural, which is the case in Japan:

Not far from three-fifths of the population gainfully occupied are engaged in tilling small plots of land, frequently as tenants paying high rents, or in agricultural labor at wages very low as compared to those earned in unskilled labor in this country. The more ambitious have tended strongly to leave the rural communities to seek better opportunities in the cities or in other countries. In the cities, however, in spite of long hours of labor, wages are still low. Consequently emigration has appealed to many of the more ambitious as the solution of their problem of limited opportunity. The western part of the United States has naturally appealed to them most strongly as the land of opportunity.[11]

Causes for Japanese immigration to America are not confined to Japan. Many Japanese went to Hawaii and Mexico as contract laborers under the supervision ef emigration companies. Dissatisfied with conditions of labor in these two destinations, they moved on to the United States.

THE JOURNEY

THE EXCLUSION of immigrant groups of any nationality has always created certain problems, many of which are connected with the journey, especially at the port of debarkation. People still want to migrate after they have been denied the privilege, since the causes for their original movement are still in operation; thus there is a tendency toward an illegal entry. Another problem growing out of an exclusion movement is that of determining the status of those who want to enter. Exemption of certain classes tends to make the whole situation more complex, resulting in some injustice for certain individuals who are entitled to come.

[10] *Ibid.*, pp. 159–160.
[11] From H. A. Millis, *The Japanese Problem in the United States* (New York: The Macmillan Company 1915), p. 8. By permission of The Macmillan Company, publishers.

Then there is the problem of interpreting the law. The legislative body that passes an exclusion measure cannot anticipate all of the multitude of problems that may arise in connection with its enforcement. The executive department, entrusted with the administration of the law, is, therefore, assigned the difficult task of interpreting its meaning. Accordingly rules and regulations are established in a rigid or a liberal manner depending upon the personal attitudes of the officials in charge. In either case the rules governing enforcement tend to become arbitrary and may produce results quite contrary to the spirit and purpose of the act. The ultimate resort in this country, of those who consider themselves injured by the law, is to appeal to the courts of the land. Through such appeals the courts participate in the interpretation of the law. In the course of time judicial decisions constitute a large part of the rules governing procedure. This complicates the problem of interpretation but it is the only release from prison wardens' methods of dealing with international problems.[12]

As with the Chinese, the most important aspect of the journey of the Japanese immigrant has to do with experiences at the port of debarkation and at places of surreptitious entry. Under the Gentlemen's Agreement, which was legislated out of existence in 1924, the Japanese government had control of emigration to the United States so that each migrant entered this country on a passport issued by his government.

But the Japanese laborer constituted a problem of entry even under the Gentlemen's Agreement. While the policy of the Japanese government was to oppose the emigration of laborers to continental United States, the individuals of this class could go to Hawaii, Canada, and Mexico, as an indirect route to the United States. It was necessary for President Roosevelt to issue a proclamation excluding Japanese or Korean laborers who held passports for these countries. The co-operation of the Japanese government was secured in this matter.

Smuggling of Japanese into the United States has been carried on most successfully across the Mexican border. Southern California, especially the Imperial Valley, has a great many Japanese agriculturists in both Mexico and the United

[12] R. D. McKenzie, *Oriental Exclusion* (The Institute of Pacific Relations, 1927), pp. 19–20.

States who often cross the border. This contiguous territory makes the " bootlegging " of immigrants an easy matter.

Once safely across the line, the contrabands find concealment at conveniently located ranches conducted by fellow countrymen, where they work for small wages until a smattering of English and an air of sophistication are acquired, when they proceed farther toward their respective ultimate destinations. When any of such contrabands are arrested, the resident Japanese who have given them asylum rush to the defense and, if necessary, do not hesitate to perjure themselves as to the period of residence in the United States of the arrested alien. Vigorous measures and unremitting zeal on the part of immigration officers, resulting in the arrest and deportation of large numbers of contrabands of this class and the prosecution of such of the ring-leaders and coconspirators of lesser importance as could be found in the United States, have served, temporarily, at least, to check the influx. The participation in this illegal traffic of domiciled aliens, without whose assistance it could not survive, has been discouraged to a no inconsiderable degree by the prosecution instituted during the past year. It should be understood, however, that the same situation has confronted the district on previous occasions and will again arise if there is any relaxation of vigilance. In order to keep the problem in hand, a sufficient force of alert, resourceful officers must at all times be maintained.

Numerous Japanese fishing boats on the Pacific Coast, operating in Mexican waters, are employed to facilitate the illegal entry of Japanese laborers.

The greater number of Japanese aliens arrested on departmental warrant during the year promptly claimed that they had been in this country in excess of three years, so that the government was unable to charge them with entry without inspection or at a place other than a regular port of entry, although there was ample reason to believe, even where the suspicion was not susceptible of proof, that they had but recently come from Mexico. When it became apparent that the government, nevertheless, intended to proceed in appropriate cases on the charge that the aliens entered and were within the United States in violation of the so-called passport provisions of the immigration act, the defendants promptly set up the defense of residence in excess of five years, that period being the one beyond which deportation proceedings could not prevail. In a few instances, all other subterfuges failing, the arrested contraband set up the claim to ownership of extensive property or business interests. Investigation developed that a majority of such claims were purely fictitious.[13]

[13] Extract from *Annual Report of the Commissioner General of Immigration* 1919.

American-born Japanese children who were sent or taken to Japan by their parents when only a few years old, frequently experience difficulty in returning to the United States. They have to prove by birth certificates that they were born in this country or secure affidavits from physicians or midwives. In some cases they are detained until authentic evidence is available.

THE JAPANESE have been described as the least urbanized immigrant group in America. On the Pacific Coast especially they are found in the agricultural districts, constituting in some communities the bulk of the population. Before they became an important element in farming, they could be found in camps; not even during their pioneer days in America were they a city population.

As farmers, the Japanese are to be found in greatest numbers in California, Oregon, Washington, Idaho, Utah, and Colorado. They are interested in crops that demand intensive agriculture.

The isolation of the Chinese in disorganized areas near the center of American cities has not caused much concern. The Japanese, however, have not been so willing to confine themselves to certain regions. Their distribution, therefore, has been a source of more worry than the location of the Chinese.

The fact that the Japanese have concentrated in truck gardening makes for their distribution around the peripheries of a few of the large cities of the coast, and in adjoining fertile valleys. The rather wide dispersion of population occasioned by any form of agriculture is also a factor for consideration. The Japanese population engaged in truck gardening seems much larger than it would if huddled together in a few blocks in the center of the city, as the Chinese are. Moreover, the leading highways radiating from the large cities pass through or by these fertile garden spots cultivated by Japanese. This enables a large number of whites to view the colored invader at work, and to compare his fine agricultural holdings with those of his less efficient white competitor, gaining thereby the impression that the Japanese are driving the whites away from the best land and forcing Americans to assume not only an inferior economic rôle, but also an inferior social rôle.

Again, in regard to residence within the city, the Japanese assume a different ecological organization from that of the Chinese. The Chinatown is as a rule a receding community. There is but little tendency to extend its boundaries or for the individual Chinese families to move into white neighborhoods. Most Japanese communities, on the other hand, are of the bursting type. Population increase constantly forces the local community to extend its boundaries, pushing out the inhabitants who occupy the fringe. But far more important is the fact that the upper economic and social classes of the Japanese are unwilling to live in the quarters occupied by Japanese coolie labor. Ever since the passing of the " Gentlemen's Agreement " in 1907, the type of Japanese male immigrant coming to this country has been of the higher economic and cultural level. This type of person is unwilling to live in the slum quarters of an American city; consequently, he is making continual efforts to find a home in a white residential section which corresponds to his own economic status. Americans have adopted the attitude that people of another color are all of the same social status, and they therefore object to the intrusion into their neighborhood of a cultured Japanese family, just as keenly as they would to that of a coolie family. This tendency on the part of the Japanese to distribute territorially in the city is quite as great a source of irritation as is the competitive occupational relation assumed by the group.[14]

Japanese colonies are tending to disappear, though it will take some time for a complete dissemination. Immigrants are not coming now in great numbers from the Orient. Business establishments owned and operated by Japanese are seeking and securing trade from whites. Many of the second generation Japanese are interested in American goods rather than things from the East. In many cases they seem more Occidental than Oriental in their tastes. It is believed by many that the Japanese, like the Chinese, will soon be found almost entirely in large cities engaged in occupations where they will not be in direct competition with whites.

SOCIAL INTERACTION AND ADJUSTMENTS

IT HAS been said repeatedly that any adjustment made by immigrants of any race or nationality must be contingent upon the attitudes of Americans concerning that group. These attitudes are the dynamic aspects of the social organization in

[14] R. D. McKenzie, "The Oriental Invasion," *Journal of Applied Sociology,* 10 (1925), pp. 127–128.

which the alien has to establish himself. The Japanese in the United States have been defined largely on the basis of economic competition, cultural and racial differences.

The economic factor attracted attention first of all because early opposition came from labor organizations. The initial contacts of the Japanese were with workingmen who had previously objected to the Chinese, also an Oriental group. The average person is not able to distinguish one from the other. The Japanese made their original adjustments in the United States in a different social situation from the one into which the Chinese came. Attitudes concerning Orientals had been crystallized into laws and organizations in an effort to exclude Chinese laborers before the Japanese government had approved emigration. The forced cessation of Chinese immigration made a place at first for the Japanese workingman just as legislation concerning all European and Asiatic immigration has provided an opening for the Mexican in so-called undesirable occupations.

Like all other newly arrived immigrant groups the Japanese went into cultural isolation. They lived apart in the social heritage of the Orient and secured work in the least desirable branches of the various industries where they were employed. They did not retreat, however, in the same meek fashion as did the Chinese when their presence was recognized through attitudes of hostility on the part of Americans. We have seen that the Chinese gradually accommodated themselves to an unfriendly environment by entering occupations where they did not have to compete with white Americans. The Japanese did not withdraw in true retiring Oriental fashion. They even refused to stay any length of time in the status of laborers.

The Japanese came to the United States for economic reasons and it is in this field that they have been most conspicuous in their adjustments. There was a place for them in the unskilled occupations since Chinese laborers were leaving outdoor activities for work in the cities. At first the Japanese were seasonal workers, but soon entered farming as the chief form of economic adjustment. In 1915 the Japanese Agricultural Association was organized to aid those who were engaged in farming by securing information from the Agricultural Experimental Station of California; this, along with the alien land laws, indicates their importance in this field.

Whenever the Japanese have gone to the cities, they have established themselves in retail trade where they can handle farm products raised in the Japanese agricultural communities. They have many fruit and vegetable markets, as well as nurseries. Since a Japanese community in America tends to be more or less self-sufficient, it is organized from an economic standpoint to care for all occupational classes. The Japanese operate many small establishments including hotels, rooming-houses, barber shops, etc. These small enterprises are in competition with similar American retail units of business, and become the basis of friction and irritation. The merchants in international trade are not competitors; rather they have merchandise not handled by white citizens and are therefore considered an asset to the community.

The present trend among the Japanese indicates that they will not remain so much in isolated settlements, but will soon be found in many American communities in numbers small enough to create little opposition to their presence. The second generation is not so definitely interested in agriculture as those who came from Japan. Their geographical distribution will be determined by the occupational fields in which they are accepted by the American public.

The most vehement demand for exclusion was on an economic basis at first, though the racial factor was probably the underlying reason for the objection to the competition with Japanese. The following statement emphasizes this point:

Because discriminations based on physical race touch human pride at its most sensitive point, there has been a tendency to protest that these exclusions are based on economic and not on racial grounds. In part, this is true. All the pressure for migration from the Orient is economic. The Oriental peoples do not come to us because they like us, but because their lands are crowded and ours have room; because we are rich and they are poor. We, in turn, object to them because their standard of living is low; because they can overwork and underlive us, and by that defeat us in economic competition. The workingmen objected to the Chinese, and then to the Japanese, when they were competitors. The small farmers objected when the Japanese began buying land. The large landowners, who want cheap and docile labor, do not object even now, but would prefer Chinese to Japanese. The merchants' objection was that " they send their money home." Now that the alien land laws are driving the Japanese back to the cities, the workingmen talk of relaxing those laws. Wherever in the world there is an Oriental working population, there is no room for a white one. And even where Orientals are fewer, they monopolize whatever occupations they enter. No one else can compete with them. All these motives are expressly economic. And economic causes doubtless also underlie much of the feeling which is more consciously racial.[15]

The cultural adjustment of the Japanese has caused more concern than the social life of the Chinese because of the composition of the population. The Japanese in the United States are not predominantly a male population and have, therefore, made better family adjustments than have the Chinese. While this is a more wholesome situation for the immigrants, it has become a cause of worry for Americans. The appearance of Japanese children in the public schools focussed the attention of whites on the birth rate of this Oriental group. Women worked in the fields with their children, making it possible for a Japanese family to become a rather self-sufficient economic unit in agricultural activities, a condition not existing with the whites. This placed an increased emphasis on the economic argument for exclusion and also raised the question of assimilation of a population rapidly increasing through a high birth rate.

The fact that many Japanese living in this country have been able to establish homes and thus enjoy normal family life has probably prevented much social disorganization. In the Orient the family is a fundamental institution and every man is expected to marry. The founding of a family is given more importance than anything else he may do. When the legislative act of 1924 made it impossible for domiciled Japanese other than government officials, ministers, professors, and treaty merchants to bring their wives and minor children, an important means of cultural adjustment was denied the Japanese.

[15] Chester H. Rowell, "Western Windows to the East," *Survey*, 56 (1926), p. 174.

Resident alien Japanese, at present, are the ones who suffer most under this law. Japanese and Chinese have not intermarried to any great extent and few Orientals have been married to members of the white population. There is a cultural as well an age gap between these alien Japanese men and those of the second generation born in the United States. Furthermore, in marrying one of these men, an American-born girl loses her citizenship in this country. This condition, however, will not be so critical with the second generation Japanese, most of whom are not yet old enough to marry.

Lack of opportunity for marriage is not the only phase of maladjustment in the family situation among the Japanese in America. The exclusion law has resulted in broken families with some members of the groups in the United States and others in Japan.

Every Japanese community of any size in America contains some households from which the mother or one or two of the children are permanently absent as a result of the exclusion law. The Japanese have had a habit of sending their children back to Japan to be with relatives or to attend school. So when the exclusion law came into effect the foreign-born children and the mothers who did not return to America in time are now separated from their families. The number of such broken families does not seem to be very great but wherever they are found they occasion severe local criticism concerning the cruelty of the law. As a result of a questionnaire sent to seven branches of the Japanese Association — all in rural districts — 65 cases were reported of families where either the mother or one or more children were in Japan and could not join the family here on account of the exclusion law. . .[16]

Although the 1924 act excludes the alien wives of Chinese and Japanese United States citizens, it does not exclude their children — born after the father has established residence in the United States — thus producing the anomalous situation that when a mother and child arrive at a United States port the child is permitted to enter but the mother is debarred. Likewise a mother is a United States citizen and is not subject to the immigration laws, but a child, born to domiciled alien parents during a temporary visit of the mother to Japan or China, is an alien and can never attain United States citizenship. This feature of the 1924

[16] R. D. McKenzie, *Oriental Exclusion*, pp. 95–96.

act occasions illogical and severe discrimination among the members of a family group and in the eyes of the ordinary person makes the law seem unnecessarily harsh and unjust.[17]

The marital status of the Japanese has aided them in their economic adjustments despite all these barriers. Their family life has been as normal as that of any immigrant group, of course in terms of the Japanese mores.

Another cultural adjustment of the Japanese that has caused alarm is the religious life of this Oriental group. While some of them are Christians, many more are Buddhists. In admitting a foreign group composed largely of adults, it is well to realize that it means the introduction of cultural elements very different from those found in the United States. It is to be expected that the Japanese would be Buddhists and Shintoists, just as one would expect the first generation of Americans to maintain their religion in a strange cultural complex. The fact that the Japanese have maintained as many of their cultural units as possible has materially aided in the adjustment process. The religious unit with the Japanese attracted much attention because of its strangeness to the American viewpoint; then, too, the Buddhist priests have evidenced considerable ethnocentrism, partly because they are specialists in one unit of culture, and loyalty to the ideals and customs of Japan was necessary to perpetuate the religion of which they were representatives.

Still another cultural accommodation resulting in apprehensive attitudes is the establishment of language schools in which the American-born Japanese learn to speak Japanese and acquire some knowledge of Oriental history, customs, and traditions which help them to live, in part, in accord with the cultural experiences of their parents. The acquisition of a foreign language does not need to infer disloyalty to the United States and it may mean an occupational accommodation for a Japanese who is too Oriental in appearance to make an adjustment where only the English language is used. As an interpreter between the East and the West he can doubtless find ready employment in the economic world of either the Occident or the Orient. So economic and cul-

[17] *Ibid.*, pp. 71–72.

tural adjustments have been the basis of objections to the presence of Japanese.

But there is also an impulse which is more than economic, and is expressly and biologically racial. Not in all the occupations into which Asiatics go do they displace workers of European race. In California the Chinese largely did work which there were no white workers to do, and the Japanese have improved lands which we left waste, and developed products which we overlooked. There is no economic conflict here, but there is still hostility. Into the places vacated by departing Orientals now flow, not Americans, but Mexicans. Nobody objects, because nobody else wants those jobs. Tropical Australia is retarded in its development because it needs labor which British immigrants will not do; yet it refuses, on racial grounds alone and to its economic loss, to admit Chinese immigrants eager to do it. When Japanese move into a city neighborhood, in California, Americans move out, not because there is any economic competition, but because they will not live where persons of a different physical race live. American farmers sell out, when Japanese buy their neighbors' farms, because they will not have their children in a school where the other children are mostly Japanese. There is nothing else against these children. They are just as bright as American children, speak as good English, and have the same manners and impulses; they are American citizens; and of course there is nothing economic in which to compete. It is sheer racial caste. But it makes the American farmer move out, even at an economic loss.[18]

Despite this widespread tendency to react to racial characteristics there was little opposition to the Japanese at first. They were even welcomed by the public press. But soon local agitation on the Pacific Coast was aroused and the Japanese were given an unfavorable definition. The movement for restriction soon became widespread and racial factors became more important along with the economic aspects. Each legislative gesture on the Pacific Coast brought the Japanese into the focus of national attention. It is to these attitudes created at an early time in their history of immigration that the Japanese have had to make their adjustments.

The discussion in the first chapter of this text shows that an individual of any race has the capacity to acquire the culture of any group if the process of socialization begins early enough. The Japanese of the second and third generations,

---

[18] Chester H. Rowell, *op. cit.*, p. 174.

if in contact with American culture, can learn the English language, even with the pronunciation peculiar to the locality in which he lives. He can take over the ideas, motives, and ideals of the cultural situation of which he is a part. Biological differences are non-essential in the acquisition of a social nature. Apparently races do not have inherent psychic characteristics. The mental organization of a person comes from his experiences in his social heritage. The Japanese from the Orient does have a different mental content from that found in the United States but that is not true of the Americanized Japanese reared in this country.

The American-born Japanese, though more Occidental than Oriental, in his social nature will remain in part Japanese because his home has an Eastern culture. He may have to learn his ancestral language and something of the history of his father's native land, but in the public schools the process of Americanization will be a factor. There will be barriers other than the culture of his home. His assimilation will depend on the manner in which educational, political, economic, and social opportunities are opened to him.

True, the Oriental from Japan has different family and national customs from those which we have. His religious convictions are not ours. He has conceived a philosophy of life peculiar in certain respects to the East. But Japan no longer sends us immigrants. Our problem then is with the second generation. The individual of this group is likely to be a marginal man through definition at least, because he will probably not be accepted by Americans although he may be Western in his thinking; certainly he will not be Oriental in his mental processes. His situation will not be entirely unique. Most people are marginal individuals, in the process of making the transition from a rural to an urban environment. Certainly the second generation of European immigrants from southern and eastern Europe is composed of individuals who are marginal men in a cultural sense. These marginal individuals who are Orientals, so far as the biological process is concerned, and Occidentals through the social process are not numerous enough to constitute a bewildering question for America, but they will be great problems to themselves as they stand on the peripheries of two cultures without complete acceptance in either.

Since Japanese immigration to the United States was terminated by the legislation of 1924, the problem connected with this racial group from the East is largely a matter of the second generation. Many of them are college graduates and many more will be trained in our universities in the future. They will be well equipped for the professions and for business. They will speak English as well as white citizens. Their habits of thinking will be American. Their whole mental organizations and philosophies of life will be Western. Yet they will be treated as foreigners; they will be unable to get themselves defined as Americans.

In the first place, these Japanese of the second generation are often not adjusted in their own families. They are not in the same universe of discourse as their fathers and mothers. The parents have not gone to American schools; their social natures were acquired in the East. They will always be Oriental to a certain extent. Their standards will be Japanese while those of the children will tend to be Western. American parents find it hard to enter the cultural world of their children and, of course, it is much more difficult for Oriental parents in the United States to do so. This means that there is a conflict of culture in a home where there is a tradition of parental domination.

In so far as Japanese parents try to live in the American cultural complex their behavior is a conscious process and they suffer in contrast with their children. Most of the time they are hopelessly confused in the presence of their children if they try to adopt American ways. It is doubtless better for their children and for them when they maintain the home according to Oriental traditions. They are supreme in that situation. They can interpret their own culture to their children after a fashion, but they would be wholly unable to interpret American life. Children would soon discover that their parents knew very little about American life. The younger generation would be superior in that realm. The parents must cling to their own culture to maintain supremacy at all. If Americans realized the merit of a foreign culture in the home in the matter of learning a language and other cultural units, the immigrant home could be a valuable institution. The child is ashamed of the customs of his parents only when they are not approved by the Americans he meets. The Oriental home could produce an ideal reciprocal relationship with the parents interpreting the Orient to their children and the children in turn introducing their parents to American life. There could be status for both in terms of a particular situation and each one could have a feeling of success in relation to cultural facts valuable to all within the group.

There is something of worth in every milieu, and the desirable aspects of any alien culture should be preserved and transmitted through the second generation of every immigrant group. As a matter of fact, this is what happens, but the process would have greater fruition if it were directed rather than opposed by the ethnocentric attitudes prevalent in any social order.

The members of the second generation Orientals in this country often feel that their problem of adjustment will be solved as soon as they can cut loose from the home moorings so replete with cultural conflicts. With their sentiments, attitudes, viewpoints, and behavior patterns almost entirely American, they believe that they are well equipped to find a place in the society of Western civilization. But they have not taken into consideration the social definition of their physical characteristics which are as Oriental as their ancestors, against whom anti-Japanese agitation was first directed. In the mind of the American public all persons with Oriental physiognomies are aliens and are possessors of all the alleged undesirable attributes that led to Japanese exclusion legislation.

The thrust into American life which these young people make by preference is made while they are in high school or college and so comparatively immature, and it meets stiff resistance. In Seattle there was quite a stir because a Japanese public school child in the fourth grade had taken the part of George Washington in a school play. The reporters would like to have made the teacher responsible for this choice, but actually it was the little boy's classmates who decided that he should play the rôle. In the high schools there is more feeling. Another Seattle boy of Japanese blood who was the valedictorian of his high school class received letters which warned him that he had better decide not to speak on commencement night. In the colleges distinctions are still more marked. An American graduate of Stanford University said, after several years' residence in Washington, D. C., " When I see American girls dancing with members of the Chinese and Japanese embassy I can't stand it or understand how they do it." [19]

The early migrants from the Orient were Japanese and Chinese in culture. They lived in isolation. But it is different with their progeny of Western birth.

The grandchildren of these Orientals will be, in every spiritual and cultural respect, exactly as American as the descendants of the Mayflower. Every difference will have gone except the physical one. But that, being hereditary, will last forever, unless obliterated by general intermarriage. In that case, it would make a new race, neither European nor Asiatic. This is the reason why the physical, in its relation to this problem, is more important than the spiritual or cultural. It alone is permanent.[20]

The Japanese of the second generation who have been educated in our colleges find it difficult to establish themselves once they have graduated. As one student has said:

. . . There is very little chance to rise, for the Americans make no distinction between the second generation Japanese and the older Japanese, and we are all treated equally badly. It is impossible, at least on the Pacific coast, to imagine a Japanese in any high position which would require Americans to work under him. If, in order to avoid troublesome contact with American workers, we man a whole industry from top to bottom with Japanese, as we have tried to do in some fields, such as farming, fishing, and in some cases the hotel and restaurant business, the cries of " yellow peril " and " peaceful penetration " are immediately raised, and august state legislators feel it their duty to safeguard the commonwealth by taking drastic steps to oust us from our business by legislative measures. Or if we limit ourselves to businesses which cater to only the Japanese community, we are accused of being unassimilable and clannish, an undesirable element in American society. But however that may be, the Japanese com-

[19] William C. Smith, "Born American, But —" *Survey*, 56 (1926), p. 168.
[20] Chester H. Rowell, *op. cit.*, p. 175.

munity here in America is too small to support many businesses or professions by itself.[21]

While the second generation Japanese are equipped culturally for adjustments in the United States they are unable to find places, for racial reasons. In Japan their racial characteristics are acceptable, but their social heritage is at variance with that found in the Orient. Consequently they may find it difficult to make an accommodation there. This is substantiated by the statement of a Japanese of the second generation:

If it is so hard for us to get into suitable vocations here, why don't we go back to Japan? we are frequently asked. Only a few days ago I was walking across the Quad on our campus with an American classmate, and he turned around to me and said: " Gee! you fellows are lucky! Look at the great advantage you American-educated fellows have over the rest of your people when you go back to the old country." I suppose his attitude reflects that of most Americans. " Well," I should like to ask, " what do you mean by going *back* to our old country? We've never been there in the first place." Most of us were born here, and we know no other country. This is " our old country " right here. As to having advantage over the people in Japan, we have the wonderful advantage of being quite unable to speak their language or read their papers, of being totally ignorant of their customs, history, or traditions, of holding different ideals, of thinking in different ways. Yes, we have as much advantage over the people in Japan as a deaf mute has over a man in possession of all his faculties. An American would have an infinitely easier time in Japan than we would, for they would excuse a foreigner if he made mistakes, but we, with our Japanese names and faces, would have to conform to their rigid standards or else be " queer." . . The trouble with us is that we have been too thoroughly Americanized. We have attended American schools, we speak English exclusively, we know practically nothing of Japan except what an average American knows; our ideals, customs, mode of thinking, our whole psychology is American. Although physically we are Japanese, culturally we are Americans. We simply are not capable of fitting into Japanese society, so we are destined to remain here.[22]

Some people have proposed amalgamation as the best form of final adjustment of the Japanese question, and others pre-

[21] Kazuo Kawai, "Three Roads, and None Easy," *Survey*, 56 (1926), p. 165.
[22] *Ibid.*, p. 165.

dict that the problem will be solved in that way. Amalgamation, however, will probably never be a direct process. First of all it is not in the mores of either the Occidental or Oriental. It will be a slow process involving only an occasional individual inside and outside the institution of marriage. If miscegenation does not take place, and it probably will not for many generations, something resembling a caste line will doubtless be drawn and future generations will find the attitudes involved a part of their social heritage and be strongly opposed to amalgamation.

Amalgamation will never be a directed process in spite of the fact that there is a realization that racial mixtures have produced the present population of the world, because cogent attitudes of opposition concerning the matter already exist. Even cases of miscegenation involving Orientals and Occidentals which have produced no ill results are not evidence that amalgamation might be a success. Our minds are impervious to facts. The people of any country do not want to be convinced that their traditional attitudes are wrong, even in matters of less importance. As one author has said, we tend to think of "race mixture as a sort of interracial adultery." [23]

With many states having legislation against marriages between Orientals and Occidentals and with public opinion against it, miscegenation is not likely to solve the problem of adjustment for the second and subsequent generations. Though American in culture, they will have to make for themselves a place in society where they can capitalize on their Oriental physical characteristics.

In time they can capitalize their physical difference in the movies, as stewards of country clubs, as managers of tea-rooms, as artists and handicraft workers; also, they can work for each other and do business with each other. American business houses will utilize them more and more as intermediaries in reaching the local community, and foreign trade houses will pay high for Americans if they can speak the languages of both America and Eastern Asia.

In the meantime they must exhibit unusual qualifications to compete successfully against Americans in the same line of work;

[23] Chester H. Rowell, *op. cit.*, p. 175.

therefore it is not surprising that well-educated persons of Oriental parentage are forced to a lower step on the occupational social ladder, because they cannot get a hold on the upper rungs.[24]

So far as Orientals are concerned the question of immigration in the United States has to do with the Japanese and Chinese already resident in this country, and those of future generations. They will be problems because they do not resemble Caucasians in physical appearance. No matter how thoroughly American they may be in culture they will always be Orientals in the minds of the white population. They will be too American and too few in numbers to endanger in any way the institutions and cultural habits in the United States.

[24] E. G. Mears, *Resident Orientals on the American Pacific Coast* (The Institute of Pacific Relations, 1927), pp. 208–209.

READINGS

GENERAL

Abbott, James F., *Japanese Expansion and American Policies.* 1916

American Academy of Political and Social Science, " Chinese and Japanese in America." *Annals*, Vol. 34, No. 2, pp. 4–203

Bennett, John Edward, *Our National Tendency and Its Goal.* 1914

Brooks, Sidney, " The Real Pacific Question," *Harper's Weekly,* Oct. 12, 1907, V. 51, p. 1484

Burgess, George F., " Speech of George F. Burgess, in the House of Representatives Feb. 18, 1907." *Congressional Record,* 1907, V. 41, pp. 3224–3225

Burnett, Albert H., " Misunderstanding of eastern and western states regarding Oriental immigration," *Annals,* V. 34, No. 2 (1909), pp. 37–41

Crow, Carl, *Japan and America; A Contrast.* 1916

Davis, J. Merle, " We Said ' Let's Find the Facts.' " *Survey,* 56, 1926

Documental History of Law Cases Affecting Japanese in the United States, 1916–24. 1925

Galbreath, Charles B., " Japanese Exclusion and the Pacific Coast," *Ohio Magazine,* July 1907, V. 3, pp. 1–10

Garis, Roy, *Immigration Restriction.* 1927

Garrett, Garet, " The Snarl of Waking Asia," *Everybody's Magazine,* May 1915, V. 32, pp. 587–600

Greene, Daniel C., "Japanese Immigration," *Outlook,* April 1911, V. 97, pp. 795–796

Gulick, Sidney Lewis, *America and the Orient.* 1916

—— "America's Oriental Immigration Problem," *Chicago City Club's Bulletin No.* 7, 1914. Pp. 173–181

—— "A New Immigration Policy," *The Public,* April 12, 1912. V. 22, pp. 369–371

—— *New Oriental Policy.* 1914

—— *The American Japanese Problem.* 1914

—— "The Problem of Oriental Immigration," *Survey,* Mar. 7, 1914, V, 31, pp. 720–722

—— "Problems in American-Japanese Relations," *Asia,* 1917, V. 17, pp. 526–528

—— "What Japan Really Wants," *Independent,* May 10, 1919, V. 98, pp. 218–219

—— "What Program Shall the United States Stand for in her Relations with Japan and China; the Problem and a Practical Solution," *Annals,* July 1916, V. 66, pp. 106–117

Hayashi, Tadasu, Count, "The Political Relations of Japan and America," *Overland,* Jan. 1910, (new series, V. 55, pp. 41–45)

Hepburn, Alonzo B., "The United States and the Orient," *Nation,* Mar. 28, 1918, V. 106, pp. 382–383

Iyenaga, Toyokichi, "Japan and America in the World War," *Proceedings of The Engineers' Club of Philadelphia,* 1917, V. 34, pp. 351–353

"Japan Alarms Our Pacific Coast," *Literary Digest,* April 5, 1919, V. 61, pp. 20–21

"Japan, America, and the Anglo-Saxon World," *Living Age,* Aug. 3, 1907, V. 254, pp. 314–317

"Japanese Wrath at Our Immigration Bills," *Literary Digest,* Feb. 7, 1914, V. 48, p. 252

Jones, Chester L., "The Legislative History of Exclusion Legislation," *Annals,* V. 34, 1909, pp. 131–139

Jordan, David Starr, "Japanese Exclusion," *Independent,* Dec. 13, 1906, V. 61, p. 1425

Kasai, Jiuji, "Relations between Japan and the United States," *Annals,* V. 54, pp. 260–269

Kawakami, Kiyoshi K., *American-Japanese Relations.* 1912

—— "Japan and the United States," *Atlantic Monthly,* May, 1917, V. 119, pp. 671–681

—— *The Real Japanese Question.* 1921

Kohler, Max J., "Un-American Character of Race Legislation," *Annals,* V. 34, 1909, pp. 55–73

Lasker, Bruno, *Race Attitudes in Children.* 1929

Lewis, William Draper, "Treaty Powers: Protection of Treaty

Rights by Federal Government," *Annals*, V. 34, 1909, pp. 93–108

McKenzie, R. D., *Oriental Exclusion*. 1927

Mahan, Alfred T., " Japan among the Nations," *Living Age*, Aug. 2, 1913, V. 278, pp. 312–315

—— " The Japanese Question," *American Law Review*, Sept. 1914, V. 48, pp. 698–713

Nevada. Legislature. Petition of the Legislature relative to the unrestricted immigration of the Japanese in the United States. *Congressional Record*, Dec. 11, 1905. V. 40, pp. 267–268

Park, Robert E. and Miller, Herbert A., *Old World Traits Transplanted*. 1921

Ozaki, Y., " Misunderstood Japan," *North American Review*, 1900, V. 171, pp. 566–576

Perkins, George C., " The Pacific Coast and the Orient," *Independent*, Feb. 21, 1907, V. 62, pp. 429–434

Pitkin, Walter B., *Must We Fight Japan?* 1921

" Points of Friction with Japan," *Literary Digest*, Dec. 18, 1915, V. 51, pp. 1417–1418

Roosevelt, Theodore, " The Japanese Question," *Outlook*, May 8, 1909, V. 92, pp. 61–62

Scherer, James A. B., *The Japanese Crisis*. 1916

Singh, Saint Nihal, " Asiatic Emigration, a World Question," *Living Age*, 1914, V. 282, pp. 387–392

Smith, Goldwin, " The World Menace of Japan," *Cosmopolitan*, Oct. 1907, V. 43, pp. 604–607

Stead, Alfred, " Racial prejudice against Japan," *Fortnightly Review*, 1907, V. 88, pp. 637–651

Treat, Payson J., *Japan and the United States*, 1853–1921. 1921

Trevor, John B., *Japanese Exclusion*. 1925

" The United States and Japan," *World's Work*, June 1916, V. 32, pp. 140–142

U. S. Congress. Senate. Committee on Immigration. *Japanese Immigration Legislation*

Weyl, Walter E., " Japan's Thwarted Emigration," *Asia*, 1918, V. 18, pp. 393–394

Whelpley, James Davenport, " Are We Honest with Japan? " *Century Magazine*, May 1914, V. 51, p. 12

" The World's Most Menacing Problem," *Collier's Weekly*, May 31, 1913, V. 51, p. 12

COMPOSITION

Anraku, Yeiji, " Oriental Immigration," *Outlook*, Oct. 1907, V. 87, pp. 455–457

Aoki, S., " Japanese Immigration," *World's Work*, V. 15, pp. 10041–10044

" Emigration from Japan," *Outlook,* July 1911, V. 98, pp. 699–700

French, B. L., " Shall the United States Exclude Japanese and Korean Laborers? " *Congressional Record,* Mar. 17, 1908, V. 42, pp. 3494–3499

Griffis, William Elliot, " Japan and the United States. Are the Japanese Mongolian? " *North American Review,* 1913, V. 197, pp. 721–733

Hyndman, Henry M., " The Rising Asiatic Tide," *Asia,* Aug. 1919, V. 19, pp. 781–784

Ichihashi, Yamato, " Japanese Students in America," *Outlook,* Oct. 1907, V. 87, pp. 295–297

The Japan Current, Printed every month for the dissemination of ideas of Japan in America. V. 1, 3, Nov. 1907. V. 2, No. 1–4, 6–7, Jan.-April, July-Aug. 1908

" Japanese as Immigrants," *Outlook,* April 1905, V. 79, pp. 862–863

" Japanese Immigration," *Outlook,* Jan. 28, 1911, V. 97, pp. 151–154

" Japanese in the United States," *Literary Digest,* Nov. 1919, V. 63, p. 40

Lauman, Charles, *The Japanese in America.*   1926

McLaughlin, Allen, " Chinese and Japanese Immigration," *Annals,* 1909, V. 34, pp. 19–26

" Oriental Immigration," *Outlook,* Jan. 14, 1911, V. 97, pp. 63–64

Rowell, Chester H., " Chinese and Japanese Immigrants," *Annals,* V. 34, No. 2, 1909, pp. 3–8

Scanlan, J. M., " The Japanese Invasion," *World Today,* Aug. 1905, V. 9, pp. 899–901

CAUSES

Kawakami, Kiyoshi K., *Asia at the Door.*   1914

Millis, H. A., *The Japanese Problem in the United States.*   1915

Yoshida, Y., " Sources and Causes of Japanese Emigration," *Annals,* 34, 1909, p. 165

THE JOURNEY

Annual Report of the Commissioner General of Immigration, 1919

McKenzie, R. D., *Oriental Exclusion.*   1927

Yoshida, Y., " Sources and Causes of Japanese Emigration," *Annals,* 34, 1909, p. 165

DISTRIBUTION

Bwinight, Ralph F., *The Japanese in Rural Los Angeles County.* 1920

Japan in New York. 1908
Kawakami, K. K., " The Japanese on American Farms," *Independent,* Oct. 27, 1907, V. 59, pp. 961–967
—— " The Japanese on Our Farms," *Forum,* July 1913, V. 50, pp. 82–93
Turner, Thomas F., " Chinese and Japanese Labor in the Mountain and Pacific States," *United States — Industrial Commission. Reports,* 1901. V. 15, pp. 745–802

SOCIAL INTERACTION AND ADJUSTMENTS

Adams, Thomas S. and Sumner, Helen L., *The Problem of Immigration.* 1908, pp. 99–107
Bogardus, E. S., " Social Distance, A Measuring Stick," *Survey,* 1926, V. 56, p. 141
Braun, Marcus, " How Can We Enforce Our Exclusion Laws? " *Annals,* V. 34, No. 2, 1909, pp. 140–142
Brown, Alice M., *Education, Not Legislation; California and the Japanese.* 1913
Buell, Raymond L., *Japanese Immigration.* 1924
" Can We Assimilate the Japanese? " *Literary Digest,* Aug. 2, 1913, V. 47, pp. 165–166
Clement, Ernest W., " Expatriation of Japanese Abroad," *Nation,* V. 102, 1916, pp. 613–614
—— " The United States and Japan," *Magazine of American History,* V. 28, 1892, pp. 129–130
Darsie, Marvin L., *The Mental Capacity of American-born Japanese Children.* 1926
Douglas, Henry C., " What May Happen in the Pacific," *Review of Reviews,* April 1917, V. 55, pp. 394–398
Eliot, Thomas L., " Moral and Social Interests Involved in Restricting Oriental Immigration," *Annals,* V. 34, 1909, pp. 80–85
Flowers, M., *The Japanese Conquest of American Opinion.* 1917
" From Citizenship to Exclusion," *Nation,* Feb. 1907, V. 84, p. 168
Glynn, Billee, " Orientals and Portola," *Overland,* Feb. 1910, V. 55, pp. 204–210
Gompers, Samuel and Gutstadt, Herman, " Meat vs. Rice. American Manhood against Asiatic Coolieism, Which Shall Survive? " *Senate Document, No. 173.* 1902
Gowen, Herbert H., " The Problem of Oriental Immigration in the State of Washington," *Annals,* V. 34, 1909, pp. 109–117
Gulick, Sidney Lewis, *American Democracy and Asiatic Citizenship.* 1918
Harwood, W. S., " Americanizing the Japanese," *World Today,* Dec. 1905, V. 9, pp. 1286–1292
Hurd, Archibald, " Racial War in the Pacific; an Imperial Peril," *Fortnightly Review,* 1913, V. 99, pp. 1031–1046

Hutchinson, Woods, " The Mongolian as a Workman," *World's Work,* 1907, V. 14, pp. 9372–9376

Ichihashi, Yamato, *Japanese Immigration, Its Status in California.* 1913

" Inferiority of the Caucasian Race," *Independent,* Feb. 1909

James, Thomas L., " Revival of the Know-Nothing Spirit," *North American Review,* Feb. 1, 1907, V. 184, pp. 268–274

" The Japanese as American Citizens," *Chautauquan,* Jan. 1906, V. 42, pp. 392–394

" Japanese Exclusion," *Sunset,* June 1916, V. 36, p. 36

" Japanese Schools in America," *Literary Digest,* Mar. 1912, V. 44, p. 585

" Japan's Immigration Grievance," *Literary Digest,* April 22, 1916, V. 52, p. 1138

Japanese and Korean Exclusion League. 1907

Jenks, J. W. and Louck, W. J., *The Immigration Problem.* 1913. Chapter XIII, pp. 231–260

Johnson, Herbert B., *Discrimination against the Japanese in California.* 1907

Jones, Rosalie, *The American Standard of Living and World Co-operation.* 1923

Kaneko, Kentaro, " The Effect of American Residence on Japanese," *Annals,* V. 54, pp. 260–269

Kawakami, K. K., *Asia at the Door.* 1914

—— " The Naturalization of the Japanese," *North American Review,* June 21, 1907, V. 185, pp. 394–402

Lusk, Hugh H., " The Real Yellow Peril," *North American Review,* V. 186, 1907, pp. 375–383

Macarthur, Walter, " Opposition to Oriental Immigration," *Annals,* V. 34 (1909), pp. 19–26

Newlands, Francis G., " A Western View of the Race Question," *Annals,* V. 34, No. 2, 1909, pp. 49–51

Noguchi, Yone, " Naturalization of Japanese," *Nation,* June 19, 1913, V. 96, pp. 616–617

Northern California Peace Society, *California Press on Anti-Alien Land Legislation.* 1915

" Not the Right Way," *Outlook,* Jan. 14, 1911, V. 107, p. 645

Park, Robert E., " Behind Our Masks," *Survey,* 56, 1926, pp. 135–139

—— *The Immigrant Press and Its Control.* 1922

Prosser, William T., " Western View of the Japanese," *World's Work,* Dec. 1908, V. 17, pp. 10989–10991

" Protection to Aliens," *Outlook,* June 8, 1907, V. 86, p. 226

Raushenbush, Winifred, " Their Place in the Sun," *Survey,* 56, 1926

Rowell, Chester H., " Orientophobia," *Collier's Weekly,* Feb. 6, 1909, V. 42, p. 13

Satoh, Henry, " The Past and Present of Japanese Emigration
    Policy," *Overland,* Jan. 1910, V. 55, pp. 108–110

Spier, Leslie, *Growth of Japanese Children Born in America and
    in Japan.* 1929

Steiner, Jesse F., *The Japanese Invasion.* 1917

Stowell, Ellery C., " The Policy of the United States in the
    Pacific," *Annals,* V. 54, 1914, pp. 245–250

" Trenchant Japanese View of Exclusion," *Review of Reviews,*
    Oct., 1907, V. 36, pp. 487–488

Young, Frederic G., " Why Oregon Has Not Had an Oriental
    Problem," *Annals,* V. 34, No. 2, 1909, pp. 86–90

Young, John R., " The Support of the Anti-Oriental movement,"
    Annals, V. 34, No. 2, 1909, pp. 9–18

Young, Joseph H., *The Anti-Japanese Movement in California
    down to* 1915

CHAPTER XVI

THE HINDUS

FROM A RACIAL standpoint the East Indians should not be included in this section on Orientals. "The Hindu is in the main a narrow headed, dark skinned Caucasian, not very different from the Mediterranean."[1] However, the immigrants from India have not been so considered in the United States. Their brown skin and turbaned heads have resulted in a definition that has placed them in a category with the nonwhite groups.

At the present time the problem concerning them involves only the small group in the United States, since they were excluded in 1917 by a legislative act. Their arrival on the Pacific Coast was probably the immediate reason for the "geographical delimitation clause" that made it impossible for them to enter this country as immigrants. The opposition to them, especially in labor organizations, has been quite as strong as against the Japanese and the Chinese, and an excellent rationalization has been found in the fact that Canada does not admit them any more, even though they are British subjects.

While there are not many Hindus in the United States, a great many were rejected at the ports of debarkation, the immigration law being rigidly enforced in their case. The following statement in the annual report of the Commissioner General of Immigration in 1910 gives some of the reasons why many were not allowed to enter the United States. This report also reveals the attitude on the Pacific Coast concerning the East Indians, since the statement was made by the Commissioner of Immigration at Seattle.

[1] A. L. Kroeber, *Anthropology* (New York: Harcourt, Brace & Co. 1923), p. 44.

334

A number of Hindus have applied for admission to the United States through this district during the year just passed. Every Hindu laborer has been rejected by a board of special inquiry on the grounds of belief in polygamy, likely to become a public charge, doctor's certificate, or as an assisted immigrant.

The Hindu laborers are certainly not a class of immigrants who can be allowed to enter the country freely. They are not fitted physically to cope with the more efficient American and European labor. They tend to lower the standard of wages and living. They are clannish to a degree. They only come here for temporary purposes, do not bring their families, and have no idea of remaining permanently in the country. They are filthy and unsanitary in their habits. They refuse to eat food prepared by any but themselves, rendering it impracticable to care for them in an immigrant station. There is a strong prejudice on the Pacific coast against the Hindus by all classes of people except among a few employers who think to profit by the procurement of cheap labor. They have been driven out of many localities on the coast and the people generally have no use for them.[2]

Like most of the groups in recent immigration, the Hindus have come for economic reasons. The prospect of industrial advancement in the United States was an inducement to leave their low economic status in India.

Practically all of these Hindus were born in the rural districts of India and are agriculturalists by occupation. In the United States they are quite largely in the rice and cotton fields and other agricultural work, with the greatest numbers concentrated in California and Washington. A considerable number of sailors are to be found in New York. Very few brought families with them, so there has been little home life in America. In any nationality the segregation of a male population leads to a certain amount of vice, and inevitably attracts the attention of the law.

The East Indians in America are the close followers of three different religions: Hinduism, Sikhism, and Mohammedanism. The majority are Sikhs. Their rigid adherence to the dictates of their religious beliefs brought them to the attention of those who had to work with them; thus religion readily became a factor around which attitudes of opposition could be organized once economic competition entered

[2] Extract from the *Annual Report of the Commissioner General of Immigration* 1910, pp. 148–149.

into the question. Like other excluded classes, the Hindus are likely to be a greater problem to themselves in an inhospitable environment than they are to the United States, since the government will have to deal with only the few now in the country.

READINGS

Braden, C. B., " Invasion of America," *Christian Cent.*, 47: 1491–2
Buchanan, A. F., " West and the Hindu Invasion," *Overland*, n.s. 51: 308–13. April 1908
Das, R. K., *Hindustani Workers on the Pacific Coast*
Dodd, W. D., " Hindus in the Northwest," *World Today*, 13: 1157–60, Nov. 1907
Drury, C. M., " Hinduism in the United States," *Mis. R.*, 44: 281–3, April 1921
Ghose, S. N., " Deportation of Hindu Politicals," *Dial*, 67: 145–7, August 23, 1919
" Hindu Invasion," *Collier's Weekly*, 45: 15, March 26, 1910
" Hindu, the Newest Immigration Problem," *Survey*, 25: 2–3, Oct. 1, 1910
" Indian Rights in the United States," *Nation*, 117: 447, Oct. 17, 1923
Johnson, A. T., " Rag Heads: a Picture of America's East Indians," *Independent*, 109: 234–5, Oct. 28, 1922
Lovett, R. M., " United States and India," *New Republic*, 66: 175–6, April 1, 1931
McCrae, L., " Birds of Passage in California," *Mis. R.*, 41: 910, Dec. 1918
—— " Self-exiled in America," *Mis. R.* 39: 525–6, July 1916
Millis, H. A., " East Indian Immigration to British Columbia and the Pacific Coast States," *Am. Econ. R.*, 1: 72–6, Mar. 1911
—— " East Indian Immigration to the Pacific Coast," *Survey*, 28: 379–86, June 1, 1912
Mukerji, G., " Hindu in America," *Review of Reviews*, 37: 604–5, May 1908
" Race Riots on the Pacific Coast," *Outlook*, 87: 89, Sept. 21, 1907
Scheffaner, H., " Tide of Turbans," *Forum*, 43: 616–8, June 1910
Schibsby, M., " Hindus and American Citizenship," *Nat. Conf. of Social Work*, 1927: 579–81
Singh, Pardanian, *Ethnological Epitome of the Hindustanees of the Pacific Coast*. 1922
Sudhindra, Bose, " American Impressions of the Hindu Student," *Forum*, 53: 251–7, Feb. 1915

CHAPTER XVII
THE FILIPINOS

INTRODUCTION

WITH European and Asiatic migrations under legislative control, it is generally believed that the problem of immigration is in a process of being solved in an adequate manner. Few citizens east of the Pacific Coast region are aware that emigration from the Philippine Islands to the United States is approaching a mass movement. Strictly speaking, the Filipinos are probably not immigrants since they were not given the status of aliens under the legislative act of 1924. They occupy a peculiar position. They are not aliens and they are not citizens. Furthermore, they are not eligible to citizenship according to the Supreme Court decision of 1925, unless they have served in the American Navy for a period of three years.

Nor are these the only unique features of the question. The Filipinos are American subjects, citizens in an Island possession of the United States. There is a cogent movement on the part of these nationals for independence. Legislation designed to regulate their movement cannot regard them as foreigners and it must be expected that it will greatly influence the growing attitude on the part of the Filipinos for self-government.

There are other factors which make this mass movement a particular problem. The Filipinos are the only non-Caucasian group invading the United States at the present time. Every legislative move is being watched as indicative of the attitude America may have concerning similar racial groups.   Furthermore the Filipinos are not coming into a situation of unorganized attitudes.   They are defined as Mongolians and must make their adjustments in the United States in terms of dynamic attitudes that were crystallized years ago around the Chinese and Japanese.

COMPOSITION

THE MOVEMENT of the Filipinos to the United States was initiated quite largely by students who wished to study in American universities.   Following the World War many who had served in the Navy were discharged at ports on the mainland and became part of the orig: al group of migrants that has established a Filipino population in the United States estimated to be about 60,000.

The racial affiliation of the Filipinos has been a debatable question since their first entrance into the United States.   It even became a court issue in the Superior Court at Los Angeles in February, 1930.

According to Dr. Fay-Cooper Cole, one of America's foremost anthropologists:

The Filipinos are Malays, who in turn are Southern Mongoloids and may be spoken of as Orientals.   To be specific, it appears that the Malay is an ancient mixture made up of a small fraction of aboriginal pygmy blacks, and a rather strong sprinkling of early Caucasoid, but all predominately Southern Mongoloid. Racially they are close to the Southern Chinese and the bulk of the Japanese population.

The migration from the Philippine Islands comprises a population unit that is almost entirely male, and whose members have not yet reached the age of thirty.   This preponderance of males has made possible a mobile population which lacks the stability characteristic of a family organization. Much of the social disorganization may be attributed to this abnormal sex distribution.   The age of the members of this group is also an important factor.   There must be a certain amount of youthful immaturity and inexperience that leads to social maladjustments.   Habits were built up in a situation very different from that in the United States and when these migrants had reached an age that would assure a certain amount of stability in their own cultural organization they moved to a strange social milieu that demanded another pattern of behavior.

CAUSES OF FILIPINO IMMIGRATION

THE CHIEF cause of Filipino emigration is economic, a desire for better living and social conditions. There is, however, or at least there has been, the usual amount of labor recruiting and propaganda regarding opportunities which have become the occasions for the movement to the United States. Steamship companies have been anxious to sell steerage passage to those who are desirous of better economic adjustments, and have maintained agents for this purpose. Finding a predisposition for emigration, the propaganda becomes very effective.

Here we must not overlook the general Americanizing influence in the Philippine Islands which has suggested a means of relief in the United States for the undesirable economic conditions at home. American schools, the press, moving pictures, and letters from those in the United States all become factors of importance, especially when there is dissatisfaction with conditions at home.

DISTRIBUTION

THERE HAS been a concentration of the Filipinos in the United States where there are definite attitudes concerning any group with Oriental physical characteristics. It is not the number of Filipinos in America that has brought them to the attention of the public as a problem, but that they have settled quite largely in one area, along the Pacific Coast.

Like other immigrants they have located in the disorganized sections of American cities, where they live under congested conditions in a few blocks adjacent to Chinatown or the central part of the city. Overcrowding has even extended to camp and ranch life. This distribution of the Filipino working men in the worst urban areas brings them into close proximity with all the demoralizing elements in American city life.

ADJUSTMENTS

THE ADJUSTMENTS made by any immigrant group are of utmost importance, since they form the basis of the attitudes
of the immigrants as well as those of the native Americans.
On the other hand, the accommodations made are contingent
upon the set of attitudes prevalent in the place of location.
In the Western States the Filipinos have to contend with attitudes that were formulated years ago concerning the Orientals. The average person does not recognize a Filipino, that
is, he is not readily distinguished from the Japanese and the
Chinese. Where he has been recognized, he is suspected of
immorality, criminal tendencies, low standards of living, and
endangering health.

Since 1927 the Filipinos have been recognized as a factor
in economic competition. The anti-Filipino riots in California and Washington in 1929 and 1930 are evidence that
there is a real feeling of opposition to them as an important
labor element in certain districts. They are to be found in
agricultural work, domestic and personal service, with a great
many in hotels and restaurants.

The chief objections raised against this group are the usual
ones. In some occupations they have replaced the whites. In
certain instances they receive a lower wage and have a lower
standard of living than American citizens of a similar class.
Being largely a male population, there is enough evidence
of vice for the Filipinos to be regarded as dangerous to the
morals of the community where they live. They must live
in rooming-houses, in areas where there is an individualiza-
tion of behavior, and a tendency toward disorganization. Intermarriage with Caucasians is contrary to the laws of some
states, since the Filipinos are classed as Orientals; intermarriage is also against the mores of most communities,
so this group is without the stabilizing influence of family
life.

The Filipinos have attracted considerable attention in
many of their social adjustments. " . . . The principal objection to the Filipino arises from the fact that they cross the

race line in their relations with white women."[1]   They are found to be frequenters of the Chinese gambling establishments, and many police officials regard them all as potential criminals.[2]   It is easy to think categorically concerning any group; as a matter of fact, that is what invariably happens. It is hard to believe that there are desirable as well as undesirable individuals in a group very different from our own.

The Filipinos differ from most immigrant groups in the United States in matters of isolation and social aggressiveness. They have come to the United States with a feeling that they belong, and expect to be accepted as nationalists rather than as foreigners.   Not only do they intend to accumulate some wealth, perhaps receive an education, but they anticipate cultural acceptance, since discriminations are not so great in the Philippines.   Associations, however, in many cases are possible only with other strangers in the United States and with Americans who are also unadjusted.

Of equal importance with the social adjustments of the Filipinos is the fact that their movement to this country is at present not controlled by any legislation so that they may come in great numbers.   No matter what their educational status, it is difficult for them to be more than skilled laborers, and in many cases college graduates must accept work in unskilled trades.   This fact alone has given organized labor much concern.

On two occasions the Federation of Labor has petitioned Congress to exclude Filipino laborers, and bills designed for that purpose were presented in 1928 and 1930.   Had this proposed legislation passed, the legality of this action probably could have been established, but there is another aspect to be considered.   Coming at a time when there is agitation for the independence of the Philippine Islands, restrictive legislation, denying entrance to the United States, would doubtless lead to an attitude of antagonism toward this country.

No immigrant group proves its worth in a single generation.   Attitudes concerning any foreign invaders are not

---

[1] *Report on Crime and the Foreign Born*, National Commission on Law Observance and Enforcement, No. 10, June 24, 1931, p. 362.
[2] *Ibid.*

based on the contribution they will be able to make or the disorganization they will be able to induce through competition in the economic process or through unapproved behavior in the social process. In reacting to the influx of Filipinos, Americans are unconsciously reacting at the same time to their experiences with the Chinese, the Japanese, and the Hindus. What the Filipinos do in the United States is no more important than the mental content that Americans have concerning people who differ from them in a racial or a cultural sense.

Filipinos attract considerable attention because they are variants in physical appearance and in cultural experiences. While opposition to them is based in part on this factor, there are also well organized attitudes of fear in all parts of the United States concerning economic competition with new arrivals. If the Western States were invaded in great numbers by native Americans from other states in the Union, the opposition would probably be as vehement, if the citizens along the Pacific Coast were endangered in their economic adjustments. The same situation would prevail if the people from the Western States migrated to states farther east and threatened the economic security of those who had been there for some time. Fear of being displaced through economic competition is not just a matter of racial prejudice, though difference in race often complicates matters.

It is hard to keep a problem like immigration in its proper perspective. There is cogent legislation in the United States against the invasion of any nonwhite group, which is really a crystallization of important attitudes. Labor groups have powerful organizations for the protection of the working men. No group, regardless of its racial or cultural attributes, can enter the United States in great numbers at present without meeting trenchant opposition. The Filipinos have encountered the great accumulation of anti-immigration sentiment now .so prevalent in the social heritage of the United States.

While there is at present some anti-Filipino opposition, the problem of this group is a matter to be worked out in the future. Unless attitudes are altered, the situation in the

United States will be about the same for them as for Chinese and Japanese. There will be certain places opened to them in various occupations, but their color will doubtless prevent complete assimilation, thus making them problems to themselves in a cultural organization where they do not have complete acceptance.

The Filipino question is one of the unsettled problems in the field of immigration. Assimilation must include co-operation on the part of Americans as well as a willingness and a capacity on the part of the Filipinos, or they will always remain an extraneous group. The fact that they are denied citizenship places them at once in a category that elicits certain definite attitudes concerning them. They would be considered undesirable if for no other reason. Restriction of type connotes inferiority to the average mind, a prejudice that makes thinking impervious to facts.

READINGS

Bogardus, Emory S., " The Filipino Immigrant Problem," *Sociology and Social Research,* May-June 1929
—— " Foreign Migrations within United States Territory," *Nat. Conf. of Social Work,* 1929: 573–9
—— " American Attitudes toward Filipinos," *Sociology and Social Research,* Sept.-Oct. 1929
—— " Filipino Immigrant Attitudes," *Sociology and Social Research,* May-June 1930
" Causes of California's Race Riots," *Literary Digest,* 104:12, Feb. 15, 1930
" Filipino Problem in California," *Monthly Labor Review,* 30:1270–2, June 1930
Goethe, C. M., " Filipino Immigration Viewed as a Peril," *Current History,* 34:353–4, June 1931
Gonzalo, D. F., " Social Adjustments of Filipinos in America," *Sociology and Social Research,* Nov.-Dec. 1929
Lasker, Bruno, *Filipino Immigration.* 1931
Malcolm, Roy, " Immigration Problems on the Pacific Coast," *Current History,* 33:726–8, Feb. 1931
Phillips, H., " Orientals on the Pacific Coast," *Nation,* 132: 12–14

Part V: *The Problem of Immigration and Conclusions*

CHAPTER XVIII

THE PROBLEM OF IMMIGRATION

PERHAPS the outstanding mistake that has been made in the study and analysis of most social problems is the fact that these problems have not been kept in their proper perspective. It is thoroughly scientific to abstract a problem from its many relationships in a configuration and talk about the problem, but when it comes to the matter of drawing conclusions regarding the effects and the importance of a question, the problem must be well oriented in its proper relationships or the person discussing the problem will find himself reacting to an isolated aspect of the whole rather than to the problem in its totality as a part of a larger situation.

There is no doubt that the United States has a problem of immigration, but it is not an isolated fact that can be considered apart from a larger situation in America. In discussing immigration most writers and lecturers have taken it away from its constitutive relationships. Also, there has always been a tendency to emphasize the pathological aspect of immigration, as has been the case in any social situation. When the increase in feeblemindedness has been under consideration there has been no effort to show how great has been the increase in the number of superior individuals. When the ill effects of immigration have been discussed, no effort has been made to show what have been the desirable results. Who is qualified to discuss scientifically the effects of immigration? Certainly there exist no objective data from which one can draw conclusions. In the first place, no one knows what would have happened if there had not been any immigration. Furthermore, one's point of view determines the manner in which he categorizes the various aspects of immigration as to their desirability. One person would say that isolated colonies of foreigners were dangerous to the safety of the United States. Many students of human behavior see these communities of European culture as a means of obviating disorganization and thus preventing the matter of immigration from becoming a greater problem than it is.

Many writers who have concerned themselves with the problem of immigration have been interested in showing that there should or should not be immigration. Consequently, certain phases have been emphasized apart from all other aspects. The undesirable features of immigration have no interpretable significance apart from the desirable aspects. The justification for the further existence of any situation is to be found in the relative importance of desirable and undesirable features. Any discussion that seeks to show the effects of immigration must include both angles of the problem. Furthermore, conditions associated with immigration are not necessarily caused by immigration. There is a well established practice in society, when two things are found together, to say that one has caused the other. Often this is not the case. For instance, the immigrant has been indicted for low wages when inadequate pay has resulted from a general industrial situation in which the employer has used the immigrant to bring his interests to actualization. This was shown by a statement in the New York *Nation* during the Lawrence strike.

For years the textile manufacturers have carried on a policy of gathering in the peasants of eastern and southeastern Europe to operate the looms of New England. The immigrants were distributed so that no more than fifteen per cent of any one race were employed in a single mill, and the apportionment was dispassionately determined so that men and women racially hostile to one another worked side by side. This was to render organization impossible and thus keep wages low." [1]

[1] Herbert A. Miller, "Treatment of Immigrant Heritages," *Proceedings of the National Conference of Social Work* 1919, p. 737.

If immigration is to be understood, it must be viewed as a part of a much larger situation. Life has changed so rapidly in the United States and there have been so many factors involved that it is impossible in many cases to determine which element has been important in any instance. If scientific caution is to be exercised, then there must be a great deal of research before much can be said about the ultimate effects of immigration. This point of view can be appreciated only with some conception concerning the manner in which immigration is a part of a much larger situation. It will be seen, then, that certain social phenomena attributed to immigration are only elements in the unprecedented social changes in the United States and the problems that attend the transition from a simple to a complex economic system.

In 1783 the United States was composed of thirteen colonies on the Atlantic seaboard with a population that was fairly homogeneous and a culture predominantly rural. A century later, the United States was a complex, industrial, urban society with a heterogeneous population.

The thirteen colonies were in the north largely farming communities about small towns; and in the south, great rural estates. There were few cities, and these were small. The largest, New York, had a population of but 29,906; and the average community was a township having under 1000 people. The members of these communities lived their lives in contact at practically all points. In relation to his neighbors, the New Englander might be on Monday the postmaster or the merchant, on Saturday the justice, and on Sunday the deacon in the church. Associations were largely face-to-face, attitudes were primary — immediate, concrete, and emotional. The community was organized more largely about sentiment than interests, and it was relatively isolated from other communities. . .

But in the three decades following the Civil War, the character of American life was completely changed. These decades witnessed a period of rapid national and industrial expansion. Factory communities began to blacken the skies from their smoking chimneys; a network of railroads and telegraphs bound communities more closely together; and great industrial and commercial cities sprang up, completely altering the nature of social life.[2]

[2] H. W. Zorbaugh, *The Gold Coast and the Slum* (University of Chicago Press 1929), pp. 253–254.

During the last half-century the range of territory stretching from Atlantic to Pacific was settled. Wave after wave of migration swept to the West, across the Mississippi, over the Missouri, beyond the mountains, along the coast, until finally the frontier disappeared.[3]

Rapid change always means a certain amount of disorganization. Since immigration has been a part of this unparalleled change, and since it was obviously an extraneous element, attention has been directed toward immigration as the explanation of many of our social problems. Ethnocentrism and the fact that the immigrant has had a geographical connection with many of the social problems in America accounts for the fact that there has been found in immigration a ready explanation for many social lesions.

In the rapid development of the United States from a wilderness to a great industrial society there was no frame of reference except a rural model to follow, consequently methods of control had to be created after changes had taken place. As Dr. Merriam has said: "A mighty process of urban and industrial concentration was going on, under the forms and traditions of rural democracy."[4] This shift, then, had no guide other than rural traditions which were *de trop* in an urban situation. Institutions were rural in their techniques and practices; customs, habits, and attitudes were rural. The immigrants as well as Americans came into this social transition with arcadian heritages and thus were poorly equipped to make adjustments. Native citizens who became a part of the change found it difficult to accommodate themselves to the rapid march of events with a mental organization that was essentially rural.

The history of the United States, from the standpoint of material culture, has been one of rapid changes with a "cultural lag" that will be discussed later. There was much material prosperity and poverty. Individual fortunes were amassed. There was an increasing concentration of popula-

---

[3] From Charles Edward Merriam, *American Political Ideas* (New York: The Macmillan Company 1920), p. 9. This quotation and those which immediately follow are reprinted by permission of The Macmillan Company, publishers.

[4] *Ibid.*, p. 34.

tion in urban centers, which created many new problems and thus social disorganization and personal demoralization.

In this process fundamental changes were made in the life and labor of men. In their housing conditions, in their working surroundings, in their facilities for leisure, and in many other ways far-reaching changes in human life were made. Not only were readjustments necessary within the city itself, but under the new conditions reconciliations of the ideals of the urban and rural communities were distinct features in the nation's life. The early prophets and statesmen of the Republic had thought of democracy as agrarian in its composition and rural in its tendencies, but by the end of the century the rush of population to great urban centers had changed in great part this portion of the foundations upon which the earlier philosophies had rested.[5]

Powerful " trusts " involving oil, steel, lumber, transportation, etc., were formed and placed the control of the industrial world into the hands of a few.

The growth of these gigantic organizations constitutes one of the most striking features in the development of American life. Into their hands flowed the control of billions of money, and the employment of millions of men. With their growth and activities there came an inevitable series of legal and political problems which demanded the attention of the lawyer, the statesman, the economist, and the philosopher.[6]

On the one side, there appeared an unparalleled concentration of activity in corporate form; on the other, the unprecedented concentration of labor in the trades unions.[7]

The unions were institutional techniques to meet certain problems that had emerged during the rapid changes and development of new systems of economic relationships. The legalization of trade unions, in itself, was a break with traditions and evidence that changes were taking place. There were organizations and movements in the field of agriculture, proof that conditions were changing in rural areas. All institutions and movements are the crystallization of the attitudes of certain individuals as to the way specific problems should be met. So the advent of any institutions, organizations, or movements may be regarded as an index of the presence of certain problems.

[5] *Ibid.*, p. 10.
[6] *Ibid.*, p. 14.
[7] *Ibid.*, p. 13.

The immigrant came to the United States as a laborer and found himself in the same situation as the American working man. His arrival did not, however, create this situation but contributed to it. He became a factor in a situation where the conditions of life were being revolutionized for most of the people in the United States and many other parts of the world. Urbanization brought great masses together and threw into contrast poverty and wealth.

So immigration must be considered along with the growth of urbanism, industrialism, unionism, corporations, feminism, etc. In its effects it cannot be understood apart from them. Without some of these there would have been very little immigration. So immigration, as a movement, is not a thing of itself but is interwoven with all that has taken place in the United States. More than this, as a problem it has an integral relationship to the nature of human nature.

Immigration of all periods has reached the United States when changes were taking place. "Conditions of life and labor were turned upside down. The ways of life were altered in a few years, while the ways of thought and the types of organization followed far in the rear. There developed new standards, new norms of conduct, new demands, new philosophies to match these new environments."[8] There were few people qualified by experience to interpret properly the economic tendencies of the times, and to develop a technique of control. Women entered industries. Child labor became a problem. Small business enterprises were swallowed up by large-scale industry. The masses became interested in an education. Old institutions encumbered by traditions failed to function. People worked against trends instead of in terms of these trends.

The attitude concerning government in this period of change was not one of respect, especially with those of power in the economic activities.

It was a situation in which the ruling powers wished to be let alone, employing the government only occasionally as in the case of the tariff, yet feeling that the government was at their disposal whenever required; but not frequently requiring it, and not much

[8] *Ibid.*, p. 21.

disposed to build up an effective government which might prove troublesome when set up and put in action. To this the prevailing popular opposition to economic concentration and the corrupt tendencies of politics of the spoils type contributed. Thus a prevailing type of thought regarding the government tended to a certain kind of contempt for it, not the type of theoretical dislike entertained by the anarchist, but a feeling that energetic government internally was more likely to make trouble than otherwise in the evolution of the nation's industries, just as labor was thought of frequently as a potential source of " trouble." Government was a necessity, but it was a corrupt, ignorant, and weak thing, to be roughly handled and sharply spoken to when contact with it became necessary — useful in times when force was needed at home or abroad for the protection of persons or property, but dangerous in that when once galvanized into action it showed a tendency to continue its activities. Its enthronement and its abdication were both awkward. Thus the political *mores* of the leading group was divided against itself. On the one hand, it preached patriotism, devotion to the state in international affairs, and in internal affairs respect for law and order as often as it became necessary to call upon the government for protection of persons and property in industrial disputes; but on the other hand the broader social interests of the state, the majesty of the public purpose, the supremacy of the common interest against the special, could not be too vigorously emphasized.[9]

Immigrants who prospered in America soon sensed this attitude and adopted it as a part of their superficial Americanization. Even the laborer realized that there was a disregard for law in the industrial world in which he worked.

In this era of rapid change the United States passed through a period when many customs, traditions, and institutions were no longer adapted to American conditions. Even the parliamentary system of government was no longer suited to the political needs.

The change in the nature of social life that has come with the city first attracted attention by the change that it brought in the nature of politics. Parliamentary government, under which elections are supposed to be based upon real issues, and carried out to decide those issues, grew out of a condition of small communities, primary contact, face-to-face associations. It is theoretically the government of the United States today. But while it was adapted to the needs of the thirteen seaboard colonies of 1790,

[9] *Ibid.*, pp. 27–28.

it is not adapted to the needs of an industrial nation of large cities.[10]

This industrial expansion brought with it problems entirely new to American life, problems with which parliamentarism was not prepared to cope. These were the days of the " captain of industry," of " concessions," and shortly of the " trust." At the same time the growth of the city, with its mobility and anonymity, its organization along lines of interest rather than sentiment, its specialization, its breaking down of local life, greatly changed the nature of political life. The old issues, which continued each four years to be written into doctrinaire party platforms, were no longer real issues — indeed, the host of social questions that came with the industrial society, and which were the real if imperfectly recognized issues of the day, were rarely acknowledged as political issues. People were no longer divided upon the formal political issues. Party struggles were no longer based upon constitutional questions. Party organizations were indifferent to social questions. Politics narrowed down to struggle for office and the booty of office. It was the day of the " spoils system " of the " ring " and the " machine." The " boss " became a power in local politics, and the " lobby " in national politics. The pursuit of " honest graft " was added to the professions.[11]

From the outset the United States has tried to function under traditions and customs that were not designed in the first place for a new country. Our cultural heritage from Europe was utilized when it was not a part of the situation in America. Especially is this true in the use of the English judicial system.

Not only were the colonial judicial organization and colonial policy as to the personnel of tribunals ill adapted to American conditions after the Revolution, but the procedure of the courts — and at that time procedure was the bulk of the legal system — was ill suited to a new and growing country, with its common law yet to shape and with institutions for training lawyers yet to be set up. . .

Nor was the substance of the English law, which we inherited at colonization or received after the Revolution, better adapted to the time and place than the court-organization and legal procedure which were to provide enforcing machinery.[12]

After a period of stability, extending from the middle of the

[10] H. W. Zorbaugh, *op. cit.*, pp. 252–253.
[11] *Ibid.*, pp. 254–255.
[12] Roscoe Pound, "The Crisis in American Law," *Harper's Monthly Magazine*, 152 : 153. 1925–1926.

last century to the present, a new era of dissatisfaction has set in. Once more our legal and judicial institutions are under fire — and justly so. And the reason is the same. We are in a period of transition, and our legal and judicial institutions, well adapted to and functioning adequately in the society for which they were devised and in which they grew up, are ill adapted to and function badly, or at best indifferently, in the society in which they find themselves. The census of 1920 showed a definite shift of the center of gravity of our population from country to city. Moreover, this growth has been chiefly in the large cities, whereas in the nineteenth century growth took place chiefly by the opening up of new areas to settlement and the building up of new agricultural communities. When we observe that the population of New York City multiplied by forty-six in one hundred years, by six in fifty years, and almost by four in the last twenty years; that Chicago was non-existent in 1820, and that its population has multiplied by nine in fifty years; that Cleveland, a village of less than one thousand inhabitants in 1820, had in 1920 a population of nearly 800,000 and had multiplied its population by more than eight in fifty years; that Detroit had multiplied its population by thirteen in fifty years, and by four in the last twenty years; and that Los Angeles had multiplied its population by one hundred in fifty years, and by almost six in the last twenty years, and had more than 576,000 inhabitants where there had been only a mission a century before — when we observe these things we may understand better the temporary breakdown of judicial justice in our large cities. A highly developed system of substantive law and a specialized machinery of prosecution, administration, judicial organization, legal procedure, and penal treatment, devised and shaped for pioneer, rural, agricultural America of the first half of the nineteenth century, are struggling with the wholly different conditions of the urban, industrial society of today. In the huge cities which have grown up all over the country in a generation the ill adaptation of the machinery to the task is acute.[13]

Recent immigrants left a more or less static peasant community and reached the United States when Americans were experimenting with a new urban life. Efforts were being made to use the social values and customs of village life in cities where they could not function. The immigrant of the recent groups came when the neighborhood as a means of social control was breaking down. Communities were in the process of disorganization. This situation is shown in the

[13] *Ibid.*, pp. 154–155.

study made by Mr. Zorbaugh of the Lower North Side in Chicago and published as *The Gold Coast and the Slum.*

> Throughout the Near North Side, then, community life, where it has not already disintegrated, is in process of disintegration. Community institutions are ceasing to function. The church, the school, the family, the occupational group, government, and the news have ceased to bear any direct relationship to local life. Behavior is individualized in the extreme. There is little or no public opinion. There is no common interest or cultural background. The greater part of the area is incapable of political action. What government there is on the Near North Side is in the hands of the social agency and the police. But neither the social agency nor the police meet with any degree of success. Life is highly disorganized — lived without the law, and without the mores of the larger society. The Near North Side is a section of the old frontier transplanted to the heart of a modern city.[14]

It is in areas similar to the Near North Side that immigrants come to live. Soon they are identified with the chaos that existed before they arrived. In the conflict of cultures they are soon involved in this disintegration and thus make a contribution to disorganization. The definition society gives the situation is that the immigrants are responsible for the disorganization. Especially is this true with those who do not understand the processes that go on day after day in the city, destroying community life and weakening the controls of traditional institutions.

The press has revealed many of the aspects of disorganization that have come through the rapid changes in America that have brought rural and urban cultures into conflict. "Periodically we witness sensational exposés of some aspect of the city's life — political corruption, festering slums, sweatshop exploitation, vice, crime."[15] "The man with the muckrake" and the "yellow press" showed to America the results of rapid changes which involved the immigrant, deteriorating neighborhood life, the failure of traditional institutions and disorganization in general. Publicity, however, showed that disorganization was a part of the rapid changes in America.

Much of the disorganization that has taken place has been

[14] H. W. Zorbaugh, *op. cit.*, pp. 198–199.   [15] *Ibid.*, pp. 268–269.

explained by the fact that not all aspects of a cultural complex change with equal rapidity. This has been called a "cultural lag."

Where one part of culture changes first, through some discovery or invention, and occasions changes in some part of culture dependent upon it, there frequently is a delay in the changes occasioned in the dependent part of culture. The extent of this lag will vary according to the nature of the cultural material, but may exist for a considerable number of years, during which time there may be said to be a maladjustment. It is desirable to reduce the period of maladjustment, to make the cultural adjustments as quickly as possible.[16]

Nowhere in society has the "lag" been greater than in the traditional institutions, the family, the church, and the school. Before the advance of material culture, life had been lived largely in terms of these three institutions, especially in the family, the chief primary group. The trend in the advance of material culture demanded some change in the family but there was a "cultural lag" in this respect. This was disorganizing for the American but even more so for the European peasant with whom the primary group exercised complete control. Under the old cultural régime, relationships were face-to-face and intimate, but the transition in America has postulated a different type of social relationship.

The advance of the material culture has broken up what Professor Cooley indicates as the primary group organization of society, and has substituted a derivative group organization as determinative in its stead. Consequently people's lives are no longer dominated chiefly by primary groups, at least in their late childhood and adult years, but by large impersonal groups, such as industrial and political units, through which we have not yet learned adequately to place responsibility or to maintain control in society. The primary groups remain, but they themselves have come under the dominance and shaping influence of the overhead impersonal or derivative groups. While they still do much to shape human nature directly, their character is increasingly determined by factors and processes that are often far removed from the direct and simple expression of human nature. Life becomes, as a consequence, increasingly regimented with respect to impersonal and non-spontaneous social and economic processes.

[16] William Fielding Ogburn, *Social Change* (New York: The Viking Press, Inc. 1923), p. 201.

This new overhead, abstract, group organization frequently changes the allegiance of the individual to the primary group or removes him from it altogether.   Thus the family is being increasingly disrupted by the demands and rewards of modern industry, and the new civic organization of the world has all but destroyed the old localism by which men were born, lived, and died in a single community, and, frequently under the same roof.

With the breaking down of the dominance of primary group organization and control has passed also the dominance of the primary attitudes and ideals which primary or face-to-face organizations sponsored.   In the old social order, before the coming of the new cultures, these primary attitudes and contacts determined our loyalties and gave emotional sanction to our principles, or even determined them for us.   All of this made for an emotional continuity of our culture which rendered social control fairly easy.   The absence of such determination and guidance of our loyalties and principles under the new social order has brought us dangerously near to social chaos. . .

The new material culture of the individual system has fostered a new institutional organization in law and in business practice, especially as respects the rights and privileges of women and children, which permits a new alignment of individuals to society as a whole or in larger units to supplant the old alignment and loyalty to the small family and neighborhood groups and to individuals.   These new social organizations we call derivative groups. They differ from primary groups in that their contacts are not face-to-face, but are indirect, and their organization is abstract rather than concrete and personal.   For example, the legal right of women to work for wages outside of the home and to retain the wages of their labor has dissolved their primary economic dependence upon the home group and has transferred it to the derivative industrial group and the derivative political group, the state.   The obvious social result here is that the primary home group becomes secondary in power of control to industry and to other derivative groups of which the worker becomes a member.   If the home retains its dominance in control under such conditions it will be because of the voluntary decision of the members; and this voluntary loyalty may snap under the strain of conflict with loyalties to wider and more derivative and compelling groups. Likewise, in case of a conflict of interests between members of the same primary group, such as the home, the revolting member may easily secede, because in most cases ready protection can be had from the derivative groups.

The new material culture in part calls the members of the primary groups away from their close contacts within the primary groups into wider and more abstract relationships in the fulfilment of their duties, and in part it makes such a transference of association possible through the fact that it has made feasible the establishment and economic support of numerous æsthetic, recreational, civic, religious, and other derivative cultural activities which are constantly clamoring for, and stimulating to, membership. Thus we observe that in cities especially there is no longer any appreciable continuity to, or permanency of, neighborhood life, and along with the new and growing tenant system on our farms the same transitoriness of neighborhood life is appearing there also. Likewise the city home, at least for large classes of our population, has come to be perhaps more nominal than real after the period of infancy and early childhood has passed. The farm family still remains fairly intact because the economic interests of the members of the farm family are likely to be concentrated upon the farm itself, until the sons and daughters go away to the city. Here, as in the preceding types of cases, the individuals in the primary groups are constantly building up new interest alignments and new loyalties to the derivative groups with which they become associated. These new interests and loyalties work in many cases to the permanent hurt of the primary group allegiances with which they are in functional conflict.

As yet we have not worked out a new philosophy of loyalties to the derivative group contacts which are as consistent and as highly socialized and moralized as were the old primary attitudes and ideals. The new relationship is too abstract and too difficult to grasp for the average mind. The old primary ideals and attitudes could be formulated in the folk mind itself in the actual process of living, of day-to-day adjustments. The new loyalties or principles of moral and social relationships on an abstract or derivative contact basis will have to be formulated by social science as the joint product of the social theorist and of the social technologist or social worker. The individual cannot do it for himself. We must build around this new body of social principles adapted to the needs of our derivative social organization a new religious and moral sanction if it is to be effective. We must also find some way of making it preserve the good and the indispensable in the old primary group loyalties and ideals. But this is not easy to do.[17]

This brief discussion of the situation in the United States shows the configuration in which immigration must be studied. It cannot be studied apart from its many relationships. The problem of immigration is only a part of the social change and advancement in material culture in the United States.

[17] Luther L. Bernard, "The Family in Modern Life," *International Journal of Ethics*, 38 : 429–432.

Immigration has given the United States problems to solve. This has been portrayed by many as a great injustice, endangering our political ideals and standards, which have outgrown their usefulness through cultural changes. Immigration has been condemned for forcing low standards of living upon the American working class when standards of living are determined not so much by the classes at the lowest industrial levels, but by those in controlling situations. This, however, does not remove the fact that America has had tremendous social problems of increasing complexity to meet, partly because of immigration. But no nation will deteriorate so long as there are problems confronting it. Give a nation problems to solve and endow it with the virility that the United States has evidenced and there will never be any nationalistic decay.

Some of the countries that have sent the recent immigrants to the United States have struggled for centuries with problems greater to them than the immigration question has ever been to the United States. A case in point would be the Bohemians who won their independence from the domination of Germany. The British Isles have been able to assimilate a diverse population and become a great nation. The United States has made her progress with a problem of immigration present at all times.

It is not possible to say just what has been the effect of immigration on the United States. Knowledge of human nature as well as knowledge of the importance of social interaction and the diffusion of culture leads to the conclusion that there have been tremendous effects, but it is hard to sort them out from other cogent influences. We know that the present status of America among civilized countries is due to her propitious natural conditions and the type of population that has come from foreign lands. If another racial group had come first, with a diverse history and culture, there is no doubt that our social organization would have been quite different. There would have been a different social, political, and economic organization.

Knowledge of the character of human nature and its dependence on the culture in which it developed produces further evidence that the United States has a problem of immigration. People do not want to change their habits, attitudes, and philosophies of life. The reason that most people do not make good anarchists or communists is that they are required to change their own human nature, and human nature, once it has developed, resists change. This is true of both native Americans and immigrants. This fact alone, without social changes and advances in material culture, would create a problem of immigration. The ethnocentrism involved results in attitudes concerning immigrants that increase the problem of adjustment, and the problem of immigration is one of accommodations.

The human nature that we find in ourselves through introspection is the criterion by which we judge the immigrant from southern and eastern Europe. If the Pole, Magyar, Czech, Jew, Russian, or Italian expresses his vanity, curiosity, pride, love, fear, and other human qualities differently from the American, it is hard to think of him as a person with the same elements of human nature or to believe that from a cultural standpoint he could have been an American had he acquired his personality organization and his social world in America.

The very character of human nature makes it difficult for any person to understand sympathetically any group whose traditions and customs differ from his own. The social heritage in which one finds himself at birth, or shortly after birth, becomes the standard by which he measures the traditions and mores of others. He can draw conclusions only in terms of his own experiences. If we do not understand the culture of others through scientific study, we shall continue to think of all other cultures as inferior to our own. We shall think of others as human, but human in an inferior sense.

A part of the problem of immigration lies in the fact that immigrants and Americans do not understand each other. Ambitious programs of Americanization have been undertaken without any knowledge of the history or culture of the group involved. Any adjustment that the immigrant makes in this country must be in terms of the human nature that he brings with him from his native land. Since his human nature is directly contingent upon his historical as well as his contemporaneous experience in his original home, Americanization workers cannot expedite immigrant adjustment without understanding his native culture.

A sympathetic knowledge of the life and hopes of the people of these un-American American neighborhoods is rare among us. An understanding of the racial history, of the social and economic development and of present political tendencies in the countries from which the inhabitants of such a neighborhood come is much more unusual. A knowledge of both their life here and their life at home is necessary for intelligent community planning. In the attempts made to help those who have been unable to make the necessary adjustments to the new conditions they encounter here, we have usually acted quite without the information which is necessary for the proper diagnosis of the source of their difficulties, and as long as individual cases are not properly diagnosed successful treatment is only a happy accident and cannot form the basis for a program of prevention.[18]

The general attitude concerning human nature is responsible for the idea that all that is needed to deal with immigrants in the Americanization process is a sentimental interest. The average citizen feels qualified to explain the most complex case of social behavior. Most Americanization workers have not understood the immigrants in relation to their culture, nor do they understand the nature of human nature.

One reason why it is difficult to develop a science of human behavior is the fact that most people feel that they understand human behavior because they possess it and because they live with it every day. But direct observation without scientific study does not equip one to understand so complex a reality as human behavior. As one author has said:

. . . There is nothing so misleading as direct observation; for numberless generations people believed that the earth was flat and stationary and that the sun revolved about it. This was a common sense generalization based on direct observation. It was a self-evident truth; everyone could see that it was so.[19]

[18] Grace Abbott, "The Immigrant as a Problem in Community Planning," *Publications of the American Sociological Society*, Vol. XII (1918), p. 169.
[19] E. B. Reuter, *The American Race Problem*, p. 66.

We have inherited the same traditional thinking regarding human behavior. The most naïve and inexperienced person feels that he is qualified to explain and does explain, to his own satisfaction, the most complex instances of human behavior. Human behavior that would require months of study before a behavior specialist could understand and explain it can be handled at once by the average person. The student of human behavior realizes the tremendous task in adjusting an adult immigrant to a strange culture, but many Americanization workers need only their ethnocentrism and maudlin sympathy.

The adjustment of the immigrant has been difficult and the problem of immigration greatly increased because the science of human behavior is not well developed. One reason why this science has progressed so slowly is the fact that there exists an attitude that the layman and the individuals who are experts in other fields are qualified to explain human behavior and direct adjustments. All the other sciences and disciplines had to pass through the same stage. The science of medicine was once in the home remedy stage and people were not interested in natural causes. But medicine has passed this emotional, superstitious stage, and we now turn to the specialist who has at his service the latest findings of the research laboratory.

To be a physician one must be well informed concerning the structure and function of the human anatomy. But that is not the case in the field where problems of human behavior are concerned. It has not been required of one to know anything about the nature of immigrant human nature and the cultural experiences of the new arrivals on our shores, to guide them through the Americanization process. This attitude has greatly increased the problem of immigration. When it comes to the matter of diagnosis and treatment, the science of human behavior is still in the " home remedy " stage, and the statesmen, the politicians, and the persons who reach the public from the platform and through the press think they know a great deal about human behavior without any training in the field. Human behavior is not a simple phenomenon, nor is it easily understood. Even among experts in the field, only the self-satisfied specialist feels that he knows a lot about human behavior. If the same requirements demanded in medicine, in law, and in engineering had been required in handling the matter of immigration and other social questions in the United States, these problems would have been greatly reduced in their results.

Those who have dealt throughout the years with the question of immigration, with rare exception, have been sentimentalists, idealists, or exploiters, both economic and political. What is needed is a realistic attitude, a realization that the character of human nature makes it impossible for an adult immigrant to become Americanized. The understanding that the isolation in colonies makes eventually for a better adjustment is likewise necessary. The immigrant, like other human beings, must make all adjustments in terms of past experience. In cultural areas of their own, the immigrants have made temporary accommodations to American life. " They conserved their religious rites and customs, they developed particular institutions, and kept alive the traditional culture, the racial consciousness, and the national genius of their people." [20] This is a statement concerning Jewish life in Central Europe, but it is descriptive of the function of immigrant colonies in America. On the basis of what we know about behavior, we can say that these colonies have prevented disorganization for the adult immigrant and minimized the problem of immigration. Mr. Cohen has shown the rôle of segregation in the transition from one culture to another in the following statement:

Socially, the ghetto in the West is necessitated by the immigration of hosts of Jews into countries whose language, conditions, and modes of life are utterly strange to them. But its inhabitants are never permanent inmates: they use it at most as a half-way house, as a transitional stage between East and West. The influences from without penetrate slowly, subtly, inevitably, luring the Jew into the outer world. By dint of industry, sobriety, and thrift he reaches a position that makes him discontented with his abode in the ghetto, and he leaves it for a more spacious quarter, where he will find more quiet and comfort. By that time he will

[20] Israel Cohen, "The Jewish Community," *The Sociological Review*, Vol. III (1910), p. 216.

have mastered the language both in speech and writing, and become pretty familiar with the principal conditions of his adopted fatherland. He possesses a gift for adaptability due in large measure to the hereditary effects of his people's migrations, whilst the process of assimilation is favoured and stimulated by his native co-religionists, who make " Anglicisation " or " Americanisation," or whatever else the local term may be, a cardinal principle in their communal policy. Thus the Western ghetto is but the preparatory school in which the orthodox Jew of the East, with all his ingrained ideas, traditions, prejudices, is gradually developed into the modern Jew of the West.[21]

Even in this somewhat shielded environment, the migration from one country to another proves to be a critical experience for immigrants. Peasants who have lived in a rural or village community where there was no doubt in their minds about their status find themselves bewildered in America where patterns of behavior are not definite. The movement from a relatively static social environment to one characterized by mobility and change is replete with difficulties. In this transition there are bound to be many pathological adjustments, especially in the economic process. With the younger generation, there is the situation involving the much emphasized conflict of cultures, in which standards are in a flux and the resultant behavior is a violation of many formal laws and ordinances.

An attitude of realism discovers the fact that many of the second generation immigrants will become disorganized because they live on the peripheries of two cultural worlds with little opportunity to develop human nature in terms of either. They become " marginal men." [22] This is true not only of the children of immigrants, but is true of any person who experiences difficulty in acquiring a world in which to live.

A realistic attitude, also, discovers that the biological process does not produce the social nature of any individual. His human nature, no matter what his racial affiliation may be, is produced in the social process and is contingent upon the

[21] *Ibid.*, p. 255.
[22] See Robert E. Park, "Human Migrations and the Marginal Man," *American Journal of Sociology*, XXXIII, May 1928.

culture in which it developed. This means that the offspring of any nationality can take on the American cultural pattern and in a few generations be just as American as anyone. Anthropologists and race specialists are agreed that "so far as innate human capacity is concerned, there is probably little choice between the different races and peoples immigrating to this country."[23] This being the case, the quality of the population will be little affected. Regarding the effects of amalgamation of the recent immigrants with Americans, dogmatic statements cannot be made since there has been little cross-breeding. Since there is not a pure race in existence there is probably little need for concern. Experts in the field of heredity have shown that the same parents may produce superior, mediocre, or inferior individuals. "From the same set of genes may be produced, by combining them in different ways, superior individuals, mediocre individuals, and inferior individuals, all of them in various diverse types."[24] The chances for superiority, mediocrity, or inferiority are many for any nationality.

It is not possible here to go into a complete discussion of the matter. But for those who feel that the immigrants from eastern and southern Europe are inferior, or that the inferior individuals from this part of Europe are coming to America, it might be well to read the recent book, *The Biological Basis of Human Nature,* by H. S. Jennings of Johns Hopkins University. He says:

From the great mass of mediocre parents arise more superior offspring than from the few distinguished parents; more inferior offspring than from the inferior parents. And superior parents often produce mediocre or inferior offspring; inferior parents at times produce mediocre or superior offspring. In consequence of this situation, decrease or even complete stoppage of the propagation of the "superior" individuals, or of the "inferior" individuals has very little effect on the average grade of the next generation.[25]

[23] E. B. Reuter, *Population Problems* (Philadelphia: J. B. Lippincott Company 1923), p. 286.
[24] Herbert Spencer Jennings, *The Biological Basis of Human Nature* (New York: W. W. Norton & Company, Inc. 1930), p. 25.
[25] *Ibid.,* p. 248.

Within the same race there are superior individuals and inferior individuals. In racial crossings the result seems to be the same.

With respect to the main features of physical structure and of physiology, the offspring of parents belonging to diverse races are as perfect and vigorous and efficient as the offspring of members of the same race. We may dismiss from consideration, so far as crosses of human races are concerned, the question of serious incompatibility of chromosomes or genes, such as we find in crosses between organisms standing far apart in their structure and physiology.[26]

Where mixture occurs among races which, though different, do not show marked superiorities and inferiorities in important ·respects, and under circumstances in which the hybrids are not at a lasting social disadvantage, we have the situation exemplified by the mixing of European races in the United States. In such cases the consequences result mainly from the fact that the diverse racial characteristics appear in many new combinations. Some of these combinations may be inharmonious, disadvantageous. Some of them manifest the combined poorer qualities of the races concerned. Others show the combined better qualities of different races, giving rise to superior individuals. All these things will occur for physical and physiological characteristics: and also for mental characteristics. Some of the hybrids will be poorer physiological machines than either parent race; some will be better. If one race has greater activity and energy, the other artistic ability, some of the offspring may have both; they are geniuses. Other offspring will get lack of energy from one race, lack of artistic ability from the other. A population derived from a mixture of races having diverse characteristics will be much more heterogeneous than a population from a single race. There may be better combinations, and worse combinations, than are found in the single races. There will certainly be many individuals showing combinations of characteristics not found in the original races. In the long run there is selective elimination of the inefficient combinations, so that finally a race emerges that is again relatively homogeneous, combining characteristics from all the original races. This process has been gone through many times in the past; through it have arisen the races of the present day.[27]

These same results are to be found within the same race. While the result of cross-breeding is a hybrid that may be superior or inferior, just as in the case of any mating within

[26] *Ibid.*, p. 278.   [27] *Ibid.*, pp. 287–288.

the same group, there may be a problem of social maladjustment. This, however, is due to social definitions and is not caused by racial mixtures. This maladjustment is in the social process and not in the biological process.

The immediate consequences of race crossing, whether for good or evil, often depend on diversity of social systems in the two races. If the two races have very diverse social systems, as have Americans and Asiatics, as have Europeans and American Indians, the hybrid individual does not fit either system; he is rejected by both. This places him in an unfortunate situation. But this need not mean that he is essentially unfit, as compared to the single races. If such hybrids could start even with members of the single races, each developing his own social system, possibly that produced by the hybrids would be as valuable as the others. But coming into a world in which social systems are already established, the hybrid between races whose social systems are diverse is at a serious disadvantage. Such difficulties are, however, from the point of view of biology, very transitory, though they may be serious while they last.[28]

The following case recorded by Dr. Sidney L. Gulick shows the result of racial mixture in one case, at least:

My parents were missionaries in the Caroline Islands from 1854-61. Among the most serious obstacles to their work were the lives of dissolute white sailors. One of them, a notorious murderer, at his death gave my father a four-year old girl born to him by one of those savage women. Could a child possibly have worse ancestry? My parents reared her as the eldest daughter. I thought of her as my oldest sister and did not know until her death, ten years later, that she was an adopted child. She learned to speak English and to be in every respect one of us. My mother said of her that she never knew her to do anything wrong; she was perfectly obedient, gentle, kind, and truthful. She evinced no tendencies to theft and deceit, not even to ill temper. She was absolutely trustworthy.[29]

Anthropologists and ethnologists find from their scientific data no reason for worry about the outcome of intermarriage between native Americans and European immigrants. So eminent an authority as Dr. Franz Boas says:

There is no reason to suppose that from the present migration from all parts of Europe and from many parts of Asia there will

[28] *Ibid.*, p. 287.
[29] Sidney L. Gulick, *The American Japanese Problem* (New York, Charles Scribner's Sons 1914), pp. 128-129.

result an inferior mixed population. All historical, biological, and sociological considerations point to the conclusion that we have at present merely a repetition on a large scale of the phenomena of mixture from which have sprung the present European nations.[30]

Much emphasis has been placed on the superiority of the colonial settlers but we do not have adequate scientific data to make anything more than vague generalizations about the early American stock. Some were superior individuals and others were not. The descendants of some early settlers have been and are outstanding individuals while others were very inferior. These statements might be applied to the immigrants of all periods. Early immigration from northwestern Europe was largely from the middle class, but in America, with equal opportunities, many superior individuals have been produced. We have seen that many of the early migrants were redemptioners and indentured servants; many others were social variants. Much of our legislation for the exclusion of undesirables was passed as a reaction to early immigrants. Out of early migrations have come many superior individuals in the United States, and out of them also have come many criminals, paupers, and other maladjusted individuals. Some who were considered desirable when they arrived have produced offspring who became undesirables. Some successful citizens today can trace their ancestry to indentured servants and to other classes not regarded as desirable when they were admitted as immigrants at the Atlantic ports.

There were superior individuals among the colonists both from the European continent and from the British Islands. There were outstanding people in the immigrant stream that followed from the same source. There were, also, mediocre and inferior individuals among those who have helped to develop the United States from a pioneer country to a world power. The composition in this respect was similar to that found in most population groups. An analysis of the early stream of immigration, considering the success of the groups

[30] Franz Boas, "Fallacies of Racial Inferiority," *Current History*, Vol. 25 (1926–27), p. 682. Reprinted by special permission of *The Current History Magazine*, the monthly periodical of The New York Times Company.

involved, makes one less apprehensive about the ultimate outcome with recent immigration.

The sociological effects of immigration on American cultural life are hard to determine. We do know that through contacts and social interaction a process of acculturation goes on and that both the natives and the immigrants experience some modifications in their cultural organization until they are eventually practically the same. The strength of ethnocentrism has probably kept each group from realizing the values that could have come from the culture of the other. There has been no conscious effort to utilize the best phases of the foreign cultures that have come to America. It was pointed out early in this book that the content of each unit of culture with the immigrants of any nationality differs from the content of the same unit in the United States. The difference is greater with the recent immigrant. Many feel that the dissimilarity is so great that the general cultural level in America is lowered.

In the discussion of the composition of recent immigration, we observed that most groups were not English-speaking. They have not had the same educational opportunities as those from northwestern Europe. They are peasants from countries that have suffered for centuries at the hands of stronger powers. Through this experience they are ethnocentric to a high degree concerning their language, religion, and other cultural elements. Their standard of living, in most cases, is regarded as very low in the United States.

These differences tend to lower the general cultural level in the United States. Naturally there is more illiteracy, but this has changed with the second generation. The average standard of living was lowered but the American-born demand a wage equal to that received by anyone. The ethnocentrism regarding language swings in the opposite direction with the children of foreign peasants in our schools; they are ashamed of the speech of their parents. The customs and habits to which they subscribe are American. Their interests are at variance with those of their ancestors. This all shows that the immediate effects are not the ultimate results of recent immigration.

What the ultimate sociological effects will be no one is prepared to say. Perhaps the coming of so diverse a population has made possible the versatility that is found in America. There must be a realization that Europeans and Asiatics are here in great numbers and that the process of interaction is going on. A realistic attitude that seeks to understand what has happened, so that the interaction of the future may be directed, will result in effects that will be desirable. Ethnocentrism, emotional sentimental reactions to the problem will increase the problem of immigration.

An attitude of realism leads to the conclusion that Americanization cannot mean trying to crowd all nationalities and all individuals into the same social mold. What we call *American* is not the result of one cultural pattern. There has always been regionalism, culturally speaking, in the United States. This country will not be weakened, culturally, economically, or politically, if the Americanization process lets each ethnic group maintain its best characteristics. On the contrary the United States will suffer if the process of assimilation operates in any other way.

In the process of Americanization, with the immigrant the problem is not that of producing incipient human nature, a process that more or less takes care of itself once it has started, rather it is a more difficult problem — that of changing human nature that has developed in a foreign culture. For this reason it is essential that the Americanization workers and others interested in assimilation should be trained. They should understand the character of human nature and the social process by which it develops. There should be training in Sociology, History of Cultures, Economics, Political Science, Heredity, and Psychology. Otherwise the work of Americanization will be on an ethnocentric, emotional basis. The development of a real science of human behavior will result in adequate social controls.

There must be a realization that there is something in the past of the immigrant that is valuable for Americanization. The immigrant has a body of socially created attitudes that must be used in the process of assimilation. American values must become identified with the sentiments of the immigrant.

The culture of the peasant is much more important for adjustments than his racial affiliation. In the process of Americanization the first adjustments will not be in terms of American culture. The immigrant does not participate directly in American life except in an economic sense. Therefore, he is not controlled by American life. The United States has never been entirely American. It has always been English-American, Irish-American, Italian-American, Slavic-American, etc. In these various cultural areas the patterns of behavior slowly become more American. In discussing the Polish group, it has been said:

> This Polish-American society as a whole is, indeed, slowly evolving from Polonism to Americanism, as is shown by the fact that its members, particularly those of the second generation, are continually acquiring more American attitudes and being more influenced by American civilization. But this " assimilation " is not an individual but a group phenomenon, to be compared with such processes as the progressive Germanization of Czech society up to a hundred years ago or the adoption of French culture by the Polish, Russian, and German aristocracies in the course of the 18th century.[31]

The process of assimilation requires new schemes of behavior, new codes of conduct, different institutional adjustments; in short, a change in human nature. This cannot take place through legislation or force, but ought to be a slow unconscious process in which the immigrant scarcely realizes that he is changing. In the isolation of immigrant communities, their ideas, attitudes, and values slowly become American. They work outside the community. Their foreign institutions were not transplanted with their original content since the situation to be met in America is not the same. The change is noticed in their language which comes to include many English words. " A good illustration is the language of the American Poles which, though still etymologically Polish, contains an increasing number of American slang words which are treated as roots and used with Polish inflexions and prefixes and whose syntax and literary appli-

[31] W. I. Thomas and F. Znaniecki, *The Polish Peasant in Europe and America* (N.Y. 1918) by permission of and special arrangement with Alfred A. Knopf, Inc., authorized publishers, V, ix.

cation (the latter more easily influenced than etymology by changes in the form of thought) are growing more and more specifically local and neither Polish nor American." [32]   This same change took place with the Germans in Pennsylvania much earlier.

It has already been pointed out that Americanization is not the same in all parts of the United States because the cultural characterization is not the same in all localities. Neither has it been the same for all periods. Americanization during the colonial period was not the same as it is today. Assimilation, furthermore, is desired on a level where immigrants have very few contacts. If they were Americanized at once it would have to be on a slum level where they live. Values have a different meaning in the slum areas of American cities from what they have in other regions.

Mention has been made of the fact that demoralization results when Americanization is forced or directed by people who do not understand the character of human nature. In a peasant community all aspects of life are closely related. If one unit of culture loses its controlling influence, then all others tend to be weakened. It has been observed again and again " that when an individual rejects any social tradition of his group all other traditions usually lose their hold upon him, so close is the association between all of them." [33]

The immigrant has been censured for living in colonies in our large cities and propagating his foreign culture. The very organization of urban life with its processes of isolation and segregation makes it impossible for him to do otherwise if he wanted to, and of course he has no such desire.

There is no way of knowing just how much disorganization has been prevented for the first generation by the fact that the migration can be made as a group and each group can settle near a European or an Asiatic neighbor. Thus, after a fashion, the immigrants are able to establish a daily social life similar to the one in some foreign village. It makes possible an objective reality which corresponds to the life organization of habits, attitudes, interests, and philosophy of life of the individual and thus prevents disorganization.

[32] *Ibid.*, V, xiii–xiv.   [33] *Ibid.*, V, 169.

It must be remembered that a sudden change in cultural affiliation does not mean stability in terms of American culture but the abandonment of standards, habits, and philosophy of life without genuine factors being put in their places. The integrating of new experiences into a personality is a gradual process and not an abrupt change. The transplantation of a foreign village to an American industrial city offers a chance for an interchange of old memories. The peasants wait together for news from the homeland which interests them more than unfamiliar affairs in the United States. They show more enthusiasm about the political situation in their native land. This is not true because they are immigrants — Italians, Germans, Bulgarians, Magyars, etc., but because of the character of human nature. They are familiar with the home situation. It is part of their life organization through their mental imagery. All people think in terms of their past experience. It is not possible to do otherwise. What would be considered group solidarity in their native land becomes a clannish spirit by definition in the United States. The relationship is not different and could not be expected to change merely because they moved. The reminiscence of their past life in an antagonistic social situation makes their old habits and customs seem more important than ever before. Once these habits were accepted; now they are emotionally cherished. The experiences of the immigrants from the time they leave home are such that they cling tenaciously to their own culture. In terms of it they can think and act; in terms of the strange situation, they are nonplused and often appear stupid. We may dislike the fact that immigrants think in terms of the past, but it is the nature of human nature to do so.

Racial or cultural prejudice is another phenomenon that needs to be defined by a realistic attitude, so that we may know just what is involved. We have reached the stage in the study of human behavior where we can no longer be emotional about cultural relationships. We need first of all to know why there is racial prejudice. This was partly answered in the discussion of ethnocentrism, but should be given further consideration here.

Racial prejudice, which is often cultural prejudice, exists as a cogent fact in the United States as it does in all parts of the world. It will continue to exist as long as human nature is developed as it is today. It will continue to exist as long as there is prejudice in human nature at all. Racial prejudice is not different from any other prejudice. It is exactly the same type of social phenomenon as color prejudice, dislikes in dress, in manners, food aversions, etc.

An educational system such as we have throughout the world keeps alive prejudice in human nature. Narrow specialists are produced everywhere. This is true of informal and formal education. A life is too short to develop it without prejudice. Economy of time is necessary if one is to accomplish anything. There must be predilections and aversions.

If we are to be moral, then we must be prejudiced against immorality. If we favor peace, then we must be opposed to war. So it is throughout all the social ramifications of our existence, and so it is in relation to our mores and traditions. If we are to have an organized personality it must be in relation to an objective world and in relation to certain mores and traditions. If we are to subscribe to certain mores, then we must have some feeling of opposition to mores that differ greatly. The only other alternative is to have a scientific understanding of human nature. Out of knowledge comes a sympathetic understanding productive of great tolerance, much greater than the pseudo-tolerance that comes because we are told that it is our duty to love everybody. If we understand human nature and the process by which it develops, and acquire this knowledge before we are too old, then there is some possibility of a certain amount of tolerance. If we have a special liking for our own traditions and mores, then for that very reason we shall have a dislike for anything that differs greatly. Ethnocentrism is the inevitable consequence of the social process by which human nature develops. Prejudice will be greater with some than with others since the experiences of some are narrow and held more by traditional thinking.

READINGS

Adams, Thomas S. and Sumner, Helen L., *The Problem of Immigration.* 1908

Arrlitt, A. H., " On the Need for Caution in Establishing Race Norms," *Jour. of Applied Psychology,* 25: 179–183. 1921

Barnes, Harry E., *Living in the Twentieth Century.* 1928

Beard, Charles A. and Beard, Mary, *The Rise of American Civilization.* 1928

Becker, Howard, " Sargasso Iceberg: A Study in Cultural Lag and Institutional Disintegration," *Amer. Jour. of Sociology,* 34: 492–506. Nov. 1928

Bernard, L. L., " Conditions of Social Progress," *Amer. Jour. of Sociology,* 28: 21–48. July 1922

—— " Inventions and Social Progress," *Amer. Jour. of Sociology,* 29: 1–33. July 1923

Boas, Franz, " Fallacies of Racial Inferiority," *Current History,* 25: 571–582. 1927

—— " The Nordic Nonsense," *Forum,* 74: 502–511. 1925

—— " The Question of Racial Purity," *American Mercury,* 3: 163–169. Oct. 1924

—— " What Is Race? " *Nation,* 120: 89–91. 1927

Bogardus, E. S., *Immigration and Race Attitudes.* 1928

Brown, Gilbert, " Intelligence as Related to Nationality," *Jour. of Educational Research,* 14: 1–20. 1922

Chapin, F. Stuart, *Cultural Change.* 1928

Cooley, C. H., *Social Process.* 1922

Davies, Maurice R., *A Constructive Immigration Policy.* 1923

Dixon, Roland B., *The Building of Cultures.* 1928

Dorsey, George A., " Race and Civilization," *Whither Mankind,* edited by Charles A. Beard, Chapter X. 1926

Fairchild, Henry P., *Immigration.* Revised ed., Chapter XXI. 1926

—— *The Melting-Pot Mistake.* 1926

Faris, Ellsworth, " Remarks on Race Superiority," *Social Service Review,* I, 36–45. March 1927

Feingold, Gustave A., " Intelligence of First Generation of Immigrant Groups," *Jour. of Educ. Psychology,* 15: 65–82. 1924

Feldman, Herman, *Racial Factors in American Industry.* 1931

Fish, Carl, *The Rise of the Common Man.* 1928

Frazier, Edward F., " The Pathology of Race Prejudice," *Forum,* 77: 856–862. 1927

Freeman, R. Austin, " Some Ethical Consequences of the Industrial Revolution," *International Jour. of Ethics,* 33: 347–368. 1923

Goldenweiser, A. A., " Some Problems of Race and Culture in the

United States," *Proceedings of the National Conf. of Social
    Work.* 1922
Grant, Madison, *The Passing of the Great Race.* 1916
Haskin, Frederick J., *The Immigrant an Asset and a Liability*
Hiller, E. T., *The Strike.* 1928
Hourwich, I. A., *Immigration and Labor.* 1912
Jenks, J. W. and Louck, W. J., *The Immigration Problem.* 1913
Lasker, Bruno, *Race Attitudes in Children.* 1929
Merriam, C. E., *American Political Ideas,* 1865–1917. 1920.
    Chapters I–II, pp. 1–70
—— *The American Party System.* 1922. Chapters IV–VII, pp.
    102–200
Miller, H. A., *Races, Nations, and Classes,* Chapter XII, pp. 129–
    145. 1924
North, C. C., *Social Problems and Social Planning.* 1932
Ogburn, W. F., *Social Change.* 1923
Randall, John Herman, Jr., *Our Changing Civilization.* 1929
Reuter, E. B., *The American Race Problem.* 1927
—— *Population Problems.* 1923. Chapters XVIII–XXI, pp.
    267–330
Speranze, Gino, *Race or Nation.* 1925
Sullivan, Mark, *Our Times: The United States* 1900–1925. 1927

CHAPTER XIX
CONCLUSION

THE QUESTION of immigration in the United States has been important for the following reasons which, of course, are not mutually exclusive.

(1) Immigration has been an important question since it is a part of a much larger problem situation in the United States, the growth of a new country involving an unprecedented transition from a relatively static, rural social order to a chaotic, complex, industrial, and urban organization. The outstanding problems in this transition exist because of the social change and advancement in material culture, and not because any particular ethnic groups were implicated.

Foreign peasants along with rural Americans have been involved as the human element in this transition. Immigration, however, has not created a single problem in this industrial growth. Without immigration the United States would have all its social lesions — unemployment, poverty, pauperism, crime, vice, etc. This statement does not remove immigration from the realm of problems; it merely orients it in its true perspective, in the inextricable, complex configuration of which it is a part.

If the immigrants have caused more concern in the cultural transition in the United States than any other group, it is not because they have created any problems in this transition but because their units of culture and human nature have been at greater variance with the demands of the new urban situation in America than those in the United States of the same educational, economic, and cultural level. They have caused very little more difficulty in the industrial world than have the mountaineers and other isolated groups in the United States. In addition to the variance of their units of human nature and culture, the chief difference can be explained by the fact that they have entered the industrial process in greater numbers and that they are an extraneous group, defined and treated as such by Americans.

(2) The United States has a problem of immigration because there has been a " cultural lag " — that is, few aspects of non-material culture have changed so rapidly as material culture with inventions, scientific accomplishments, discoveries, etc. Furthermore, related aspects of non-material culture have not changed with the same rate of speed. This " lag " on the part of certain cultural elements has resulted in considerable disorganization, and the immigrant has been identified with many phases of this disintegration.

The real significance of a " cultural lag " is seen when we realize that the attitudes of the people in America and the character of human nature are responsible for it. Dr. C. C. North has given reasons for this cultural inertia that throw some light on the situation making immigration such a tremendous problem.

A second reason for a slower rate of change in the non-material culture is that the dissemination of new patterns meets stronger resistance than does that of change in material culture. This resistance is of two sorts, an emotional one on the part of those whose interests lie in the direction of maintaining the *status quo*. The emotional resistance arises from the fact that matters of ethical and religious principles, political theories, forms of human relations, such as class and race, lie much closer to the inner citadel of personality than do the use of material objects or the technique of economic activity.[1]

In this " cultural lag " a large percentage of the native population become problems, especially in those areas of social life where there is the greatest change in material culture. In this relationship one finds most of the recent immigrants since they are nearly all involved in the industrial

[1] Reprinted by permission of the publishers from C. C. North, *Social Problems and Social Planning*, McGraw-Hill Book Company, Inc. 1932.

process where change is taking place. With their cultural ideas the product of a foreign peasant social order, they become an important element in the inertia back of cultural changes and thus we have a problem of immigration.

(3) The problem of immigration in the United States is complex because the rapid change from a rural culture to an industrial social order has created areas of disorganization in urban centers in which are concentrated most of the social problems in American life. It is in these areas of disintegration that the immigrants of the first generation have to live — they have no choice. In this ecological distribution the immigrants become identified with all the disorganization of the slum area in which they reside. This in itself gives the United States a problem of immigration through no particular fault of the immigrant.

Any group living in a poverty belt of an industrial city will experience a certain amount of poverty. Delinquency areas produce delinquents, irrespective of nationality; bright-light areas are regions of demoralization. Adjustments are always to social situations and as soon as the immigrant leaves the European or Asiatic cultural area that he has transplanted in America, his adjustments are to situations of disintegration, since he does not have *entrée* to areas that are more desirable. As we have already observed, immigration is a problem because of this area. The immigrant has been condemned for living in foreign colonies in these areas of disorganization, but he could not live elsewhere if he chose. "The immigrant is often criticized for living in segregated groups. No criticism could be more unjust. Is it not perfectly natural everywhere for social groups having something in common to try to live in the same neighborhood? Even should they try to avoid segregation, their American neighbors would not allow it. The result is that every effort is made to keep them from getting into a new section." [2] It is this criticism of an unavoidable situation that accentuates the question of immigration.

Furthermore, when Americans discover the recent immi-

[2] H. A. Miller, *The School and the Immigrant*, p. 57.

grants living in the slums they make the question of immigration a greater problem by assuming that they are there because of a low mentality, or other inadequacies. Their slum occupancy is evidence of inferiority and a basis for intolerance.

(4) The problem of immigration in the United States has been complex because techniques of social control were not worked out for the unprecedented change that was taking place in America. Unpredicted trends were initiated, to which the first reactions were those of opposition. Consequently trends were opposed, but not directed.[3] Instead of getting into these trends and working out social controls in terms of them, all energy was wasted in an effort to return to the good old days.

There were no precedents to follow in the transition from a rural to an urban social organization. People developed their human nature in terms of the neighborhood, the traditional family, and other institutions and organizations, only to find that an irrepressible trend was under way that threatened to change the social order to which they had made adjustments. Not understanding the irresistible nature of trends, they tried to check them. Trends can be directed and social controls worked out in terms of them, but once they are under way, they cannot be stopped. Immigrants were involved in all these trends where there were no adequate means of preventing disorganization and demoralization. Consequently the problems of immigration were greatly increased by a force outside of immigration itself.

(5) The character of human nature and its inextricable relationship to the culture in which it developed, with both Americans and immigrants, have greatly complicated the problem of immigration in the transitional situation of which it was a part. Even in a relatively static social order the nature of human nature would make it impossible for the adult immigrant to make the transition from one culture to another. In a changing social order such as exists in the United States, there has not been a culture stationary enough

---

[3] From an unpublished manuscript by author on "Non-Direction of Social Trends."

for an adequate social adjustment for many Americans. For the foreign peasants the situation has been even more difficult.

The social nature of the immigrant varies in every unit from that found in America. The immigrants are different — no one can deny that fact. They are different because they have had a history in which they have developed a mentality and characteristics peculiar to their experiences. Americans have behaved toward them as though they were different in an inferior sense, and the immigrants have come to think of themselves as unique. The realization of the fact that a situation is strange to one must be met by rationalization, by some method that will lead to self-respect in terms of the difference.

Where immigrants have felt inferior because of their cultural variation they have become disorganized and presented a much greater problem than they otherwise would have done. A feeling of high regard on the part of the immigrant for his own group is an attitude much desired by those who understand human nature. Any group that accepts a definition of inferiority always becomes maladjusted. There has to be some respect in which a group feels equal or superior, or social disorganization is the result. We need not expect immigrants to be exceptions. If they think well of themselves and their heritages they will become better Americans, because they feel that they have some contribution to make. Immigration has been a great problem because it is the character of human nature for disorganization to result when self-respect is disturbed. Cultural variations have been defined as a matter of inferiority and the immigrants often have made themselves conspicuous in struggling against the definition.

The contents of the units of human nature in the immigrants are more at variance with the demands of urban life than with the rural Americans. With recent arrivals this is particularly true in the unit of language. This one phase is discussed here because it is the unit of culture most used in making adjustments. Not only is language important for adjustments, but it plays a specific rôle in the development of all other units of social nature.   Every phase of human nature materializes through the utilization of language, and once it has been created, it in turn contributes to the development of language.

The human nature of the immigrants and the cultural adjustments they have made are related to language, which singles them out as different in America; this comes to be the greatest barrier to adjustments.   Along with religion, language has been the most important element around which Americans could organize their emotional attitudes of ethnocentrism.   At birth the European or Asiatic peasants could have learned English as readily as they learned to speak their native language, but once their random vocalizations had been defined, the learning of English became a difficult, conscious process.   It is the language of the immigrant that has attracted so much attention in the industrial world and magnified his presence as a factor in low wages and other industrial evils.

Other units of human nature might be similarly discussed to reveal the way in which the social nature of the immigrant makes it impossible for him to become assimilated, and thus he is defined as a problem.   The process by which human nature develops creates the emotional attitudes of ethnocentrism with foreign peasants and Americans.   Out of it grows the racial prejudice, a part of human nature as it is developed at the present time, which makes the problem of immigration as great as it is.

(6) Immigration has been a complex problem because the behavior of the immigrant has been measured by American norms that were changing.   If the customs or habits of the immigrants varied from the accepted customs and habits in the United States they were regarded as abnormal and undesirable; they were customs and habits that should be suppressed without any understanding of their adjustment value for the immigrant.   If the moral, political, or religious views of the immigrants differed from similar views in America, then they were regarded as dangerous to American institutions — an attitude that eclipsed any value that might incur in these views, either for the process of accommodation for

the immigrant or as a contribution to the American cultural complex.

Behavior developed in one cultural complex cannot be evaluated in terms of the norms of another social organization. It is one of the disconcerting facts that must be accepted when a country progresses economically and industrially through the utilization of an alien ethnic group, no matter what the nationality may be. It is even a greater mistake to determine the worth of the culture of a new group by norms that are already obsolete in the country receiving the newcomer, which has often been the case in reactions to immigrants. Norms change slowly in some societies but in the United States and other countries where the industrial revolution has been important this is not the case. It is hard to believe that some old standards have lost their significance. But such is the case. "Traditions and customs, morality and religion, undergo an evolution that is more and more rapid, and it is evident that a sociology proceeding on the assumption that a certain norm is valid and that whatever does not comply with it is abnormal finds itself absolutely helpless when it suddenly realizes that the norm has lost all social significance and that some other norm has appeared in its place. This helplessness is particularly striking in movements of great social crisis [industrial revolution and urban trend[4]] when the evolution of norms becomes exceptionally rapid."[5] The practice of measuring the behavior of immigrants by American norms has greatly increased the problem of immigration.

(7) Immigration has been a disconcerting problem because there has been a tendency to evaluate the culture of the immigrant in terms of the social situation in the United States. Immigrant institutions have been compared with similar institutions in America. The fallacy of this practice is seen when there is a realization that institutions transplanted from peasant communities in Europe or Asia are the crystallization of the attitude as to the way situations should be met in the native habitat of the immigrant. It has been

[4] Inserted by author.
[5] W. I. Thomas and F. Znaniecki, *The Polish Peasant in Europe and America*, I, 10.

customary to react to immigrant institutions apart from the cultural complex in which they had their inception and development; thus the institutions have not been understood.

This mistake has been accentuated by the fact that the culture of the immigrant has been compared with the culture of Americans who were on a much higher social and economic level. Their culture has not been compared with a peasant social organization in America or with that of industrial workers on the same economic level. There has also been a tendency to compare the adjustment of immigrants when America was a rural country with the adjustment in the present urban organization which has made immigration seem a growing problem in itself.

(8) Immigration has been an alarming problem because each individual of the second generation has to be a " marginal man." [6] He is forced to live on the peripheries of two cultural worlds and finds it impossible to establish a life organization in terms of either. He is not a part of the peasant culture of his home, nor can he identify himself with the American culture of the school. With him the development of human nature, ordinarily an unconscious process, becomes a conscious process, with the realization that he is not a part of any social order.

In this predicament he becomes demoralized, his behavior is random and not organized toward any particular adjustment end. Without a world in which to live, he may enter the unconventional world of the gang where his social variant patterns of behavior make him a part of the underworld milieu, where he has status and a well defined rôle to play. He becomes adjusted in the only cultural world where he can have a feeling of belonging, and thus develops a conception of himself as a person who counts. In the gang world of our industrial cities, the immigrant boy of the second generation finds an approval group made up of those who understand him after a naïve fashion, because they have had similar experiences in trying to make an adjustment to life.

[6] See Robert E. Park, "Human Migration and the Marginal Man," *American Jour. of Sociology*, XXXIII, 881–893. May 1928.

This attitude has made immigration a great problem because the second generation of the foreign-born has furnished most of our juvenile delinquency. Studies have shown, however, that the rate of delinquency for these areas has been practically the same for all nationalities. It is a conflict between rural and urban cultures. It is a conflict between personalities developed in static, peasant communities and personalities that are trying to amplify themselves in the disorganized areas of an urban environment. This same conflict exists between every parent and every child generation in the United States but it is greater in immigrant homes because the parents, culturally speaking, are not even in America. It is characteristic of human nature to be contingent upon some culture, and when it is forced to develop in conflicting cultures, it creates a culture of its own.

(9) Immigration has been a great problem because of the tendency to emphasize the pathological aspects of the question. It has been a practice in the study of human behavior to pay attention to behavior that varies from the accepted norms in a particular situation without considering other aspects. It is true that in most cases the pathological may be the normal magnified, but the abnormal in itself is usually an isolated aspect of a total situation. Therefore, the behavior of any group cannot be understood just through either variant or approved behavior alone. In industry or in social accommodation the immigrants have been evaluated by their pathological adjustments. Likewise, immigrants have judged Americans by superficial traits, vices, techniques of exploitation, and characteristics that they could not understand.

While pathological facts in cultural relationships attract more attention than others they are not any more significant for understanding a social situation than the less startling phases.

The scientific value of a fact depends on its connection with other facts, and in this connection the most commonplace facts are often precisely the most valuable ones, while a fact that strikes the imagination or stirs the moral feeling may be really either isolated or exceptional, or so simple as to involve hardly any problems. Again, by separating the abnormal from the normal we deprive ourselves of the opportunity of studying them in their connection with each other, while only in this connection can their study be fully fruitful. There is no break in continuity between the normal and the abnormal in concrete life that would permit any exact separation of the corresponding bodies of material, and the nature of the normal and the abnormal as determined by theoretic abstraction can be perfectly understood only with the help of comparison.[7]

(10) We have seen that immigration has been a great problem because of the emphasis placed on the pathological aspects. It has been a complex problem, also, because there has been a tendency to consider all facts of immigration in isolation. Immigrant societies as a whole have been little studied. Knowledge of the Black Hand activities of Italians was sufficient data to regard them as undesirable. The history of this activity in relation to a Sicilian or southern Italian culture was not thought necessary, nor were other facts concerning the Italians considered essential. During an earlier period a similar reaction was made concerning the Irish because of the operations of the Molly Maguires and the fact that the Irish tended to settle in cities and enter politics. The tong organizations of the Chinese provide an excellent basis for forming opinions concerning Orientals.

The Jews have been excoriated for their economic proclivities because this interest has been considered as an isolated phenomenon. This *penchant* has not been considered along with other Jewish traits, nor has this interest been considered in relation to the experiences of the Jews where it developed. During the early history of the Hebrews, usury was one of the few occupations open to the Jews. The Christian church had connected it with sin as far as the gentiles were concerned. The important thing to remember is the fact that every trait with any nationality has a history that can be understood only in terms of that history.

In our thinking concerning all immigrant groups, facts have been considered apart from their history and isolated from other social data. The immigrant has been regarded as desirable or undesirable through a consideration of one unit

[7] W. I. Thomas and F. Znaniecki, *The Polish Peasant in Europe and America*, I, 9, by permission of and special arrangement with Alfred A. Knopf, Inc., authorized publishers.

of culture rather than the total culture of the group. Equally important is the mistake whereby a whole group has been judged through an unfortunate experience with one member of a nationality. In this respect the immigrants have been at fault quite as much as the Americans. Mistreatment by one American has led, in many cases, to the generalization that all Americans are mean and unworthy.

(11) The problem of immigration has been critical because there has been an emotional rather than a realistic, scientific attitude concerning immigration as well as other social problems. The frame of reference for thinking about immigration has been the traditional conception of a hierarchy of nationalities and races in which groups differing most from Americans in the contents of their units of culture were placed at the lowest level, with presumably the least capacity for American culture. Scientific data accumulated by race specialists have been ignored, as shown by the belief that race is the dominant factor in culture accomplishments.

A realistic attitude would have discovered a real problem in immigration because of the nature of human nature which is socially acquired, but not because of innate capacity where all races are equal. A realistic attitude discovers a difference between race and nationality. While European immigrants belong to the same race (the Caucasian) as native Americans, they are not of the same nationality. They speak a different language, have a different political organization, etc. They are of a different nationality because the contents of their units of culture are not the same as those found with Americans. The biological process has not been responsible for the difference; it is due to the fact that European peasants have different cultures and different social natures because they have had different experiences and have made adjustments to different situations. The same statement holds true for Asiatics.

A realistic attitude toward the problem of immigration would have evidenced the fact that immigration has not created problems but intensified them. It would have discovered that the early American stock had both superior and inferior individuals; likewise all immigrant groups. American culture is not uniform, throughout, consequently assimilation could not be the same everywhere. All Americans are not alike in their cultural patterns and philosophies of life. Americanization, as a process of adjustment, is, therefore, a relative thing so far as results are concerned.

An objective attitude toward the problem of immigration could show that many things for which immigrants have been criticized have prevented their complete social disorganization, notably the colonies in which they live so that they can make some adjustment use of their past experiences. Many problems for which they have been condemned were not produced by them, but intensified by their presence. In fact, a realistic attitude would have defined every aspect of immigration differently from the way it has been defined and thus the problem of immigration would not have been so great.

(12) Immigration has been a complex problem because there has been a belief that Americanization could be a reality for adult immigrants unless they came from a group inferior to native Americans. While this was a reaction to a wish it was believed that America was to be a great melting pot. When it was discovered during the World War and on other occasions that foreign peasants, culturally speaking, had not become Americans, immigration was defined as a greater problem than it had been before. Immigrants became undesirables and were regarded as endangering American institutions. A knowledge of the character of human nature would have obviated the belief that Europeans or Asiatics could become Americans in any complete sense.

(13) Immigration has been a great problem because Americans have not tried to make use of the desirable aspects of immigrant culture but have tried to suppress them. Instead of appreciating the importance of the immigrant child's learning the native language of his parents there has been opposition to it. Such a practice was regarded as un-American. The inconsistency of this attitude is seen in our educational system where we spend a great deal of money every year trying to teach foreign languages in our schools. The attitude concerning the language of the immigrant

is typical of the attitude toward all other aspects of his culture.

Although this text is not concerned with international-mindedness, an ability to appreciate the culture of Europeans and Asiatics whom we accept as citizens in America might be an important step in that direction. With Americans appreciating the best of their own culture and the desirable aspects of immigrant culture and a reciprocal attitude with the immigrants, there could develop a fine relationship between the nations involved. There is no doubt in the minds of most people concerning the desirability of world peace. However, human nature as it has developed often stands in the way. " The chief obstacles in the way are *race prejudice* and *national jealousy*. The former in most cases is but another name for ethnological ignorance." [8] When we realize that international-mindedness is a " consequence of contact and communication," we can see the desirability of making use of any valuable units of culture brought to the United States by immigrants.

(14) Immigration has been a great problem because those who have presented the question of immigration to the public from the lecture platform and through the press did not understand the nature of human nature and were not, therefore, qualified to discuss immigrant behavior for the purpose of influencing public opinion. Every community has had its litterateurs, journalists, travelers, statesmen, and lecturers, who have discussed immigration because of their positions and not because they were qualified through study to make authoritative statements. Social nature has been confused with inherent nature. Racial affiliation has been the explanation of any retardation.

(15) Immigration has been defined as a great problem because there have not been any reliable data from which to draw conclusions. We have been reacting to traditional prejudices and antiquated ideas and to wishes and desires growing out of age-long misconceptions. Enough is known about human nature and the capacity of races to formulate

[8] Griffith Taylor, *Environment and Race* (Oxford: Oxford University Press 1927), p. 341.

some new hypotheses, but before definite conclusions are reached concerning immigration there will have to be extensive research.

Research will not change the problem of immigration but it will give it a different definition and make possible the scientific handling of the problem and better controls in human relationships. As yet most aspects of the immigration problem are untouched by research.

(16) Immigration has been a greater problem because the Science of Human Behavior has not been well developed. The materialization of the study of human behavior with a scientific technique has been greatly delayed by the fact that it is believed that any person, important because of wealth or education, is qualified to deal with problems of human behavior. Human behavior, however, is extremely complex and the only person equipped to deal with it in any adequate fashion is the behavior specialist who has been trained to understand the character of human nature in all of its ramifications, as it is produced through social interaction.

Immigration has been a great problem because there have been few persons trained to understand all of the intricacies of immigration and the complex changing social situation of which it is a part.

The United States has always had a problem of immigration and will have for some time to come even though there may be legislation in the future to exclude immigrants entirely. The country will continue to have this problem because there are in the United States at the present time thousands of unassimilated Mexicans, French-Canadians, Europeans, and Asiatics. Without immigration in recent years when the immigration question has been so vital, the United States would have had the same problems, in a slightly lesser degree, that it has had with immigration.

APPENDIX

CHAPTER I

WRITTEN ASSIGNMENTS

1. Each student should read an Immigrant Autobiography and write a paper on it, dividing the paper into the following sections: (1) cultural isolation (the experience of the individual in his native land) ; (2) the journey (the experiences of the trip including those at the ports of embarkation and debarkation) ; (3) segregation (isolation in the United States) ; (4) competition; (5) conflicts; (6) accommodation; and (7) assimilation.

2. The following assignment will give each student a chance to study immigration in relation to his major subject.

(*a*.) Have majors in *Anthropology* and *Ethnology* trace the racial origin of immigrant groups and the development of their culture.

(*b*.) Have majors in *Business Administration* study problems of management with various immigrants in industrial plants.

(*c*.) Students in *Dramatics* and related fields may study the dramatic work of immigrant groups in the United States and in their native countries.

(*d*.) Have *Economics* majors contrast the economic organization of peasant groups with their economic adjustments in this country.

(*e*.) *Education* majors may investigate the problems of education with immigrant children and with adults of the same nationalities.

(*f*.) Those working in the field of *Fine Arts* will be interested in peasant art and the contributions of each nationalistic group in art.

(*g*.) Have majors in *Cultural Geography* study the relationship between culture and geographical factors.

(*h*.) Have *History* majors write papers on the historical aspects of immigration.

(*i*.) Have *Home Economics* majors prepare papers on the food habits of certain immigrant groups as well as on their contributions in furniture and clothing.

(*j*.) *Journalism* majors may study the immigrant press in the United States.

(*k.*) *Language* majors may classify all immigrant groups in the United States on the basis of the origin of language.

(*l.*) *Literature* majors may interest themselves in the peasant contributions of each country in literature.

(*m.*) *Music* majors may study the contributions of each nationality in music.

(*n.*) Majors in *Philosophy* may write papers on philosophical contributions of the various countries sending immigrants to America.

(*o.*) *Physical Education* students may study the folk-dances and recreational activities of immigrants.

(*p.*) Majors in *Physical Sciences* may write papers on the lives and contributions of scientists in the various fields for different nationalities.

(*q.*) Have *Political Science* majors write papers on the political activities of the different nationalities in the United States as well as their European or Asiatic antecedents.

(*r.*) *Psychology* majors may write papers on the mental characteristics of various groups.

(*s.*) *Religion* majors may study the religion of each group and the various sects that have developed with each nationality.

(*t.*) *Sociology* majors may compare the contents of the units of culture of two or more groups: language, religion, marriage customs, familial organizations, etc.

QUESTIONS

1. What are the chief factors in the problem of immigration in the United States?

2. What aspect of the question of immigration is of most interest to the sociologist?

3. In what respect is human nature everywhere the same?

4. In what way does human nature differ in each cultural situation?

5. What is there in the nature of human nature that makes social intercourse possible between two individuals of divergent cultures?

6. Why is assimilation difficult for adult immigrants?

7. What is meant by a *monogenetic* origin of man?

8. What impersonal objects are acquired through experience by individuals in society which have a different meaning in each social heritage?

9. Under what conditions can an Oriental by birth become an Occidental in culture?

10. What is an example of ethnocentrism?

11. Why is assimilation in any culture not checked by the biological process?

12. What are some of the needs prevalent with every racial or nationalistic group?

13. How have situations been met by every ethnic group?

14. What social processes are important in immigration?

15. What is meant by the statement that an individual starts life without a social nature?

16. What is the significance of the affirmation that the life organization of an individual is contingent upon the culture in which it has developed?

17. How would you explain the statement that one's culture really becomes a part of him through mental imagery?

18. In what sense is the personality of an individual the subjective aspect of his culture?

19. How do artifacts from his native habitat help the immigrant in his American adjustment?

20. What is the difference between denationalization and re-nationalization?

21. What are some cultural values accruing from ethnocentrism?

22. Why is an immigrant who has lived in America maladjusted when he returns to the country of his birth?

CHAPTER II

WRITTEN ASSIGNMENTS

1. Make a list of the cultural changes in the United States since colonial days and show the significance of them in relation to the question of immigration.

2. Write a paper on the economic changes in the United States since the colonial period, showing the importance of these changes in relation to the problem of immigration.

3. Make a study of population changes in terms of the various periods of immigration.

QUESTIONS

1. Why has the stream of immigration been divided into " old " and " new " ?

2. What change has taken place in the control of immigration?

3. What general change has taken place in the United States since early immigration?

4. In what respects were cultural adjustments less difficult for the early immigrants?

5. Why must the adjustments of any group be considered only in terms of the period in which they arrived in the United States?

6. What has been the nature of the interest in immigration?

7. What are the periods of immigration?

CHAPTER III

WRITTEN ASSIGNMENTS OR CLASS REPORTS

Students write papers or make class reports on the following topics:

1. English emigration to the United States.

2. German Palatines and the causes of their emigration to America.

3. Cultural characteristics and the first adjustments made by the Scotch-Irish in America.

4. The historical experiences of the French Huguenots that led to emigration.

5. The indentured servants and redemptioners during colonial days.

6. The experiences of the journey for immigrants during the colonial period.

7. Immigration legislation for the colonial period.

8. Religious conflicts during the colonial period.

QUESTIONS

1. How do you distinguish between colonization and immigration?

2. Who were the colonists during the colonial period?

3. Why was the colonial cultural pattern not entirely English?

4. What two adjustments did immigrants have to make in the United States during this period?

5. What was the basis of the objections to immigration during the colonial period?

6. What immigrant groups came to the United States during this period?

7. What were the chief religious sects during colonial days?

8. What distinction do you make between redemptioners and indentured servants?

9. What two undesirable classes attracted the most attention in the early days of immigration?

10. What were the chief reasons for emigration during the colonial period?

11. What factor in Europe made indentured servitude possible?

12. What was the basis of rationalization for indentured servants?

13. Why was the journey an important experience for adjustments in America?

14. What were the evils of indentured servitude?

15. What is the relationship between the distribution of immigrants and their adjustments?

16. What four experiences of the immigrants before they reach America are important for their adjustments in the United States?

17. How do you explain the differences in attitudes in the various colonies concerning immigration?

18. What were the conditions at the port of debarkation during the colonial period?

19. How do you distinguish between accommodation and assimilation?

20. What do you understand by the term " cultural conflict "?

21. What cultural unit received the most attention during the colonial period?

22. What two religious groups met the most opposition during colonial days?

CHAPTER IV

WRITTEN ASSIGNMENTS

Students write papers on the following topics:

1. Legislative acts for the period of unrestricted immigration.
2. The economic conditions in Ireland leading to emigration.
3. The hardships attending the journey for this period.
4. Chief problems of adjustments.

QUESTIONS

1. What projects in America needed European immigrants for their development?

2. Why was there a period of unrestricted immigration?

3. Why was there a cessation of immigration at this time?

4. Why was the system of indentured servitude discontinued?

5. What were the causes of emigration for this period?

6. What were the conditions during the journey?

7. What section of the country was considered undesirable for the settlement of immigrants at this time?

8. What were the chief objections to immigration between 1783 and 1830?

9. The passage of what Bill shows the attitudes of fear on the part of native Americans?

10. Why was naturalization for aliens feared by Americans?

11. How were immigrants defined by native Americans?

12. What means of exploitation were used against immigrants?

13. Was the adjustment for this period accommodation or assimilation?

14. What were the pathological adjustments for this period?

CHAPTER V

WRITTEN ASSIGNMENTS OR CLASS REPORTS

Students prepare papers or class reports on the following subjects:

1. The legislation that was enacted while immigration was under state control.
2. Scandinavian immigration to the United States.
3. Compare the journey of this period with the two previous periods of immigration.
4. The influence of German life and thought on American civilization.
5. The German, Scotch-Irish, Irish, and Scandinavian press in the United States.
6. The Molly Maguires, a conflict group in the United States.
7. The economic and social conditions in Europe in countries furnishing emigration for this period.
8. The societies established in the United States for the protection of immigrants.
9. Immigrant organizations in the United States for this period.
10. The political activities of the various immigrant groups for the period of state regulation.
11. The Native American Party and its relationship to immigrant adjustments.
12. The Know-Nothing Party and its rôle in the question of immigration.
13. The pathological adjustments, pauperism, dependency, criminality, and insanity, made by immigrants.
14. The adjustments of the second generation.

QUESTIONS

1. What factors in America offered some amelioration from the economic conditions in America?
2. In what field was there a demand for immigrants?
3. What were the causes of emigration from 1830 to 1860?
4. What were regarded as the chief dangers of immigration at this time?
5. What were the chief nationalities emigrating during this period?
6. What country sent the largest number?
7. Why did the Irish furnish the greatest problem of adjustment?
8. What change was there in the composition of immigration from Germany?

9. What undesirable classes were found in the stream of immigration for this period?

10. What evidence have we that many desirable individuals were emigrating from Europe to the United States during this time?

11. What two laws in the United States were to the advantage of the immigrants coming during state regulation?

12. What were the four important stages in the journey of the immigrants?

13. What were some of the problems at the port of embarkation and how were they related to adjustments in America?

14. What parasitic classes were found at the port of debarkation?

15. What were some of the frauds practiced upon the immigrants at the port of debarkation?

16. What were the activities of the immigrant brokers for this period?

17. What group settled in great numbers in urban communities at this early date?

18. What were some of the problems in society for which immigration was blamed?

19. What three problems dominated the fears of Americans concerning immigration?

20. What two events in the United States led to a cessation of immigration?

21. What were some of the indices that assimilation had not taken place during this period?

22. Why did slave-holding states object to European emigration?

23. Why were European immigrants opposed to slavery?

24. What was the nature of the legislative acts for this period?

25. What was the program of the Native American Party?

26. What was the purpose of the Know-Nothing Party?

27. What were the types of adjustments made by immigrants between 1830 and 1860?

28. What were some institutions maintained by the immigrants in their cultural isolation?

29. What were the chief pathological adjustments made by immigrants in the United States at this time?

30. Why was the process of adjustment difficult with the second generation?

CHAPTER VI

WRITTEN ASSIGNMENTS OR CLASS REPORTS

Students prepare papers or class reports on the following subjects:

1. The Danes in America.
2. Contrast the journey of this period with previous periods.
3. The contribution of the various Scandinavian groups to American life.
4. The attitudes involved in the passage of the Liberal Homestead Act of 1862.
5. The immigration from Switzerland.
6. The activities of the Western States in an effort to secure emigrants from European countries.
7. The development of the Middle West by immigrant groups.
8. The pathological adjustments of immigrants for this period.
9. The immigrant press for this period.

QUESTIONS

1. What event opened the South to immigration?
2. What legislation led to Western settlements on the part of immigrants?
3. Why was there a demand for laborers in the Eastern States at this time?
4. What was done to encourage immigration between 1860 and 1882?
5. What countries provided the greatest numbers of immigrants for this period?
6. What were the chief causes of immigration for this period?
7. What were the chief inducements in the United States which led to immigration?
8. What were the activities of the Western States designed to attract emigration from European countries?
9. What important changes were made in shipping conditions for this period?
10. How did immigration help the development of systems of transportation in the United States?
11. What is meant by the statement: " Culturally speaking, the immigrant is not in America "?
12. Why are so many members of the second generation of immigrants disorganized in American cities?
13. What factors were important in the process of adjustment during this period?
14. What were some of the social lesions in American society for which immigrants were blamed?

15. What is the distinction between poverty and pauperism?
16. What were the chief economic adjustments made by immigrants?
17. What immigrant groups pursued their European occupations in the United States?
18. In what locations were there real problems of adjustment for immigrants?

CHAPTER VII

WRITTEN ASSIGNMENTS OR CLASS REPORTS

Students write papers or make class reports on the following subjects:

1. Immigration Laws under Federal Control.
2. The History of the Literacy Test.
3. The National Origins Plan of Immigration Restriction.

QUESTIONS

1. What policies were included in the immigration laws during Federal Control?
2. What methods have been used to control immigration?
3. What important factors distinguish the period of Federal Control from previous epochs of migrations?
4. What changes had taken place in the United States which were closely related to the problem of immigration?
5. What occupational changes had taken place in the process of adjustment for immigrants?
6. What great crisis led to the cessation of immigration during the period of Federal Control?
7. What reason was given by three presidents for vetoing the immigration law which embodied the literacy test?
8. What is meant by the statement that Americanization is a relative thing?
9. How can immigration be properly evaluated?
10. What was accomplished by the quota plan of restriction?

CHAPTER VIII

WRITTEN ASSIGNMENTS OR CLASS REPORTS

Students prepare papers or give class reports on the following subjects:

1. The experiences of the Jews in Russia and other eastern European countries.

2. The economic and cultural life in Greece.

3. The struggle of the Czechs for independence.

4. The political, economic, and cultural lives of the Finns under Swedish and Russian domination.

5. The experience of the Albanians with their Balkan neighbors.

6. The economic life of the Russian peasant before the World War.

7. The political and cultural life of the Jugo-Slavs.

8. The experiences of the Bulgarians in the political history of the Balkans.

9. The experience of the Esthonians under the German land-owners.

10. The political domination of the Russians and the economic and cultural domination of the Germans over the Letts.

11. The history of the Lithuanians during the union with Poland.

12. The influence of Russia in Lithuania.

13. The cultural life of the Polish peasants.

14. The political experiences of the Poles under Austria, Germany, and Russia.

15. Make a classification of all the Slavic groups.

16. The ethnocentrism of the Slavs.

17. The " oppression psychoses " with eastern Europeans.

18. The political situation in Austria-Hungary.

19. The racial and nationalistic situation in Austria-Hungary.

20. The peasant population of Roumania.

21. The religious situation in Jugo-Slavia.

22. The economic and cultural life of the southern Italians.

23. The economic and cultural life of the northern Italians.

24. The Portuguese peasants.

25. Anti-Semitism in eastern Europe.

26. The Jewish ghetto.

27. Pogroms in Russia and Roumania.

28. The religious experiences of the Armenian immigrants.

29. The position of the Syrians between the East and the West.

30. The Christian Persians.

31. Composition of the Mexican emigration to the United States.

32. The religious and cultural ethnocentrism of French-Canadians.

QUESTIONS

1. What immigrant groups are included in " new " immigration?

2. What is the distinction between immigrants and non-immigrant aliens?

3. What is the distinction between emigrant and nonemigrant aliens?

4. In what age groups were most of the recent immigrants?

5. What is significant about the age of immigrants for adjustments in America?

6. What was the nature of oppression with immigrant groups from eastern Europe?

7. What is an " oppression psychosis "?

8. What has been the effect of Swedish domination in Finland?

9. What two countries have dominated the Esthonians?

10. What country was responsible for the system of landlordism in Latvia?

11. In what sections of Lithuania was the Lithuanian language preserved during the union with the Poles?

12. How many Lithuanians are there in the United States?

13. What country offers the most highly developed example of nationalism?

14. Under the rule of what three countries was Poland divided?

15. What is the chief religion of the Poles?

16. What is the chief occupation in Ukrainia?

17. What is chauvinism?

18. What are the chief religions in Ukrainia?

19. What group of peasants was most ignorant and degraded before the World War?

20. What three groups came as immigrants from Russia, according to Jerome Davis?

21. What three nationalistic groups dominated Czechoslovakia for years?

22. Which is the most self-conscious Slavic group, according to Miss Balch?

23. What is the attitude of many Bohemians concerning religion?

24. What were some of the measures used by the Magyars in dealing with the Slovaks?

25. What are the minority groups in Austria-Hungary?

26. What are the major nationalistic groups in Austria-Hungary?

27. What are the population elements in Roumania?

28. What countries have been important in Bulgaria through domination?

29. What is the chief religion in Bulgaria?

30. What are the chief ethnic groups in Jugo-Slavia?

31. What are the minor ethnic groups in Jugo-Slavia?

32. What for many years stood in the way of the development of a Jugo-Slavia state?

33. What countries have exercised an influence in Albania?

34. What countries have struggled to preserve their nationalities with language and religion the most important cultural elements?

35. What are the chief symbols of national unity?

36. What three languages have been forced on Slavic groups in Europe?

37. What is the definition given a foreign language in the United States when spoken by immigrants?

38. What knowledge concerning each group is necessary for directing the process of Americanization?

39. With what countries have the Greeks had conflicts?

40. What section of Italy has furnished most of the immigration to the United States?

41. What important internal situations in Italy have led to emigration?

42. From what regions have the Portuguese come?

43. What group of Portuguese have " colored " blood?

44. From what countries have Jews come to the United States in recent years?

45. What were some of the events in Europe responsible for the attitude of anti-Semitism?

46. What were some of the restrictions placed on the Jews late in the eighteenth century?

47. What factors within the ghetto and outside of the ghetto have given the Jews their characteristics?

48. What is the religious affiliation of the Armenians?

49. What is the geographical location of the Syrians in Asia?

50. What is the basis of the nationalistic spirit in Syria?

51. How do you account for the religious egocentrism of the Persians?

52. What are the most cherished units of culture with the French-Canadians?

53. What is the importance of discussing the cultural experiences of each immigrant group?

CHAPTER IX

WRITTEN ASSIGNMENTS OR CLASS REPORTS

Students prepare class reports on the cause of immigration for the different groups, using the books given in the bibliography of this chapter.

QUESTIONS

1. What is the relationship between the causes of emigration and the adjustments made in the United States?

2. What is the chief cause of emigration from eastern and southern Europe?

3. To what minor causes is the chief cause of emigration related?

4. What has been the change in Poland regarding the object of work?

5. What type of ownership gives the peasant status in many European countries?

6. What was the nature of the economic transition in Russia when the Russian peasants were emigrating?

7. What three causes have been important in emigration from Austria-Hungary?

8. What is the nature of the economic cause of emigration from Bulgaria?

9. What is the cause of emigration from Greece?

10. What has been the relationship between production and population increase in Italy?

11. What are the causes in nature in Italy leading to emigration?

12. What is the nature of the system of landlordism in Italy?

13. What are the conditions of the hired laborer in Italy?

14. In what sense have the Jews been the scapegoats in eastern Europe?

15. What were some Jewish monopolies in eastern Europe?

16. What facts separated the Jews from the Slavic population in eastern Europe?

17. What were some of the laws applicable only to Jews?

18. What was the area in which Jews were confined in Russia?

19. What is the nature of a pogrom?

20. Why were Jews not citizens in the countries of eastern Europe?

21. What were some crises which led to an increase of Jewish emigration?

22. What are the causes of French-Canadian emigration?

23. Why have Mexicans come to the United States as immigrants?

CHAPTER X

WRITTEN ASSIGNMENTS OR CLASS REPORTS

Students prepare papers or give class reports on the following subjects:

1. Compare modern transportation methods with those of earlier years of emigration.

2. Laws in foreign countries for regulating emigration.

3. Steerage conditions.

4. Ellis Island as a port of debarkation.
5. Conditions at ports of embarkation.
6. Surreptitious entry of aliens.
7. The journey of the eastern Europeans.
8. Medical examinations at the ports of embarkation and debarkation.
9. The control of emigration in Italy.
10. The surreptitious entry of immigrants from Europe into the United States.
11. Problems connected with Mexican immigration at the border.

QUESTIONS

1. Why are the experiences of the journey important for adjustments of the immigrant?
2. What is the nature of most of the legislation connected with migrations?
3. What is the nature of the examination at the port of embarkation?
4. What part has the United States in the examinations at the port of embarkation?
5. What is the nature of the vessel inspection?
6. What is the procedure step by step at Ellis Island?
7. How many buildings are there on Ellis Island?
8. How does the present size of Ellis Island compare with its original size?
9. How does Ellis Island compare with other immigrant stations in the world?
10. Why is the problem of handling immigration at the port of debarkation so difficult?
11. What are some of the hardships endured at Ellis Island?
12. What undesirable attitudes are developed with immigrants at the port of debarkation in certain cases?
13. What recommendations were made in 1922 regarding improvements at Ellis Island?
14. What are the reasons for the illegal entry of Mexican immigrants into the United States?
15. Why are smugglers so successful on the Mexican border?
16. What is the procedure for a legal entry at the Mexican border?

CHAPTER XI

WRITTEN ASSIGNMENTS OR CLASS REPORTS

Students should write papers or give class reports on the following subjects:

1. Chart on a map and describe the immigrant areas of some city.
2. Jewish ghettos in the United States.
3. The slums of American cities.
4. Satellite industrial cities.
5. Mining communities.
6. French-Canadian communities.
7. Settlements in American cities.

QUESTIONS

1. What factors have increased the problem of adjustments in the United States?
2. In what sections of industrial cities can immigrants settle?
3. What factors create the transitional zone in a city?
4. What do you understand by the statement: " The slum is a mosaic of cultural areas "?
5. What are some of the social variant types found in the slum?
6. What are some of the radical types in the slum?
7. What are some of the social problems found in or near the immigrant areas in American cities?
8. What two types of social disorganization are most important with immigrants in the United States?
9. What is the popular assumption regarding native ability and poverty?
10. Against what two factors do immigrants have to struggle in leaving the slum?
11. What adjustment prevents the disorganization and demoralization of the immigrant in city life?
12. What is the value of the isolated settlements to the immigrants?
13. What three adjustments are made by the second generation of immigrants?
14. Why is a conflict of cultures important in the development of human nature?

CHAPTER XII

WRITTEN ASSIGNMENTS OR CLASS REPORTS

Students write papers or give class reports on the following subjects:

1. Americanization: A process of adjustment.
2. Economic adjustments of immigrants.
3. Accommodation: A process of adjustment.
4. Naturalization: A factor in adjustments.

5. Race attitudes in children.
6. The immigrant and our courts.
7. The immigrant and patriotism.
8. Education of the immigrant.
9. Religious life of the immigrant in the United States.
10. The standard of living of immigrant groups.
11. Adjustments of second generation immigrants.
12. Agricultural adjustments of the Mexicans.
13. The Melting Pot.
14. The padrone system in operation in the United States.
15. Housing conditions among immigrant groups.
16. The contract labor system and the laws regulating it.
17. The peonage system in America.
18. Immigrant banks.
19. The sweatshop system.
20. Employment agencies and immigrants.
21. The immigrant press as a means of adjustment.
22. The function of immigrant churches.
23. The rôle of the synagogue in Jewish life in America.
24. The rôle of parochial schools in America.
25. Nationalistic organizations in the United States.
26. Immigrant theaters and plays.
27. Insanity and immigration.
28. Pauperism and immigration.
29. Crime and immigration.
30. Delinquency and the second generation of immigrants.

QUESTIONS

1. What two factors help create the problem of immigration in the United States?
2. Why had the peasants not been used to cultural conflicts before they came to America?
3. Why do adjustments tend to be easy in a peasant community?
4. What are some of the factors that make adjustments difficult in a complex cultural situation?
5. How is the adjustment process affected by new arrivals year after year?
6. What is significant for adjustments about the fact that many immigrants do not expect to remain in the United States?
7. What are the different types of economic adjustments made by immigrants in the United States?
8. What are the cultural adjustments made by immigrants?
9. At what level does a new immigrant group enter a particular industry?
10. What determines the standard of living of an immigrant group?

11. In what sense are housing conditions an adjustment to a social situation?

12. What well developed systems have been used for the exploitation of immigrants?

13. What is the padrone system?

14. What nationalistic groups have used the padrone system?

15. What is the contract labor system?

16. What is the peonage system as it refers to immigrants?

17. Why do foreigners trust immigrant banks rather than American banks?

18. What are the services performed for the individual by immigrant banks?

19. In what way has the immigrant banker occasionally exploited the immigrant?

20. What is the chief evil of the sweatshop system?

21. What are the forms of exploitation practiced by some employment bureaus?

22. What institutions have been important in the adjustments of immigrants in this country?

23. How does the immigrant press aid in accommodations in America?

24. According to A. Koupas, what is the most powerful bond for uniting immigrants in this country?

25. In what sense is the church " a little corner of the distant fatherland "?

26. What are the three traditional functions of the synagogue in Jewish life?

27. In what way is the religious attachment of the recent immigrants similar to the attitudes of the Pilgrim Fathers?

28. According to Thomas and Znaniecki, what is the most essential point in the value of the parochial school in America?

29. What is the advantage for the immigrant of the parish school over the public school?

30. With what groups have parochial and foreign language schools been important?

31. Why should a school teacher understand the cultural history and characteristics of the different national groups under her supervision?

32. What elements are there in the nationalistic sentiments of the immigrants as evidenced in their nationalistic organizations?

33. What is the nature of the process of accommodation through nationalistic organizations?

34. What are the pathological adjustments with recent immigrants?

35. How should proneness to any social inadequacy be determined?

36. What is the social aspect of insanity?

37. In what sense is crime or delinquency an adjustment to life?

38. How do you explain the statement: " Social variants are produced in cultural conflicts and not where one is controlled by a definite cultural pattern "?

39. What is the chief problem of the second generation of immigrants?

40. Why are immigrants not successful in an effort to lose their identity as members of a certain group?

CHAPTER XIII

WRITTEN ASSIGNMENTS OR CLASS REPORTS

Students prepare papers or give class reports on the following subjects:

1. Racial differences between Mongolians and Caucasians.

2. The contrast between the Chinese religions and the Christian religions.

3. The contrast between the Japanese religions and the Christian religions.

4. A comparative study of the Chinese family life and family life in America.

5. A comparative study of the Japanese family life and family life in America.

6. Oriental philosophies and Occidental philosophies.

7. Social values in the Orient and social values in the Occident.

8. Oriental laws vs. Western laws.

9. Oriental art compared with the art of the Western world.

10. Oriental industrial life compared with industrial life in the United States.

11. The systems of education in the Orient and in the United States.

12. The position of women in the Orient and in the Western world.

QUESTIONS

1. Why are the Orientals not discussed with other immigrants?

2. What is the " geographical delimitation clause "?

3. What countries are in the barred zone?

4. Why are the Filipinos and the Hindus discussed with the Orientals?

5. Does emigration solve the population problems of a country?

CHAPTER XIV

WRITTEN ASSIGNMENTS OR CLASS REPORTS

Students write papers or make class reports on the following subjects:

1. Legislative acts concerning the Chinese.
2. The early experiences of the Chinese on the Pacific Coast.
3. Treaties w'th China regulating immigration.
4. The Congressional investigation of the Chinese situation.
5. The political aspect of the Chinese question along the western coast.
6. Extra-legal activities against the Chinese (massacres, riots, etc.).
7. Economic conditions in China leading to emigration.
8. Smuggling of Chinese immigrants.
9. Chinatowns in America.
10. Activities of the Workingmen's Party of 1877.
11. The rôle of the press in anti-Chinese agitation.
12. Present economic adjustments of the Chinese in the United States.
13. The "Six Companies" in America.
14. Tongs in America.
15. Orientals of the second generation.

QUESTIONS

1. What were the conditions in western United States when the Chinese first came to this country?
2. What was the nature of the competition on the Pacific Coast during pioneer days?
3. What were the early attitudes concerning the Chinese in America?
4. What were some of the early occupations of the Chinese?
5. What were some of the personal qualifications for which the Chinese were praised during the pioneer days in California?
6. What were some undesirable attributes found in the Chinese after the anti-Chinese agitation had begun?
7. What were the municipal laws passed against the activities of the Chinese?
8. What were some of the state laws of California concerning the Chinese?
9. What were the objections raised concerning the Chinese which led eventually to their exclusion?
10. What group is most important in the composition of Chinese immigration?

11. What is abnormal about the sex distribution of the Chinese in the United States?

12. What classes of Chinese are admitted as nonimmigrants?

13. What class of Chinese can become citizens of the United States?

14. What are some of the absurdities arising under the citizenship law?

15. In what ways are families often disrupted by the exclusion laws?

16. What was the chief cause of emigration from China?

17. What were the chief means of making surreptitious entries into the United States?

18. What have been some of the cases of mistreatment growing out of the practice of smuggling?

19. What were some of the handicaps under which the immigration officials had to work in enforcing the exclusion laws?

20. What were the most used routes for the " bootlegging " of Chinese immigrants?

21. What means of transportation have been used for smuggling Chinese immigrants into the United States?

22. In what sense is a Chinatown a cultural area?

23. What were the chief crisis situations that led to anti-Chinese legislation?

24. What were some of the dissimilarities between the Chinese and the Americans that made the Chinese objects of attack in the early economic crisis situation on the Pacific Coast?

25. With what group did anti-Chinese agitation originate?

26. How did politicians capitalize on the anti-Chinese attitude?

27. What were some of the techniques used to influence public opinion concerning the Chinese?

28. What is the present attitude toward the Chinese on the Pacific Coast, according to Dr. Park?

29. From what occupations have the Chinese withdrawn?

30. What are the parasitic occupations in which Chinese have made adjustments?

31. What is the purpose of the " Six Companies " in America?

32. What American institutions have been important in Chinatowns in the United States?

33. What is the chief rôle of the language schools in the Chinatowns of the United States?

34. What Chinese organization is interested in the political life in the United States?

35. What are some of the important festivals in Chinatowns?

36. What is the function of the festivals with the Chinese in a strange environment?

37. What rôle does the clan organization play in the adjustments of Chinese in America?

38. What is the definition of a tong given by Dr. Wu?

39. What is the chief problem of the second generation Chinese?

40. What is an atomized individual?

CHAPTER XV

WRITTEN ASSIGNMENTS OR CLASS REPORTS

Students should prepare papers or give class reports on the following subjects:

1. The Gentlemen's Agreement.
2. Amalgamation as a solution to the Japanese question.
3. The treaty relationships between Japan and the United States.
4. The anti-Japanese activities of the School Board in San Francisco.
5. The successive steps in Japanese exclusion.
6. Alien land legislation in California.
7. The rôle of the Hearst papers in the exclusion of the Japanese.
8. Japanese opposition to the legislation of 1924.
9. Japanese Emigration Companies.
10. " Picture brides."
11. Smuggling of Japanese immigrants into the United States.
12. Japanese agriculture in the United States.
13. The second generation of Japanese in the United States.
14. The adjustments of American-born Japanese in Japan.

QUESTIONS

1. When did the Japanese immigration to the United States have its origin?

2. What were the chief differences between the United States which the Chinese entered and the United States which the Japanese entered?

3. What was the nature of the early attitudes concerning the Japanese?

4. What event led to the formation of the Japanese Association of America?

5. What were the chief aspects of the Gentlemen's Agreement as revealed by Ambassador Hanihara's note to Secretary Hughes?

6. What situations were important in the development of anti-Japanese legislation?

7. What were the demands made by the Exclusionists on the Pacific Coast?

8. What conclusions were reached in the conference between President Roosevelt and the California School Board?

9. What means were used by the Japanese to evade the alien land law of California?

10. What classes of Japanese may still enter the United States after the legislation of 1924?

11. What was the attitude in Japan concerning the legislative acts of 1924?

12. What have been the sources of Japanese immigration to the United States?

13. What was the chief occupational class in Japanese immigration?

14. Are American-born Japanese citizens of the United States?

15. What conditions in Japan are the causes of emigration?

16. What are the chief problems of the journey which have grown out of the exclusion of the Japanese?

17. Where are most of the Japanese located in the United States?

18. In what respect does the distribution of the Japanese make them a greater problem than the Chinese?

19. What are the chief bases for objections to the presence of Japanese in the United States?

20. How does the family adjustment of the Japanese in the United States compare with that of the Chinese in America?

21. In what sense is the Japanese family a self-sufficient economic unit?

22. In what way have the Buddhist priests hindered assimilation?

23. What is the important aspect of the rôle of the Japanese language schools?

24. What is evidence to show that races do not have inherent psychic characteristics?

25. Why will the second generation of Japanese be a problem in the future?

26. Why are American-born Japanese treated as foreigners?

27. What are the chief barriers to amalgamation with the Japanese in this country?

CHAPTER XVI

WRITTEN ASSIGNMENTS OR CLASS REPORTS

Students write papers or give class reports on the following subjects:

1. An anthropological study of the Hindus.
2. The religions of the Hindus in the United States.
3. The economic adjustments of the Hindus in the United States.

QUESTIONS

1. To what race do the Hindus belong?
2. By what legislation were the Hindus excluded from the United States?
3. What were the chief reasons for excluding the Hindus?
4. What is the chief reason for the Hindu migration to the United States?
5. What are the chief religions among the Hindus of the United States?

CHAPTER XVII

WRITTEN ASSIGNMENTS OR CLASS REPORTS

Students prepare papers or give class reports on the following subjects:

1. Racial affiliation of the Filipinos.
2. Objections to Filipinos on the part of Americans.

QUESTIONS

1. What is the racial affiliation of the Filipinos?
2. What is the citizenship status of the Filipinos?
3. What are the chief objections to Filipinos?
4. What moves have been made to exclude the Filipinos from the United States?
5. In what sense is the situation for the Filipinos different from that which other groups have had to face?

CHAPTER XVIII

WRITTEN ASSIGNMENTS OR CLASS REPORTS

Students prepare papers or make class reports on the following subjects:

1. Social changes in the United States.
2. Racial superiority and inferiority.
3. The differences between race and nationality.
4. Intelligence as related to nationality.
5. Race and civilization.
6. The Melting Pot.

7. Racial prejudice.
8. Population problems.
9. The control of social change.
10. Social problems in relation to social change.
11. "Cultural lag" as a factor in maladjustment.
12. The relation of immigration to urbanism.
13. The relation of immigration to industrialism.
14. The relation of immigration to unionism.
15. The relation of immigration to corporations.
16. Immigration and American politics.
17. Read H. S. Jennings: *The Biological Basis of Human Nature.*
18. Racial prejudice.

QUESTIONS

1. What are the difficulties in the way of drawing conclusions regarding the effects of immigration?
2. Why does disorganization usually accompany rapid social changes?
3. Why has immigration been given as the explanation of many of our social problems?
4. What is the nature of the institutions, customs, and habits in urban life in America that lead to maladjustment?
5. What do you understand by "cultural lag"?
6. What is the relationship between immigration and industrialization?
7. In what sense are institutions and movements the crystallization of attitudes?
8. With what movements is immigration as a problem identified?
9. What new standards have grown out of the social changes in America?
10. What is the result of working against trends?
11. What new attitude came into existence regarding law in the process of industrialization?
12. What is the relationship between immigration and political changes?
13. In what institutions has the "cultural lag" been the greatest?
14. What is the criterion by which we evaluate the human nature of an immigrant?
15. How do we evaluate the traditions and mores of immigrant groups?
16. What is essential to a program of Americanization?
17. Why is the human nature of the immigrant so often misunderstood?

18. What is the value of a realistic attitude in handling any problem of human behavior?

19. What is the difference between the innate capacity of different immigrant groups according to Reuter?

20. What are Jennings' findings regarding the offspring of diverse races?

21. What is the chief problem with the hybrid?

22. What are the sociological effects of immigration?

23. What in the past experience of the immigrant is important for Americanization?

24. What is required by the process of assimilation?

25. What is the result in a sudden change in cultural affiliation?

26. How does racial prejudice differ from other types of prejudice?

CHAPTER XIX

WRITTEN ASSIGNMENTS OR CLASS REPORTS

Students should prepare papers or give class reports on the following subjects:

1. Knowledge acquired concerning immigration of value for future work.

2. Criticism of the conclusions reached by the author.

3. New attitudes developed through the study of immigration.

QUESTIONS

1. What human elements have been involved in the economic and cultural transition in the United States?

2. What problems in American life have been created by immigration?

3. Why have immigrants caused more concern in the cultural transition in the United States than other groups?

4. What groups of Americans have found industrial adjustments difficult?

5. What causes a " cultural lag "?

6. What reasons does Dr. C. C. North give for cultural inertia?

7. What relationship is assumed to exist between the dwelling place of the immigrant and his native ability?

8. How are trends in society usually handled?

9. In what way have trends increased the problem of immigration?

10. Why are the immigrants different in a cultural sense from Americans?

11. What is the result of a feeling of group inferiority?

12. What two cultural units of immigrants form the bases for ethnocentrism with Americans?

13. Why is it impossible to evaluate behavior developed in one cultural complex in terms of the norms of another social organization?

14. What is the problem of the " marginal man "?

15. What is peculiar about the cultural situation of the second generation?

16. What facts in cultural relationships attract the most attention?

17. What mistake is made in studying cultural factors in isolation?

18. What would a realistic attitude concerning immigration reveal?

19. What has been the result of believing that an adult immigrant could be Americanized?

20. What has been the American attitude concerning desirable aspects of immigrant culture?

21. Why is it necessary to understand the nature of human nature in order to understand the problems of immigration?

INDEX